FIGURING
RELIGIONS

FIGURING
RELIGIONS

Comparing Ideas, Images, and Activities

EDITED BY

Shubha Pathak

Cover Art: "Angel Caryatids," photograph by Esther Kutnick, © Exploratorium, www.exploratorium.edu
Cover Artist: Amane Kaneko

Published by State University of New York Press, Albany

© 2013 State University of New York

For information, contact State University of New York Press, Albany, NY
www.sunypress.edu

Production by Laurie Searl
Marketing by Michael Campochiaro

Library of Congress Cataloging-in-Publication Data

Figuring religions : comparing ideas, images, and activities / edited by Shubha Pathak.
    p. cm.
  Includes bibliographical references and index.
  ISBN 978-1-4384-4537-3 (hardcover : alk. paper) 1. Religions. I. Pathak, Shubha, 1972-
  BL87.F54 2013
  200—dc23

2012009850

10 9 8 7 6 5 4 3 2 1

For my womenfolk, whose love lives on . . .

Contents

Acknowledgments

T HIS BOOK BEGAN as a thematic paper session that I organized for the Comparative Studies in Religion Section at the 2004 meeting of the American Academy of Religion. Since then, the project grew into an intergenerational and international endeavor that could not have been completed without the efforts of many people. Above all, I am grateful to the volume's other contributors for allowing me to include their work. Among them, I am especially thankful to Laurie L. Patton, who gave me the idea to expand our AAR paper session into an edited volume and who went on to cheer it on at its various milestones; to Wendy Doniger, my then dissertation advisor, who generously agreed to pen her pithy foreword even before the book's contents were complete; and to Glen Alexander Hayes, who provided an illuminating afterword and strong moral support as the manuscript approached its completion under duress. I would like to acknowledge as well American University's Department of Philosophy and Religion for the material and technical support that helped make this work possible—many thanks indeed to Shelley Harshe, the Department's stellar senior administrative assistant, who helped me print and package the manuscript in preparation for its trips to the publisher; and to Bree del Sordo and William Brandon, the diligent graduate research assistants who tracked down much-needed resources for me. Additionally, I appreciate the patience and expertise of Nancy Ellegate and her colleagues at the State University of New York Press as they guided this volume into its final form and brought it to the public's attention. Also invaluable was the frank feedback offered by the Press's anonymous readers, who identified areas in the initial version of *Figuring Religions* that warranted further reflection and elucidation. For the index, I thank Jim Blenko.

Four chapters of the volume were reprinted, with minor revisions, from previously published works:

Chapter 1: "Marking Religion's Boundaries: Constitutive Terms, Orienting Tropes, and Exegetical Fussiness," by Thomas A. Tweed, © 2005 by the University of Chicago Press, Chicago, Illinois. Published in *History of Religions* 44, no. 3: 252–76.

Chapter 3: "Conceptions of the Self in the *Zhuangzi*: Conceptual Metaphor Analysis and Comparative Thought," by Edward Slingerland, © 2004 by the University of Hawaii Press, Honolulu, Hawaii. Published in *Philosophy East & West* 54, no. 3: 322–42.

Chapter 7: "Poetry, Ritual, and Associational Thought in Early India: The Theories," pp. 38, 45–58 of chapter 2 in *Bringing the Gods to Mind: Mantra and Ritual in Early Indian Sacrifice*, by Laurie L. Patton, © 2005 by the Regents of the University of California. Published by the University of California Press, Berkeley, California.

Chapter 9: "In Search of Equivalence: Conceiving Muslim-Hindu Encounter through Translation Theory," by Tony K. Stewart, © 2001 by the University of Chicago Press, Chicago, Illinois. Published in *History of Religions* 40, no. 3: 260–87.

These four essays appear in *Figuring Religions* with the permission of the University of Chicago, University of Hawaii, and University of California Presses.

In the time during which this book took shape, I lost many loved ones in my matriline, including my great-grandmother, grandmother, and mother. Although I am sad that they have not lived to see this work, it bears marks of the strength and persistence of these remarkable women and is dedicated to them for this reason. I also am indebted to my menfolk—my father, my husband, and my brother—for their unremitting love and unrelenting good cheer over these challenging years. Finally, I would like to thank for their time everyone who has read or will read this book, a collaboration of comparative religion scholars for their colleagues within and without classrooms present and future.

Foreword

WENDY DONIGER

SHUBHA PATHAK'S introduction speaks of the earlier wave of comparatists, the worst of whom (the universalizers) tried to reduce various religions to a much too common denominator, and the very worst of whom (the hierarchizers) strove primarily to demonstrate how their own religion was better (which usually meant older and/or Truer) than all the others. Mircea Eliade was the prime mover of this generation of comparatists, with C. G. Jung and Joseph Campbell providing less and less acceptable (and more and more popular) versions of the universalist approach. Reacting against them, a second wave—a generation of younger scholars—sought to emphasize difference (in order not to universalize) and/or cultural context (in order not to hierarchize, but also to nuance still admitted resemblances). Jonathan Z. Smith carried the banner for this generation.[1]

The problem of the same and the different had become a crucial issue within the field of comparative religion. My own response to this problem included a challenge to difference and a cautious defense of sameness:

> . . . any discussion of difference must begin from an assumption of sameness; Wilhelm Dilthey has said that "Interpretation would be impossible if expressions of life were completely strange. It would be unnecessary if nothing strange were in them."[2] If we start with the assumption of absolute difference there can be no conversation. . . .

. . . Either similarity or difference may lead to a form of paralyz-
ing reductionism and demeaning essentialism, and thence into an
area where "difference" itself can be politically harmful. For where
extreme universalism means that the other is exactly like you, extreme nominalism means that the other may not be human at all.
Many of the people who argued (and continue to argue) that Jews
or blacks or any other group defined as "wogs" were all alike (that
is, like one another) went on to argue (or, more often, to assume)
that they were all different (that is, different from us white people,
us Protestants), and this latter argument easily led to the assertion
that such people did not deserve certain rights like the rest of us.
Essentialized difference can become an instrument of dominance;
European colonialism was supported by a discourse of difference.[3]

The present volume presents a much more complex response to the
problem of the same and the different, and amounts to a third wave. It seizes
a moment when the pendulum has swung back again from the extreme emphasis on difference, to recapture some of the good parts of the old agenda
of comparatism—without falling into the worst of the deep pits that it dug
for itself. I think the volume succeeds admirably. It swings just far enough
to make responsible comparison possible, but never sinks into romantic universalizing, let alone arrogant or even just inadvertent hierarchizing. And,
by gathering together a team of scholars who study different cultures and,
moreover, employ a wide range of different theoretical approaches to comparison, this collection makes possible a far wider scope of comparison than
any single scholar could ever responsibly muster. The volume also demonstrates a number of ways to compare not merely texts (in the broad sense of
the word—including rituals, visual icons, and media events, as well as words,
both written and oral) but also contexts. More precisely, the individual essays compare the relations of texts to their contexts in two or more cultures,
an agenda that allows the comparatists to reach a kind of middle ground
between old-fashioned morphological comparison and newfangled micro-
historical comparison.

This volume also does something more, and important, in advancing the
comparatist agenda. The book focuses on metaphor and metonymy, both in
theories about comparison and in the precise tropes that can be compared
across cultures. The first chapters use the concept of metaphor to illuminate
some of the most basic challenges to the comparative enterprise, starting

from the realization that there is a natural, but lamentable, human tendency to use our own world as the dominant metaphor for other worlds, so that their gods are more or less "like" our gods, their religions more or less like ours—a tendency that the first-wave comparatists often failed to resist. But metaphor can function in a more positive way when it flows in the other direction, when we allow our own metaphors to be refreshed by infusions of images from other religions. This is one of the many benefits that come to us from engaging in comparison, since comparison functions as a kind of metaphor, a more self-conscious version of the sort of metaphorical thinking that we all do—often unconsciously—all the time.[4]

Figuring Religions begins with Thomas A. Tweed's essay, located firmly in the second-wave, anti-universalist camp: he alerts us to the insidious effects of definitions, and the ways in which they constrain our thoughts. He sounds the clarion call to clarify or replace the metaphors used by our predecessors, who must necessarily include the comparatists of the first wave. But Edward Slingerland's essay takes a very different tack. Moving between the two stunningly disparate examples of the modern discipline of cognitive linguistics and the Daoist text the *Zhuangzi*, he lands in the middle so resoundingly that he can argue for a quasi-universalist theory of comparison, in the very tradition of Eliade that much of *Figuring Religions* sets out to correct. For Slingerland argues, and demonstrates, that there is a shared corpus of human experience at the heart of the metaphor of the self as a container, and likewise at the heart of the metaphor of the self as an object. It is a fine measure of the open-mindedness of the volume as a whole, its breadth and its willingness to embrace competing views, that Slingerland's argument takes its place beside harder-line arguments such as Tweed's. James Egge then picks up the ball and offers confirmations, correctives, and extensions of Slingerland's position, adding examples from another culture—Theravāda Buddhism—to deepen as well as nuance the argument.

Pathak's chapter shows how the tendency to take our own cultural tropes as metaphors for other peoples' tropes informs the particular example of epics, the very word for which requires us to use the Homeric poems as metaphors for all other poems of that type, including the ancient Sanskrit poems (which their authors and audiences call poems or histories rather than epics). Two chapters that follow deal with other cross-textual religious metaphors that function in a variety of different ways. Ellen Haskell demonstrates how the image of a suckling mother, in two Kabbalistic texts, structures the mystic's understanding of his relationship to God, and how this understanding both coincides with and differs from the ways that Christian traditions use the same basic metaphor. Terhi Utriainen compares the ways in which Biblical and Finnish Lutheran stories use the metaphor of a human being dressing and undressing to construct both specifically Christian identities and more generally human identities.

The final section of the book looks at religious activities through the lenses of theories of metaphor and metonymy. Laurie L. Patton analyzes the relationship between words and actions in Vedic rituals, but first sets the scene with numerous examples from our modern Western culture—first assuming, and then arguing in terms of modern metonymical theories of interpretation, that we and the authors of the Vedic hymns share numerous assumptions about the relationships between words and the human and divine worlds. Yiqun Zhou shows how the contrasting roles of ancient Greek women in public festivals and ancient Chinese women in domestic rites are expressed and enhanced by spatial metaphors in different sorts of texts—literary, ritual, and historical.

And, finally, in Tony K. Stewart's chapter, we see cultures other than our own comparing themselves with cultures other than their own. For everyone in Bengal grows up speaking Bangla, which is also the local language of Hinduism, derived in large part from Sanskrit (the classical language of Hindu scriptures), with a heavy input of Persian (one of the languages of Islam). And Bangla is the language that Bengali Muslims use to explain their religion to Hindus. Stewart thus uses the metaphor of translation rather than of syncretism (which has often been used in this situation), and concentrates on process rather than on product, to explain the rapprochement between these two religious groups.

Translation is intrinsically linked with metaphor: both words are derived from related Greek and Latin words that mean "bringing across" (Greek *phérō*, Latin *ferō*, *lātus*—"to bring"; Greek *metá*, Latin *trāns*—"across"). In a very real sense, even when we speak to someone in our own language, we are translating our thoughts; and this translation is simply compounded when we speak to someone in a foreign language, and to someone who comes from a foreign culture.[5] *Figuring Religions* demonstrates—often in surprising and eye-opening ways—how metaphor, even more basically than translation, lies at the heart of the comparative enterprise. This volume also shows how complicated metaphor is and how many different, fruitful ways there are to approach it.

NOTES

1. The observant reader will have noted that both of my exemplary scholars, the editor of this volume, the authors of its foreword and afterword,
and five of the other volume contributors are University of Chicago–af-
filiated or –trained. Swift Hall has indeed been one of the main battle-
fields of this war.
2. Dilthey 1961: 77.
3. Doniger 2010: 75, 75–76.
4. Doniger 2010: 4. See also Doniger [1988] 1995.
5. Doniger 2010: 4.

REFERENCES

Dilthey, Wilhelm. 1961. *Pattern and Meaning in History: Thoughts on History and Society*, edited by H. P. Rickman, 77. New York: Harper and Row. Quoted in Doniger 2010: 75.

Doniger, Wendy. 1995. *Other Peoples' Myths: The Cave of Echoes*. New York: Macmillan, 1988. Reprint, with a new preface, Chicago: University of Chicago Press.

———. 2010. *The Implied Spider: Politics and Theology in Myth*. Rev. ed. New York: Columbia University Press.

Introduction

SHUBHA PATHAK

Although the field of religious studies long has been a province of comparativists, their current representatives now turn a critical eye to the projects of their predecessors. Comparative religionists today eschew their antecedents' tendencies to reduce different religions to their common denominator (to see only one religion where there are many) and to assert the superiority of their own faith tradition (to see one religion over and above all others). Correctives to these universalizing and hierarchizing tendencies include attending carefully to the differences as well as similarities among religions and appreciating the richness of religions' respective cultural contexts. Indeed, these remedies recur as themes in two earlier volumes on comparative religious studies, *A Magic Still Dwells: Comparative Religion in the Postmodern Age* and "Comparison in the History of Religions: Reflections and Critiques."[1]

As works that simultaneously describe the state of comparative religious studies today and prescribe ways to improve this subfield, both volumes, by necessity, are broad. They consider comparison at a theoretical level, taking up the questions of why scholars should compare aspects of religions and how they can better do so. By contrast, *Figuring Religions* shows how current comparativists can apply the general lessons that they have learned about examining differences and contexts, while adopting a particular set of approaches appropriate for studying a variety of religious expressions. To clarify religious ideas, images, and activities, the contributors to *Figuring Religions* focus on the figures of metaphor and metonymy in religious thought, art, and rituals. These authors offer fresh outlooks on these aspects of religions, by applying trope theories developed recently in the disciplines of philosophy, linguistics, and anthropology.

These three types of theories allow comparative religionists to adapt the tacks that they take to religious forms. In choosing one of these frameworks to study such forms, a scholar indicates both the scale of her analysis and the relative importance that she will ascribe to similarity and difference as she compares the forms in question.

If, for instance, she follows in the footsteps of philosopher Paul Ricoeur, she will focus on metaphorical statements and will emphasize similarity and difference equally in her comparison. This comparison initially is implicit in a metaphorical assertion "x is y," where the metaphor lies in the copula "is" that connects a subject (x) to whatever is predicated of it (y). Yet the comparativist can make the comparison explicit, by recognizing that, in this metaphor, the term "is" means both "is not" and "is like." Once she is aware of this double meaning, she sees that the metaphorical statement contains three sorts of tension: (1) tension between the statement's subject (x) and predicate (y), (2) tension between the statement's literal (x is y) and metaphorical (x is like y) interpretations, and (3) tension between the asserted identity of x and y and their obvious difference.[2] When the subject and predicate of the metaphorical statement come from different cultures, adopting Ricoeur's philosophical perspective allows the scholar to examine closely both the intersections and the disjunctures between these terms. The same holds true, if the statement in her sights is metonymical rather than metaphorical, though the relationship that the metonymy asserts is the contiguity rather than resemblance of the subject and predicate.[3]

If, however, the scholar is concerned primarily with a broader kind of comparison, with comparing the conceptual systems of different cultures rather than their key terms, she more likely will look at these networks of notions through the lens of the cognitive linguistics applied by George Lakoff and Mark Johnson. On this view, the most salient features are metaphor, which is the "understanding and experiencing [of] one kind of thing in terms of another," and metonymy, which is the conceiving of a thing via its generally "physical or causal" relation to another thing.[4] These kinds of cognition underlie and thereby structure the conceptual systems that people employ, the assemblages of ideas that arise as people encounter their environments. The scholar comparing such metaphorical or metonymical systems is more sensitive to their similarities than to their differences. While she, like Lakoff and Johnson, allows that distinct cultures and distinct physical conditions give rise to different nexuses of concepts, she especially is interested in the similar sets of thoughts that emerge across cultures as human beings sense their surroundings with their bodies in the same ways.[5]

Yet she can explore a still wider area, if she steps back from conceptual systems to see more clearly the distinct cultures in which they are located. From this vantage point, she examines the cultural dynamics that condition the tropes and concepts before her. These tropes thus are a starting point for her inquiry, rather than its end. Therefore, seeing the tropes in spatial terms is helpful to her. In these terms, a metaphor arises where an element of "some source domain" is mapped onto a similar-seeming element of "some target domain," a semantic field that appears to be "abstract," because it includes elements that can be observed less readily than the contents of the source domain, a semantic field whose concreteness makes it seem more "familiar." A metonymy, however, occurs between contiguous elements of a semantic field, when one of these elements is substituted for another. But, even as these two tropes differ, both are influenced by cultures. Because specific cultures structure the semantic domains from which these tropes draw, by determining continuously which elements the domains contain and the relative positions of these elements within the domains, a scholar cannot understand completely the tropes that she observes, unless she knows their surrounding cultures. Even if she sees similarities among different cultures' tropes, only by appreciating the cultures' particularities can she attain access to the complete complexity of the individual figures in front of her.[6]

Employing philosophical, linguistic, and anthropological approaches such as the ones just outlined enables the comparativists contributing to *Figuring Religions* to study statements, conceptual systems, and cultural contexts concerning religious tropes. By examining such facets of religious figures, these scholars figure religions more effectively, seeing their central ideas, their central images, and their central activities distinctly yet collectively.

These forms of religion form the themes of this volume's three parts. Part I, "Figuring Religious Ideas," treats not only notions native to religious traditions, but also categories that scholars apply as they study religious traditions. In chapter 1, Thomas A. Tweed examines philosophically the tropes that theorists have used to define religion, and the effects that metaphors for religion have on the scholars who use them. As he surveys such orienting tropes, he notes that religion has been represented in ways enabling its observers to focus on certain of its aspects rather than on others. Likening theorists' metaphors to lenses, he concludes that scholars of religion are obligated to devote at least some of their exegetical energy to clarifying and—if necessary—to replacing their intellectual forebears' metaphors for religion, because this constitutive term demarcates their discipline as definitely and definitively today as before.

In chapter 2, I take a philosophical approach to comparing the designations of Homeric and Hindu works as epics. In my view, the statement that the *Iliad* and *Odyssey* are epics is an identity because the English word "epic" derives from a Greek term that interpreters used for the Homeric poems in ancient times. The statement that the *Rāmāyaṇa* and *Mahābhārata* are epics, however, is a metaphor because modern English-speaking critics transferred the term "epic" to the Hindu poems centuries after they were composed. While resembling their Greek counterparts in their enormous poetic forms and heroic themes, the Sanskrit epics repeatedly embed narratives within narratives and express in their encapsulated tales a devotionalism and a moral didacticism that do not mark the Greek epics. By distinguishing the senses in which the Greek and Indian texts may be considered epics, I recognize the contributions that the poems of each culture make to this rubric for religious literary works.

In chapter 3, Edward Slingerland argues that cognitive linguistics applies to metaphorical conceptions of the self in the *Zhuangzi*, a Daoist text. This application's ease indicates that the embodied existence characteristic of all human beings accounts for metaphors for the self that are common to classical China and modern America. Thus, human interactions with bounded areas and containers give rise to a metaphor of the self as a container that may be filled with virtues, vices, inclinations, and knowledge; and human experiences with manipulating physical objects bring forth a metaphor of the self as an object. The commonness of these metaphors across cultures distinguished by disparate histories and environments points to the shared human experience that can serve as the theoretical point of departure for comparative religious projects.

James Egge evaluates in chapter 4 Slingerland's proposal that conceptual metaphor theory be adopted as a methodology for the comparative study of religion. Contending that the flaws in the current formulation of conceptual metaphor theory are correctable, Egge extends its central idea of image-schematic projection, the use of image schemas—patterns of practical knowledge derived from sensory data about concrete objects, such as one's own body and physical environment—as the terms in which to understand more abstract items. He analyzes key practical concepts in two Theravāda Buddhist texts—passion and asceticism in the *Dhammapada* and meditation in the *Visuddhimagga*—and demonstrates that these texts provide strong evidence of the usefulness and validity of conceptual metaphor theory for comparing religions.

Part II, "Figuring Religious Images," focuses on the representations evoked by religious texts. In chapter 5, Ellen Haskell examines two kabbalistic texts that make extensive use of the metaphor of God as a suckling mother: Ezra of Gerona's *Commentary on the Song of Songs* and the *Sefer ha-Zohar*. In her inquiry Haskell works from anthropological assumptions that a metaphor, by locating its referents in only a small portion of the zone comprising a culture's characteristic ranges of various attributes, demonstrates that additional metaphors are needed to span this space; and that a person, by seeking to make metaphorical sense of his entire cosmos, can transform himself in such a way that he may become one with the whole of physical and cultural experience. For Haskell, then, the Jewish mystical works employ the metaphorical connotations and metonymical structures of the suckling-mother image, in order to relocate the kabbalists with respect to God. This relocation, which establishes a metaphysical social connection, conceptually transforms the kabbalists into beings capable of standing in the profoundly interdependent relationship with divinity that kabbalistic theology advocates. While Jewish images of God and Christian images of the Virgin Mary share the basic metaphor of suckling as spiritual transmission, the Jewish and Christian traditions differ as to the nature of the transmission and as to the relationships that it constructs between humanity and divinity.

In chapter 6, Terhi Utriainen argues philosophically that readers should regard as both metaphors and images the depictions of people in various states of dress and undress that appear in certain Biblical stories and in Finnish Lutheran sermons and hymns. More precisely, a dynamic notion of metaphor elucidates the processual aspects of human and Christian identities as they are constructed through the acts of dressing and undressing. Yet an even better understanding of these means of constructing identities arises by applying an idea of image. While a metaphor condenses information about a referent and makes it easier to grasp, by highlighting its resemblance to another phenomenon, an image opens up onto the fullness of envisioned existence. Therefore, identifying dressing and undressing as images reveals not only the multiple ways in which to conceive the identities associated with these acts, but also the nuances of the contexts in which these identities are constructed.

In part III, the focus shifts from religious images to religious activities. The particular practices with which Laurie L. Patton is concerned in chapter 7 are the Hindu rituals originating in the Vedic period, many of which continue to be enacted today. She offers a fresh fivefold philosophical interpretation of the mantras recited during these rituals, by analyzing the metonymies that constitute these poetic chants. Thus, she illuminates (1) the mental world that frames Vedic rituals for their performers, (2) the pragmatism of the technical terms that these performers use as shorthands for sequences of ritual acts, (3) the specific ways in which the elements of the mantras' compound words refer to one another as they express implicit grammatical relationships, (4) the modeling of ritual acts on prototypes, and (5) the identification of ritual actors with the rituals' prototypical performers. In doing so, she demonstrates a metonymical method that can be used to study the interactions of word and act in other religions.

Religious practices are similarly central in chapter 8, where Yiqun Zhou studies in literary, ritual, and historical texts the spatial metaphors mirroring and influencing ancient Greek and Chinese women's participation in public festivals and domestic rites. Assuming anthropologically that spatial metaphors (the physical representations of social arrangements and hierarchies) both map and shape social relationships, Zhou argues that, although sexual separation—formulated typically as a spatial contrast between "inside" (read "female, domestic") and "outside" (read "male, public")—underlay and organized the Greek and Chinese societies, their female religious practitioners challenged differently the physical limits that such separation set. While the prestige and emotional satisfaction of Greek women grew when the women entered and forged friendships within the communities participating in extradomestic public festivals, authority and honor accrued to Chinese women who engaged in domestically located ancestor worship. This contrast between women's roles as reflected and constructed ritually in two paradigmatic classical civilizations bears on a better understanding of the civilizations' distinct legacies for Western and Eastern gender relations.

Whereas Zhou compares and contrasts the religious activities of two historically unrelated communities, Tony K. Stewart considers in chapter 9 the actual encounter between Muslims and Hindus in sixteenth-, seventeenth-, and eighteenth-century Bengal. More precisely, he clarifies the process whereby Bengali Muslim theologians use the non-Islamic vocabulary of their native language, Sanskritically derived Bengali, to explain Islamic practices in terms that Bengali Hindus and Muslims alike can understand. Stewart, by taking a cognitive-linguistic approach to such works as the *Āgama* of Āli Rajā, substitutes a translation model for the syncretistic models that would have been applied by certain scholars preceding Stewart, had they interpreted the interreligious encounters among Āli Rajā and his peers. Specifically,

Stewart takes issue with his predecessors' overemphasis on the products yielded when the practitioners of different religions interact with one another, because adopting this product orientation—which is predicated on four problematic types of metaphor (borrowing, cultural overlay, alchemy, and reproduction)—obscures the processes that constitute the interreligious interactions. By categorizing these interactions as four kinds of translation (literal, approximate, analogous, and cultural), Stewart elucidates the dynamism inherent in interreligious expressions.

Figuring Religions thus offers new ways to compare prominent features of the world's religions, an experience that globalization has made common. In illuminating salient aspects of Hinduism, ancient Greek religions, Judaism, Buddhism, Daoism, Confucianism, Christianity, and Islam, this volume's contributors demonstrate that metaphor and metonymy theories from the fields of philosophy, linguistics, and anthropology can serve as lenses through which religious ideas, images, and activities—key characteristics of today's rapidly changing yet increasingly smaller world—can be seen more clearly.

These three features, perhaps the most common components of faith traditions, have been treated individually in earlier trope-focused inquiries across religions. These studies, while landmarks in their own rights, evince by omission the signal contributions of *Figuring Religions*.

The first of these works, *God and the Creative Imagination: Metaphor, Symbol and Myth in Religion and Theology*, sets forth a theological analysis of the figurative language in which Christian conceptions of truth are couched.[7] This text, while examining metaphors for the relationship between the Christian God and human beings, and addressing symbolic and mythic representations of this relationship, does not delve into theories of metaphor. Moreover, the book acknowledges that divine/human encounters are depicted similarly in Judaism, Christianity, and Islam, but does not extend its focus on figures to other faiths. Instead, this work asserts that truly understanding Christianity's teachings requires appreciating the richness of their representations, because such metaphors, symbols, and myths bring believers into contact with the divine. Centering on the figurative expressions of Christian truth-claims in scripture, theology, belief, and liturgy, the inquiry does not consider the tropes that constitute the categories used by scholars who study Christianity from without rather than from within.

Whereas *God and the Creative Imagination* views religious ideas more narrowly than does *Figuring Religions*, *The Sacred Gaze: Religious Visual Culture in Theory and Practice* devotes more attention to religious visual images.[8] This study of Christian uses of visual representations worldwide in the nineteenth and twentieth centuries shows that applying art-historical theories of visual culture can bring to light the religious beliefs and practices attending the creation and observation of religious images in all faith traditions. Yet, while *The Sacred Gaze* lingers productively on material representations (and adduces in passing an admirable array of visual manifestations of religions other than Christianity), the work skims over textual imagery and the disciplinary approaches suited to its interpretation.

If the practices of different religions are prominent in *Figuring Religions*, the practice of religion in general comes to the fore in *Ritual and Religion in the Making of Humanity*, an anthropological essay that accords primacy to ritual as the source of ontology, morality, and theology.[9] Regarding ritual as the fundamental human behavior, as the means by which societies preserve their conventions, *Ritual and Religion* distinguishes three levels of ritual meaning: (1) the low-order meaning of the taxonomic distinction of linguistic terms, (2) the middle-order meaning of metaphorical similarity between icons and the objects that they indicate, and (3) the high-order meaning of the participatory unification of actors with entities beyond them. Although this elegant schema conduces to nuanced interpretations of ritual performances, the schema's adoption circumscribes metaphor within the sphere of material symbols and leads observers to overlook the metaphorical aspects of statements and mystical experiences.

At the same time that *Figuring Religions* advances new views on cognitive, visual, and ritual forms from a variety of faith traditions and historical periods, this volume suggests ways in which the earliest of its constituent investigations already have shaped the subfield of comparative religious studies. More precisely, the previously published essays that appear in the volume have broken paths of inquiry from which the volume's most recent essays have set forth in new directions.

Thus, just as Tweed's "Marking Religion's Boundaries: Constitutive Terms, Orienting Tropes, and Exegetical Fussiness" treats the metaphors associated with "religion" (a term that is constitutive of the discipline of religious studies), my "'Epic' as an Amnesiac Metaphor: Finding the Word to Compare Ancient Greek and Sanskrit Poems" centers on the metaphorical nature of "epic" (a constitutive term of the subdiscipline of religion and literature). In regard to religious traditions' own ideas, Egge's "Theorizing Embodiment: Conceptual Metaphor Theory and the Comparative Study of Religion" evaluates and elaborates the argument made in Slingerland's "Conceptions of the Self in the *Zhuangzi*: Conceptual Metaphor Analysis and Comparative Thought" for conceptual metaphor theory as a methodology for comparing religions. The process whereby religious texts are embodied and enacted is examined in terms of metonymies in Laurie L. Patton's "Poetry, Ritual, and Associational Thought in Early India and Elsewhere" and in terms of metaphors and images in Utriainen's "Metaphors and Images of Dress and Nakedness: Wrappings of Embodied Identity." And the ways in which metaphors inform religious communities' distinctive self-constructions are explored in view of Muslims and Hindus in pre- and early colonial Bengal in Stewart's "In Search of Equivalence: Conceiving Muslim-Hindu Encounter through Translation Theory," Jews and Christians in medieval Europe in Haskell's "Bathed in Milk: Metaphors of Suckling and Spiritual Transmission in Thirteenth-Century Kabbalah," and ancient Greek and Chinese women in Zhou's "Spatial Metaphors and Women's Religious Activities in Ancient Greece and China."

Taken together, then, the earlier and later studies that appear in *Figuring Religions* constitute a thought-provoking conversation across academic generations—a colloquy that can be comprehended completely only upon hearing both of its sides. This conversation, I hope, will continue with you.

NOTES

1. Patton and Ray 2000; Carter 2004.
2. Ricoeur 1977: 25, 7, 248, 298–99, 313.
3. Brown [1927] 1966: 149–50.
4. Lakoff and Johnson [1980] 2003: 5 (emphasis removed), 39.
5. Lakoff and Johnson [1980] 2003: 146, 247.
6. Fernandez 1991: 57, 123, 161, 192, 151, 196.
7. Avis 1999.
8. Morgan 2005.
9. Rappaport 1999.

REFERENCES

Avis, Paul. 1999. *God and the Creative Imagination: Metaphor, Symbol and Myth in Religion and Theology*. London: Routledge.

Brown, Stephen J. 1966. *The World of Imagery: Metaphor and Kindred Imagery*. London: Routledge & Kegan Paul, 1927. Reprint, New York: Russell & Russell.

Carter, Jeffrey, ed. 2004. "Comparison in the History of Religions: Reflections and Critiques." Special issue, *Method & Theory in the Study of Religion* 16, no. 1.

Fernandez, James. 1991. *Beyond Metaphor: The Theory of Tropes in Anthropology.* Stanford: Stanford University Press.

Lakoff, George, and Mark Johnson. 2003. *Metaphors We Live By.* Chicago: University of Chicago Press, 1980. Reprint, with a new afterword, Chicago: University of Chicago Press.

Morgan, David. 2005. *The Sacred Gaze: Religious Visual Culture in Theory and Practice.* Berkeley: University of California Press.

Patton, Kimberley C., and Benjamin C. Ray, eds. 2000. *A Magic Still Dwells: Comparative Religion in the Postmodern Age.* Berkeley: University of California Press.

Rappaport, Roy A. 1999. *Ritual and Religion in the Making of Humanity.* Cambridge: Cambridge University Press.

Ricoeur, Paul. 1977. *The Rule of Metaphor: Multi-disciplinary Studies of the Creation of Meaning in Language.* Translated by Robert Czerny, Kathleen McLaughlin, and John Costello. Toronto: University of Toronto Press.

PART I

Figuring Religious Ideas

Marking Religion's Boundaries

Constitutive Terms, Orienting Tropes, and Exegetical Fussiness

Thomas A. Tweed

Religion cannot reasonably be taken to be a valid analytical category since it does not pick out any distinctive cross-cultural aspect of human life.
  —Timothy Fitzgerald, *The Ideology of Religious Studies*

When everyone around you is demonstrating that no one can walk, it's a good time to get up quickly and start running.
  —Michel Serres to Bruno Latour, *Conversations on Science, Culture, and Time*[1]

Despite warnings about the futility of efforts to define religion, many scholars still choose to "get up and start running." In this essay I warm up for the sprint by discussing constitutive terms and arguing for scholars' role-specific obligation to define them. Meeting that obligation, I suggest, means being clear about the type of definition offered and attending carefully to the choice of orienting trope, since definitions imply theories and employ tropes. Interpreters of religion have relied on a wide range of orienting metaphors, and I consider some of the most influential ones as I point to some implications of those choices.

For good reasons, nonspecialists start to snooze when definitions come up; scholars of religion, who've heard it all before, exhale a knowing sigh. Not another (doomed) attempt to characterize religion! And there is a long and lofty lineage of scholarly suspicion, even contempt, for definitional attempts. Consider this excerpt from a 1901 article by an influential American scholar of religion, James H. Leuba, who recorded a familiar complaint: there are lots of definitions and none of them seem to agree.

> It has been a favorite custom with [scholars] to put up the concentrated results of their toil with little formulae, commonly called *definitions* of religion. Although they evince most astonishing divergencies, extending even to hopeless contradiction, they will, when considered together and compared with each other, at least warn us away from certain false conceptions which have obscured the view of otherwise clear-sighted men. It must be confessed that the definitions of religion would afford a happy topic for a malicious person bent upon showing the quackery of the Doctors in religion.[2]

I don't think I'm driven by any "malicious" impulses—though readers can decide that for themselves—and I certainly don't think it's "quackery" for scholars to propose definitions, even "astonishing[ly] divergen[t]" and "hopeless[ly] contradictory" ones. On the contrary, I suggest that scholars have a role-specific obligation to define constitutive disciplinary terms: "art" for art history, "music" for musicology, "literature" for literary studies, "culture" for anthropology, "space" for geography, and "language" for linguistics.[3]

"EXEGETICAL FUSSINESS" AS ROLE-SPECIFIC DUTY

Constitutive terms are those that constitute or mark the boundaries of a field of study. Practitioners—artists, musicians, poets, and the pious in the pews—don't have to define these constitutive terms. It is enough that they know how to produce a painting, play the flute, write a sonnet, or recite the Lord's Prayer. Scholars who have been trained to participate in an academic conversation, however, have a role-specific obligation to reflect on their work—and on the constitutive terms of their discipline. They have a professional duty to be self-conscious in their use of central categories—art, religion, literature, or music. So when poet and literature professor John Hollander composed the poems collected in *The Night Mirror* he was properly focused on his art, but when he wrote *Rhyme's Reason*, his brilliant guide to verse, he rightly also pondered poetry and its "formal structures." When the ethnomusicologist John Blacking—who confided to readers that he was also a musician—played Chopin on his living-room piano on a Saturday afternoon, he had no duty to ponder whether "humanly ordered sound" was an inclusive enough definition of music. Only when he stepped into his study to write about the *mankuntu* dance song of the Gwembe Tonga of Zambia did he have an obligation to reflect on his field's central category.[4]

But the problems of defining these categories can be so great that some scholars feel unable to meet their role-specific professional duties. In some instances, well-grounded worries about the adequacy of disciplinary idiom have led scholars to silence. The 1980 edition of *The New Grove Dictionary of Music and Musicians*, which had plenty of room in its twenty hefty volumes, included no entry for "music"; the 2000 edition of *A Handbook to Literature* failed to define "literature"; and the editors of the 1997 edition of the *Oxford Dictionary of Art* didn't even take a stab at defining "art."[5]

Even when scholars do reflect on these categories they often find themselves befuddled. Those struggling with their role-specific obligation encounter the disorienting diversity of previous definitions. As the author of the entry on "religion" in *The HarperCollins Dictionary of Religion* noted, "Defining religion is often held to be difficult. Introductions to the study of religion routinely include long lists of definitions of religion as proof of this."[6] Definers also confront other difficulties, including the constitutive term's alleged inability to include all instances in all times and places: this clan does not seem to have art, those people write no literature, that culture has no word for music.

Some who confront these difficulties eschew definitions but self-consciously reflect on the prior attempts and the conceptual problems. For example, a group of musicologists and philosophers of music who took on the task in the ambitiously titled volume *What Is Music?* noted that "the question 'what is music?' has no easy answer." As the book's editor suggested, "'music' seems . . . to be a culturally unstable term, likely to remain a contested concept within our own civilization where the term covers a wide range of practices." In the same spirit, though the latest edition of *The New Grove Dictionary of Music and Musicians* includes an entry on "music" (my friends in musicology tell me it's because of the "uproar" generated by its omission from the previous edition), this standard reference work avoids defining it: "Imposing a single definition flies in the face of the broadly relativistic intercultural and historically conscious nature of this dictionary." That account ends by restating the definitional problem: "It ought to be possible to define music in an interculturally valid way, but the fact that definers inevitably speak with the language and from the cultural viewpoint of their own societies is a major obstacle. Only a few societies have a word whose meaning corresponds roughly to the English 'music'; and it is questionable whether the concept of music in the breadth it enjoys in Western cultures is present in the cognitive maps of all cultures." Other constitutive terms don't seem to be found on all cognitive maps either. After noting the difficulties in discerning whether all cultures have a term or concept for art, the entry in *The Dictionary of Art* makes a similar point: "the question of whether art is or is not . . . an integral part of human society remains undecided."[7]

The geographer David N. Livingstone, while discussing attempts to define "geography," explains why faces flush during vigorous disciplinary debates about (apparently) small differences in usage and meaning: "To have command of definition is to have control of discourse. For this reason it is not surprising that *exegetical fussiness* over the precise meaning of terms is characteristic of those apologetic works that aim to fix disciplinary identity." Scholars can't—and shouldn't—avoid reflecting on the terms that "fix disciplinary identity," and it is the academics who use them who get to define them. As the religion scholar Jonathan Z. Smith noted, "'Religion' is not a native term; it is a term created by scholars for their intellectual purposes and therefore is theirs to define. It is a second-order, generic concept that plays the same role in establishing a disciplinary horizon that a concept such as 'language' plays in linguistics or 'culture' plays in anthropology. There can be no disciplined study of religion without such a horizon." So even if not all interpreters have a duty to construct theories and propose definitions— for then what would anyone have to theorize?—our professional obligations nudge us to enter the debate about the meaning and usefulness of constitutive terms. Those of us who claim a lineage in the academic conversation about religion should be clear about how we use the term. In that sense, we are called to the task of defining—and to contesting definitions. We are called to offer self-conscious sightings from where we stand, reflexive surveys of the disciplinary horizon. We are called to "exegetical fussiness."[8]

TYPES OF DEFINITIONS: LEXICAL, EMPIRICAL, AND STIPULATIVE

As we get "fussy" about the meaning of terms, we might find that we're appealing to either cartographic or visual analogies: definition is "the setting of bounds or limits" or the rendering of "an object or image distinct to the eye." And however scholars have defined definition—and some linguists and philosophers have spent a good deal of energy doing precisely that—most note the variety of methods employed. Among scholars of religion, Robert D. Baird has presented a helpful typology of definitions. He distinguishes lexical, real, and functional (or stipulative) definitions. For Baird, a "lexical definition" mirrors ordinary usage. It explains "the actual way in which some actual word has been used by some actual person." We may think of this as the dictionary definition. An example may include the long entry from the *Oxford English Dictionary*, which documents seven primary uses of "religion" and includes, with each, a chronologically arranged list of quotations from texts that use it that way. So, for example, the fifth definition is: "Recognition on the part of man of some higher unseen power as having control of his destiny, and as being entitled to obedience, reverence, and worship; the general mental and moral attitude resulting from this belief, with reference to its effect upon the individual or the community; personal or general acceptance of this feeling as a standard of spiritual and practical life." Below that definition are ten quotations and citations from texts published between 1535 and 1877, including passages from works by Thomas Hobbes (1651) and Adam Smith (1776).[9]

A "real definition," which might be labeled an empirical or inductive definition, "is a true statement about things that are." Such definitions offer propositions about the nature of things, and they can be true or false. Truth in this approach often, though not always, means correspondence with mind-independent objects. An example may be found in Rodney Stark and Roger Finke's *Acts of Faith*. Although the authors suggest that their sociological theory of religion is not a "fully deductive theoretical system," they offer ninety-nine "propositions" and thirty-six "definitions" throughout the book, from assertions that excavate the "micro foundations" of religion to those that help explain how religious institutions transform from sect to church. Consider, for example, proposition six: "In pursuit of rewards, humans will seek to utilize and manipulate the supernatural." Or definition five: "Religion consists of very general explanations of existence, including terms of exchange with a god or gods." In these and other propositions and definitions, Stark and Finke offer proposals about what religion is and how it functions. They offer an empirical definition.[10]

Finally, scholars can propose "stipulative definitions," which somewhat arbitrarily stipulate "that a certain word means a certain thing." Stipulative definitions cannot be true or false; they can be only more or less useful. The psychologist and philosopher William James decided on this approach near the start of his influential Gifford Lectures, *The Varieties of Religious Experience*:

The field of religion being as wide as this, it is manifestly impossible that I should pretend to cover it. My lectures must be limited to a fraction of the subject. And, although it would indeed be foolish to set up an abstract definition of religion's essence, and then proceed to defend that definition against all comers, yet this need not prevent me from taking my own narrow view of what religion shall consist in *for the purposes of these lectures*, or out of the many meanings of the word, from choosing the one meaning in which I wish to interest you particularly, and proclaiming arbitrarily that when I say "religion" I mean *that*.[11]

In this self-consciously stipulative approach, James says that he offers the definition "*for the purposes of these lectures*," and italicizes the phrase for emphasis. He acknowledges, without remorse or apology, that it is an "arbitrar[y]" account designed for a particular purpose. And he reminds readers of that a few pages later when he offers his famous definition: "the feelings, acts, and experiences of individual men in their solitude, so far as they apprehend themselves to stand in relation to whatever they may consider the divine." Yet scholars usually omit—or at least deemphasize—the introductory phrase of that sentence: "Religion, therefore, as I now ask you arbitrarily to take it shall mean for us . . ." Note the function of several words here: "I," "now," "arbitrarily," "you," "us." James tried to make clear, then, that a particular scholar was stipulating an arbitrary definition for particular purposes and a particular audience.[12]

One way to clarify the differences between stipulative and empirical approaches to defining constitutive terms is to consider a recent contribution to the ongoing debate over the term "culture" in the field of anthropology. In an imaginative article in *American Anthropologist* four scholars coauthored a piece that juxtaposed four positions that, taken together, created a published "conversation about culture." Most important, they reframe the issue of definition in a very helpful way by shifting the question from "what form of the concept one might apply" to "when to apply the concept." They ask, "Does one lean more toward induction or deduction in applying the cultural concept?" Two of the authors suggest that we introduce the constitutive term only at the end of a study (an empirical or inductive definition); the other two favor proposing a definition at the start of the work (a stipulative or deductive definition). Nomi Maya Stolzenberg, who defends the stipulative approach, acknowledges the "lack of precision" in the term "culture": "No one could seriously deny that 'culture' is an exceedingly vague and ambiguous term." But, she suggests, "it is precisely because of its lack of precision that culture remains a useful concept, for both anthropologists and those outside the field." Stolzenberg, a legal scholar, suggests that we reimagine "culture" and other constitutive terms and "cease to think of [them] as the name for a thing and come to view [them] instead as a placeholder for a set of inquiries—inquiries which may be destined never to be resolved."[13]

CONSIDERING OBJECTIONS TO DEFINITIONS

Whether interpreters have offered lexical, empirical, or stipulative definitions—and empirical definitions have predominated—some religion scholars have challenged any attempt to define the field's constitutive term. Still, there have been many attempts at definition, as Leuba noted in his 1901 article. Eleven years later, Leuba reprinted a revised version of that essay in *A Psychological Study of Religion* and listed more than four dozen definitions of religion in an appendix to that volume. Using Leuba's list and other evidence of the diversity of definitions, some scholars have rejected definition altogether on the grounds that scholars have been unable to agree on the meaning and use of the term. This lexical objection, which focuses on linguistic use, is only one of several. A second sort of objection, which focuses on the term's historical origins, suggests that we should abandon the term—and attempts at definition—because "religion" is a Western (and Christian) category that arose (or gained wider usage) in a colonial context. Even if the term has a much longer history, Western missionaries, traders, soldiers, and civil servants advanced its use in a discourse that still informs the academic study of religion. A third objection, closely related to the second, assesses the category using pragmatic criteria and highlights its moral implications. As one interpreter has suggested, the Western term has "mediated the value-charged and deeply inequitable encounters between 'us' and 'them,' the 'West' and the 'Orient,' the present and the past." A fourth objection to defining religion repeats concerns about defining other constitutive terms, like "music": critics point to its lack of cross-cultural breadth or universal applicability. They note either that the term "religion" is not found in all languages and cultures, or that the announced features of religion are not found in all cultures. This position assumes that all definitions are empirical and thereby entail true or false claims that can be assessed by considering whether they correspond with a mind-independent state of affairs. It also assumes that "universality" is a reasonable criterion for definitions. Finally, as with art historians who propose that "visual culture" replace "art" in academic conversations, some religion scholars don't object to the view I have supported here—that disciplines employ constitutive terms and we should define them. Instead, they chronicle the limitations of the category "religion" while advocating an alternative. So "politics," "ritual," "soteriology," "faith," and "tradition" are nominated as better interpretive categories. Or, in a related approach, religious studies is reimagined as cultural studies, and scholars suggest that "culture" should be taken as the central analytical term.[14]

To consider the final objection first, even if we were to seek alternative categories, none of the proposed alternatives overcomes the other four objections or dissolves definitional problems. *Culture*, the classic 1952 work by anthropologists A. L. Kroeber and Clyde Kluckhohn, and many other contributions to the anthropological conversation about that field's constitutive term show that "culture" is at least as contested as "religion." And Fitzgerald's proposed alternatives to the latter—"soteriology," "politics," and "ritual"— are not much better. In *The Ideology of Religious Studies*, Fitzgerald suggests that "[r]eligion cannot reasonably be taken to be a valid analytical category since it does not pick out any distinctive cross-cultural aspect of human life." Drawing from several of the standard objections to definition, Fitzgerald argues "for deleting the word 'religion' from the list of analytical categories entirely" not only because it does not identify a cross-cultural practice and so has no analytical use for those who study, for example, Japan and India, where no term parallels "religion." The term also deserves to be dumped, Fitzgerald argues, because it is "ideologically charged," having arisen in the context of nineteenth-century European colonization. He proposes that religious studies be reimagined as cultural studies and that we turn to other, less problematic analytical categories.[15]

But Fitzgerald's three categories and all constitutive disciplinary terms (including "religion") have their limits. Consider a few observations about the proposed terms that might suggest that, at the least, they are not self-evidently more adequate, even without highlighting a primary objection—that "religion" has been the primary category used by scholars in this professional conversation since the mid-nineteenth century and cannot be replaced easily. Like the term "religion," "soteriology," "politics," and "ritual" arose in particular social contexts for particular purposes, and they don't seem to have cross-cultural equivalents in all societies. "Politics," meaning "the science and art of government," comes from a Greek root pertaining to citizens, and it was connected with ancient Greek conversations about citizenship, the state, and (more broadly) the social good.[16] This term is no less idiosyncratic or situated for having had wide influence, and to pencil in this term at the top of the religion scholar's lexicon is to evoke certain notions about what religion is and how it functions. To talk about religion in terms of politics is to foreground the collectivity more than the individual and to highlight power more than meaning. Such an approach may be useful. Collectivity and power are important. But this strategy is not free of definitional—or ideological—difficulties.

"Ritual," a term of Latin origin that refers to "a prescribed order of performing religious or other devotional service," is a slightly better alternative category, since it seems to make sense of a wider range of practices across cultures and periods. Yet it too arose in a particular cultural context and, like "politics," is not as inclusive as the maligned term "religion." Anthropologist Roy A. Rappaport and others who have argued that "ritual is taken to be the ground from which religious conceptions spring" can offer a compelling account of practices. Yet they still confront the difficulties of identifying "religion's most general and universal elements" (for Rappaport, "the Holy") as they also try to find creative ways to illumine traditional religious features that "ritual" ("the performance of more or less invariant sequences of formal acts and utterances not entirely coded by the performers") seems to obscure—for example, artifacts, narratives, and institutions.[17]

And Fitzgerald's third proposed category, "soteriology," seems even more problematic. It is a Greek term that has been used primarily in Western Christian theology to describe "Christ's saving work" or the "doctrine of salvation." But the Baktaman of New Guinea don't talk much about soteriology. Neither do Theravāda Buddhist monks in Sri Lanka. Moreover, even if some interpreters might respond by suggesting that theoretical terms need not follow vernacular use or that the Buddhists and the Baktaman do share some notion of salvation or, more broadly, some concept of an ultimate goal, we have only returned to the sort of fundamental definitional problems that drove many to befuddlement—or silence—when attempting to characterize religion. For now we must ask if "salvation" is inclusive enough to make sense of both the Buddhist monk's striving for *nirvāṇa*, the cessation of suffering and release from rebirth, and the Baktaman's hope that their *finik* (spirit) can be transformed through a nonviolent death into a *sabkār* (deceased spirit) that is transported to the land of the dead. We are not far from where we began as we started to ponder the difficulties of the term "religion."[18]

That shouldn't surprise us. No constitutive disciplinary term is elastic enough to perform all the work that scholars demand of it. But that means we should continually refine and revise our understanding of the term for different purposes and contexts, not abandon it. As sociologist Max Weber noted, broad categories—he called them "ideal types"—are theoretical constructs that function as more or less useful interpretive tools. We shouldn't be surprised that they fail to conform to the full range of historical or contemporary cases. And their effectiveness isn't challenged when we find some instances that don't seem to "fit"—whether analyzing Shintō in Japan, Hinduism in India, or any other particular cluster of spiritual practices. As the anthropologist Melford E. Spiro has argued, interpretive terms need not be "universal" to be useful: "From what methodological principle does it follow that religion—or, for that matter, anything else—must be universal if it is to be studied comparatively?" The term "religion" has not failed us when we decide that it obscures some features we want to highlight. It has directed our attention to practices that we may otherwise have missed. It has prompted further conversation, more contestation. It has done its work. We know something we did not know. We have been reminded—and we always need reminding—that there are other sites that offer other sightings.[19]

If we shouldn't be surprised—or disappointed—by the "discovery" that constitutive terms, while elastic, still don't stretch to cover all we can see from where we stand, we shouldn't abandon them either, simply because our scholarly idiom arose in particular social contexts. All constitutive disciplinary terms—including "music," "art," "literature," "culture," and "religion"—are located and contested. All arose, and have been used, in particular social sites for particular purposes.

So, to return to the five objections to defining religion, only the last—that another term would be better—seems to be without much merit, and the other four objections, though useful as correctives, are not significant enough to abandon the definitional task. First, as critics have pointed out, "religion" has been defined in a variety of ways. Yet definitional variety indicates that the term *can* be defined, not that it cannot, since agreement is not necessary, possible, or useful. "It was once a tactic of students of religion," Jonathan Z. Smith argued in challenging Winston King's dismissive claim, "to cite the appendix of James H. Leuba's *Psychological Study of Religion* (1912), which lists more than fifty definitions of religion, to demonstrate that 'the effort clearly to define religion in short compass is a hopeless task.'" But the task is not hopeless, just demanding. Note that the widely consulted religious-studies reference work that acknowledged the diversity of definitions still went on to offer one: religion is "a system of beliefs and practices that are relative to superhuman beings." And the entry's author justified the attempt: "the lists [of definitions] fail to demonstrate that the task of defining religion is so difficult that one might as well give up on the task. What the lists show is that there is little agreement on an adequate definition."[20]

The second and third objections to definition also seem right, although they too don't preclude attempts to set out the meaning of the term: even if the term has an earlier origin, scholarly discourse about religion did emerge in a colonial context and has been employed unjustly to marginalize some groups. Many studies, including those by Talal Asad, David Chidester, Donald Lopez, and Richard King, have shown that. But, as Chidester notes, that is not grounds to abandon the term: "After reviewing the history of colonial productions and reproduction on contested frontiers, we might happily abandon *religion* and *religions* as terms of analysis if we were not, as the result of that very history, stuck with them." If, as even Wilfred Cantwell Smith and Timothy Fitzgerald acknowledge, constitutive terms establish disciplinary horizons, religion scholars need such terms. We are "stuck" with them. The disorienting variety, ambivalent history, and inequitable function of definitions only make scholars' obligations to assess previous accounts and to self-consciously redefine the category more complicated—and more morally urgent. Definitions matter.[21]

DEFINITIONS, TROPES, AND THEORIES

Definitions matter, in part, because they offer hints about theories. The widely read reference book I quoted earlier, *The HarperCollins Dictionary of Religion*, notes that "a specific definition of religion usually comes from a particular discipline or theory of religion."[22] I agree that definitions and theories are linked, although I would challenge the misleading causal claim implied in the phrase "comes from," since that phrasing obscures the complex ways that definitions also shape theories. And I would go further. Definitions and theories also intertwine with tropes. Definitions, in my view, imply theories and employ tropes. This reciprocal triadic relation involves a constant crisscrossing of influences among definition, theory, and trope.

Consider Sigmund Freud's famous definition of religion in *The Future of an Illusion*, which appeared in 1927. Freud had begun his analysis of religion in 1907, with the publication of "Obsessive Actions and Religious Practices," and he continued it in other writings until he died in 1939 at the age of eighty-three. Although his theories have been vigorously and widely challenged, inside and outside the field of religious studies, his lexicon and interpretations have remained influential. For that reason one prominent interpreter said of the psychoanalyst, "Freud is inescapable."[23] I suppose we could try to avoid him, but that would be unwise here, since his *Future of an Illusion* usefully illustrates the reciprocal interactivity among definition, trope, and theory. In that volume, Freud—like most authors of theoretical works on religion—actually employs several tropes. For example, in a passage that recalls Karl Marx's famous definition of religion as an "opiate," the Viennese therapist suggests that "the effects of religious consolations may be likened to that of a narcotic." But more central to the book's argument than this simile is a metaphor that compares religion to illness, or individual psychological dysfunction. Religion is "the universal obsessional neurosis of humanity; like the obsessional neurosis of children, it arose out of the Oedipus complex, out of the relation to the father." As with all definitions to some extent, and especially those of complex cultural practices, Freud reaches for figurative language to establish some contiguity, if not identity, between the *definiendum* (the unknown that is defined) and the *definiens* (the known that is used to define the term). Although I do not agree with many of Freud's explanations of religion's nature and function, I am not criticizing him here for turning to figures. All of religion's scholarly interpreters have done that, and Freud is actually much more self-conscious than many. He ends the paragraph—after going on to suggest that religion, in this approach, becomes "a system of wishful illusions" comparable to amentia (a state of acute hallucinatory confusion)—by acknowledging the function and limits of his metaphor: "But these are only analogies, by the help of which we endeavour to understand a social phenomenon; the pathology of the individual does not supply us with a fully valid counterpart."[24]

So, if Freud self-consciously employed figurative language in his definition of religion, the definition he fashioned from this primary trope (children's psychological pathology) evokes in turn the outlines of a theory of religion. Even without recourse to the rest of the book—which I think would support this reading—we can tentatively identify several implicit claims in this brief definition. First, since Freud compares religion to a psychological dysfunction, the origin of religion is psychic rather than social, cultural, political, or economic. Second, since it is a "universal" pathology of "humanity," religion seems to be a transcultural form that crosses chronological and spatial boundaries. Third, religion is "like the . . . neurosis of children," so in this simile religious adherents are analogous to children. Fourth, since Freud juxtaposes religion and children, who are not developmentally advanced, it seems to follow that religion represents a lower stage of cultural development. (Freud confirms this in the next sentence: "If this view is right, it is to be supposed that a turning-away from religion is bound to occur with the fatal inevitability of a process of growth, and that we find ourselves at this very juncture in the middle of that phase of development.") Fifth, since religion arises from "the relation to the father," it must reproduce in some ways that dependent relation (at least as that relation is imagined in a particular model of the family). Sixth, although Freud insists earlier in the book that "to assess the truth-value of religious doctrines does not lie within the scope of the present enquiry," religion seems to be a bad thing. Either, at best, humanity is just going through a stage it will outgrow, or we need to plop humanity on the couch for what promises to be a very long series of therapeutic interventions.[25]

I could go on. I could say more about the outlines of a theory of religion embedded in the tropes found in this one passage or in many other classic formulations of religion's meaning. You may want to quarrel with this or that in my reading of Freud's definition, but I hope that I have at least established that definition, theory, and trope seem to shape each other reciprocally. I will refer to the relation between definition and theory later, but so far I have talked about tropes without considering what they are or how they function—or how tropic analysis can be useful in the humanities and the social sciences, especially in the study of religion.[26]

As I hinted in my reading of Freud's definition of religion as psychological pathology, tropes are figures of speech that depart from the ordinary form, use, or arrangement of words. They involve figurative, or nonliteral, language. As James W. Fernandez noted in his introduction to *Beyond Metaphor*, cultural interpreters who have taken figurative language seriously often have highlighted one type of trope, metaphor. Scholars have taken several approaches in their efforts to understand metaphor. First, some have turned to "the Aristotelian-derived strain of metaphor theory," which "focuses upon the transfer of features of meaning from one domain of understanding to another." A second interpretive tradition that is "much influenced by the American critic and philosopher Kenneth Burke . . . concentrates on how experience in culture and position in society are constructed through metaphoric predication."[27] A third approach, which highlights metaphors' effects or uses and challenges the notion that they contain hidden or nonliteral meaning that needs to be decoded, emerges from the philosopher Donald Davidson's 1978 essay "What Metaphors Mean" and has been endorsed and revised by, among others, Richard Rorty and Nancy K. Frankenberry.[28]

As Fernandez and his colleagues suggested, the first two approaches have been most influential, and since the 1980s metaphor theory in the social sciences has focused more on the variety of tropes and their "foundations" in culture. Rhetoricians have identified more than two hundred figures of speech, including simile, symbol, allegory, personification, apostrophe, synecdoche, and metonymy. So Paul Friedrich, one of the contributors to Fernandez's volume, was right to emphasize "polytropy" and to urge scholars to recall the full range of figurative language at play in cultural practices. Yet of the five "macrotropes" that Friedrich identifies—image tropes, modal tropes, formal tropes, contiguity tropes, and analogical tropes—it is analogical language, especially metaphor, that can be especially useful in cultural analysis.[29]

The metaphors that cultural analysts interpret can be direct or indirect. Consider examples from the well-known poem by T. S. Eliot "The Love Song of J. Alfred Prufrock." "And I have seen the eternal Footman hold my coat, and snicker" is a direct metaphor that identifies the divine with an attendant or servant. An indirect metaphor, in which the comparison is implied but not stated, appears in an earlier line: "The yellow fog that rubs its back upon the window panes."[30] This image implies, but does not declare, that the fog is a cat. Or, to use examples from Freud's definition, neurosis is the direct metaphor. He says that religion is "the universal obsessional neurosis of humanity." Because the next sentence parallels religion with a "neurosis of children," the passage also includes an indirect evolutionary or developmental metaphor that—as discussed earlier—portrays religion as childish, a lower stage of cultural development.[31]

To demarcate religion's boundaries, interpreters of religion have employed many different kinds of tropes. Some have used symbols: G. W. F. Hegel's "consciousness of God," F. Max Müller's "perception of the Infinite," and Rudolf Otto's "experience of the Holy."[32] Metaphor, however, is a widely used trope. Although one philosopher has suggested that "a definition must not be expressed in metaphor or figurative language"[33]—one of his thirteen rules for constructing definitions—this seems to be a principle that no scholar who risks a definition can follow. Many contemporary theorists would acknowledge that most language is figurative in some sense, and metaphor is an important figure.

Using metaphor to define metaphor—and, unrepentant, breaking that rule of definition—I suggest that metaphor is a lens and a vehicle. It directs language users' attention to this and not that, and transports them from one domain of language, experience, and practice to another. In my terms, it prompts new sightings and crossings. As Davidson proposed, it can be helpful to think about "the effects metaphors have on us" and talk about what metaphors do. What do they do? They redirect our attention. Drawing on analogy for their power, metaphors illumine some features of the terrain and obscure others. To use an example from my study of Cuban American devotion at the shrine of Our Lady of Charity, Bishop Agustín Román, the shrine's director, turned to metaphor to address race relations in Miami, a city that had been unsettled by ethnic and racial tension for years. Consider my earlier account of the event:

> In 1994 Román arranged for a bus filled with white Cubans from the shrine to visit the Haitian Catholic Center, where they would participate in a mass and procession on the feast of Corpus Christi. During the ride to Little Haiti the shrine director tried to prepare the Cubans for what they soon would experience: the only white faces in a crowd of several hundred, all eyes on them. And he tried to promote tolerance. Noting the differences in skin color, he turned to an analogy from Cuban foodways to persuade. He reminded the white Cubans—no one needed reminding—of their traditional love for black beans and white rice. Extending that analogy to Cuban history and identity, the shrine director suggested that "Cuba is beans and rice, black and white."

The Cuban leader's metaphor redirected the attention of the white devotees to food, a beloved traditional dish. Cuba is a plate on which black beans and white rice have been mixed. The metaphoric utterance associated language, experience, and practice about food with language, experience, and practice concerning race. As some cognitive scientists have proposed, the metaphor made a "class-inclusion assertion." In other words, the analogy established a grouping or relation between two categories—food and race—and, I would add, between two domains of practice. It highlighted the ways that racial comminglings, like culinary combinations, have been part of Cuban history. In contrast, to return to the passage from Freud again, the direct metaphor of psychological pathology and the indirect metaphor of evolutionary stages prompt readers to highlight dysfunction and immaturity and obscure the ways that religion may arise from or cultivate mental or physical health and may inspire or reflect a mature engagement with the world.[34]

Metaphor can redirect attention because it functions as a mode of transport. It prompts a linguistic crossing that can create associations, stir affect, and prompt action. The shrine director induced nostalgia, even triggered sense memory, as he used the culinary metaphor to prescribe and transform the white Cubans' behavior when they entered the Haitian church—and after they left. He transferred memories, values, and emotions from the realm of food to the realm of social relations as he talked about black beans. So, in this metaphor and in others, more than a single term ("beans," "neurosis," or "children") is transferred from one use to another, transported from one cultural domain to another. Metaphors propel language—and language users—between frames of reference, to borrow a phrase from physics. Or, in Nelson Goodman's terms, there is a "migration of concepts." But metaphor is a reciprocal interactive process. It is not a matter of transferring one static and bounded "scheme" to another. As some interpreters of metaphor have noted, it is the reciprocal and relational dynamics of metaphor that characterize this trope. Victor Turner, for example, suggested that "the two thoughts are active together, they 'engender' thought in their coactivity." So, when Freud appealed to the metaphor of children and, indirectly, to the evolutionary model positing progressive linear "stages" of nature and culture, he put that organic image in dynamic reciprocal relation with the scholarly discourse about religion. In the same way, in that brief passage in Freud's *Future of an Illusion*, a confluence of concepts from depth psychology (obsession, neurosis, Oedipal complex) "migrated" back and forth between a discourse about religious life and a discourse about psychic life.[35]

Analogical language, as well as this sort of figurative process, is inscribed in many other scholarly definitions of religion. Freud was not the only interpreter of religion to employ tropes. Sherry Ortner's "key metaphors," Turner's "root metaphors," Fernandez's "organizing metaphors," or what I call orienting metaphors appear in many other definitions.[36]

ORIENTING METAPHORS: TROPES IN DEFINITIONS OF RELIGION

At least a dozen orienting metaphors have had some influence in the history of scholarly definitions of religion. Most definitions employ more than one of these, so there is no pure type, only hybrid forms that approximate the categories in this taxonomy. And some orienting metaphors have had much more influence than others. Religion has been analogized as capacity, organism, system, worldview, illness, narcotic, picture, form of life, society, institution, projection, and space.

The first approach—to define religion by identifying it with one or more psychic capacities—has been especially popular. In fact, this has been the favorite method of classifying religion's definitions. In some premodern philosophical approaches, interpreters talked about psychological faculties, and some (even into the late nineteenth century) posited a distinctive religious faculty. Even if the idiom has changed over time, many interpreters have defined religion by emphasizing one or another psychic capacity: believing, willing, or feeling. In other words, there are—as Friedrich Schleiermacher, James Leuba, and many others have proposed—intellectualist, volitional, and affective definitions. For example, religion is belief for many scholars, as in the anthropologist Edward B. Tylor's famous definition: "the belief in spiritual beings." But the object of belief varies to some extent. Religion has been imagined as belief in an ever-living God (James Martineau), the super-human (C. P. Tiele), God and spiritual beings (Robert Crawford), human-like beings (Stewart Guthrie), or a world of counterintuitive supernatural agents (Scott Atran). In a related intellectualist approach, not only Guthrie and Atran but several other scholars have applied the findings of cognitive science and have taken cognition as the central metaphor.[37] Volitional defini-tions, which have exerted less influence, emphasize either moral action (Im-manuel Kant) or ritual action (Roy Rappaport). In a similar way, although sociologist Christian Smith acknowledges the significance of "beliefs, sym-bols, and practices," the core of his definition emphasizes the ways in which religions are "superempirically referenced wellsprings of moral order." Affec-tive definitions, however, associate religion with a feeling, for example, ab-solute dependence (Schleiermacher), *mysterium tremendum* (Otto), or hopes and fears (Hume).[38]

Affective definitions are closely aligned with another capacity metaphor: religion is about experiencing. This association derives in part from the mul-tiple terms that Schleiermacher employed: although he marked off religion's distinctive terrain with the term *Gefühl* (feeling), he also used related terms such as *Anschauung* (intuition) and *Empfindung* (experience).[39] The latter became a central analogue in many definitions. Religion is noncognitive; it does not, as in the Tylorian tradition, make claims about the nature of things. In this view, religion is an experience of the Holy (Otto), the sacred (Eliade), the Infinite (Müller), or invisible things (Jevons).[40]

Other affective definitions frame religion as a desire or, better, as a con-cern. Hume claimed religion was "an anxious concern for happiness," but in a more influential formulation the theologian Paul Tillich suggested that religion was one's "ultimate concern." Scholars before him anticipated Til-lich's approach: religion is, for George Malcolm Stratton, a "bearing toward what seems to [him] the Best, or Greatest," and, for Bernard Bosanquet, the "objects, habits, and convictions . . . he would die for." And many who have followed Tillich, including Baird and John Wilson, have found "ultimate concern" a compelling analogue. As Jonathan Z. Smith notes, Tillich's definition is one of two—the other is Spiro's, which I introduced earlier and will return to later—that "command widespread scholarly assent."[41]

Many influential accounts define religion by pointing to several psychic capacities: religion as belief and feeling (Morris Jastrow Jr.) or as emotions, conceptions, and sentiments (C. P. Tiele). Some definitions that combine intellectualist, affective, and volitional approaches imagine religion not only as believing or feeling but also as doing—by trading on the notion of religion as will. Consider James's definition of religion as "feelings, acts, and experiences" or Emile Durkheim's account of religion as "beliefs and practices."[42]

Other definitions appeal to other orienting metaphors, even if they simultaneously appeal to one or another capacity metaphor. For instance, there are definitions that have appealed to organic tropes, even imaging religion as an organism. In a direct metaphor of this type, the American scientist Edward O. Wilson talked about "religion as superorganism." In somewhat less direct ways, many scholars since the late nineteenth century, like Freud, have implied an analogy to the development of the individual or the evolution of the natural world (or both). To mention only two famous examples, Tylor spoke of "the natural evolution of religious ideas" and Müller claimed to trace "the origin and growth of religion." In a similar vein, several definitions turn to a term from the natural sciences, "system," to understand religion. This analogy highlights the assumption that religion includes parts that form a whole. Here "system" is often interpreted more statically than in the field of physics, which understands systems as groups of bodies moving in space according to some dynamic law. Applied to the task of definition, religion becomes "a system of willful illusions" (Freud), "a unified system of beliefs and practices" (Durkheim), "a cultural system of symbols" (Clifford Geertz), or "a complete system of human communication" (Gerald James Larson).[43]

There are still other orienting metaphors that have had varying influence. In one formulation that has been affirmed (or assumed) by many scholars in recent decades, religion is a worldview (Peter L. Berger and Ninian Smart) or form of life (Ludwig Wittgenstein and Gerald James Larson). Emphasizing the ways that religious language differs from other language, some interpreters have emphasized that religions use pictures (Wittgenstein) or, as in Hegel's view, religions appeal to *Vorstellung* or pictorial thought.[44] Emphasizing religion's negative individual or social effects, some have compared religion to an illness (Freud) or narcotic (Marx). Some theorists who have been hostile to religion, as Van A. Harvey persuasively argues, also have imagined religion as projection. Using the indirect metaphor of a projected beam, Harvey suggests, a number of theorists from Hume and Ludwig Feuerbach to Robin Horton and Guthrie have turned to this trope.[45] Many beam projection theorists focus on the individual, but other definers of religion have emphasized religion's social or cultural origins and functions. Religion is society, in one way or another, for a range of social scientific accounts that began at least as early as Durkheim's *Elementary Forms of Religious Life*, in which the French sociologist claimed that religion was "an eminently collective thing." Others who have followed in that broad and varied interpretive tradition have defined religion as one or another cultural form, as with Spiro's influential definition of religion as "an institution consisting of culturally patterned interaction with culturally postulated superhuman beings." Finally, just as those who have embraced organic images about "evolution" or "growth" have highlighted (wittingly or unwittingly) change over time, there is another tradition of definition that directly or indirectly draws on spatial metaphors. Spatial figures are implied in some psychological accounts that focus on the individual and posit "levels of consciousness" (for instance, Freud, James, and Jung). Some interpreters (Charles H. Long and Gordon D. Kaufman) have appealed to indirect spatial images as they talk about religion as "orientation." Spatial metaphors are more explicit, and even more influential, in a tradition of interpretation that goes back to Durkheim and circulated widely in van der Leeuw's *Religion in Essence and Manifestation* and Eliade's *Sacred and the Profane*. This approach begins with a distinction between sacred and profane space—or, in Durkheim's phrase, "*things set apart*."[46]

If these varied tropes intertwine with definitions, the orienting metaphors that authors select also inscribe theoretical commitments, as I have tried to show in my analysis of Freud's definition. Metaphors, as I have indicated with my analogy of the lens, illumine some things and obscure others. Definitions that highlight a single human capacity (e.g., Tylor's religion as belief) tend to obscure other components of religion and other aspects of embodied human life. Definitions that foreground the individual (e.g., Alfred North Whitehead's "religion is what the individual does with his own solitariness") obscure the social, just as collectivist metaphors (e.g., Spiro's religion as institution) illumine the social character of religion but deemphasize its function for individuals. And metaphors have implications. Consider one of the most obvious examples. As other scholars have noted, organic metaphors about the "origin and growth" of religion have been associated with evolutionary models that propose a taxonomy of religions that privileges one tradition and dismisses others as lower "stages" on the cultural ladder. Those taxonomies—primitive and civilized, ethnic and universal, and lower and higher religions—have had negative, sometimes disastrous, moral and social implications. It is much easier to colonize and displace peoples who are aligned with children and imagined as "lower." For this and other reasons, as Turner suggested, "one must pick one's root metaphor carefully."[47]

Religion scholars, I have argued, have role-specific obligations not only to consider root metaphors—and their implications—but also to enter the debates about how to define their field's constitutive term. We are stuck with the category "religion" because it fixes the disciplinary horizon, and our use of it can be either more or less lucid, more or less self-conscious. So we are obliged to be as clear as possible about the kind of definition we are offering and the orienting tropes that inform it. Whether we imagine theory as our primary professional work or not, we are called to exegetical fussiness. All of us.

NOTES

This essay originally appeared in *History of Religions* (vol. 44, no. 3 [2005]: 252–76) and is reprinted here in a slightly modified form with the permission of the University of Chicago Press.

1. Fitzgerald 2000: 4; Serres with Latour 1995: 121. Of course, other scholars also have suggested that we drop the term "religion" and stop trying to define it, including Wilfred Cantwell Smith in his compelling and influential 1962 volume: "Neither religion in general nor any one of the religions, I will contend, is in itself an intelligible entity, a valid object of inquiry, or of concern whether for the scholar or the man of faith. . . . My own suggestion is that the word, and the concepts, should be dropped" (Smith [1962] 1978: 12, 50). More recently, like Fitzgerald, other scholars have advocated the abandonment of the term "religion." See Dubuisson 1998; Sabbatucci 2000.

2. Leuba 1901: 201.

3. Although it has not happened in religious studies, a discipline's constitutive term can change over time. Geography provides a good example. From the founding of the Association of American Geographers through the 1920s, scholars in that field focused on "human ecology," or the interaction between humans and land. Under the influence of Richard Hartshorne's methodological statement of 1939, "The Nature of Geography," "region" was widely accepted as geography's central term from the 1930s through the 1950s. While some professional geographers

endorse "place" or "location," most today would suggest that since the 1960s "space" has functioned as the discipline's constitutive term. This disciplinary history is traced in Taaffe 1974 and Hartshorne 1939. That influential work was reprinted and revised in 1946 and 1959, when its vision of the field still enjoyed widespread acceptance. See Hartshorne 1959.

4. Hollander 1971; Hollander 1981: 1; Blacking [1973] 1976: 32, 42–43.
5. Sadie 1980; Harmon 2000; Chilvers and Osborne 1997.
6. Smith 1995: 893.
7. Alperson 1994: 9–10; *The New Grove Dictionary of Music and Musicians*, s.v. "music"; *The Dictionary of Art*, s.v. "art," http://www.groveart.com.
8. Livingstone 1992: 304 (emphasis mine); Smith 1998: 281–82.
9. Baird 1991: 6; *Oxford English Dictionary Online*, s.v. "religion," http://dictionary.oed.com. As the philosopher Alexander Matthews (1998: 45) notes in *A Diagram of Definition*, scholars have enumerated many types of definitions. One philosopher distinguishes circular, coordinative, eliminative, explicative, and contextual definitions; another talks about prescriptive, ostensive, verbal, implicit, recursive, nominal, and real definitions. If nonspecialists—and more than a few specialists— find themselves disoriented by definitions, it seems almost impossible to avoid getting completely lost as they machete their way through the thicket of definitions of "definition." But gaining some clarity on this fundamental point can help in the long run, since readers need to know precisely what scholars are claiming for their definitions. How else can they be in a position to offer informed and judicious assessments? (The first list of types of definitions Matthews cites is from Pap 1958; the second, from the *Dictionary of Philosophy*, 2nd ed., s.v. "definition.") For a helpful anthology of philosophers' reflections on definition that ranges from Plato to Heinrich Rickert, see Sager 2000. For a collection of more recent essays on definition, see Fetzer, Shatz, and Schlesinger 1991.
10. Stark and Finke 2000: 85. The propositions and definitions are all listed in the "Appendix," pp. 277–86.
11. James [1902] 1982: 28.
12. James [1902] 1982: 31.
13. Borofsky et al. 2001: 434, 443–44.
14. Leuba [1912] 1969: 339–63. This framing of the third kind is from Sands 2002: 70. Among the scholars who have raised these five objections, or at least some of them, are Wilfred Cantwell Smith and Timothy Fitzgerald. See Smith 1978: 1–60, 119–92; and Fitzgerald 2000: 3–32.

There have been a number of recent attempts to consider the task of defining religion. For examples, see Smith 1998, Idinopulos and Wilson 1998, and Arnal 2000. As to art history, Chris Jenks (1995: 16) argues, "Within the academy, 'visual culture' is a term used conventionally to signify painting, sculpture, design, and architecture; it indicates a late-modern broadening of that previously contained within the definition of 'fine art.'" And he and his colleagues broaden the term still further to include advertising, photography, film, television, and propaganda. See also Morgan and Promey 2001: xiii.

15. Kroeber and Kluckhohn 1952; Fitzgerald 2000: 4, xi. For a discussion of some of the problems with "culture," see Brightman 1995: 509–46. In another important piece, anthropologist Lila Abu-Lughod (1991: 143, 154, 157) tries to "disturb the culture concept," since it has "problematic connotations," including "homogeneity, coherence, and timelessness." For a critique in cultural geography, see Mitchell 1995: 102–16. Other scholars who favor abandoning "religion" also have proposed alternate terms, such as "*formations cosmographiques*" (Dubuisson 1998). For a cross-cultural study of "religion" and allegedly analogous concepts, see Haussig 1999.

16. *Oxford English Dictionary Online*, s.v. "politics," http://dictionary.oed.com.

17. *Oxford English Dictionary Online*, s.v. "ritual," http://dictionary.oed.com; Rappaport 1999: 3, 1, 24.

18. *The Concise Oxford Dictionary of the Christian Church*, s.v. "soteriology"; Barth 1975: 124–27.

19. Spiro 1966: 88. Weber used "ideal types" in a variety of ways in his works. For a helpful theoretical discussion, see Weber 1949: 49–112 and 1978, 1:4–7, 20–22. Of course, if a category illumines nothing that interests an interpreter, the term will be judged of little use. But this is a matter of degree, and a term rarely will offer no interpretive benefits at all.

20. Smith 1998: 281; Smith 1995: 893.

21. Asad 1993; Chidester 1996: 259; Lopez 1998; King 1999. The British theologian Graham Ward, who also acknowledges the colonialist and capitalist origins of "religion" as well as its recent commodification, offers a genealogy of the social production of "religion." Yet he resists definition (and use) of the term and—unlike Asad, Chidester, Lopez, and King—predicts and champions a theological turn. "The turn to theology offers the only possible future for faith traditions," Ward has suggested,

although those traditions will need to avoid fetishizing their faith as they do battle in the ever more widespread and ferocious "culture wars" that will follow (Ward 2003: vii–5).
22. Smith 1995: 893.
23. Gay 1989: xiii.
24. Freud [1961] 1989: 62, 55, 56.
25. Freud [1961] 1989: 55, 42.
26. This is not to say that tropic analysis is not useful in the sciences too. Consider the work of Gerald Holton, the scholar of physics and historian of science who wrote the influential *Thematic Origins of Scientific Thought* (Holton 1973). In a more recent piece, Holton (2001: 24) proposes, "[I]n studying major scientists, I have repeatedly found the same courageous tendency to place one's bets early on a few nontestable but highly motivating presuppositions, which I refer to as themata." Holton goes on to note how certain tropes (or "themata")—including symmetry and unity—functioned in the work of Albert Einstein.
27. Fernandez 1991: 6, 7. See also Holland and Quinn 1987, an earlier interdisciplinary volume that explores the role of metaphor and metonymy in constructing "cultural models" that organize cultural knowledge. Harris 1992—a very helpful account of the major approaches to the theory of metaphor, especially in the humanities—chronicles four stages from the publication of I. A. Richards's *The Philosophy of Rhetoric* in 1936 to the appearance of John Searle's *Expression and Meaning* in 1979.
28. Davidson 2001: 245–64; Rorty 1991: 162–72; Frankenberry 2002: 171–87.
29. Friedrich 1991: 17–55.
30. Eliot [1952] 1971: 6, 4. Edward Quinn (1999: 192) gives the useful example of the indirect metaphor from Eliot's poem.
31. Freud [1961] 1989: 55.
32. Hegel 1979: 2; Müller 1879: 1; Otto [1958] 1976: 11.
33. Angeles 1981: 56–59.
34. Davidson 2001: 261; Harris 1992: 224; Black 1955: 288; Tweed 1997: 67. My own view of tropes, and of metaphor in particular, has been shaped to some extent by the Davidsonian tradition's emphasis on metaphor's uses. I also have profited from the "interactionist" theory of I. A. Richards, Max Black, Nelson Goodman, and others, as well as from Robert J. Fogelin's reflections (1988) on figures (especially his defense of metaphor as "elliptical similes") and Eva Feder Kittay's refinement (1987) of the interactionist theory and proposal of a "perspectival"

theory of metaphor. Empirical and theoretical studies in cognitive science also offer interesting angles of vision on metaphor. On metaphors as "class-inclusion assertions" see Gluckberg and Keysar 1990. For an introduction and overview, see *Encyclopedia of Cognitive Science*, s.vv. "metaphor," "metaphor processing, psychology of." For a summary of research and theory on analogy more broadly, including metaphor, see Gentner, Holyoak, and Kokinov 2001.

35. Harris 1992: 224; Goodman 1976: 71–73; Turner 1974: 29. Turner (1974: 29–33) endorses the "interaction view" of Richards (1936) and Black (1955). I have reservations about Black's talk about "filters" and Goodman's talk about "schemes" for a variety of reasons, especially because I am persuaded by Davidson's critique (2001: 183–98) of the usual notions about divergent "conceptual schemes" and Terry F. Godlove Jr.'s challenge (1989) to the strong version of the "framework model" of religious belief.

36. Fernandez 1991: 5; Ortner 1973: 1338–46; Turner 1974: 25–26; Fernandez 1974: 119–45. As Turner notes, he borrowed the phrase "root metaphor" from Stephen C. Pepper (1942: 91–92).

37. Tylor [1871] 1920: 424; Martineau 1888: 1; Tiele 1897: 4–6; Crawford 2002: 201; Guthrie 1993: 178; Atran 2002: 4. Atran actually uses the term "commitment," not "belief": "Roughly, religion is (1) a community's costly and hard-to-fake commitment (2) to a counterfactual and counterintuitive world of supernatural agents (3) who master people's existential anxieties, such as death and deception." For examples of cognitive approaches, see Lawson and McCauley 1990, Whitehouse 2000, Boyer 2001, and Pyysiäinen 2001.

38. Kant 1960: 142; Rappaport 1999: 3; Smith 2003: 98, 104; Schleiermacher 1963: 12–18; Otto [1958] 1976: 12; Hume 1993: 140.

39. Schleiermacher 1958: 44–45, 241. John Oman translates *Empfindungsweise* as "type of feeling," but the term may be rendered better as "type of experience" to distinguish it from the other two words that Schleiermacher uses most often to mark the essential nature of religion: *Gefühl* and *Anschauung*.

40. Otto [1958] 1976: 5; Eliade 1959: 8–18; Müller 1879: 20–21; Jevons 1896: 9–10.

41. Hume 1993: 159; Tillich 1959: 7–8; Stratton 1911: 343; Bosanquet 1902: 456; Smith 1998: 280.

42. Jastrow [1901] 1981: 171; Tiele 1899: 2:14; James [1902] 1982: 31; Durkheim 1995: 44.

43. Wilson 1999: 280; Tylor [1871] 1920: 425; Müller 1879: i, 131–32; Freud [1961] 1989: 55–56; Durkheim 1995: 44; Geertz 1973: 90; Larson 1978: 443.

44. Berger 1969: 3–25; Smart 1989: 9; Wittgenstein [1958] 1968: 11; Larson 1978: 443. Wittgenstein did not employ the phrase "form of life" to describe religion in *Philosophical Investigations*, but others, including Larson, have applied that phrase in their accounts of religion. Wittgenstein ([1966] 1972: 55, 59, 63, 66–68, 71–72) did talk a good deal about religion in terms of pictures, however. See also Hilary Putnam's insightful analysis (1991) of Wittgenstein's use of "picture" as an orienting metaphor for understanding religion. For Hegel (1979: 33, 35–36), as notes his translator Peter C. Hodgson (Hegel 1979: xxv), the *Vorstellung* of religion "produces synthetic images based on sense perception." It is in this sense that *Vorstellung* can be understood as "pictorial thinking" or "representation."

45. Harvey 1995: 229–80. In an extremely useful typology, Harvey distinguishes "beam" projection theories and "grid" projection theories. I've borrowed the first term but not the second, though not because I don't think both provide insights. Many interpreters whom Harvey classifies as grid theorists I've classified in other ways, although I see his point. While some of his grid theorists (e.g., Berger, Geertz, Marx) do appeal to the indirect metaphor of a grid, I classify them here by noting what I take to be the direct metaphors that orient their definitions (e.g., worldview, system, narcotic). Of course, as I've noted, multiple tropes are usually at work in the most complex and satisfying definitions.

46. Durkheim 1995: 44; Spiro 1966: 96; Long 1999; Kaufman 1993: 36–37, 70, 432; van der Leeuw [1938] 1963: 2:393–402; Eliade 1959: 20–65.

47. Whitehead [1954] 1960: 16; Turner 1974: 25.

REFERENCES

Abu-Lughod, Lila. 1991. "Writing Against Culture." In *Recapturing Anthropology: Working in the Present*, edited by Richard G. Fox, 137–62. Santa Fe: School of American Research Press.

Alperson, Philip, ed. 1994. *What Is Music? An Introduction to the Philosophy of Music.* University Park: Pennsylvania State University Press.

Angeles, Peter A. 1981. "Definition." In *Dictionary of Philosophy*. New York: Barnes & Noble Books.

Arnal, William E. 2000. "Definition." In *Guide to the Study of Religion*, edited by Willi Braun and Russell T. McCutcheon, 21–34. London: Cassell.

Asad, Talal. 1993. *Genealogies of Religion: Discipline and Reasons of Power in Christianity and Islam*. Baltimore: Johns Hopkins University Press.

Atran, Scott. 2002. *In Gods We Trust: The Evolutionary Landscape of Religion*. Oxford: Oxford University Press.

Baird, Robert D. 1991. *Category Formation and the History of Religions*. 2nd ed. Berlin: Mouton de Gruyter.

Barth, Fredrik. 1975. *Ritual and Knowledge among the Baktaman of New Guinea*. Oslo: Universitetsforlaget; New Haven: Yale University Press.

Berger, Peter L. 1969. *The Sacred Canopy: Elements of a Sociological Theory of Religion*. Garden City, NY: Doubleday.

Black, Max. 1955. "Metaphor." *Proceedings of the Aristotelian Society*, n.s., 55: 273–94.

Blacking, John. 1976. *How Musical Is Man?* Seattle: University of Washington Press, 1973. Reprint, London: Faber and Faber.

Borofsky, Robert, Fredrik Barth, Richard A. Shweder, Lars Rodseth, and Nomi Maya Stolzenberg. 2001. "WHEN: A Conversation about Culture." *American Anthropologist* 103, no. 2: 432–46.

Bosanquet, Bernard. 1902. "Religion (philosophy of)," 456. In *Dictionary of Philosophy and Psychology*, edited by James Mark Baldwin, vol. 2, 454–58. New York: Macmillan. Quoted in Leuba [1912] 1969: 353.

Boyer, Pascal. 2001. *Religion Explained: The Evolutionary Origins of Religious Thought*. New York: Basic Books.

Brightman, Robert. 1995. "Forget Culture: Replacement, Transcendence, Relexification." *Cultural Anthropology* 10, no. 4: 509–46.

Chidester, David. 1996. *Savage Systems: Colonialism and Comparative Religions in Southern Africa*. Charlottesville: University Press of Virginia.

Chilvers, Ian, and Harold Osborne, eds. 1997. *The Oxford Dictionary of Art*. New York: Oxford University Press.

Crawford, Robert. 2002. *What Is Religion?* London: Routledge.

Davidson, Donald. 2001. *Inquiries into Truth and Interpretation*. 2nd ed. Oxford: Clarendon Press.

Dubuisson, Daniel. 1998. *L'Occident et la religion: Mythes, science et idéologie*. Brussels: Éditions Complexe.

Durkheim, Emile. 1995. *The Elementary Forms of Religious Life*. Translated by Karen E. Fields. New York: Free Press.

Eliade, Mircea. 1959. *The Sacred and the Profane: The Nature of Religion.* New York: Harcourt Brace Jovanovich.

Eliot, T. S. 1971. *The Complete Poems and Plays, 1909–1950.* New York: Harcourt Brace & Company, 1952. Reprint, New York: Harcourt, Brace & World.

Fernandez, James [W]. 1974. "The Mission of Metaphor in Expressive Culture." *Current Anthropology* 15, no. 2: 119–45.

———, ed. 1991. *Beyond Metaphor: The Theory of Tropes in Anthropology.* Stanford: Stanford University Press.

Fetzer, James H., David Shatz, and George N. Schlesinger, eds. 1991. *Definitions and Definability: Philosophical Perspectives.* Dordrecht, The Netherlands: Kluwer Academic Publishers.

Fitzgerald, Timothy. 2000. *The Ideology of Religious Studies.* New York: Oxford University Press.

Fogelin, Robert J. 1988. *Figuratively Speaking.* New Haven: Yale University Press.

Frankenberry, Nancy K. 2002. "Religion as a 'Mobile Army of Metaphors.'" In *Radical Interpretation in Religion*, edited by Nancy K. Frankenberry, 171–87. Cambridge: Cambridge University Press.

Freud, Sigmund. 1989. *The Future of an Illusion.* Edited and translated by James Strachey. New York: W. W. Norton, 1961. Reprint, New York: W. W. Norton.

Friedrich, Paul. 1991. "Polytropy." In Fernandez 1991: 17–55.

Gay, Peter. 1989. Introduction to *The Freud Reader*, edited by Peter Gay. New York: W. W. Norton.

Geertz, Clifford. 1973. *The Interpretation of Cultures.* New York: Basic Books.

Gentner, Dedre, Keith J. Holyoak, and Boicho N. Kokinov, eds. 2001. *The Analogical Mind: Perspectives from Cognitive Science.* Cambridge: MIT Press.

Gluckberg, Sam, and Boaz Keysar. 1990. "Understanding Metaphorical Comparisons: Beyond Similarity." *Psychological Review* 97, no. 1: 3–18.

Godlove, Terry F., Jr. 1989. *Religion, Interpretation, and Diversity of Belief: The Framework Model from Kant to Durkheim to Davidson.* Cambridge: Cambridge University Press.

Goodman, Nelson. 1976. *Languages of Art: An Approach to a Theory of Symbols.* 2nd ed. Indianapolis: Hackett Publishing Company.

Guthrie, Stewart. 1993. *Faces in the Clouds: A New Theory of Religion.* New York: Oxford University Press.

Harmon, William, ed. 2000. *A Handbook to Literature*. 8th ed. Saddle River, NJ: Prentice Hall.

Harris, Wendell V. 1992. "Metaphor." In *Dictionary of Concepts in Literary Criticism and Theory*, 222–31. Westport, CT: Greenwood Press.

Hartshorne, Richard. 1939. "The Nature of Geography: A Critical Survey of Current Thought in the Light of the Past." *Annals of the Association of American Geographers* 29, no. 3: 173–645.

———. 1959. *Perspective on the Nature of Geography*. Chicago: Rand Mc-Nally for the Association of American Geographers.

Harvey, Van A. 1995. *Feuerbach and the Interpretation of Religion*. Cambridge: Cambridge University Press.

Haussig, Hans-Michael. 1999. *Der Religionsbegriff in den Religionen: Studien zum Selbst- und Religionsverständnis in Hinduismus, Buddhismus, Judentum und Islam*. Berlin: Philo.

Hegel, G. W. F. 1979. *The Revelatory, Consummate, Absolute Religion*. Pt. 3 of *The Christian Religion: Lectures on the Philosophy of Religion*. Edited and translated by Peter C. Hodgson. Missoula, MT: Scholars Press.

Holland, Dorothy, and Naomi Quinn, eds. 1987. *Cultural Models in Language and Thought*. Cambridge: Cambridge University Press.

Hollander, John. 1971. *The Night Mirror: Poems*. New York: Atheneum.

———. 1981. *Rhyme's Reason: A Guide to English Verse*. New Haven: Yale University Press.

Holton, Gerald. 1973. *Thematic Origins of Scientific Thought: Kepler to Einstein*. Cambridge: Harvard University Press.

———. 2001. "Einstein and the Cultural Roots of Modern Science." In *Science in Culture*, edited by Peter Galison, Stephen R. Graubard, and Everett Mendelsohn, 1–44. New Brunswick, NJ: Transaction Publishers.

Hume, David. 1993. *Dialogues and Natural History of Religion*. Edited by J. C. A. Gaskin. New York: Oxford University Press.

Idinopulos, Thomas A., and Brian C. Wilson, eds. 1998. *What Is Religion? Origins, Definitions, and Explanations*. Leiden: E. J. Brill.

James, William. 1982. *The Varieties of Religious Experience: A Study in Human Nature*. New York: Longmans, Green, 1902. Reprint, with a new introduction by Martin E. Marty, New York: Penguin Books.

Jastrow, Morris, Jr. 1981. *The Study of Religion*. London: Walter Scott, 1901. Reprint, Chico, CA: Scholars Press.

Jenks, Chris, ed. 1995. *Visual Culture*. London: Routledge.

Jevons, F. B. 1896. *An Introduction to the History of Religion.* London: Methuen.

Kant, Immanuel. 1960. *Religion within the Limits of Reason Alone.* Translated by Theodore M. Greene and Hoyt H. Hudson. New York: Harper & Brothers.

Kaufman, Gordon D. 1993. *In Face of Mystery: A Constructive Theology.* Cambridge: Harvard University Press.

King, Richard. 1999. *Orientalism and Religion: Postcolonial Theory, India, and the Mystic East.* New York: Routledge.

Kittay, Eva Feder. 1987. *Metaphor: Its Cognitive Force and Linguistic Structure.* Oxford: Clarendon Press.

Kroeber, A. L., and Clyde Kluckhohn. 1952. *Culture: A Critical Review of Concepts and Definitions. Papers of the Peabody Museum of American Archeology and Ethnology, Harvard University* 47.

Larson, Gerald James. 1978. "Prolegomenon to a Theory of Religion." *Journal of the American Academy of Religion* 46, no. 4: 443–63.

Lawson, E. Thomas, and Robert N. McCauley. 1990. *Rethinking Religion: Connecting Cognition and Culture.* Cambridge: Cambridge University Press.

Leuba, J[ames] H. 1901. "Introduction to a Psychological Study of Religion." *Monist* 11, no. 2: 195–225.

———. 1969. *A Psychological Study of Religion: Its Origin, Function, and Future.* New York: Macmillan, 1912. Reprint, New York: AMS Press.

Livingstone, David N. 1992. *The Geographical Tradition: Episodes in the History of a Contested Enterprise.* Oxford: Blackwell.

Long, Charles H. 1999. *Significations: Signs, Symbols, and Images in the Interpretation of Religion.* Aurora, CO: Davies Group.

Lopez, Donald. 1998. *Prisoners of Shangri-La: Tibetan Buddhism and the West.* Chicago: University of Chicago Press.

Martineau, James. 1888. *A Study of Religion, Its Sources and Contents.* Rev. ed. Vol. 1. New York: Macmillan.

Matthews, Alexander. 1998. *A Diagram of Definition: The Defining of Definition.* Assen, The Netherlands: Van Gorcum.

Mitchell, Don. 1995. "There's No Such Thing as Culture: Towards a Reconceptualization of the Idea of Culture in Geography." *Transactions of the Institute of British Geographers*, n.s., 20, no. 1: 102–16.

Morgan, David, and Sally Promey, eds. 2001. *The Visual Culture of American Religions.* Berkeley: University of California Press.

Müller, F. Max. 1879. *Lectures on the Origin and Growth of Religion, as Illustrated by the Religions of India*. New York: Charles Scribner's Sons.

Ortner, Sherry. 1973. "On Key Symbols." *American Anthropologist* 75, no. 5: 1338–46.

Otto, Rudolf. 1976. *The Idea of the Holy*. Translated by John W. Harvey. 2nd ed. London: Oxford University Press, 1958. Reprint, London: Oxford University Press.

Pap, Arthur. 1958. *Semantics and Necessary Truth*. New Haven: Yale University Press.

Pepper, Stephen C. 1942. *World Hypotheses*. Berkeley: University of California Press.

Putnam, Hilary. 1991. "Wittgenstein on Religious Belief." In *On Community*, edited by Leroy S. Rouner, 56–75. Notre Dame, IN: Notre Dame University Press.

Pyysiäinen, Ilkka. 2001. *How Religion Works: Towards a New Cognitive Science of Religion*. Leiden: E. J. Brill.

Quinn, Edward. 1999. "Metaphor." In *A Dictionary of Literary and Thematic Terms*, 192–93. New York: Facts on File.

Rappaport, Roy A. 1999. *Ritual and Religion in the Making of Humanity*. Cambridge: Cambridge University Press.

Richards, I. A. 1936. *The Philosophy of Rhetoric*. New York: Oxford University Press.

Rorty, Richard. 1991. "Unfamiliar Noises: Hesse and Davidson on Metaphor." In *Philosophical Papers*. Vol. 1. Cambridge: Cambridge University Press.

Sabbatucci, Dario. 2000. *La prospettiva storico-religiosa*. Formello, Italy: Edizioni SEAM.

Sadie, Stanley, ed. 1980. *The New Grove Dictionary of Music and Musicians*. London: Macmillan.

Sager, Juan C., ed. 2000. *Essays on Definition*. Amsterdam: John Benjamins Publishing Company.

Sands, Kathleen. 2002. "Tracking Religion: Religion Through the Lens of Critical and Cultural Studies." *Council of Societies for the Study of Religion Bulletin* 31, no. 3: 68–74.

Schleiermacher, Friedrich. 1958. *On Religion: Speeches to Its Cultured Despisers*. Translated by John Oman. New York: Harper & Row.

———. 1963. *The Christian Faith*. Edited by H. R. Mackintosh and J. S. Stewart. Vol. 1. New York: Harper & Row.

Serres, Michel, with Bruno Latour. 1995. *Conversations on Science, Culture, and Time*. Ann Arbor: University of Michigan Press.

Smart, Ninian. 1989. *The World's Religions*. Englewood Cliffs, NJ: Prentice Hall.

Smith, Christian. 2003. *Moral, Believing Animals: Human Personhood and Culture*. Oxford: Oxford University Press.

Smith, Jonathan Z. 1998. "Religion, Religions, Religious." In *Critical Terms for Religious Studies*, edited by Mark C. Taylor, 269–84. Chicago: University of Chicago Press.

———, ed. 1995. *The HarperCollins Dictionary of Religion*. San Francisco: HarperSanFrancisco.

Smith, Wilfred Cantwell. 1978. *The Meaning and End of Religion: A Revolutionary Approach to the Great Religious Traditions*. San Francisco: Harper & Row, 1962. Reprint, San Francisco: Harper & Row.

Spiro, Melford E. 1966. "Religion: Problems of Definition and Explanation." In *Anthropological Approaches to the Study of Religion*, edited by Michael Banton, 85–126. London: Tavistock Publications.

Stark, Rodney, and Roger Finke. 2000. *Acts of Faith: Explaining the Human Side of Religion*. Berkeley: University of California Press.

Stratton, George Malcolm. 1911. *Psychology of the Religious Life*. London: G. Allen & Company.

Taaffe, Edward J. 1974. "The Spatial View in Context." *Annals of the Association of American Geographers* 64, no. 1: 1–16.

Tiele, C. P. 1897–99. *Elements of the Science of Religion*. 2 pts. Edinburgh: William Blackwood.

Tillich, Paul. 1959. *Theology of Culture*. Edited by Robert C. Kimball. New York: Oxford University Press.

Turner, Victor. 1974. *Dramas, Fields, and Metaphors: Symbolic Action in Human Society*. Ithaca: Cornell University Press.

Tweed, Thomas A. 1997. *Our Lady of the Exile: Diasporic Religion at a Cuban Catholic Shrine in Miami*. New York: Oxford University Press.

Tylor, Edward B. 1920. *Primitive Culture*. Vol. 1. London: John Murray, 1871. Reprint, London: John Murray.

van der Leeuw, G. 1963. *Religion in Essence and Manifestation*. Translated by J. E. Turner. 2 vols. London: George Allen & Unwin, 1938. Reprint, New York: Harper & Row.

Ward, Graham. 2003. *True Religion*. Oxford: Blackwell.

Weber, Max. 1949. "'Objectivity' in Social Science and Social Policy." In *The Methodology of the Social Sciences*, edited and translated by Edward A. Shils and Henry A. Finch, 49–112. New York: Free Press.

———. 1978. *Economy and Society*. Edited by Guenther Roth and Claus Wittich. Vol. 1. Berkeley: University of California Press.

Whitehead, Alfred North. 1960. *Religion in the Making.* New York: Meridian Books, 1954. Reprint, New York: Meridian Books.

Whitehouse, Harvey. 2000. *Arguments and Icons: Divergent Modes of Religiosity.* Oxford: Oxford University Press.

Wilson, Edward O. 1999. *Consilience: The Unity of Knowledge.* New York: Vintage Books.

Wittgenstein, Ludwig. 1968. *Philosophical Investigations.* Translated by G. E. M. Anscombe. 3rd ed. New York: Macmillan, 1958. Reprint, New York: Macmillan.

———. 1972. *Lectures & Conversations on Aesthetics, Psychology, and Religious Belief.* Edited by Cyril Barrett. Berkeley: University of California Press, 1966. Reprint, Berkeley: University of California Press.

"Epic" as an Amnesiac Metaphor

Finding the Word to Compare
Ancient Greek and Sanskrit Poems

SHUBHA PATHAK

AMONG THE RICHEST sources of ancient mythology available today are the protracted praise poems that capture heroes' quests to live (and die) up to the ideals of their societies. Such poems now are known commonly as "epics," and the assumption that they, as members of the same genre, share certain characteristics underlies any cross-cultural comparison of these works. Yet, until now, scholars' oft-rehearsed act of assuming that the epics share enough to be compared has shifted attention away from what the poems of particular cultures contribute to this category overarching them. These poems have been placed in the epic category so consistently and persistently that critics do not ask what this classification entails. But posing this question is important because equating poems with epics is a way for scholars to sort out the poetic features that they see fit to study from the attributes that they consider less crucial to compare. Asking what it means to identify works as epics thus illuminates the nature of the comparative analyses that are founded on this identification.

Such analyses may focus, in fact, on poems that have disparate histories as epics. Such is the case when critics compare the earliest heroic poems of Greece and of India. While the *Iliad* and *Odyssey* have been known as epics for nearly as long as they have existed, the *Rāmāyaṇa* and *Mahābhārata* have acquired this rubric only relatively recently. Even so, the Sanskrit poems have enlarged the conception of epic conceived originally for their Greek counterparts. Examining what each pair of poems offers to the epic idea casts the differences between the Greek and Sanskrit works into relief from their similarities and thereby sets the stage for nuanced comparison of the four poems.

One way to see what the notion of epic owes to these Greek and Sanskrit poems is to study each poem pair's relationship to this term. Because "epic" originated as an appellation for the *Iliad* and *Odyssey*, the statement that these texts are epics amounts to an identity. Yet to say that the *Rāmāyaṇa* and *Mahābhārata* are epics is to make a metaphor. Thus, as I will show further on, these two equations provide distinct perspectives on the epic genre, outlooks that make works of this kind clearer.

THE *ILIAD* AND *ODYSSEY*: "EPIC" AND GENERIC IDENTITY

THE *ILIAD* AND *ODYSSEY* AS EPICS

The *Iliad* and *Odyssey*, poems composed collectively in the latter half of the eighth century BCE, do not describe themselves as epics. Instead, each poem suggests that it should be classified among the *kléa andrôn*, or accounts of men's glorious deeds.[1] Nonetheless, it is understandable why some people, even without examining any evidence, may sense that these poems are inextricable from the idea of epic. For most readers schooled in the Western tradition, the *Iliad* and *Odyssey* epitomize epic poetry, as they are the first epics that students of this tradition encounter (though perhaps in abridged form[2]). Their assumption is borne out insofar as the Homeric poems have taken precedence etymologically as well as experientially. The English word "epic" ultimately derives (via the Greek adjective *epikós*) from the Greek noun *épos*,[3] the meaning of whose plural form *épea* expanded by neology to encompass "epic poetry or poem" in addition to "words." More precisely, *épos* in the late eighth century BCE was "used widely in Homer to designate words, in contrast to *mûthos*, which applies instead to the content of the words."[4] But, by the early fifth century BCE, *épos* had come in its plural form to mean epic poetry as well, as attest works of the lyric poet Pindar (518–c. 440 BCE) and the historian Herodotus (c. 485–425 BCE).[5] Classicist Gregory Nagy has noted that, "[a]s in the songs of Pindar, the figure of Homer is treated as the ultimate representative of epic in the prose of Herodotus."[6] I would go a step further to stress that the foremost epic exemplars for both Pindar and

Herodotus were Homer's *Iliad* and *Odyssey*. Although the two later authors each count among Homer's epic compositions at least one component of the Epic Cycle (a number of now-lost poems that were composed separately c. seventh century BCE but subsequently collected as accounts of the creation of the gods, the Theban War, and the Trojan War), the *Iliad* and *Odyssey* are the paradigmatic epics in Pindar's and Herodotus's eyes.[7]

The emphasis that these authors place on this pair of poems echoes in their recent treatments. Twentieth-century critics, like the early exponents of Homer, single (or perhaps double) the *Iliad* and *Odyssey* out from the Greek epic corpus, with labels as lofty as "the noble epithets"[8] that the two poems themselves employ. Thus, the *Iliad* and *Odyssey* are "great epics,"[9] "monumental compositions"[10] of "influence."[11] In comparison suffer their successors, the Cyclic epics. In the current absence of these works, contemporary critics assume that ancient exegetes assessed the poems correctly. On this assessment, the Cyclic epics are dismissed as being derivative: "Aristotle, Callimachus, and everyone else who mentions the Epic Cycle poems remark on their obvious inferiority to the Homeric poems. They seem to have been composed in order to create a chronology in epic narrative of all the events from the origin of the world to the death of Odysseus, which is what we might call the end of the heroic period."[12] Seeing the Cyclic epics simply as supplements to the *Iliad* and *Odyssey* allows their modern readers to elevate this pair of earlier poems above subsequent works. From the perspective of these interpreters, not only were the Cyclic epics "clearly inferior to the *Iliad* and *Odyssey*," but the "distinction between Homeric and Cyclic [works] . . . was due to the exceptional genius that went into the creation of the two Homeric epics."[13] This perspective thus proceeds from the assumption that the *Iliad* and *Odyssey* are *magna opera sui generis*, the acme of all poetic compositions past and to come: "The utter collapse of the creative epic spirit as shown in the poetry of the Epic Cycle, if we base our opinion of the merits of these poems on the estimate of competent ancient authorities, shows that Homer had no successors. The Iliad and the Odyssey represent the golden age of epic poetry, and golden ages are always brief."[14] At least part of the luster of the Homeric poems is lent by their "Panhellenic" outlook. While the Cyclic epics take up topics local to particular city-states, the *Iliad* and *Odyssey* meld the traditions of these areas into an amalgam that reflects local colors in the light of close examination but that combines them to emit its own characteristic spectrum.[15]

Yet, separating the Homeric epics radically from their Cyclic counterparts uproots both sets of poems from the common ground of their shared mythological tradition. While both the Homeric works and the Cyclic works

likely grew at least partly independently out of an older body of heroic stories, considering the *Iliad* and *Odyssey* as this corpus's crowning glory requires
reconceiving and relocating the Cyclic epics as limbs newly added to connect the Homeric canopy to its onetime trunk. In this misguiding light, the
Cyclic poems seem to have been transplanted after the fact, as missing links
between the Homeric epics and their narrative antecedents. It is more likely,
however, that the Cyclic epics are the younger offshoots of a largely separate
branch belonging to the same storied tree.[16]

Misconstruing the relationship between the Homeric and Cyclic epics
as one of sheer dependence of the latter on the former offers the distinct
advantage of pinpointing in the *Iliad* and *Odyssey* the pinnacle of the ancient
Greek poetic tradition. To this effect, Cedric H. Whitman suggests that in
spite of subsequent literary production the Homeric epics endure as their
culture's most prominent representatives: "In the long run, both Iliad and
Odyssey contributed their share to the perfecting of what we call the classical spirit. Embodying as they do the polarities of that spirit, they remain for
us the archetypes of the Classical, the Hellenic."[17] In the eyes of yet other
readers, including Charles Rowan Beye, the influence of the Homeric epics
is even wider, crossing cultural and temporal divides. Thus, "for [these] literary historians and theorists the very notion of epic poetry ultimately derives
from the Homeric texts."[18]

But, although Whitman and Beye consider the *Iliad* and *Odyssey* to be
prototypes, these critics do not claim that the poems possess no predecessors. While Whitman emphasizes the immense contribution that the *Iliad*
and *Odyssey* have made to ancient Greek culture, he acknowledges their own
debt to earlier works. In a later study, he states that "Homer's poems bear on
every page the tokens of oral composition within a traditional verse medium
reaching back for centuries into the unexplorable dimness of the Indo-European past." By the same type of token, Beye allows that "one may argue that
the Greeks inherited epic poetry in dactylic hexametric rhythm from their
Indo-European ancestors," even after he has identified the Homeric works as
the source of the epic idea.[19]

The *Iliad* and *Odyssey* thus imitate as well as innovate, as their identification as epics implies. As a particular kind of composition, the *Iliad* and *Odyssey* resemble poems that preceded them, but at the same time have brought
something new to the literary world that has become inextricable from the
idea of what an epic is. This apparent paradox of originary model poems
made in the mold of older ones is useful because it highlights the constructed
character of the Homeric compositions' archetypicality. Recognizing that the

Iliad and *Odyssey* themselves have poetic ancestors in spite of being represented as the first forebears of a poetic tradition reveals that interpretative pains have been taken to portray the Homeric poems as prototypes. This portrayal probably arose from two attributes of the *Iliad* and *Odyssey*. First, they are the earliest attested works of ancient Greek literature, so it is convenient for critics studying this corpus to see these extant compositions as its head and to ascribe an identity to this body on the basis of their features. Second, the *Iliad* and *Odyssey* long have inspired aesthetic appreciation and thus seem to be suitable exemplars for subsequent literary efforts.[20] Even if somehow recovered and proved to precede the Homeric poems, the Cyclic epics would be pressed hard to dethrone them as standards of artistic beauty, because, no matter what current critics beheld, they probably still would heed the dissatisfaction with the Cyclic poems that has been resounding for centuries.

The longstanding influence that the *Iliad* and *Odyssey* have had on later literary composition and criticism explains why identifying what these works contribute to the conception of epic that they inaugurated is important. This conception, which would serve as a standard of composition and comparison not only for ancient Greek authors and exegetes but also for their counterparts in later periods and other lands, can be clarified by applying philosopher Panayot Butchvarov's idea of generic identity.

Generic Identity and the Homeric Epics

"Generic identity" is a relationship between the quality of one individual and the quality of another, such that the characteristic specific to each quality and thus not possessed by the other depends logically on the characteristic that these qualities share (i.e., their generic characteristic). In the "classical example of [the] generic identity . . . of an equilateral [triangle] and an isosceles triangle," the generic characteristic common to the qualities of these figures, which are equilateral triangularity and isosceles triangularity, is triangularity itself; and the specific characteristic of each quality, having three equal sides in the case of equilateral triangularity or having two equal sides in the case of isosceles triangularity, is contingent on the generic characteristic, triangularity. Therefore, equilateral triangularity and isosceles triangularity are generically though not specifically identical.[21]

This account of generic identity applies to the classification of the *Iliad* and *Odyssey* as epics. "Iliadness" and "Odysseyness," the respective qualities of the Homeric poems, share "epicness," their generic characteristic; and the specific characteristics of these qualities—namely, being unique to the *Iliad* and being unique to the *Odyssey*—are a subset of epicness.

Also pertinent to the equation of epic poetry and the Homeric texts is another aspect of generic identity: the fact that the quality of an individual has a generic characteristic means that this quality must have only one of a limited range of specific characteristics. Stated another way, the generic characteristic of the quality must manifest as one of the specific characteristics that the quality can possess. Take, for example, triangles again:

> [W]hile an instance of being a figure enclosed by three lines need not be an instance of equilateral triangularity, it must be an instance of *some* one of the logically possible species of being a figure enclosed by three lines, i.e., the lengths of its three sides must be proportioned in one of the several ways which alone are logically possible. It cannot be an instance of triangularity unless it is an instance . . . of equilateral or isosceles or scalene triangularity.[22]

For those who see epic poetry and the Homeric works as being synonymous, the generic characteristic of epicness is instantiated in Iliadness or Odysseyness. Epicness, or the conception of epic that originates with the Homeric works, is constructed from the attributes common to the *Iliad* and the *Odyssey*, and therefore amounts to the overlap of Iliadness and Odysseyness.

Inspecting the features that the Homeric poems share shows that these traits compose portraits of epic form and content. The form that epic assumes consists in similarities between the *Iliad* and the *Odyssey* in scale, structure, and style. In scale, the compositions are extensive, each containing twenty-four books averaging somewhat less than 660 lines each in the *Iliad* and over 500 lines each in the *Odyssey*. Yet, the epics' extent is a matter not merely of length but additionally of depth. If "[e]verything is presented [in the poems] on a huge canvas[,] . . . sketched in . . . large outlines,"[23] these lines have been filled in with detailed designs rather than broad brushstrokes. The expanse of the epics' forests fails to overshadow the intricacy of the veins in their leaves.

The extent of the epics is supported by their structure, an outgrowth of repetition, ring composition, and multiplication. About one-third of the lines in the *Iliad* appear elsewhere in the poem, and the same goes for the *Odyssey*. Additionally, the story line of each epic comes full circle. For instance, the *Iliad*'s first and last books both feature an angry Achilles speaking with his mother, divine Thetis, the sea nymph who intercedes for him with Zeus, the king of the gods. Similarly, the *Odyssey* opens and closes with the goddess Athena descending from Mount Olympus to the island of Ithaca in order to aid Odysseus and his son Telemachus. Yet, as patly as the epics end, they delay their denouements, sustaining narrative tension through the climaxes of their twenty-second books. What postpones the peaking of their plots until the eleventh hour is the incessant interposition of episodes. In each poem, approximately 2,200 lines separate the turning point from the climax, so there is a similar prolonging of the plot line between Odysseus's return to his palace and slaying of the suitors in the *Odyssey* as between Achilles' decision to avenge Patroclus and killing of Hector in the *Iliad*.[24]

Thus, the structure of the Homeric epics is such that audiences wending their way through the woods of the *Iliad* and of the *Odyssey* retrace some of their steps and sidetrack as they circumambulate. Both paths beneath the strollers' feet parallel the styles of these poems and thus are made of the same materials. The *Iliad* and *Odyssey* exhibit like styles, relying on like types of poetic formulae and language.

The ground common to the epic forests that underlies their trees as well as their paths is their poetic tradition. The plot of this land on which the *Iliad* and *Odyssey* stand yields four types of trees, four themes that constitute columns of epic content: (1) the hero's need to separate himself from his social surroundings, (2) their destabilization by conflict, (3) his ability to reorder his life, and (4) his mortal limits.

To make a name for himself, an epic hero has to act exceptionally. Yet action in the epics is inextricable from a nexus of social relationships. The strong connections between warriors and their families and compatriots put recognizable faces on the society that would celebrate the successes of these fighters or deride their defeats, and provide a social context for their individual deeds.[25] A man who hopes to be a hero, however, can cement his local status only by isolating himself from others.

> Whether for wealth or reputation or by a code that demands leadership in adventure, a hero cannot tamely stay home. In the so-called shame-society and at a time before the protections of formal law, a man's standing with dependents and rivals turns on his will to demonstrate his power. Nothing will protect him if he fails to do so. But if he leaves home, he moves into a world the width and complexity of which only the gods fully know, yet which as a man of position he expects to master. The task will prove impossible on those

assumptions. Great heroes will owe their fame to their self-fidelity in face of the fact. True to themselves, they will have moved out toward command and glory and will die when it becomes evident that safe return was not among the first conditions. On this view, the Iliad as much as the Odyssey concerns the relationship of home to the world. Both poems turn on the hard paradox that to stay home will, by a man's loss of wealth and reputation, undermine home and obscure its relation to the gods' wide world, yet to venture out will reveal enormity and danger and make return unlikely.[26]

Yet venture out the Homeric heroes must, and enter the fights forged by their aspirations, for conflict creates opportunities for these men to prove their martial prowess. While the seizure of the Spartan queen Helen and its aftermath incite Achilles to lay down the lives of legions as well as his own on the Trojan battlefield, the suitors' encroachment upon Odysseus's Ithacan estate spurs him to slaughter them after his arduous journey home.

But, even though the heroes ultimately mend rends in their societies' social fabrics by working to reunite Helen and Penelope with their husbands, there is more to the *Iliad* and *Odyssey* than their third "theme of restored order."[27] The paradox in which the poems' heroes are placed as they exchange the ill-regarded security of home for the prestigious prospect of faraway success that necessarily remains unreachable has even larger implications to which John H. Finley Jr. has pointed. Once epic heroes leave home, they strive to prove themselves while discovering that they are less than divine.[28] Whitman develops this idea by describing these characters' condition as "the heroic paradox," the contradiction that they live as they attempt to emulate gods, in spite of confronting human constraints.[29] The route to which Achilles and Odysseus resort in order to escape this paradox is a path to poetic immortality. Although the men themselves cannot elude death, they can achieve *kléos*, or heroic glory, and thereby live on in epic song.

Nevertheless, the Homeric heroes do not transcend their paradox, which actually is a prerequisite of their stories. Epics, as Wendy Doniger has discussed, are associated intimately with myths, narratives that "raise religious questions"[30] and that "wrestle with insoluble paradoxes[—]as Claude Lévi-Strauss noted long ago[—]that] they inevitably fail to pin . . . to the mat."[31] If, as Lévi-Strauss asserts, "the purpose of myth is to provide a logical model capable of overcoming a contradiction (an impossible achievement if, as it happens, the contradiction is real),"[32] and if the *Iliad* and *Odyssey* address the heroic paradox, then it makes sense that these epics (like their counterparts in other cultures) feature, in Doniger's words, "the constant interaction of the two planes, the human and the divine,"[33] without allowing them to merge. By interacting with their anthropomorphic gods, Achilles and Odysseus become aware of the full measure of the power which they themselves may aspire to if only imperfectly personify.

Although Olympus-like heights lie off-limits to Achilles and Odysseus, the *Iliad* and *Odyssey*—as I have described—occupy a privileged place atop their poetic tradition. Yet losing sight of the critical influences that have lifted the *Iliad* and *Odyssey* above other literary works leaves the Homeric poems aloft at an Archimedean point in the heavens, with these epics' connections to subsequent texts unwitnessed. Seeing such works as the *Iliad* and *Odyssey* as nearly unreachable benchmarks of the epic genre has two drawbacks, as J. B. Hainsworth has observed. First, such single-minded sight blinds onlookers to later uses of the term "epic" in senses that may be separate from the poems that first bear its standard. Second, the spectators regard as deficient those works that differ from these Platonic forms of epics.[34]

These two problems threaten to cloud the surroundings of the Homeric poems in such a way that they seem likely to soar in mid-air above not only other texts of the same tradition but also similar texts of other traditions. Fortunately, however, the fresh zephyrs of two analyses keep clear the epics' rarified air and account for their abstraction from works of their own and other cultures. One analysis, involving generic identity, has shown how the notion of epic has been built from the attributes of the *Iliad* and *Odyssey* rather than later Greek texts, and thus indicates that this concept could be reconstructed from the characteristics of other apparently ur-works. The other analysis, which will make use of metaphor, exhibits the reconstruction of the epic idea on the basis of two ancient Indian poems.

THE *RĀMĀYAṆA* AND *MAHĀBHĀRATA*: "EPIC" AND METAPHOR

THE *RĀMĀYAṆA* AND *MAHĀBHĀRATA* AS EPICS

Like the *Iliad* and *Odyssey*, the *Rāmāyaṇa* and *Mahābhārata* now are considered to be epics. Yet this label does not suit the Sanskrit poems as well as it does the Greek works, for Sanskrit, unlike Greek, has no etymon for the word "epic." Rather, the *Rāmāyaṇa* and *Mahābhārata*, which were composed circa 200 BCE–200 CE, refer to themselves in a variety of ways and emphasize particular epithets in the myths about their own making—*kāvya* (or a poem that expresses emotion) in the case of the *Rāmāyaṇa* and *itihāsa* (or an account of the way things had been) in the case of the *Mahābhārata*.[35]

"Epic" probably was adopted as a rubric for the *Rāmāyaṇa* and *Mahābhārata* in the twentieth century for two reasons. Certainly the term serves as a convenient catchall for this pair of self-distinguishing poems that, despite their disparities, share traits. Moreover, opening the umbrella term "epic" over these two texts expresses that they are similar to the Homeric works with which Western audiences already are familiar.

In categorizing the *Rāmāyaṇa* and *Mahābhārata* as epics,[36] twentieth-century critics all take after E. Washburn Hopkins (1857–1932), the philological pioneer whose work informed English-speakers of these poems. Hopkins not only refers to the poems as epics and to their authors as epic poets,[37] but also acknowledges that he orients himself to these texts by turning to their Greek analogues. True to his training as a classicist,[38] he contrasts the *Mahābhārata* and the *Rāmāyaṇa* thus: "beside the huge and motley pile that goes by Vyāsa's name stands clear and defined the little Rāmāyaṇa of Vālmīki, as (in this respect) besides Homer's vague Homerica stands the distinct Argonautika of Apollonius."[39] Although it is Vyāsa whom Hopkins overtly views as "[t]he Hindu Homer," as the "*poiētès epôn*" who "out-Homers Homer," Hopkins implicitly cloaks Vālmīki with the Homeric mantle as well—by likening the composition of the *Mahābhārata* and *Rāmāyaṇa* to the making of the *Iliad* and *Odyssey*: "As the two Greek epics were both based to a certain extent on the general rhapsodic phraseology of the day, so the two Hindu epics, though there was without doubt borrowing in special instances, were yet in this regard independent of each other, being both dependent on previous rhapsodic and narrative phraseology."[40]

Scholars who style the Sanskrit poems as epics after Hopkins evince varying levels of self-consciousness in doing so. While P. V. Kane, Barend A. van Nooten, and John D. Smith do not mention the connection between the term "epic" and Homer's works, David Shulman and John Brockington do, and Brockington advances still farther by suggesting that this relationship is worthy of further study.

Both Shulman and Brockington see the Sanskrit texts in the light of their Greek antecedents. Shulman recognizes that the complementarity of the *Rāmāyaṇa* and the *Mahābhārata* recalls that of "the prototypical epic poems of Homer," the *Iliad* and the *Odyssey*.[41] Brockington is similarly explicit in associating the *Mahābhārata* and the *Iliad*. He observes "broad similarities between the battles of the *Mahābhārata* and the *Iliad*," remarking that "the whole of India took part" in the fighting featured in the *Mahābhārata*, "in the same way that in the *Iliad* all the Greek world took part in the siege of Troy." Brockington also interrelates the *Rāmāyaṇa* and the Homeric works, albeit less overtly. In the course of explaining away inconsistencies in the *Rāmāyaṇa* narrative, he adduces the "even Homer nods" aphorism. And, as Brockington describes the tendency of the *Rāmāyaṇa* to refer to precious metals rather than the baser ones that already were employed by the time the poem was composed, he cites "adherence to the older pattern on precisely this point" as "a well known feature of Homer."[42]

Even more importantly, Brockington raises a question that anyone studying the Sanskrit poems today should attempt to answer: "It is . . . worth asking from the start whether designation of the *Mahābhārata* and the *Rāmāyaṇa* as 'epics' affects our understanding of them, generating expectations derived from ideas about the *Iliad* and *Odyssey*."[43] To respond to Brockington's query, I will draw from the resources of metaphor theories from the fields of philosophy and literary criticism.

Metaphor and the Sanskrit "Epics"

I turn to these theories because I believe that identifying the implications of asserting that the *Rāmāyaṇa* and *Mahābhārata* are epics requires recognizing that this assertion is a metaphor. The statement's metaphorical aspect stems from the fact that the term "epic," as I have discussed, is inextricable from the *Iliad* and *Odyssey*. Characterizing the Sanskrit poems as epics, then, constrains their definition in the manner mentioned by Slavicist David E. Bynum. For Bynum, "the name 'epic' is only a more or less metaphorical expression as applied to oral poetry in many parts of the modern world," because the term indicates a "long verse narrative sharing qualities of the *Iliad* and *Odyssey*" and excludes "the peculiar features of particular modern [poetic] traditions."[44]

Yet, the metaphorical equation of poems with epics does more than merely reduce non-Greek narratives to the characteristics that they have in common with Homeric works. Three of this equation's implications are indicated by theories of metaphor.

The first implication enables the act of discerning that the equation indeed is a metaphor. Implicit in this kind of equation—in the analysis of Jacques Derrida[45]—is the equation's "primitive meaning," the equation's original import, which makes patent the equation's metaphorical nature. Thus, the primitive meaning of the equation of the Sanskrit poems with epics is that the *Rāmāyaṇa* and *Mahābhārata* are equivalent to the *Iliad* and *Odyssey*. But, as the equation becomes current and the Sanskrit compositions commonly come to be called epics, this primitive meaning is "forgotten" and "[t]he metaphor is no longer noticed." By this point, the primitive meaning has been supplanted by a less particular "proper meaning": hence the *Rāmāyaṇa* and *Mahābhārata* are epics insofar as they are long verse narratives.[46]

The process of retrieving an equation's primitive meaning and thereby of perceiving the equation as a metaphor has been portrayed metaphorically itself, in the image of a resurrection. I. A. Richards, for instance, speaks of "wak[ing] . . . up" metaphors that seem "stone dead"; and Paul Ricoeur similarly refers to the "reanimation" or "rejuvenation of dead metaphors."[47] But I think that this recognition process is characterized more aptly by a metaphor that captures the reversal of the memory failure discussed by Derrida: to discern a metaphor, then, is to remind an amnesiac metaphor that it is a metaphor.

Once the metaphorical aspect of the equation of Sanskrit poems with epics is remembered, the equation's second and third implications become apparent. If the equation's first implication is that the equation possesses a primitive meaning, then the equation's second implication is that the primitive meaning accentuates those characteristics of the Sanskrit poems that accord with this meaning. Therefore, to equate the *Rāmāyaṇa* and *Mahābhārata* with epics is not only to suggest that the Sanskrit poems are equivalent to the *Iliad* and *Odyssey* (which is the primitive meaning of the aforementioned equation), but also to foreground the features of the Sanskrit works that are analogous to attributes of the Greek ones. The metaphorical equation—to borrow an image from Max Black[48]—thus functions as a filter composed of stripes of clear and opaque glass: if the Sanskrit poems are the night sky and their features are stars, then the stars most clearly visible through the filter (which stands for the equation of the Sanskrit poems with epics) align with the lines of clear glass in the filter (which represent the attributes of the Greek poems that evidence the equation's primitive meaning).

Yet, those of the Sanskrit poems' characteristics that have no Greek counterparts are not obscured for long. Indeed, the third implication of the metaphorical equation of the *Rāmāyaṇa* and *Mahābhārata* with epics is that the semantic domain of the term "epic" expands so as to encompass the Sanskrit compositions' unique characteristics. This broader definition of "epic" ensues from a productive tension inherent in the predication that makes the metaphor possible. Two theorizations of this type of tension indicate how it operates with respect to the Sanskrit poems. According to Ricoeur, the tension is "between an 'is' and an 'is not,'" between the "literal interpretation restricted to the established values of words" in a statement (this interpretation being that the Sanskrit poems are epics in the original Greek sense by virtue of resembling the *Iliad* and *Odyssey*) and the "metaphorical interpretation resulting from the 'twist' imposed on these words in order to 'make sense' in terms of the statement as a whole" (this interpretation being that the Sanskrit poems are not epics in the original Greek sense but are epics in some other sense).[49] The process whereby predicative tension produces the metaphorical interpretation has been elaborated on by Monroe C. Beardsley. Just as the term "tension" itself denotes stretching as well as conflict, the "clash between sameness and difference" in a metaphor "twist[s]" the meaning of the predicate nominative that is metaphorically attached to a subject.[50] Consequently, the original sense of the predicate nominative "epics" shifts from "poems similar to the *Iliad* and *Odyssey*" to a new connotation that conforms to the two Sanskrit works that constitute the subject, namely, "poems resembling the *Rāmāyaṇa* and *Mahābhārata*."

Reminding the amnesiac equation of the Sanskrit poems with epics that it is a metaphor, then, does not—contrary to Bynum's contention—simply highlight the Sanskrit poems' correspondences to their Greek analogues. The "entities" between which a metaphor "posit[s] an illuminating resemblance" are not—pace anthropologist Fitz John Porter Poole—"apparently disparate,"[51] but actually are so; and their differences, which also are elucidated by the metaphor, are as enlightening as their similarities. More precisely, the interplay of likeness and unlikeness in the epic metaphor for the Sanskrit poems provides a guide to exploring attributes of the *Rāmāyaṇa* and *Mahābhārata* that the *Iliad* and *Odyssey* do not exhibit, as well the features common to the Greek and Sanskrit poems.

Before I describe what the Sanskrit poems have contributed to the idea of epic, let me characterize what these works share with their Homeric counterparts. The *Rāmāyaṇa* and *Mahābhārata* are epics in the original Greek sense insofar as they display traits analogous to those of the *Iliad* and *Odyssey*. Thus the Sanskrit epics are immense, intricate works that arise from the repetition of lines, ring composition, and the multiplication of episodes and that both use the same metrical language and treat some of the same themes by virtue of belonging to the same storytelling tradition.

Turning first to the form of the Sanskrit poems, I see immediately that both are enormous. Although the *Mahābhārata*, with a total of almost 75,000 verses in its 18 *parvans* (books), is a "great epic" in comparison with the "little epic" of the *Rāmāyaṇa*,[52] the latter, which contains just under 20,000 verses in its 7 *kāṇḍas* (parts), is lengthy itself. Unsurprisingly for works of such sizes, they include certain lines more than once and elaborate on the events that they address. Moreover, the story line of each epic comes full circle, being extended along the way by the inclusion of additional incidents.

The *Rāmāyaṇa* is ringed by two pairs of "pictures of ideal society"[53] and by two portrayals of the ritual during which the poem itself is recited. As Nārada informs Vālmīki about the hero, Rāma, at the beginning of the *Rāmāyaṇa*, the celestial sage describes the prosperity of Rāma's people and the monarch's entry into heaven, images that reappear at the *Rāmāyaṇa*'s end. Not long after Nārada departs, Vālmīki has his disciples—Rāma's twin sons, Kuśa and Lava—recite the *Rāmāyaṇa* to Rāma at his horse sacrifice (*aśvamedha*); and the poem revisits the ritual context of their performance, soon before re-presenting the ultimate successes of Rāma's reign. The image of "righteous rule" also recurs in Kuśa and Lava's rendition: between the bookends that are the scenes of Rāma's horse sacrifice, Kuśa and Lava praise both Rāma's father, Daśaratha, and Rāma himself for doing right by the subjects in their sovereignty, Ayodhyā.[54]

The *Mahābhārata* similarly is encircled by two rings that relate to the sacrifice at its center:

> The epic opens [and closes] with Janamejaya's snake sacrifice, which provides the setting for its narration; the action proper commences with the *rājasūya* [royal consecration], which is so fatefully interrupted by [the hero] Yudhiṣṭhira's defeat at the dice-game;[55] the main narrative is then concluded by the Aśvamedha, the other, even greater sacrifice of kingship; and . . . [between these two royal sacrifices that are recounted between the scenes of the snake sacrifice is] the awesome sacrifice of battle.[56]

The narrative of the *Mahābhārata* thus seems to be arranged so as to have a ripple effect that enlarges the poem plot's ritual dimensions. The sacrificial war at the core of the story is compassed most closely by the *rājasūya* and *aśvamedha* observances and more remotely by the serpent ceremony that surrounds them.

Separating each set of concentric circles whose radii compose the story line of the *Rāmāyaṇa* or *Mahābhārata* are tangential tales that diverge from this plot line in many directions. The multiplication of such narrative interludes in both poems leads one critic to conclude, "The available texts of the two Sanskrit epics are thus—and this is especially true of the *Mahābhārata*—gargantuan hodge-podges, literary pile-ups on a grand scale."[57]

The similar developments of the *Rāmāyaṇa* and the *Mahābhārata* result from a shared tradition at the levels of tongue and tale alike. The epics speak not the classical Sanskrit of later courtly literature, but an earlier idiom that is sparer in style and is not governed rigidly by the grammatical rules that crystallize only subsequently. Moreover, as Hopkins has observed,[58] both works employ many of the same poetic formulae.

The *Rāmāyaṇa* and the *Mahābhārata* overlap narratively as well as linguistically. While the *Rāmāyaṇa* notes a number of characters whom the *Mahābhārata* describes in more detail, the *Mahābhārata* offers its own rendition of Rāma's story and also tells tales about other actors in the *Rāmāyaṇa*. These narrative interconnections probably reflect the epics' reliance on the same stock of older stories, in addition to the epics' influence on each other. Other evidence of this stock includes the verses that texts other than the two epics cite that appear to be from them but are not.

Even though the "ground of literary allusion"[59] that the *Rāmāyaṇa* and *Mahābhārata* have in common is located in the particular context of ancient India, the epics cover four of the themes that the *Iliad* and *Odyssey* explore. First, the *Rāmāyaṇa* and *Mahābhārata* treat the hero's need to separate himself from his usual social surroundings. The two works highlight the forest exiles of the warriors who are the epics' heroes, because being displaced from their regular royal roles affords these rulers opportunities to marshal the martial resources that the men need ultimately to defeat their foes.

Second, the Sanskrit epics address the destabilization of social order by strife, for the two poems feature families torn apart that cannot be restored in the wake of war. In the *Rāmāyaṇa*, in deference to Daśaratha, Rāma relinquishes his right to rule Ayodhyā to his younger half-brother Bharata and agrees to be exiled to the forest for fourteen years. While there, Rāma's devoted wife, Sītā, is abducted by the demon Rāvaṇa, whose refusal to return her brings about bloodshed across the country. By the time Rāma reclaims his kingdom, Daśaratha is long dead and Sītā, soon to be banished by her husband through no fault of her own. In the *Mahābhārata*, Yudhiṣṭhira, his four brothers, and Draupadī, their wife, are forced to go to the forest for twelve years and to spend another year incognito, after he is cheated of his kingdom, Indraprastha, by his cousin Duryodhana during a dice match. The hostilities that erupt worldwide when Duryodhana refuses to return Indraprastha eradicate almost the entire family.

Third, each Sanskrit poem spotlights its hero's ability to reorder his life in the aftermath of societal ruptures. Thus, the *Rāmāyaṇa*'s Rāma becomes king and eventually embraces the sons whom Sītā, unbeknownst to him, bore during her banishment. The *Mahābhārata*'s Yudhiṣṭhira, too, is crowned and reigns righteously over the other survivors of warfare.[60]

Fourth, the *Rāmāyaṇa* and *Mahābhārata* underscore the mortal constraints on their heroes by exploring the extents of their god-given gifts. Rāma (a human manifestation of the divine sustainer Viṣṇu) and Yudhiṣṭhira (the human son conceived by mortal Kuntī when she coupled with immortal Dharma) attest that the epic "world of men [has] close kinship with the gods."[61] Simultaneously, however, the heroes' mortality circumscribes their exceptional success. Although Rāma outdoes the gods by getting rid of Rāvaṇa, sets a moral example for his subjects over his long reign, and leads them to heaven at the end of his life, he cannot bring Sītā back to this world once she has buried herself alive. In like manner, Yudhiṣṭhira cannot keep his brothers and Draupadī from predeceasing him and falling temporarily into an illusory hell, even though he has demonstrated righteousness (which his divine father personifies) regularly enough to earn the honor of ascending into heaven in his human body. The ends of Rāma and Yudhiṣṭhira thus illustrate the challenge of achieving within the confines of the human condition.

At the same time that the *Rāmāyaṇa* and *Mahābhārata* resemble the *Iliad* and *Odyssey*, these Sanskrit works remain distinct from the Greek ones. The characteristics particular to the Sanskrit poems constitute their contribution to the category of epic. At least three traits set apart the Sanskrit epics from their Greek analogues. The first is formal and invites consideration of the second and third, which concern content.

The most prominent formal feature of the *Rāmāyaṇa* and *Mahābhārata* is their repeated embedding of narratives within narratives. One such nested story is the account of Rāvaṇa's rise to power in the *Rāmāyaṇa*'s seventh part. This tale is told by the sage Agastya in the tale told by Kuśa and Lava in the tale told by an unnamed narrator. The tendency to embed tales is even more marked in the *Mahābhārata*.[62] For instance, the action on the battlefield in books 6 through 9 is recounted by Saṃjaya—the charioteer-bard of Duryodhana's father, Dhṛtarāṣṭra—in the story recounted by Vyāsa's student Vaiśaṃpāyana in the story recounted by the charioteer-bard Ugraśravas in the story recounted by an unidentified narrator.[63]

Two types of material that are taken up in the embedded tales of the Sanskrit epics reflect the poems' particular devotional and didactic thrusts. Theologically speaking, the pointed polytheism of the *Rāmāyaṇa* and *Mahābhārata* preserves a pantheon that includes Vedic deities such as Indra (the gods' king), Agni (the fire god), Yama (the god of the dead), and Varuṇa (the water god),[64] while promoting Viṣṇu above them all. Evidence of this Vaiṣṇavite preference occurs in the aforementioned embedded stories.

For example, the narrative about Rāvaṇa, which Rāma hears after he has done away with this demon, both protects and perfects Viṣṇu's reputation. The account describes the boon creator god Brahmā bestowed on Rāvaṇa that made him invulnerable to all beings except humans and other mammals[65] and explains thereby why mighty Viṣṇu needed to become a man in order to destroy the demon. Additionally, the account implicitly extols Viṣṇu by expounding on the power of the enemy whom Rāma readily defeated. Indeed, lesser deities than Viṣṇu—namely, the Lokapālas Kubera (the god of wealth), Yama, Varuṇa, and Indra—had lost to Rāvaṇa in battle. Moreover, the Rāvaṇa narrative makes Rāma's victory seem to be a matter of course. Immediately after relating early on in the story that Viṣṇu slew a slew of Rāvaṇa's ancestors who were stronger than their demonic descendant, Agastya reveals to Rāma that he is Viṣṇu and has been born on earth to dispose of demons.

As for Saṃjaya's wartime tale, its most famous excerpt is the *Bhagavadgītā* (Song of the Lord), the dialogue between Yudhiṣṭhira's brother Arjuna and their cousin Kṛṣṇa, who is another human manifestation of Viṣṇu and has been giving them military advice. Arjuna and Kṛṣṇa's conversation begins when Arjuna balks at killing his kinsmen in battle. Kṛṣṇa convinces Arjuna to rejoin the fray, not simply by citing his soldierly obligations but by recasting his military service as a form of Vaiṣṇava worship. "Emphasis on the deity [Viṣṇu] reaches its climax . . . in the theophany in the eleventh chapter, where Kṛṣṇa reveals to Arjuna his universal form (the *viśvarūpadarśana*), after he has identified himself in the previous chapter with the most essential aspects of every part of the cosmos. This revelation produces in Arjuna a spirit of humble adoration, summed up as the way of devotion (*bhakti*)."[66] Even though Arjuna appears to forget Kṛṣṇa's dazzling self-display in order to resume a familiar relationship with him, the theophany throws a different light on the events of the epic, casting into relief their religious features. Specifically, Viṣṇu's temporary reemergence implicitly rebroaches the question of why he has been reborn as a man, to begin with. According to the *Mahābhārata*'s opening book, his human rebirth is a response to that of demons who intend to overrun the earth. When the distressed goddess of the earth beseeches Brahmā to lighten her load, he tells the gods to take birth themselves as men to oppose their demonic foes. Before doing so, the divinities ask Viṣṇu to supervise their effort, which he does after becoming Kṛṣṇa. By enabling Yudhiṣṭhira and his similarly godlike brothers to win the cataclysmic war, Kṛṣṇa relieves the earth of her burden and ensures that righteousness will prevail.

In addition to Viṣṇu narratives, the Sanskrit epics embed stories that promote proper human conduct. Among the occasions for these moral tales are the forest exiles of the epics' heroes, whose distance from their realms during these periods frees them to reflect on how to behave even better. Rāma, for example, is reminded by Sītā—at the beginning of their exile— that he should use violence only to protect others, not to terrorize those who have not provoked him. To make her point, she tells him about an ascetic who became so attached to a sword that Indra had given him, that he grew to enjoy attacking others without cause. A similarly instructive story for Yudhiṣṭhira emphasizes munificence and asceticism. The visiting Vyāsa narrates to the monarch how a man named Mudgala, who gets by merely by gleaning rice, goes without food so that he can host hospitably a hungry hermit who actually is Durvāsas in disguise. For satisfying this infamously irascible sage, Mudgala is granted the right to go to heaven in his human body. Knowing, however, that he will fall from heaven as soon as he finishes relishing the karmic fruit of his beneficence leads him to eschew heaven in favor of performing austerities by which he can gain the even greater reward of release from the round of rebirth.

These and the other parables in the *Rāmāyaṇa* and the *Mahābhārata* also point to the texts' broader tendency to incorporate more explicit teachings about ritual and moral subjects: "The two great Epics of India, the Mahābhārata and the Rāmāyaṇa, contain (particularly the first) numerous passages bearing on many topics of Dharmaśāstra,"[67] the body of treatises on *dharma*. Even though this pattern of interpolation is much less pronounced in the *Rāmāyaṇa*,[68] other of the poem's elements made it nearly as influential a religious authority as the *Mahābhārata*: "The Rāmāyaṇa is a Kāvya, yet, on account of the noble ideals that it sets up in the chief characters, it was very popular and is relied upon as a source in digests on Dharma, though not so frequently and profusely as the Mahābhārata."[69] This lingering indication of a difference between the Sanskrit epics points to parts of their interrelationship to which I have yet to turn.

THE AMNESIAC METAPHOR AND OTHER COMPARISONS:
A NOTE TO COMPARATIVISTS

The metaphorical method that I have employed here does not shed light on all the sorts of similarities and differences among the Greek and Sanskrit epics. So far, I have summarized intracultural similarities between the *Iliad* and the *Odyssey* and between the *Rāmāyaṇa* and the *Mahābhārata* as well as intercultural similarities and differences between the Greek poems and the Sanskrit poems. But I have delved into neither the intracultural differences between the *Iliad* and the *Odyssey* or between the *Rāmāyaṇa* and the *Mahābhārata* nor the intercultural similarities between the *Iliad* and the *Rāmāyaṇa* or between the *Odyssey* and the *Mahābhārata*.[70]

I raise these omissions not simply to specify the sphere of my approach, but to reach this conclusion as well: reminding an amnesiac metaphor that it is a metaphor is a method designed to be a point of analytical departure, not a terminus. As a starting point for a cross-cultural comparative study, this method may not lead you to all of the areas that you want to explore, but it can show you some of the directions in which your terminological choices can take your comparison. As such, my metaphorical method is not a map depicting analytical destinations but rather a guide for comparativists to consult before moving across cultures.

More precisely, reminding an amnesiac metaphor that it is a metaphor amounts to one possible solution to a problem that confronts most comparativists at the outset of their projects. The problem is one of terminology. Assuming that you seek to compare two items that belong to different cultures, you are likely to find two circumstances. First, even if the items that you aim to compare are similar in any way, they probably will have the audacity to go by names that are quite different. Furthermore, one of these names—by accident of your own heritage and education—probably is more familiar to you than is the other.

Such familiarity is problematic insofar as it inhibits your critical self-consciousness. If already part of your vocabulary, one of the names all too easily suggests itself to you, as a term not only for the one item to which it already refers but also for the other item to which it has not yet referred. And, if you select the more familiar term over the other without reflecting on your choice, then you miss something important about the comparison that you are about to undertake.

Those who do consider your selection may assume at first that you are stretching your chosen rubric beyond its denotative breaking point, because you are ascribing a semantic flexibility to this word that it simply does not have. To be sure, your transfer of the term from its customary cultural context to a less usual one rightly rings somewhat false to those of your colleagues who are attuned to cultural particularity. Those who hold dear the distinctive forms of a culture understandably fear its decline when the culture's own terms for these forms are overlooked deliberately.

Yet choosing a term other than the culture's own does not necessarily imply a lack of attention to or interest in the term that is specific to the culture. Indeed, it is precisely in order to understand better both an aspect of the culture and the label that the culture has applied to this aspect, that you can temporarily set aside the culture's own label for its aspect. So, rather than saying that something is what it is, you say that it is what it is not, substituting a less suitable label from another culture. In so speaking, you make a metaphor. But, if someone else already has made this metaphor, then your task may be twofold. First, if the metaphor has been forgotten, then you should bring it to light. Second, you should give the metaphor the careful consideration that it deserves—assuming that no one already has done so.

At this point, you and others may ask why you should try to make or retrieve a metaphor in your comparative study, why you should style what you are studying in a way that fits only imperfectly. By saying that an item is what it is not, you can see better both what the item is and how it compares with what it is not, namely, its analogue from another culture whose name it has just borrowed. More specifically, the metaphor shows you three things: (1) the inextricable link between the name newly borrowed by the item and the analogue that has lent this name to the item, (2) the attributes of the item being lent this name that come to the fore as a result of this loan, and (3) the new attributes that the borrowed name acquires in its new cultural context. By examining the shift in the meaning of the borrowed name as it moves across cultural contexts, you become more aware of the similarities and differences between the item to which the name originally belonged and the item to which the name newly has been attached. With this awareness, you can compare the two items in a nuanced way. And in this quest—whether epic or not—I wish you every success.

NOTES

1. *Iliad* 9.519–26; *Odyssey* 8.72–78. All translations are my own unless otherwise noted.
2. Summaries of the *Iliad* and *Odyssey* include those prepared by Bulfinch ([1912] 1942: 220–32, 241–62) and by Hamilton ([1942] 1969: 178–92, 202–19) for their popular mythological compendia. An even briefer account of the epics that is addressed to even younger readers appears in D'Aulaire and D'Aulaire 1962: 183–84.

3. *Oxford English Dictionary Online*, s.v. "epic, *a.* and *n.*," http://dictionary. oed.com/cgi/entry/00076701 (accessed June 25, 2003).
4. Chantraine 1990: s.v. "*épos*": "*employé largement chez Hom. pour désigner les paroles, à côté de* mūthos *qui s'applique plutôt au contenu des paroles.*"
5. Liddell, Scott, and Jones 1940: s.v. "*épos*," IV.a.
6. Nagy 1990: 215.
7. For additional discussion of this idea, see Pathak 2007.
8. Crotty 1994: 159. On epic epithets, G. S. Kirk (1962: 80) comments,

> The use of conventional decorative epithets is an essential part of the Greek epic style, and lends to the Homeric poetry much of its rich and formal texture. Each individual character, object or event is treated as a perfect member of its species, and is expressed in the way determined as best for the species as a whole. This tendency to describe individuals in generic terms implies a certain way of looking at things: a simplified, synthetic way.

I will take up the Homeric poems' generic aspects shortly.
9. Kirk 1962: 159, 265; Griffin 1977: 39, 52; Thalmann 1984: 182.
10. Nagy 1999: 15; Redfield 1983: 218; Pucci 1994: 18.
11. Griffin 1987: 86.
12. Beye 1993: 30. Earlier, Kirk (1962: 98, 254) similarly asserted that these works were "designed [expressly] to fill gaps left by Homer, . . . to fill in those aspects of the Trojan adventure not described in the Iliad or Odyssey."
13. Griffin 1977: 52, 53.
14. Scott 1921: 243.
15. On this striking contrast between the Homeric and Cyclic epics, see Huxley 1969, Finley 1978: 73, and Nagy 1999: 7–8.
16. Burgess 2001: 1, 5, 174–75, 134–45, 154–56.
17. Whitman 1965: 309.
18. Beye 1993: x.
19. Whitman 1982: 92; Beye 1993: 5.
20. If imitation is the sincerest form of flattery, then the Homeric poems have been complimented constantly as primary epics by the conscious composition of secondary, tertiary, quaternary, and quinary epics on their basis over succeeding centuries. For a survey of such developments, see Preminger et al. 1993: s.v. "EPIC."

21. Butchvarov 1966: 163–64, 165.
22. Butchvarov 1966: 164, 166.
23. Scott 1921: 267.
24. Scott 1921: 262–63, 257–58.
25. Dodds 1951: 17–18; Crotty 1994: 211.
26. Finley 1978: 42–43.
27. Finley 1978: 194.
28. Finley 1978: 211.
29. Whitman 1982: 25, 22.
30. According to David Tracy (1981: 4), "religious questions" are

> the most serious and difficult questions, both personal and commu-
> nal, that any human being or society must face: Has existence any
> ultimate meaning? Is a fundamental trust to be found amidst the
> fears, anxieties and terror of existence? Is there some reality, some
> force, even some one, who speaks a word of truth that can be recog-
> nized and trusted? Religions ask and respond to such fundamental
> questions of the meaning and truth of our existence as human be-
> ings in solitude, and in society, history and the cosmos. . . . Lurking
> beneath the surface of our everyday lives, exploding into explicit-
> ness in the limit-situations inevitable in any life, are questions which
> logically must be and historically are called religious questions.

31. Doniger 1998: 9, 2, 95.
32. Lévi-Strauss 1963: 229.
33. Doniger 1998: 9.
34. Hainsworth 1991: 3–4.
35. *Rāmāyaṇa* 1.2.3, 9–17, 22, 26–41; *Mahābhārata* 1.1.8–10, 1.1.52–60, 1.54.17–24. The Sanskrit poems' self-depictions are explicated in Pathak 2007.
36. Kane 1966: 11; van Nooten 1978: 49; Smith 1980: 48; Shulman [1991] 2001: 21; Brockington 1998: 1.
37. Hopkins [1901] 1993: 58, 244; Hopkins [1915] 1974: 1, 11.
38. Hopkins taught Latin at Columbia University and Greek at Bryn Mawr College before becoming a Sanskrit professor at Yale University.
39. Hopkins [1901] 1993: 58. Although each of the Sanskrit poems ascribes itself to one author, many people contributed to these works during the centuries over which they were composed. Thus, the putative authors of

the *Rāmāyaṇa* and the *Mahābhārata*, Vālmīki and Vyāsa, can be seen as "culture heroes" akin to Homer himself, whom Nagy (1996: 21) characterizes thus:

For the ancient Greeks, . . . Homer was not just the creator of epic par excellence: he was also the culture hero of epic itself. Greek institutions tend to be traditionally retrojected, by the Greeks themselves, each to a protocreator, a culture hero who is credited with the sum total of a given cultural institution. It was a common practice to attribute any major achievement of society, even if this achievement may have been realized only through a lengthy period of social evolution, to the episodic and personal accomplishment of a culture hero who is pictured as having made his monumental contribution in an earlier era of the given society. Greek myths about lawgivers, for example, whether the lawgivers are historical figures or not, tend to reconstruct these figures as the originators of the sum total of customary law as it evolved through time. So also with Homer: he is retrojected as the original genius of epic.

40. Hopkins [1901] 1993: 379, 4, 58, 65.
41. Shulman [1991] 2001: 23.
42. Brockington 1998: 77, 26, 386, 411.
43. Brockington 1998: 1.
44. Bynum 1976: 45, 54, 45.
45. Derrida 1974: 8–9.
46. I do not mean to imply here that all genre classifications necessarily are metaphors, merely those taxonomies in which the generic term has been coined with such a small number of species in mind, that the term, in order to be used in another context, must be transferred across significant cognitive space.
47. Richards 1936: 101; Ricoeur 1977: 291, 292.
48. Black 1962: 39, 41.
49. Ricoeur 1977: 248, 296.
50. Ricoeur 1977: 196; Beardsley 1962: 294.
51. Poole 1986: 421.
52. Hopkins [1901] 1993: 58.
53. Brockington 1998: 400.
54. Brockington 1998: 400–401. Here, Brockington refers to only one of

the three rings surrounding the *Rāmāyaṇa* story—the circle comprising Daśaratha's and Rāma's kingships—and not the loops including Rāma's celestial ascension or Kuśa and Lava's sacrificial recitation.

55. For discussion of this interruption and similar occurrences, see Minkowski 2001.

56. Brockington 1998: 45–46. The sacrificial aspects of the Mahābhārata war have been analyzed by Alf Hiltebeitel ([1976] 1990: 287–96, 312–35).

57. Smith 1980: 50. While I too believe that the *Rāmāyaṇa* and *Mahābhārata* probably were pieced together from a number of sources, I do not intend to suggest that the authors of these works assembled their contents at random. Rather I would argue that the epic authors incorporated into the plots of their poems tangential tales that illuminated important aspects of the poems' central stories.

58. For his catalogue of parallel phrases in the *Rāmāyaṇa* and the *Mahābhārata*, see Hopkins [1901] 1993: 403–45.

59. Hopkins [1901] 1993: 79.

60. Yet the reign of Yudhiṣṭhira—unfortunately if fittingly for this hero of an interrogative epic that questions whether the Hindu religious ideal of *dharma* (righteousness) actually can be realized—is fraught with far more misfortune than is Rāma's (Pathak 2006).

61. Hopkins [1915] 1974: 3.

62. Accordingly, the term that the *Mahābhārata* uses most often for itself—*ākhyāna*, or "tale"—calls attention to the *upākhyāna*s, or "subtales," that the poem embeds. See Hiltebeitel 2005: 466–76.

63. Minkowski (1989: 420) seems to suggest that this unnamed narrator is Vyāsa, arguing that his identification as "a transcendent figure in the epic" obviates the "infinite regression of frames, each one the story of the previous narration." But I imagine the anonymous narrator as someone who has heard the story from Ugraśravas and is relating it at some later time, because seeing the narrator as such accentuates the antiquity of the story, in keeping with its self-presentation as an *itihāsa*.

64. These four gods also are known as Lokapālas (World Protectors).

65. To vanquish Rāvaṇa's army, Rāma enlists the aid of monkeys. The popular notion that Rāma received ursine, as well as simian, assistance probably postdates Vālmīki's *Rāmāyaṇa* (Goldman 1989).

66. Brockington 1998: 274–75. For more on this theophany, see Hiltebeitel [1976] 1990: 114–21, 124–28, 139, 257–58, 310; and Laine 1989: 115–16, 168, 226–30, 232–34, 240–42, 244–49, 272.

67. Kane 1966: 11.

68. The *Rāmāyaṇa* contains "nothing corresponding to the material of the *Śānti* and *Anuśāsana parvans* [books 12 and 13 of the *Mahābhārata*] with their pronouncements on ethical and social issues, discourses on [such philosophies as] Sāṃkhya and Yoga, and so on" (Brockington 1998: 441).
69. Kane 1966: 53. References to the *Rāmāyaṇa* and the *Mahābhārata* in these *dharma* texts are recapitulated in Kane 1966: 49–50, 58.
70. But I have treated these types of differences and similarities elsewhere (see Pathak 2007).

REFERENCES

Beardsley, Monroe C. 1962. "The Metaphorical Twist." *Philosophy and Phenomenological Research* 22, no. 3: 293–307.

Beye, Charles Rowan. 1993. *Ancient Epic Poetry: Homer, Apollonius, Virgil.* Ithaca: Cornell University Press.

Black, Max. 1962. *Models and Metaphors: Studies in Language and Philosophy.* Ithaca: Cornell University Press.

Brockington, John. 1998. *The Sanskrit Epics.* Leiden: E. J. Brill.

Bulfinch, Thomas. 1942. *The Age of the Fable.* Rev. ed. London: J. M. Dent & Sons, 1912. Reprint, New York: E. P. Dutton.

Burgess, Jonathan S. 2001. *The Tradition of the Trojan War in Homer and the Epic Cycle.* Baltimore: Johns Hopkins University Press.

Butchvarov, Panayot. 1966. *Resemblance and Identity: An Examination of the Problem of Universals.* Bloomington: Indiana University Press.

Bynum, David E. 1976. "The Generic Nature of Oral Epic Poetry." In *Folklore Genres*, edited by Dan Ben-Amos, 35–58. Austin: University of Texas Press.

Chantraine, Pierre. 1984–90. *Dictionnaire étymologique de la langue grecque: Histoire des mots.* New ed. 4 vols. Paris: Éditions Klincksieck.

Crotty, Kevin. 1994. *The Poetics of Supplication: Homer's* Iliad *and* Odyssey. Ithaca: Cornell University Press.

D'Aulaire, Ingri, and Edgar Parin D'Aulaire. 1962. *Book of Greek Myths.* Garden City, NY: Doubleday, Zephyr Books.

Derrida, Jacques. 1974. "White Mythology: Metaphor in the Text of Philosophy." Translated by F. C. T. Moore. *New Literary History* 6, no. 1: 5–74.

Dodds, E. R. 1951. *The Greeks and the Irrational.* Berkeley: University of California Press.

Doniger, Wendy. 1998. *The Implied Spider: Politics & Theology in Myth*. New York: Columbia University Press.

Finley, John H., Jr. 1978. *Homer's Odyssey*. Cambridge: Harvard University Press.

Goldman, Robert. 1989. "Tracking the Elusive Ṛkṣa: The Tradition of Bears as Rāma's Allies in Various Versions of the *Rāmakathā*." *Journal of the American Oriental Society* 109, no. 4: 545–52.

Griffin, Jasper. 1977. "The Epic Cycle and the Uniqueness of Homer." *The Journal of Hellenic Studies* 97: 39–53.

———. 1987. "Homer and Excess." In *Homer: Beyond Oral Poetry*, edited by J. M. Bremer, I. J. F. de Jong, and J. Kalff, 85–104. Amsterdam: B. R. Grüner.

Hainsworth, J. B. 1991. *The Idea of Epic*. Berkeley: University of California Press.

Hamilton, Edith. 1969. *Mythology*. Boston: Little, Brown, 1942. Reprint, New York: New American Library, Mentor.

Hiltebeitel, Alf. 1990. *The Ritual of Battle: Krishna in the* Mahābhārata. Ithaca: Cornell University Press, 1976. Reprint, Albany: State University of New York Press.

———. 2005. "Not without Subtales: Telling Laws and Truths in the Sanskrit Epics." *Journal of Indian Philosophy* 33, no. 4: 455–511.

Hopkins, E. Washburn. 1974. *Epic Mythology*. Strassburg: Trübner, 1915. Reprint, Delhi: Motilal Banarsidass.

———. 1993. *The Great Epic of India: Character and Origin of the Mahabharata*. New York: Scribner, 1901. Reprint, Delhi: Motilal Banarsidass.

Huxley, G. L. 1969. *Greek Epic Poetry, from Eumelus to Panyassis*. Cambridge: Harvard University Press.

Iliad. 1920. In *Homeri Opera*, edited by Thomas W. Allen. 3rd ed. Vols. 1, 2. Oxford: Oxford University Press.

Kane, P. V. 1966. "The Two Epics." *Annals of the Bhandarkar Oriental Research Institute* 47: 11–58.

Kirk, G. S. 1962. *The Songs of Homer*. Cambridge: Cambridge University Press.

Laine, James W. 1989. *Visions of God: Narratives of Theophany in the Mahābhārata*. Vienna: Institut für Indologie der Universität Wien.

Lévi-Strauss, Claude. 1963. *Structural Anthropology*. Translated by Claire Jacobson and Brooke Grundfest Schoepf. New York: Basic Books.

Liddell, Henry George, Robert Scott, and Henry Stuart Jones, eds. 1940. *A Greek-English Lexicon*. 9th ed. Oxford: Oxford University Press.

The Mahābhārata. 1933–1966. Edited by Vishnu S. Sukthankar, S. K. Belvalkar, and P. L. Vaidya. 19 vols. Poona: Bhandarkar Oriental Research Institute.

Minkowski, Christopher Z. 1989. "Janamejaya's Sattra and Ritual Structure." *Journal of the American Oriental Society* 109, no. 3: 401–20.

———. 2001. "The Interrupted Sacrifice and the Sanskrit Epics." *Journal of Indian Philosophy* 29, nos. 1–2: 169–86.

Nagy, Gregory. 1990. *Pindar's Homer: The Lyric Possession of an Epic Past*. Baltimore: Johns Hopkins University Press.

———. 1996. *Homeric Questions*. Austin: University of Texas Press.

———. 1999. *The Best of the Achaeans: Concepts of the Hero in Archaic Greek Poetry*. Rev. ed. Baltimore: Johns Hopkins University Press.

Odyssey. 1917. In *Homeri Opera*, edited by Thomas W. Allen. 2nd ed. Vols. 3, 4. Oxford: Oxford University Press.

Pathak, Shubha. 2006. "Why Do Displaced Kings Become Poets in the Sanskrit Epics? Modeling *Dharma* in the Affirmative *Rāmāyaṇa* and the Interrogative *Mahābhārata*." *International Journal of Hindu Studies* 10, no. 2: 127–49.

———. 2007. "The Things Kings Sing: The Religious Ideals of Poetic Rulers in Greek and Sanskrit Epics." PhD diss., University of Chicago.

Poole, Fitz John Porter. 1986. "Metaphors and Maps: Towards Comparison in the Anthropology of Religion." *Journal of the American Academy of Religion* 54, no. 3: 411–57.

Preminger, Alex, T. V. F. Brogan, Frank J. Warnke, O. B. Hardison Jr., and Earl Miner, eds. 1993. *The New Princeton Encyclopedia of Poetry and Poetics*. 3rd ed. Princeton: Princeton University Press, 1993.

Pucci, Pietro. 1994. *Odysseus Polutropos: Intertextual Readings in the* Odyssey *and the* Iliad. Ithaca: Cornell University Press.

The Vālmīki-Rāmāyaṇa. 1958–1975. Edited by G. H. Bhatt and U. P. Shah. 7 vols. Baroda: Oriental Institute.

Redfield, James M. 1983. "The Economic Man." In *Approaches to Homer*, edited by Carl A. Rubino and Cynthia W. Shelmerdine, 218–47. Austin: University of Texas Press.

Richards, I. A. 1936. *The Philosophy of Rhetoric*. New York: Oxford University Press.

Ricoeur, Paul. 1977. *The Rule of Metaphor: Multi-disciplinary Studies of the Creation of Meaning in Language.* Translated by Robert Czerny, Kathleen McLaughlin, and John Costello. Toronto: University of Toronto Press.

Scott, John A. 1921. *The Unity of Homer.* Berkeley: University of California Press.

Shulman, David. 2001. "Toward a Historical Poetics of the Sanskrit Epics." In *The Wisdom of Poets: Studies in Tamil, Telugu, and Sanskrit,* 21–39. New Delhi: Oxford University Press. Originally published in *International Folklore Review* 8 (1991): 9–17.

Smith, John D. 1980. "Old Indian (The Two Sanskrit Epics)." In *The Traditions,* 48–78. Vol. 1 of *Traditions of Heroic and Epic Poetry,* edited by A. T. Hatto. London: Modern Humanities Research Association.

Thalmann, William G. 1984. *Conventions of Form and Thought in Early Greek Epic Poetry.* Baltimore: Johns Hopkins University Press.

Tracy, David. 1981. *The Analogical Imagination: Christian Theology and the Culture of Pluralism.* New York: Crossroad Publishing Company.

van Nooten, Barend A. 1978. "The Sanskrit Epics." In *Heroic Epic and Saga: An Introduction to the World's Great Folk Epics,* edited by Felix J. Oinas, 49–75. Bloomington: Indiana University Press.

Whitman, Cedric H. 1965. *Homer and the Heroic Tradition.* Cambridge: Harvard University Press, 1958. Reprint, New York: W. W. Norton.

———. 1982. *The Heroic Paradox: Essays on Homer, Sophocles, and Aristophanes.* Edited by Charles Segal. Ithaca: Cornell University Press.

Conceptions of the Self in the *Zhuangzi*

Conceptual Metaphor Analysis and Comparative Thought

EDWARD SLINGERLAND

Language belongs in its origin to the age of the most rudimentary form of psychology: we find ourselves in the midst of a rude fetishism when we call to mind
the basic presuppositions of the metaphysics of language—which is to say, of
reason. It is *this* which sees everywhere deed and doer; this which believes in will
as cause in general; this which believes in the 'ego,' in the ego as being, in the ego
as substance, and which *projects* its belief in the ego-substance on to all things—
only thus does it *create* the concept 'thing.' . . . 'Reason' in language: oh what a
deceitful old woman! I fear that we are not getting rid of God[,] because we still
believe in grammar.
—Friedrich Nietzsche, *Twilight of the Idols*[1]

MY PURPOSE in this chapter is to explore Nietzsche's "metaphysics of
language" as understood by a fairly new field of inquiry, cognitive linguistics
and the conceptual theory of metaphor, with metaphorical conceptions of
the self in the *Zhuangzi,* a Chinese text that dates from the fourth century
BCE, serving as my case example. I will argue that the conceptual theory
of metaphor provides scholars with an exciting new theoretical grounding
for the study of comparative thought, as well as a concrete methodology for
undertaking the comparative project. Examining the *Zhuangzi* from the perspective of metaphor theory shows that conceptions of the self portrayed in
this text are based upon a relatively small set of interrelated conceptual metaphors and that the metaphysics built into the *Zhuangzi*'s classical Chinese

metaphors resonates strongly with the (mostly unconscious) metaphysical assumptions built into the metaphors of modern American English. Such resonance is not surprising, considering the claims of contemporary cognitive linguists that the metaphorical schemas making up the foundation of our abstract conceptual life are not created arbitrarily ex nihilo, but rather emerge from common human embodied experience and are conceptual rather than merely linguistic in nature. Thus, the stubbornness of the "belief in grammar"[2] that so troubled Nietzsche is located not in language or grammar but in thought itself and—ultimately—in the unavoidable facticity of our embodied existence.

CURRENT METHODOLOGIES IN COMPARATIVE THOUGHT

One previously more common method of conducting comparative work that is now falling out of favor is based upon a kind of word fetishism: a term, such as "rationality," "mind," or "truth," is taken from the source language (e.g., English), and then an equivalent is sought in the target language (e.g., classical Chinese). Finally, the failure to find an equivalent or near-equivalent word in the target language is cited as evidence of some sort of deeper cognitive incommensurability. The theoretical assumption upon which this approach is based—that a culture cannot possess a given idea without having a specific word for it—is rather problematic, as A. C. Graham has demonstrated in the Sinological context.[3] The more common approach nowadays is to undertake comparison at a theoretical level. In this approach, a particular philosophical theory is taken from the source culture and compared with a particular philosophical theory from the target culture. A lack of fit between these theories is taken to represent cognitive incommensurability or at least profound difference.[4] In the field of Western-Chinese comparative studies of the "self," the source theory is generally the Cartesian conception of the self, which is seen—quite rightly—as being quite different from traditional conceptions of the self, whether ancient Greek or ancient Chinese. As Charles Taylor notes in his now classic *Sources of the Self*, it has become something of a truism in the humanities that "our" conception of the self is a peculiarly modern, Western achievement.[5] The idea of "the" self as an object that can be found or lost and a sharp distinction between inner and outer (mapped onto a mind-versus-body dichotomy) are the hallmarks of this "historically limited mode of self-interpretation,"[6] the genealogy of which Taylor so skillfully traces from Augustine to Descartes and Locke.

Thus, the assumption guiding most recent studies of early Chinese conceptions of the self has been that we in the modern West are all thoroughgoing Cartesians, and most of these studies see as their task to demonstrate just how alien and non-Cartesian these conceptions are. David L. Hall and Roger T. Ames, for instance, declare that "the interpretative vocabulary associated with Chinese constructions of what we would identify as 'self' or 'person' is radically distinct from that drawn from the primary semantic contexts forming the major interpretative constructs in our tradition," and conclude that from a Western perspective "the Chinese are, quite literally, 'selfless.'"[7] Moreover, in discussing the Chinese conception of physicality, Roger T. Ames goes so far as to assert that "the Chinese are truly a different order of humanity."[8]

My purpose here is neither to minimize the gulf between Descartes and, say, the author of the *Zhuangzi* nor to deny the influence that Enlightenment philosophical theories of the self have had on our modern Western self-conception. My claim, rather, is that philosophical theories concerning such abstract concepts as "the self" are parasitic on previously existing folk theories of the self,[9] which in turn arise from conceptual metaphorical structures built into colloquial language. For example, despite the surface differences between the Cartesian and Zhuangzian conceptions of the self, both of these philosophical conceptions grow out of and make use of a deeper metaphysical grammar that has its roots in a common human embodied experience. In this respect, I concur with Eliot Deutsch, who has argued that comparative work carried on at either the level of specific terminology or the level of philosophical theory misses the important level in between that represents a "common core" or "deep grammar" of human experience.[10] I claim not that "the self" as some manipulable, bounded object is "real" in the same sense that my infant nephew's milk bottle is real, but only that our common human history of interactions with a host of such objects as milk bottles and bodies makes the emergence of such metaphors for the self almost inevitable for creatures like us.

COGNITIVE LINGUISTICS AND CONCEPTUAL METAPHOR THEORY

Before proceeding to my examination of the *Zhuangzi*, let me introduce the comparative methodology that I am proposing. Cognitive linguistics and metaphor theory are perhaps most familiar to the general academic public through the works of George Lakoff and Mark Johnson, who see themselves as being engaged in a kind of "descriptive or empirical phenomenology"

aimed at sketching out a "geography of human experience."[11] One of the
basic tenets of the cognitive-linguistics approach to metaphor is that human
cognition—the production, communication, and processing of meaning—
depends heavily upon mappings between mental spaces, with "mapping"
understood as "a correspondence between two sets that assigns to each element in the first a counterpart in the second."[12] Another tenet is that human
cognition is independent of language: linguistic expressions of cross-domain
mappings are merely surface manifestations of deeper cognitive structures
that have an important spatial or analogue component.[13] These mappings
take several forms, but perhaps the most dramatic form is what Lakoff and
Johnson refer to as "conceptual metaphor," where part of the structure of
a more concrete or clearly organized domain (the source domain) is used
to understand and talk about another domain that usually is more abstract
or less clearly structured (the target domain). Metaphor understood in this
manner thus encompasses simile and analogy as well as metaphor in the
more traditional literary sense.

According to conceptual metaphor theory, our primary and most highly
structured experience is with the physical realm. Therefore, the patterns that
we encounter and develop through our bodies' interactions with the physical environment serve as our most basic source domains. We then call upon
these source domains to provide structure when our attention turns to the
abstract realm. Sensorimotor structures thus play a crucial role in shaping
our concepts and modes of reasoning.[14] The most basic of these structures,
"primary schemas," come to be associated with abstract target domains
through experiential correlation, resulting in a set of "primary metaphors."
Lakoff and Johnson, following Joseph Edward Grady, provide a short list
of representative primary metaphors—such as AFFECTION IS WARMTH, IM-
PORTANT IS BIG, MORE IS UP, and so on—specifying not only the primary
experience correlations that give rise to them but also their sensorimotor
source domains.[15]

Traditional theories usually portray metaphor as a relatively rare and
somewhat deviant mode of communication that is thrown in to add rhetorical spice but is reducible fully to some equivalent literal paraphrase.[16] On
this view, metaphor is a purely optional linguistic device. Yet, an important
claim of the cognitive-linguistics approach to metaphor is that metaphor
is, in fact, primarily a matter of thought, not language, and that conceptual metaphor is ubiquitous and unavoidable for creatures like us.[17] Indeed,
conceptual metaphor serves as one of our primary tools for reasoning about
ourselves and the world—especially about relatively abstract or unstructured

domains. While abstract concepts such as "time" or "death" may have a skeleton structure that conceptually is represented directly (i.e., nonmetaphorically), in most cases this structure is not rich or detailed enough to allow us to make useful inferences. Therefore, when we attempt to conceptualize and reason about abstract or relatively unstructured realms, we flesh out this skeleton structure (usually automatically and unconsciously) with additional structure provided by the primary metaphors that we derive from our basic bodily experience, which are often invoked in combination with other primary schemas to form complex metaphors or conceptual blends. When primary or complex source domains are activated in such cases and mapped onto the target domain, most aspects of the source-domain conceptual topology—that is, inference patterns, imagistic reasoning patterns, and salient entities, among others—are preserved, thereby importing a high degree of structure into the target domain.[18]

As an illustration of this process, consider the question of how we are to comprehend and reason about something as abstract as "life." Lakoff and Johnson note that English-speakers, when reasoning or talking about life, often invoke the complex metaphor A PURPOSEFUL LIFE IS A JOURNEY, which provides them with a complex schema drawn from embodied experience.[19] This schema is based upon two primary metaphors—PURPOSES ARE DESTINATIONS and ACTIONS ARE SELF-PROPELLED MOTIONS—that have become a part of our conceptual toolbox through experiential correlation. When these two primary metaphors are combined with the simple fact (derived from our common knowledge of the world) that a long trip to a series of destinations constitutes a journey, we have the complex metaphor schema A PURPOSEFUL LIFE IS A JOURNEY, which Lakoff and Johnson map as follows:

Journey	→	Purposeful Life
Traveler	→	Person Living a Life
Destinations	→	Life Goals
Itinerary	→	Life Plan

The PURPOSEFUL LIFE IS A JOURNEY metaphor thus arises out of our basic embodied experience and gives us a way to think and reason about this abstract "entity,"[20] which in itself is unstructured and therefore difficult to reason about. The full practical import of a metaphor such as this, as Lakoff and Johnson observe,[21] lies in its entailments: the fact that the metaphorical link between abstract life and a concrete journey allows us to draw upon our large stock of commonplace knowledge about journeys and apply this knowledge to understanding "life." For instance, we unconsciously assume that life, like a physical journey, requires planning if one is to "reach" one's "destination," that one will "encounter" difficulties "along the way," that one should avoid being "sidetracked" or "bogged down."

As we can see from this example, a single, complex conceptual-metaphor structure can inform a whole series of specific linguistic expressions. This, indeed, is a crucial proposition of cognitive linguistics: that metaphorical expressions are not simply fixed linguistic conventions but the surface manifestations of deeper, active, and largely unconscious conceptual structures. Therefore, a complex metaphorical structure such as A PURPOSEFUL LIFE IS A JOURNEY exists independently of any specific metaphorical expression of it and thus can generate new and unforeseen expressions continuously. Anyone familiar with the PURPOSEFUL LIFE IS A JOURNEY schema instantly can grasp the sense of such metaphors as "dead-end job" and "going nowhere" upon hearing them for the first time and also can draw upon the conceptual schema to create related but entirely novel metaphorical expressions. For example, a country singer may write a song entitled "The Airplane of Life Is About to Depart the Gate, and I Don't Have a Boarding Pass" that draws upon the PURPOSEFUL LIFE IS A JOURNEY schema but employs it in an entirely novel (albeit somewhat painful) linguistic expression.

Scholars studying metaphor from a cognitive-linguistics perspective cite several types of phenomena as evidence that metaphors in fact represent conceptually active, dynamic, language-independent structures. Lakoff and Johnson review some of the linguistic evidence, which includes "novel-case generalization," the ability to comprehend entirely novel linguistic expressions by drawing upon a shared conceptual structure; polysemy, the fact that we find systematically related meanings of single words or expressions such as "dead end" or "lost"; historical semantic change in Indo-European languages, which suggests that conceptual metaphors such as KNOWING IS SEEING have been active in the minds of speakers of these languages; and inference patterns—that is, the fact that reasoning patterns from well-structured source domains (physical travel, for instance) are used commonly to draw conclusions about abstract target domains (e.g., life).[22] In addition, a growing body of psychological and neuroimaging studies are bolstering the case for the cognitive reality of metaphor schemas. The psychological inquiries include spontaneous-gesture studies,[23] priming experiments,[24] reasoning-constraint studies,[25] forced-choice and free-form drawing tasks,[26] and predictions of the image-schematic structures of various concepts.[27] On the neuroimaging side, several recent fMRI studies have suggested how cognitive mappings are instantiated neurologically in the brain.[28] All of this convergent evidence implies that conceptual metaphor is not only a very real phenomenon but also an inevitable part of embodied human cognition.

This implication leads us to the "experiential realist" or "embodied realist" stance that informs the cognitive-linguistics approach and that I believe to be the most significant aspect of this approach for scholars engaged in comparative work. Conceptual metaphors are understood as "interactive[,] structured modes of understanding" that arise as a result of our embodied minds having to adapt to "our physical, cultural, and interpersonal environments."[29] Because much of human understanding of abstractions is shaped both conceptually and emotionally by basic embodied image schemas, it would not be unreasonable to expect to find a high degree of similarity with regard to conceptual metaphors across human cultures and languages, especially with regard to primary metaphors. For instance, it is likely that all human beings—regardless of culture, language, or era—have had the experience of needing to move from point A to point B in order to realize some purpose. Thus, we should not be surprised if the primary metaphor PURPOSES ARE DESTINATIONS is universal or near-universal among human cultures. Indeed, findings in cognitive science and evolutionary psychology suggest that some primary-metaphor schemas through evolutionary time may have become part of the innate structure of the human brain, being deployed universally to structure naive or folk theories of physical causality, biology, and psychology.[30] Conceptual metaphor analysis thus can serve as a bridge to the experience of "the other," because metaphors function as linguistic "signs" of otherwise inaccessible, shared, deep conceptual structures.

Of course, since these gestalt patterns arise through the interactions of our embodied minds with our environment, we also would expect that dramatic changes in environment would be reflected in the creation of novel conceptual metaphors. Nonetheless, despite the great strides in technology that have been made over the centuries and the large impact that these technologies have had on our lives, the basic shared human environment has remained remarkably stable. We still have to move physically in order to get something that we want, we still obtain most of our information about the world through our sense of sight (the experiential basis of the common primary metaphor KNOWING IS SEEING), and overall the basic repertoire of motions and physical interactions possessed by a modern American is not terribly different from that possessed by, say, a Chinese person in the fourth century BCE. Despite the advent of electricity, movable type, computers, and the Internet, then, the basic stability of the human body and the environment with which it interacts across cultures and time would lead us to expect a large overlap in basic metaphor schemas.

METAPHORS FOR THE SELF IN THE *ZHUANGZI*

We rely upon a variety of metaphorical conceptions to understand ourselves. These various metaphors, however, draw upon a fairly small number of source domains such as space, object possession, exertion of physical force, and social relationships.[31] Although these various schemas are inconsistent literally at times, they generally are not incompatible—that is, they supplement one another and thereby fit together to form a coherent conception of self. We will see that the same is true of metaphors for the self in the *Zhuangzi*. Further on, I will use some metaphor schemas for the self identified by Lakoff and Johnson as the framework for discussing conceptions of the self in the *Zhuangzi*. I also will explore how some of the metaphorical entailments of each schema relate to soteriological goals, conception of the perfected state, and so forth. This exploration will illustrate the process of metaphorical reasoning whereby entailments based upon physically grounded metaphorical schemas are projected and used to reason about the abstract realm of "the self." In fact, as we will see, the inconsistent yet compatible schemas for the self in the *Zhuangzi* provide inference patterns that fit together to motivate a coherent soteriological strategy.

To begin with, it is necessary to examine the most general metaphorical structure for conceptualizing the self, the SUBJECT-SELF schema.[32] In 1991, Andrew Lakoff and Miles Becker examined a wide variety of metaphors for the self in modern American English and concluded that English-speakers each experienced themselves fundamentally in terms of a metaphorical split between a Subject and one or more Selves.[33] In this SUBJECT-SELF schema, the Subject always is conceived of as person-like and as having an existence independent from the Self or Selves; the Subject is the locus of consciousness, subjective experience, and an individual's characteristic "essence"—everything that makes her who she is. The Self encompasses everything else about the individual, and can be represented by a person, object, location, faculty, physical organ, body, emotion, social role, and personal history, among other entities. The basic SUBJECT-SELF schema can be mapped out as follows:

A Person	→	The Subject
A Person or Thing	→	The Self
A Relationship	→	Subject-Self Relationship

Many of the metaphors for the self that I will describe here merely are special cases of this single general metaphor system.[34] Phenomenologically, this fact is very significant; as Lakoff and Johnson note, "this schema reveals not only something deep about our conceptual systems but also something deep about our inner experience, mainly that we experience ourselves as a split."[35] The precise manner in which this split is conceptualized depends upon the source domain that is invoked.

The Locational Self

This schema arises from our interactions with bounded spaces and containers. As projected onto our conception of the self, the Self as Container schema can be mapped as follows:

A Person	→	The Subject
A Container	→	The Self
Objects in Container	→	Qualities of the Self

This schema, very common in English (e.g., "I didn't think he had it *in him*"), also is found throughout the *Zhuangzi*. We often see virtues, vices, tendencies, and knowledge understood metaphorically as substances that can be "put into," "stored in," or "taken out of" the container of the Self.[36]

The metaphorical container can be the Self in the most general sense, as in such phrases as "The perfected people of ancient times first *stored it up in themselves* [*cun zhu ji* 存諸己] before they tried to give it to [lit., store it in] others"[37] or "I saw something strange *in him* [*yan* 焉]; I saw damp ashes *in him*" (W95/G299; emphases added). Alternatively, the container can be an instantiation or part of the self, such as the heart-mind (*xin* 心) or the vital essence (*qi* 氣). For instance, in the "fasting of the mind" passage in chapter 4, the heart-mind is likened to a stomach that can be made tenuous or empty (*xu* 虛) through metaphorical fasting. Once the fasting is complete, the only thing left will be the *qi*, which in turn is described as being so tenuous a substance that it has space to "receive things" and serve as a reservoir for the *dao*: "The *qi* is something that is tenuous and so can receive things. Nothing other than the Way gathers in tenuousness" (W58/G147).

In both English and classical Chinese, this SELF AS CONTAINER metaphor is combined very commonly with the schema of the ESSENTIAL SELF.

THE ESSENTIAL SELF

As Lakoff and Johnson describe,[38] the ESSENTIAL SELF metaphor is based upon a "folk theory of essences," that is, the idea that every object has "within it" an essence that makes it the kind of thing it is, and that this essence is the causal source of every object's "natural" behavior.[39] The "essence" of human beings usually is associated vaguely with the Subject. There are, however, situations in which "our concept of who we are essentially . . . is incompatible with what we actually do."[40] Such situations are explained by invoking the ESSENTIAL SELF metaphor:

Person 1	→	The Subject, with the Essence
Person 2	→	Self 1, the Real Self (fits the Essence)
Person or Thing 3	→	Self 2, not the Real Self (does not fit the Essence)

An example of this metaphor in English is the apology "I'm sorry, I just wasn't myself yesterday," where "I" corresponds to the Subject, "myself" to Self 1 (the Real Self), and whoever or whatever "I" actually was yesterday to Self 2 (the False Self).

Lakoff and Johnson note three special cases of the ESSENTIAL SELF metaphor, but the one that is the most relevant to my project is the metaphor of the INNER SELF, which involves combining the ESSENTIAL SELF metaphor with the SELF AS CONTAINER schema:

| Inside of container | → | Self 1 (fits Subject/Essence) |
| Outside surface of container | → | Self 2 (does not fit Subject/Essence) |

This metaphor is very common and immediately comprehensible in both modern English and classical Chinese. "She seems friendly," we might say, "but that is just a façade [concealing her real (i.e., internal) self]." Similarly, in chapter 4 of the *Zhuangzi*, Yan Hui explains his plan to be "inwardly straight [*neizhi* 內直] while outwardly compliant [*waiqu* 外曲—lit., bent, crooked]" (W56/G143)—that is, seeming on the (false) outside to be agreeing with a wicked ruler while on the (real) inside maintaining his own correctness. Confucius's criticism of this plan ("Outwardly he will accord with you, but inside he will be unrepentant" [W56/G141]) also invokes this combination of metaphors, and indeed the container terminology of "inner" and "outer" is used systematically throughout Warring States Chinese texts in combination with the ESSENTIAL SELF metaphor.[41]

In the *Zhuangzi*, things that properly are "inside" are related to the Real Self, whereas things that properly are "outside" are related to the False Self. We can summarize some of these associations as follows:

Properly Internal Things	Properly External Things
heaven (*tian* 天)	human (*ren* 人)
qi	"full" heart-mind
spirit (*shen* 神)	knowledge or scheming
virtue (*de* 德)	fame or achievements
true self (*shen* 身)[42]	cultural standards
the numinous (*ling* 靈)	likes and dislikes
	life and death
	the (political) world (*tianxia* 天下)
	the physical form (*xing* 形)

This metaphor schema is powerful insofar as it motivates a variety of entailments that have crucial soteriological significance and yet can be accepted without need for justification or argument by anyone familiar with the use of containers. Six such entailments are

1. Properly external things   →   Subject in a bad state
   inside the container

This entailment, in addition to motivating the perceived danger of allowing "likes and dislikes to harm the true self internally" (W75/G221), the undesirability of "hoarding up [*zang* 藏] benevolence and using it to make demands upon others" (W92/G287), and the admonition not to "serve as a storehouse [*fu* 府] for schemes" (W97/G307), provides the reasoning pattern for the statement "Death and life, preservation and destruction, failure and success, poverty and wealth . . . all these represent the vagaries of affairs and the movement of fate. Day and night they alternate before you . . . but they are not worth disturbing your harmony, they should not be allowed to enter into [*ru* 入] the Storehouse of the Numinous [*lingfu* 靈府]" (W73–74/ G212).

2. Properly internal things   →   Subject in a bad state
   outside the container

Hence the perceived danger of "allowing virtue to be agitated [*dang* 蕩] by fame" (W55/G134) and the warning that "now you are putting your spirit on the outside" (W76/G222).

3. Properly external things   →   Subject in a good state
   outside the container

This entailment motivates the description of the sage as progressively "putting on the outside" the world, things, and life, and finally reaching the point where he can "enter into [the realm of] no-death and no-life" (W82–83/ G252).

4. Properly internal things   →   Subject in a good state
   inside the container

One of the most interesting illustrations of this entailment is the metaphorical conception of virtue, which often is conceived of as a liquid substance. In the *Zhuangzi*, this liquid substance is something with which the Self originally is filled through the action of heaven, and it is important not to let the liquid leak out or become agitated. Hence the admonition "internally preserve it and do not let it become agitated [by] outside [forces] [*neibaozhi er waibudang* 內保之而外不蕩]" (W74/G214) and the fascinating description in chapter 7 of a sage who is portrayed as having a "mechanism" that "plugs up" the Self so that his virtue does not leak out: the "plugging-up-virtue mechanism" (*tude ji* 杜德幾) (W95/G299). Heaven fills up the Self with a full tank of virtue at birth. If this tank of virtue does not leak or is not agitated, a person can use it all up herself, "preserve" her true self, and live out her full life in accordance with the following teaching: "use up completely [*jin* 盡] all that you have received from heaven" (W97/G307).

On the basis of entailments 1 through 4 and our common knowledge of the behavior of substances in containers, we obtain two further entailments:

5. Pervious barrier between   →   Undesirable state
   inner and outer

Hence the problem of "entanglements" resulting from the fact that, "when asleep, people's *hun* 魂 spirits interact [*jiao* 交];[43] when awake, their bodies open up wide [*kai* 開]" (W37/G51).

6. Impervious barrier between   →   Desirable state
   inner and outer

This entailment motivates the explanation that the sage Song Rongzi could reach a state where "the whole world could praise him and he would not be encouraged, and the whole world could condemn him and he would not be discouraged," because he "firmly [had] established the distinction between inner and outer and clearly [had] marked off the boundary between glory and disgrace" (W31/G16). Similarly, after the sage Liezi is shocked into an awareness of his own ignorance and thus reaches the highest stage of understanding, he returns home, does not go out for three years, and finally enters a spiritual state in which all selfishness and socially defined distinctions have been expelled and a tight "seal [*feng* 封]" between inner and outer has been established (W97/G306). Consider also the admonition to "make it so that day and night you are without cracks [*xi* 郤]" (W74/G212) or the description of the True Person of ancient times, who is said to have "preferred to close himself off [*bi* 閉]" (W79/G234).

THE PHYSICAL-OBJECT SELF

Manipulating physical objects is one of the first things that we learn to do and also is something that we continue to do frequently throughout our lives. Thus we should not be surprised that object manipulation serves as the source domain for many SUBJECT-SELF metaphors in the *Zhuangzi*. The basic schema is SELF-CONTROL IS OBJECT CONTROL. Because the most common way to control an object is to exert force upon it, this schema often is formulated as SELF-CONTROL IS THE FORCED MOVEMENT OF AN OBJECT and can be mapped as follows:

A Person	→	The Subject
A Physical Object or Agent	→	The Self or an Instance of the Self (body part, organ, faculty, etc.)
Forced Movement	→	Control/Manipulation of the Self by the Subject

English examples of this metaphor include the following statements: "I *lifted* my arm. . . . The yogi *bent* his body into a pretzel. . . . I *dragged* myself out of bed. I *held* myself *back* from hitting him."[44] This metaphor occurs throughout the *Zhuangzi* as well, as in the following phrases: "rectify yourself [lit., straighten your body] [*zhengrushen* 正汝身]" (W62/G165) and "recklessly [lit., lightly] use my self [*qingyongwushen* 輕用吾身]" (W71/G202). In all of the cases just cited, we are dealing with a unitary Self that is manipulated in some way by the Subject. In many cases, though, that which is being manipulated is one or more instances of the Self (we might call them "component selves"). A nice example of this type of control is found in the story of the sage butcher Cook Ding in chapter 3: "I [your servant] encounter it [an ox] with my spirit and do not look with my eyes.[45] . . . [M]y vision is stopped and my actions slowed down" (W50–51/G119). Here we see Cook Ding (the Subject) manipulating (*yi* 以), stopping (*zhi* 止), or slowing down (*chi* 遲) his organs (eyes), an agency within the Self (the spirit *shen*), a faculty (vision), and his bodily movements.

Generally, control of the object Self by the Subject is desirable, but even in English we sometimes speak of noncontrol of the Self in a positive sense, as when a person who—perhaps after much effort and no progress in learning how to dance—at last succeeds and explains, "I finally was able to *let* myself *go*." As a reader familiar with the *Zhuangzi* would expect, it often is the lack of forced movement that is emphasized in the text. The idea seems to be that certain positive instantiations of the Self—the spirit, the *qi*, and virtue (all of which are associated by the philosopher Zhuangzi with heaven)—normally are repressed or restrained and need to be released, resulting in the metaphor schema FORCE EXERTED UPON AN OBJECT = REPRESSION OF AN OBJECT:

| A Person | → | The Subject |
| A Physical Object or Agent | → | The Self or Instance of the Self (body part, organ, faculty, etc.) |

Force Exerted upon an   →   Repression of the Self
Object or Agent
Lack of Force Exerted upon   →   Freedom of the Self
an Object or Agent

An example of this schema is found in the Cook Ding story, where certain negative instantiations of the Self are restrained while other positive instantiations are released from control: "My sensory knowledge is stopped [restrained] and my spiritual desires set in motion [*xing* 行 (lit., allowed to move)]" (W50/G119). This theme is echoed in a passage where Confucius (acting as a mouthpiece for Zhuangzi) describes the great sage Wang Tai (the Subject) as ignoring the opinions of his sense organs and allowing his heart-mind to wander free under the influence of virtue: "He does not know what his ears and eyes find suitable, but rather lets his heart-mind wander [*you* 遊] in the harmony of virtue" (W69/G191).

This ideal of a lack of forced motion is conceptualized most generally in terms of the famous metaphor *wu wei* 無為 (effortless action). *Wu wei* sometimes is used in its literal sense of "absence of doing" and thus in certain situations may be rendered as "no-doing" or "inaction." More commonly, however, *wu wei* involves quite a bit of "doing" and in such contexts must be understood metaphorically. The *wu wei* metaphor sometimes is based upon the Subject-Self and Self-Control as Forced Movement schemas, and as such refers to a lack of forced movement imposed by the Subject upon the Self: there is "no doing," because the Subject is not doing anything to the Self, although the Self or Selves may be (and usually are) very active. Alternatively, *wu wei* can refer to a unitary Subject "doing nothing," usually because the world (the Way or the "inevitable movement" of things) is providing the motive force and "carrying" the Subject in the proper direction.

Although *wu wei* appears only a few times in the "Inner Chapters" of the *Zhuangzi*, the term can serve as a general expression for a host of metaphors having to do with a lack of exertion: "being at ease" (*an* 安), "wandering" or "playing" (*you* 遊), "following" (*yin* 因 or *sui* 隨) or "leaning upon" (*yi* 依), "flowing with" (*shun* 順), and "riding upon" (*cheng* 乘). In chapter 2, it is said that the sage *yinshi* 因是 ("following 'this is'") and in this way refraining from *weishi* 為是 ("making 'this is'") is like the "hinge of the Way" (*daoshu* 道樞), something that remains at rest while the door moves around it. The "flowing with" metaphor often is invoked in reference to the Way (*dao* 道, frequently represented metaphorically as a river) or the natural tendency (*ziran* 自然)

of things.[46] The successful tiger trainer is one who "flows with [*shun* 順]" the tiger's nature and does not try to "swim upstream [*ni* 逆]" against it (W63/ G167). Similarly, Zhuangzi himself advises us in chapter 5 "always [to] follow along with the natural [*yinziran* 因自然] and . . . not [to] add anything to life" (W76/G221). These *wu wei* metaphors often are used in conjunction with one another in a single phrase, an indication of their close affinity.

SELF-CONTROL IS OBJECT POSSESSION

Object manipulation is not the only way to conceptualize self-control. Another common way, found in English[47] as well as classical Chinese, is in terms of object possession. This S<small>ELF-</small>C<small>ONTROL</small> I<small>S</small> O<small>BJECT</small> P<small>OSSESSION</small> schema can be mapped as follows:

A Person	→	The Subject
A Physical Object	→	The Self
Possession	→	Control of the Self
Loss of Possession	→	Loss of Control of the Self

Examples from English include "losing yourself" or "getting carried away," which generally is understood in a negative sense. We find such negative portrayals of loss of object possession in classical Chinese as well. For example, we read of the second-rate shaman who is confronted with a true Daoist master: "before [the shaman] had even come fully to a halt, he *lost himself* [*zishi* 自失] and ran away" (W96/G304; emphasis added). Similarly, in chapter 6 a person who is seduced by fame and external concerns is described as having "lost himself [*shiji* 失己]" and "ruined his true self [*wangshen* 亡身]" (W78/G232). This second expression is significant, for the *shen* 身 is an instance of the Self whose possession is extremely important for the Subject—we read repeatedly in the text that the *shen* is something that must not be damaged or "forgotten [*wang* 忘]" (e.g., W60/G155).

Nonetheless, the loss of self-control is not always given a negative valuation. For instance, "losing oneself" in the enjoyment of a book or work of art is a desirable and pleasurable experience. In such cases, the ordinary state of "possessing" the self metaphorically is conceived of as a restriction or burden, and the elimination of self-possession understood as a kind of release. In light of this alternative valuation of object possession, we may reformulate

the SELF-CONTROL IS OBJECT POSSESSION schema as SUBJECT ESCAPES CON-
TROL OF THE SELF BY ELIMINATING OBJECT POSSESSION:

A Person	→	The Subject
A Physical Object	→	The Self
Possession	→	Control of the Subject by the Self
Loss of Possession	→	Subject Freed from Control by the Self

Applying the SUBJECT-SELF and OBJECT POSSESSION schemas to Warring States texts such as the *Zhuangzi* allows us to understand more clearly
such stories as that of Zi Qi of Southwall, who—after making his body like
dead wood and his mind like dead ashes through some sort of meditative
technique—declares, "I have lost myself [*wu sang wo* 吾喪我]" (W36/G45).
Much has been made of this passage by scholars such as Kuang-ming Wu
and David L. Hall, who see it as evidence of two different types of self in
the *Zhuangzi*: the *wu*-self and the *wo*-self.[48] As Paul Kjellberg has noted,
however, the phrase *wu sang wo* simply is proper classical Chinese, *wu* being
the standard first-person subject pronoun and *wo* usually serving as the first-
person object pronoun.[49] Moreover, the sense of *wu sang wo* could have been
expressed equally with interchangeable first-person reflexive pronouns (as in
wu sang ji 吾喪己 or *wu zisang* 吾自喪), and the resulting phrase is neither
more nor less freighted with philosophical significance than is the English
phrase "I lost myself." Yet, even this English expression is significant in that
it expresses the SUBJECT-SELF and OBJECT POSSESSION conceptual schemas,
as does its classical Chinese counterpart. Metaphorically, then, Zi Qi's meditative technique has allowed him (the Subject) to escape the control of the
Self, this schema being a common way to understand Zhuangzian spiritual
attainment.[50]

CONCLUSIONS

In this brief sketch I by no means have exhausted the source domains used
for conceptualizing the SUBJECT-SELF relationship. For example, another very
common schema that appears both in English and in the classical Chinese
of the *Zhuangzi* is the SOCIAL SELF metaphor, in which our vast experience
of interpersonal relationships allows us to map knowledge about evaluative
qualities of specific social relationships onto our inner lives. This schema, for

instance, informs Confucius's warning to Yan Hui in chapter 4, "You are still taking the heart-mind as your teacher!" (W57/G145). It is hoped, however, that this short discussion has helped to illuminate the shared, metaphorical "deep grammar" underlying the superficially quite different conceptions of the self expressed in the classical Chinese of the *Zhuangzi* and in modern American English. While the degree of similarity that we see here even with regard to quite abstract and presumably culturally contingent domains such as the "self" may seem surprising or unlikely from the perspective of neo-Cartesian postmodern theory—according to which, linguistic-cultural systems are conceived of (metaphorically!) as *sui generis*, autonomous structures—such cross-cultural similarity is rather to be expected from the standpoint of cognitive linguistics.

The cognitive-linguistics approach thus not only represents a powerful and concrete new methodology for cross-cultural comparative work but also provides a convincing and coherent theoretical grounding for the comparativist project itself. That is, if the embodied realist claims of cognitive linguistics are correct—if our basic conceptual schemas arise from embodied experience—then such claims explain why we would expect to find a high degree of cross-cultural similarity with regard to deep conceptual structures. Such similarity provides an escape from the postmodern "prison-house of language." Under the cognitive-linguistics model, the basic schemas underlying language and other surface expressions of conceptual structure are motivated by the body and the physical environment in which it is located, which—shared in all general respects by any member of the species *Homo sapiens*, ancient or modern—provides a bridge to the experience of "the other." As Lakoff and Johnson note, "Though we have no access to the inner lives of those in radically different cultures, we do have access to their metaphor systems and the way they reason using those metaphor systems."[51] At the same time, the recognition that these structures are contingent upon bodies and the physical environment, that no set of conceptual schemas provides unmediated access to the "'things in themselves,'"[52] and that some degree of cultural variation in schemas is to be expected allows us to avoid the sort of rigid universalism that characterizes Enlightenment-inspired approaches to the study of thought and culture. Ideally, at least, the methods of cognitive linguistics give scholars in the humanities access to a shared conceptual grammar that can allow them to engage in genuine conversation with other cultures.

NOTES

This essay originally appeared in *Philosophy East & West* (vol. 54, no. 3 [2004]: 322–42) and is reprinted here in a slightly modified form with the permission of the University of Hawaii Press.

 1. Nietzsche 1968: 38.
 2. Nietzsche [1990] 2003: 66.
 3. Graham 1989: 396.
 4. The boundaries between this approach and the first, more term-oriented approach often are blurred by the fact that a lack of shared technical vocabulary is cited commonly as evidence of theoretical incommensurability.
 5. Taylor 1989: 111.
 6. Taylor 1989: 111.
 7. Hall and Ames 1998: 23.
 8. Ames 1993: 149. See also Elvin 1993, where it is claimed that anything like "our" (read: Cartesian) conception of the self is a very recent development in China, and Jochim 1998, where it is asserted that the *Zhuangzi* in particular lacks anything like the "modern" (read: Cartesian) conception of the self. Jochim's account is particularly interesting because some of the features that he describes as central to the modern Western self—particularly substantiality (being able to be "possessed," "lost," and so forth) and the inner-outer distinction—are in fact some of the most common ways in which the self is conceptualized metaphorically in the *Zhuangzi*, as we will see further on.
 9. For discussions of the relationship between "folk" and "expert" theories, see Lakoff and Johnson 1981: 205 and Wolf 1994: 81–109.
10. Deutsch 1992: 95–97. This type of comparative work has been done by Ames, who cites the use of physicalist metaphors for the self in Chinese thought as evidence that for the Chinese, unlike for us modern Western-ers, "body and mind were not regarded as different 'kinds' of existence in any essential way" (Ames 1993: 163). Ames does note the existence of such mappings in modern Western language but views them as remnants that "might hark back to a pre-dualistic interpretation of [the] person." As we will see, this type of cross-domain mapping, according to cognitive linguistics, is the rule rather than the exception, and such mappings in fact are conceptually alive and constantly active in modern Western

languages. Nonetheless, Ames's observation is interesting because what he is perceiving arguably is not a difference between ancient (nondualistic) and modern (dualistic) Western conceptions of the self but rather a difference between everyday conceptual structure and modern Western philosophical theories. Scholars that focus on the level of theory will tend, like Ames and Hall, to emphasize difference, and for good reason. But such a focus on the theoretical tip of the iceberg overlooks the vast region of deeper cognitive similarities upon which philosophical theories are based, and thus may tend to exaggerate cultural and historical differences.

11. Johnson 1987: xxxviii. See Wolf 1994: 38–41 for a discussion of the link between phenomenology and the work of Lakoff and Johnson. For a basic introduction to conceptual metaphor theory, refer to Lakoff and Johnson 1980 and 1999; Johnson 1981 and 1987; Kövecses 1986 and 1990; Lakoff and Turner 1989; Sweetser 1990; and Turner 1991. Lakoff 1993 is perhaps the best article-length, general introduction to the conceptual theory of metaphor, and Ortony 1993 is a helpful resource that provides a variety of theoretical perspectives on metaphor. For the more general theory of mental spaces and conceptual mapping, see Fauconnier and Sweetser 1996 and Fauconnier 1997.

12. Fauconnier 1997: 1.

13. See Fauconnier 1997: 1–5 for a brief discussion of how this treatment of language as mere "signals" connected to a deeper, nonlinguistic structure differs from structural- or generative-linguistic approaches. See Johnson 1987; Lakoff 1987; Langacker 1987; and Barsalou 1999 for arguments that linguistic representations have an analogue, spatial component rather than being amodal, formal symbols. For empirical evidence favoring these views, see Damasio 1989; Tranel, Damasio, and Damasio 1997; Martin and Chao 2001; Gibbs 2003; and Zwaan 2004.

14. See especially Johnson 1987 for a discussion of this phenomenon.

15. Grady 1997; Lakoff and Johnson 1999: 50–54.

16. For a helpful account of the traditional view of metaphor in literary and philosophical studies, see Johnson 1981: 4–18.

17. See Lakoff and Johnson 1999: 122–27 for criticisms of the views that metaphors are linguistic, not conceptual; that metaphor has to do with unusual (poetic) or otherwise "deviant" usages; and that conventional metaphors are "dead" (i.e., fixed literary expressions).

18. I say "most" aspects because the skeletal structure of the target domain that is represented directly in consciousness constrains not only what

source domains can be mapped onto it but also which aspects of the source domain can be mapped successfully and which aspects can be ignored (see Lakoff 1993: 228–35 and 1990: 67–73).

19. Lakoff and Johnson 1999: 60–62.
20. Of course, even seeing life as an entity already involves the basic Object-Event Structure metaphor schema whereby events are conceptualized as physical things. For a discussion of this schema, see Lakoff and Johnson 1999: 196–97.
21. Lakoff and Johnson 1999: 62.
22. Lakoff and Johnson 1999: 81–89.
23. McNeill 1992.
24. Gibbs 1994; Gibbs and Colston 1995; Boroditsky 2000 and 2001.
25. Gentner and Gentner 1983.
26. Richardson et al. 2001.
27. See review in Gibbs 2003.
28. See Rohrer 2005.
29. Fesmire 1994: 152.
30. See Damasio 1994: 226–30 for a discussion of the "body-minded brain" and its probable evolutionary origins; Hirschfeld and Gelman 1994, a collection of essays making the case for universal human domain-specific structures of understanding; Lakoff and Johnson 1999: 17–18, 95 for some discussion of evolutionary pressures on the embodied mind; and Carroll 1999 for the argument that cognitive linguistics needs to pay more attention to the findings of evolutionary psychology.
31. Lakoff and Johnson 1999: 267.
32. The Subject-Self schema was identified first in Lakoff and Becker 1991 and elaborated in Lakoff and Johnson 1999: 268–70.
33. "Subject" and "Self" will be capitalized when used in this technical sense.
34. Lakoff and Johnson claim that *all* metaphors for the self are based upon this schema, but in fact there are many cases in Warring States Chinese texts where one finds a unitary Subject interacting metaphorically with an external entity, as in such metaphors for *wu wei* (effortless action) as "flowing with" (*shun* 順) the *dao* (or Way) and "riding upon" (*cheng* 乘) the transformation of things.
35. Lakoff and Johnson 1999: 269.
36. Pace Ames (1993: 165), who notes Deutsch's observation (1993) that container metaphors for the self are common in the West, but claims that, "by contrast, the notion of body in the Chinese tradition tends to

be couched in terms of 'process' rather than substance language." As we will see later, however, substance metaphors are the primary means for conceptualizing the self in classical Chinese as well as in modern Western languages.

37. W54/G134 (emphasis added). Citations from the *Zhuangzi* will be in the format "Wxxx/Gxxx," where "Wxxx" refers to the page number in Watson 1968, and "Gxxx" refers to the page number in Guo 1961. All translations are my own unless otherwise noted.

38. Lakoff and Johnson 1999: 282–84.

39. Lakoff and Johnson 1999: 214–15. As Lakoff and Johnson note, this folk theory is the basis of such diverse phenomena as the Aristotelian concept of "material cause" and the common expression "Boys will be boys." While remaining vague about the origin and universality of such "folk theories," evolutionary psychologists such as Tooby and Cosmides (1992: 71) cite experimental evidence on the perceptions of prelinguistic children (e.g., Keil 1989) that strongly suggests that it is an innate cognitive human trait to distinguish between animate and inanimate beings and to view animate beings as belonging to "natural kinds" possessing invisible "essences" that are related causally to the beings' behaviors and appearances. It is likely that many of the "folk theories" and primary metaphor schemas mentioned by Lakoff and Johnson can be grounded similarly in human evolutionary psychology. See, for instance, Keil 1979 for evidence that basic concepts such as "event," "physical object," "living thing," and "person," among others, are conceptual structures that human beings are predisposed to develop.

40. Lakoff and Johnson 1999: 282.

41. Pace Fingarette (1972), who argues that inner-outer metaphors in texts like the *Analects* of Confucius are merely ad hoc and not significant conceptually.

42. While referring literally to the trunk of the body, *shen* often has the extended meaning of "self" in Warring States Chinese texts. In the *Zhuangzi*, *shen* seems to be identified with the Real Self (as we will see further on, it always must be "preserved" and never must be "lost" or "forgotten"), and therefore will be translated as "true self."

43. Usually translated as the "cloud soul," *hun* is the part of the soul that drifts up into the sky, as opposed to the *po* 魄 soul, which stays with the corpse.

44. Lakoff and Johnson 1999: 271.

45. Lit., "taking and by means of my spirit encountering [it] [*yishenyu*

以神遇]" and "not taking and by means of my eyes seeing [it] [*yimushi* 以目視]." The original and most literal meaning of *yi* 以 is "to grasp with the hand."

46. The combination of ESSENTIAL SELF + SELF AS CONTAINER is the conceptual basis for the metaphor "so-of-itself" or "natural" (*ziran*). Meaning literally "so-out-of-itself," *ziran* refers to the way a thing is when it follows its own internal Essence. Metaphorically, the image evoked by the term *ziran* is of actions emerging "naturally" out of the container of the Self—an example of the NATURAL CAUSATION IS MOTION OUT metaphor (e.g., "The chaos in Eastern Europe *emerged from* the end of the cold war") noted by Lakoff and Johnson (1999: 214) in their discussion of events and causes. This metaphor simply is an extension of the CONTAINER + ESSENCE schema: the end of the Cold War is being conceptualized as a container with an internal essence (chaos) that emerges in the way a plant emerges from a seed or a child from the womb. Arguably, this NATURAL CAUSATION IS MOTION OUT metaphor arises from our experience with mammalian birth and the germination of seeds.

47. Lakoff and Johnson 1999: 272–73.

48. Wu 1990; Hall 1994.

49. Kjellberg 1993: 133. See Pulleyblank 1995: 76–77 for a discussion of the *wu*/*wo* distinction.

50. See also the metaphor of "forgetting" (i.e., losing from consciousness) in, for instance, W49/G108 or W207/G663.

51. Lakoff and Johnson 1999: 284.

52. Lakoff and Johnson 1999: 392.

REFERENCES

Ames, Roger T. 1993. "The Meaning of Body in Classical Chinese Philosophy." In Kasulis, Ames, and Dissanayake 1993: 157–78.

Barsalou, Lawrence W. 1999. "Perceptual Symbol Systems." *Behavioral and Brain Sciences* 22, no. 4: 577–660.

Boroditsky, Lera. 2000. "Metaphoric Structuring: Understanding Time through Spatial Metaphors." *Cognition* 75, no. 1: 1–28.

———. 2001. "Does Language Shape Thought? English and Mandarin Speakers' Conceptions of Time." *Cognitive Psychology* 43, no. 1: 1–22.

Carroll, Joseph. 1999. "The Deep Structure of Literary Representations." *Evolution and Human Behavior* 20, no. 3: 159–73.

Damasio, Antonio R. 1989. "The Brain Binds Entities and Events by Multiregional Activation from Convergence Zones." *Neural Computation* 1, no. 1: 123–32.

———. 1994. *Descartes' Error: Emotion, Reason, and the Human Brain.* New York: G. P. Putnam's Sons.

Deutsch, Eliot. 1992. "The Comparative Study of the Self." In *Selves, People, and Persons: What Does It Mean to Be a Self?* edited by Leroy S. Rouner, 95–105. Notre Dame, IN: University of Notre Dame Press.

———. 1993. "The Concept of the Body." In Kasulis, Ames, and Dissanayake 1993: 5–20.

Elvin, Mark. 1993. "Tales of *Shen* and *Xin*: Body-Person and Heart-Mind in China during the Last 150 Years." In Kasulis, Ames, and Dissanayake 1993: 213–94.

Fauconnier, Gilles. 1997. *Mappings in Thought and Language.* Cambridge: Cambridge University Press.

Fauconnier, Gilles, and Eve Sweetser, eds. 1996. *Spaces, Worlds, and Grammar.* Chicago: University of Chicago Press.

Fesmire, Steven A. 1994. "What Is 'Cognitive' about Cognitive Linguistics?" *Metaphor and Symbolic Activity* 9, no. 2: 149–54.

Fingarette, Herbert. 1972. *Confucius: The Secular as Sacred.* New York: Harper & Row.

Gentner, Dedre, and Donald R. Gentner. 1983. "Flowing Waters or Teeming Crowds: Mental Models of Electricity." In *Mental Models*, edited by Dedre Gentner and Albert L. Stevens, 99–129. Hillsdale, NJ: Lawrence Erlbaum Associates.

Gibbs, Raymond W., Jr. 1994. *The Poetics of Mind: Figurative Thought, Language, and Understanding.* Cambridge: Cambridge University Press.

———. 2003. "Embodied Experience and Linguistic Meaning." *Brain & Language* 84, no. 1: 1–15.

Gibbs, Raymond W., Jr., and Herbert L. Colston. 1995. "The Cognitive Psychological Reality of Image Schemas and Their Transformations." *Cognitive Linguistics* 6, no. 4: 347–78.

Grady, Joseph Edward. 1997. "Foundations of Meaning: Primary Metaphors and Primary Scenes." PhD diss., University of California, Berkeley.

Graham, A. C. 1989. *Disputers of the Tao: Philosophical Argument in Ancient China.* La Salle, IL: Open Court Press.

Guo, Qingfan 郭慶藩. 1961. *Zhuangzi Jishi* 莊子集釋. Beijing: Zhonghua Shuju.

Hall, David L. 1994. "To Be or Not to Be: The Postmodern Self and the *Wu*-Forms of Taoism." In *Self as Person in Asian Theory and Practice*, edited by Roger T. Ames, Wimal Dissanayake, and Thomas P. Kasulis, 213–34. Albany: State University of New York Press.

Hall, David L., and Roger T. Ames. 1998. *Thinking from the Han: Self, Truth, and Transcendence in Chinese and Western Culture.* Albany: State University of New York Press.

Hirschfeld, Lawrence A., and Susan A. Gelman. 1994. *Mapping the Mind: Domain Specificity in Cognition and Culture.* Cambridge: Cambridge University Press.

Jochim, Chris. 1998. "Just Say No to 'No Self' in *Zhuangzi.*" In *Wandering at Ease in the* Zhuangzi, edited by Roger T. Ames, 35–74. Albany: State University of New York Press.

Johnson, Mark, ed. 1981. *Philosophical Perspectives on Metaphor.* Minneapolis: University of Minnesota Press.

———. 1987. *The Body in the Mind: The Bodily Basis of Meaning, Imagination, and Reason.* Chicago: University of Chicago Press.

Kasulis, Thomas P., Roger T. Ames, and Wimal Dissanayake, eds. 1993. *Self as Body in Asian Theory and Practice.* Albany: State University of New York Press.

Keil, Frank C. 1979. *Semantic and Conceptual Development: An Ontological Perspective.* Cambridge: Harvard University Press.

———. 1989. *Concepts, Kinds, and Cognitive Development.* Cambridge: MIT Press.

Kjellberg, Paul. 1993. Review of *The Butterfly as Companion: Meditations on the First Three Chapters of the Chuang Tzu,* by Kuang-ming Wu. *Philosophy East & West* 43, no. 1: 127–35.

Kövecses, Zoltán. 1986. *Metaphors of Anger, Pride, and Love: A Lexical Approach to the Structure of Concepts.* Amsterdam: John Benjamins Publishing Company.

———. 1990. *Emotion Concepts.* New York: Springer-Verlag.

Lakoff, Andrew, and Miles Becker. 1991. "Me, Myself, and I." Manuscript, University of California, Berkeley.

Lakoff, George. 1987. *Women, Fire, and Dangerous Things: What Categories Reveal about the Mind.* Chicago: University of Chicago Press.

———. 1990. "The Invariance Hypothesis: Is Abstract Reason Based on Image-Schemas?" *Cognitive Linguistics* 1, no. 1: 39–74.

———. 1993. "The Contemporary Theory of Metaphor." In Ortony 1993: 202–51.

Lakoff, George, and Mark Johnson. 1980. *Metaphors We Live By.* Chicago: University of Chicago Press.

———. 1981. "The Metaphorical Structure of the Human Conceptual

System." In *Perspectives on Cognitive Science*, edited by Donald Norman, 193–206. Norwood, NJ: Ablex Publishing Corporation.

———. 1999. *Philosophy in the Flesh: The Embodied Mind and Its Challenge to Western Thought*. New York: Basic Books.

Lakoff, George, and Mark Turner. 1989. *More Than Cool Reason: A Field Guide to Poetic Metaphor*. Chicago: University of Chicago Press.

Langacker, Ronald W. 1987. *Theoretical Prerequisites*. Vol. 1 of *Foundations of Cognitive Grammar*. Stanford: Stanford University Press.

Martin, Alex, and Linda L. Chao. 2001. "Semantic Memory and the Brain: Structure and Processes." *Current Opinion in Neurobiology* 11, no. 2: 194–201.

McNeill, David. 1992. *Hand and Mind: What Gestures Reveal about Thought*. Chicago: University of Chicago Press.

Nietzsche, Friedrich. 1968. *Twilight of the Idols and The Anti-Christ*. Translated by R. J. Hollingdale. Baltimore: Penguin Books.

———. 2003. *Beyond Good and Evil: Prelude to a Philosophy of the Future*. Translated by R. J. Hollingdale. London: Penguin Books, 1990. Reprint, London: Penguin Books.

Ortony, Andrew, ed. 1993. *Metaphor and Thought*. 2nd ed. Cambridge: Cambridge University Press.

Pulleyblank, Edwin G. 1995. *Outline of Classical Chinese Grammar*. Vancouver: University of British Columbia Press.

Richardson, Daniel C., Michael J. Spivey, Shimon Edelman, and Adam D. Naples. 2001. "Language Is Spatial: Experimental Evidence for Image Schemas of Concrete and Abstract Verbs." In *Proceedings of the Twenty-Third Annual Conference of the Cognitive Science Society*, edited by Johanna D. Moore and Keith Stenning, 873–78. Mahwah, NJ: Lawrence Erlbaum Associates.

Rohrer, Tim. 2005. "Image Schemata in the Brain." In *From Perception to Meaning: Image Schemas in Cognitive Linguistics*, edited by Beate Hampe and Joseph E. Grady, 165–96. Berlin: Mouton de Gruyter.

Sweetser, Eve. 1990. *From Etymology to Pragmatics: Metaphorical and Cultural Aspects of Semantic Structure*. Cambridge: Cambridge University Press.

Taylor, Charles. 1989. *Sources of the Self: The Making of the Modern Identity*. Cambridge: Harvard University Press.

Tooby, John, and Leda Cosmides. 1992. "The Psychological Foundations of Culture." In *The Adapted Mind: Evolutionary Psychology and the Generation of Culture*, edited by Jerome H. Barkow, Leda Cosmides, and John Tooby, 19–136. New York: Oxford University Press.

Tranel, Daniel, Hanna Damasio, and Antonio R. Damasio. 1997. "A Neural Basis for the Retrieval of Conceptual Knowledge." *Neuropsychologia* 35, no. 10: 1319–27.

Turner, Mark. 1991. *Reading Minds: The Study of English in the Age of Cognitive Science.* Princeton: Princeton University Press.

Watson, Burton, trans. 1968. *The Complete Works of Chuang Tzu.* New York: Columbia University Press.

Wolf, Hans-Georg. 1994. *A Folk Model of the 'Internal Self' in Light of the Contemporary View of Metaphor: The Self as Subject and Object.* Frankfurt am Main: Peter Lang Publishing.

Wu, Kuang-ming. 1990. *The Butterfly as Companion: Meditations on the First Three Chapters of the Chuang Tzu.* Albany: State University of New York Press.

Zwaan, Rolf A. 2004. "The Immersed Experiencer: Toward an Embodied Theory of Language Comprehension." In *The Psychology of Learning and Motivation*, edited by Brian H. Ross, 44: 35–62. San Diego: Elsevier Academic Press.

4

Theorizing Embodiment

Conceptual Metaphor Theory and the Comparative Study of Religion

JAMES EGGE

In this chapter I take up Edward Slingerland's claim that conceptual metaphor theory and the field of cognitive linguistics of which it is part offer not only a powerful methodology for comparison, but also "a convincing and coherent theoretical grounding for the comparativist project itself."[1] In making this proposal, Slingerland addresses a conspicuous deficit in the history of religions: its lack of a shared theory of comparison. Despite historians of religions' significant contributions to the knowledge and understanding of religion in recent decades, the lack of a dominant paradigm—or even competing paradigms—has limited religious studies' ability to influence larger discussions in the academy and to establish itself as an autonomous academic discipline. The last theory of comparison to be embraced widely as a disciplinary model, the phenomenology of Mircea Eliade, lost favor for failing to explain the significance of the recurring forms it identified. Although Eliade asserted that the object of his study was humanity (understood as *homo religiosus*), his attempts to shield religion from scientific explanation fed suspicions that his true commitments were theological and antiscientific.[2] Unlike him, the proponents of conceptual metaphor theory present their approach as a falsifiable theory. Moreover, the larger field of cognitive science within

which their theory is located has become, in recent years, the most productive source of general explanations of religion.[3] Conceptual metaphor theory
thus promises to revitalize the comparative study of religious symbol and to
bring such study into the center of current debates on religion, on culture,
and on cognition.[4]

In this chapter I first discuss three of the most significant criticisms lev-
eled against the theory: (1) that culture plays a larger role in the formation
and transmission of metaphor than the theory's exponents, George Lakoff
and Mark Johnson, acknowledge; (2) that empirical evidence does not support Lakoff and Johnson's claims about children's acquisition of metaphor;
and (3) that abstract concepts are understood directly rather than largely
through metaphor, as Lakoff and Johnson claim. I then examine the idea
of image-schematic projection, which I consider to be the most important
contribution of conceptual metaphor theory. Finally, I use this theory to
analyze some important metaphors from two Theravāda Buddhist texts: (1)
the *Dhammapada*, a collection of 423 verses that belongs to the Pāli canon
and dates from between the fifth and first centuries BCE; and (2) the *Visuddhimagga*, the great commentator Buddhaghosa's fifth-or-sixth-century-CE
guide to the religious life.

CONCEPTUAL METAPHOR THEORY AND ITS CRITICS

As Slingerland describes in his chapter of this volume, the central premises
of conceptual metaphor theory are that metaphor is an important feature of
not only language but also thought and that metaphor is essential to most
abstract thinking.[5] Metaphors do not merely suggest or illustrate abstract
concepts, such as notions of the self, the mind, events, causation, and time.
Rather, abstract concepts are constituted largely by metaphors that emerge
from our experiences of our bodies and physical environments.[6] In metaphor, we use one area of human experience, which Lakoff and Johnson call
the source domain, to understand another, usually more abstract area of experience, which they call the target domain. They refer to this process as
cross-domain mapping or cross-domain projection. For example, vision is
a basic metaphor for knowledge. This metaphor underlies such expressions
as "I see your point," "clarity of thought," "point of view," and "insight."
Moreover, concepts as important as knowledge usually are understood in
terms of several metaphors. In English, images of physical manipulation,
such as "grasping" or "getting" an idea, shape the notion of knowledge as

understanding. In contrast, the concept of knowledge as memory largely is structured by storage metaphors, as in such phrases as "filling one's mind" or "retrieving information." These different physical activities of seeing, grasping, and storing do not form a single image in our minds. Rather, different aspects of several source domains collectively structure the complex abstract concept of knowledge. When we employ such metaphors as those for knowledge, our brains recruit for abstract thought neural structures developed for sensory and motor functions (like seeing and grasping). Because human beings have similar bodies and ways of functioning in the world, there is likely to be a large degree of similarity among the metaphor systems of different cultures.

Unsurprisingly, Lakoff and Johnson's ambitious claims have attracted both support and criticism, including questioning of the claim that conceptual metaphor theory is a falsifiable hypothesis well supported by empirical evidence.[7] Lakoff and Johnson have responded by claiming that, since the publication of *Metaphors We Live By* in 1980, researchers have produced a large body of empirical evidence for conceptual metaphor—evidence obtained using at least nine distinct research methodologies, such as studies of gesture and of historical semantic change.[8] More recently, in a pioneering brain-imaging study, Tim Rohrer has shown that many of the same sensorimotor areas activated by tactile stimulation of the hand are activated by reading metaphorical and literal sentences involving the hand, a finding that suggests that the sensorimotor cortices indeed are recruited by the brain in metaphorical thinking.[9] Neurological studies will play an increased role in future debates over the validity of conceptual metaphor theory, but linguistic and behavioral data will also be central to the discussion. In the remainder of this section, I consider three objections to the theory that have been raised by critics in the social sciences and humanities.

The first of these criticisms is that Lakoff and Johnson understate the role of culture in the formation and transmission of metaphor.[10] While acknowledging significant cultural variation in metaphor systems, Lakoff and Johnson maintain that hundreds of the most important metaphors directly emerge from correlations learned in childhood experiences of functioning in our physical environments and therefore are universal.[11] Such basic metaphors include KNOWING IS SEEING, MORE IS UP, and AFFECTION IS WARMTH (which is said to be learned from the experience of being held as an infant).[12] Lakoff and Johnson do allow "that all experience is cultural through and through" and that there is no precultural moment of pure physical experience.[13] Yet, they assign no significant role to culture in their accounts of how basic metaphors emerge from childhood experiences. Christopher Johnson suggests an alternative explanation, that children may acquire these metaphorical mappings not from correlations in their own physical experience but from adults' use of linguistic expressions that call attention to these correlations in experience.[14] Furthermore, culture may play a more significant role in shaping children's physical experiences than Lakoff and Johnson imply. For example, Chris Sinha and Kristine Jensen de López have shown that, even prior to the acquisition of language, Danish and Zapotec children form significantly different conceptualizations of containment, because of the different ways in which containers are used in the children's cultures.[15] Lakoff and Johnson's claim that the high degree of similarity among all human beings places a strong constraint on the formation of metaphor is no doubt correct, and many metaphors may indeed be universal. Yet, there also may be significant cultural variation even in basic body-based concepts and in the metaphors that they motivate.

The second criticism of conceptual metaphor theory is that, contrary to the theory's predictions, several metaphors' target domains are formed earlier in a child's development than are their corresponding source domains.[16] Such a metaphor often cited from Lakoff and Johnson's analyses is ARGUMENT IS WAR. Since children normally have earlier and more direct experiences of arguments than of wars, this metaphor's source domain clearly is not developmentally prior to its corresponding target domain. Lakoff and Johnson have responded to this point by clarifying that this metaphor is actually an extension of the metaphor ARGUMENT IS STRUGGLE, which is learned in childhood.[17] But, as John Vervaeke and John M. Kennedy have observed, this watered-down version is not a metaphor but a literal class-inclusion statement.[18] Despite such criticisms, Lakoff and Johnson have maintained that the source domain's developmental priority is a feature of the cognitively most important metaphors, or primary metaphors. Drawing on work by Joseph E. Grady and by Srinivas Narayanan, Lakoff and Johnson define primary metaphors as neural circuits that link neural ensembles corresponding to source and target domains. Therefore, primary metaphors are fundamentally not linguistic or even conceptual entities, but structures of the brain. Lakoff and Johnson claim that primary metaphors are formed "unconsciously and automatically" on the basis of correlations in human beings' childhood experiences of their bodies and physical environments, and that human beings share hundreds of these primary metaphors, many of which are universal.[19]

Unfortunately, there are some problems with Lakoff and Johnson's formulation of the primary-metaphor hypothesis. For one, extending the meaning of the term "metaphor" to include brain structures introduces an unnecessary and confusing ambiguity into the discussion. For example, in their 2003 afterword to *Metaphors We Live By*, Lakoff and Johnson define domains as "highly structured neural ensembles," but elsewhere they assert that domains are made up of concepts, as when they say that the target domain of a metaphor "is constituted by the immediate subject matter" of the metaphor.[20] Yet, there is no one-to-one correspondence between conceptual domains and their neural instantiations. A particular concept or metaphor could be realized very differently in the brains of two different individuals. In addition, what Lakoff and Johnson call primary metaphors—namely, the neural connections formed by correlations in childhood experience—actually give rise to a variety of cognitive and linguistic phenomena in addition to metaphors, such as metonymies, prototypes, and classifications. Lakoff and Johnson's redefinition of metaphor thus glosses over some significant issues requiring clarification.

Even more problematic are Lakoff and Johnson's claims about the acquisition of primary metaphor, which are based largely on Christopher Johnson's 1999 study of children's acquisition of the metaphor KNOWING IS SEEING. According to Lakoff and Johnson, Christopher Johnson demonstrates that children acquire this metaphor through a three-stage process:

> He studie[s] how the Knowing Is Seeing metaphor develops, demonstrating that children first use "see" literally, that is, only about vision. Then there is a stage when seeing and knowing are conflated, when children say things like "See Daddy come in" or "See what I spilled"; seeing occurs together with knowing. Only later do clear metaphorical uses of "see" like "See what I mean" occur. These uses are about knowledge, not literal seeing.[21]

But, in fact, Christopher Johnson does not distinguish between literal and conflation stages in the acquisition of the term "see," and instead suggests that children's earliest understanding of "see" includes both vision and awareness:

> The data above suggest that children assimilate various uses of *see*, including those that are typically non-visual for adults, to their understanding of visual experiences, including the mental dimensions

of those experiences. That is, they may map *see* onto a situational representation—a *frame* (Fillmore 1982) or *prototypical scene* (Slobin 1985)—that is richer than the adult visual sense, in that it exemplifies both vision and the states and changes of awareness associated with metaphorical uses of *see*. What makes this likely is the very high frequency of uses in the input [i.e., adults' speech] that can be assigned either a visual or a mental meaning.[22]

In Christopher Johnson's account, a child does not distinguish between the meanings of "see" in expressions like "I see a dog" and "I see what you mean." These meanings are "conflated" only from an analytical perspective: for the child, there is only a single complex idea. Adults' concept of "see" retains much of the prototypical structure of children's idea of "see," as adults' concept includes both sense contact and apperception.[23] Thus, an adult looking at a line drawing that can be interpreted as either a rabbit or a duck may say, "I see the rabbit but not the duck."[24] In this case, the relevant meaning of "see" is not "to receive a visual sense impression," but "to recognize."

If Christopher Johnson's account is correct, then learning the adult senses of "see" is "a process of differentiating use-types from one another," rather than of metaphorically "extending an established use-type to a new conceptual domain."[25] Only when a child restricts the literal meaning of "see" to acts involving vision does she come to understand other uses of "see" as metaphorical. Consequently, while a fully formed metaphor comprises distinct source and target domains, the neural ensembles to which these domains correspond need not be distinct anatomically. The same critique applies to other primary metaphors discussed by Lakoff and Johnson, such as MORE IS UP and AFFECTION IS WARMTH. Whether these correlations learned in childhood are transmitted culturally or apprehended independently of culture, they commonly motivate not only metaphors but also nonmetaphorical cognitive and linguistic phenomena, such as metonymies and categories, in which the correlated concepts belong to a single conceptual domain rather than two distinct domains. Therefore, correlations experienced in childhood do not, in themselves, provide sufficient motivation for the formation of metaphors.

The third criticism of Lakoff and Johnson challenges their central claim that abstract concepts are largely constituted by metaphors and not merely expressed by them. In Lakoff and Johnson's view, the content of abstract concepts is primarily metaphorical and is represented directly only in part. Moreover, they maintain that metaphor generally is not motivated by the perception of similarity between source and target domains. Rather, "metaphor is . . . typically based on cross-domain correlations in our experience, which give rise to the perceived similarities between the two domains within the metaphor."[26] Several critics, however, have argued for an alternative explanation: that speakers create and select metaphors in order to express already-formed ideas.[27] Quinn has supported her argument for this view with an analysis of interviews regarding marriage, and Andrew Ortony has taken this position in criticizing Zoltán Kövecses' work on metaphors for the emotions.[28] Quinn and Ortony argue that, in these cases, speakers understand the topic concept (marriage or emotions) directly and literally, and they select different metaphors to convey their thoughts about the topic. As another alternative to conceptual metaphor theory, Gregory L. Murphy has hypothesized that metaphors arise from a preexisting structural similarity between two concepts.[29] Similarly, Vervaeke and Kennedy have asserted that a target domain, in order to motivate the creation of a metaphor in the first place, must have considerable premetaphorical structure.[30]

This debate's terms can be clarified by noting first that applying the term "structure" to target concepts implies a metaphorical understanding of concepts as complex, multidimensional entities. This metaphor is not very apt if—as Raymond W. Gibbs Jr. recommends—concepts are understood "not as fixed, static structures but as temporary representations that are dynamic and context-dependent. Under this view, concepts are temporary, independent constructions in working memory created on the spot from generic and episodic information in long-term memory."[31] As Gibbs goes on to argue, when a topic is understood in terms of multiple metaphors (such as LOVE IS A JOURNEY, LOVE IS INSANITY, LOVE IS AN OPPONENT, etc.), such metaphors do not form an integrated whole, but instead provide alternative ways of thinking about the target concept. Similarly, Lakoff and Johnson observe that multiple metaphors for a single target concept rarely are consistent (in the sense of forming a single image) but typically are coherent (meaning that they have shared entailments).[32] For example, in the *Dhammapada*, the passions are represented metaphorically as—among other things—plants that quickly become overgrown, currents that threaten to carry people away, and fetters that may ensnare.[33] Although passions are not simultaneously pictured as growing out of control, carrying away, and ensnaring, all three metaphors are employed to assert that passions are dangerous and to be cut (*chindati*). Although the bare concept "passion" has no inherent structure that would attract these metaphors, the source domains' physical structures give form to our pragmatic relationships with the target domain. Therefore, metaphors are motivated not by the perceived similarity between the inherent structures of source and target domains, but by the perceived similarity between our pragmatic relationships with source and target domains. In the case of an aspect of human experience (such as marriage or emotions), a person may have a rich direct knowledge of the target concept, but this knowledge may be inchoate and unarticulated. For example, a child may know well how it feels to be angry and how angry people typically act, but still have little ability to reason about anger in general. As he grows, he will acquire concepts—many of them metaphorical—that will enable him to reason and talk about anger better. The claim that we rely on metaphors when thinking about abstractions is more obviously valid when the target concept is something of which we do not have direct sensory knowledge, such as subatomic particles or nirvana. In such cases we rely so strongly on metaphors that we are liable to take them literally, such as by thinking of electrons as orbiting spheroids or of nirvana as a place.[34]

IMAGE-SCHEMATIC PROJECTION

The examples given in the preceding paragraph all belong to the most important class of metaphors: those that prompt human beings to use their working knowledge of their bodies and physical environments to think about other, generally more abstract domains of experience. Lakoff and Johnson refer to the practical knowledge drawn from physical source domains as "image schemas," which Mark Johnson defines as "the recurring patterns of our sensory-motor experience by means of which we can make sense of that experience and reason about it, and that can also be recruited to structure abstract concepts and to carry out inferences about abstract domains of thought."[35] For Mark Johnson, "[t]he central idea is that image schemas, which arise recurrently in our perception and bodily movement, have their own logic, which can be applied to abstract conceptual domains. Image-schematic logic then serves as the basis for inferences about abstract entities and operations. From a neural perspective, this means that certain connections to sensory-motor areas are inhibited, while the image-schematic structure remains activated and is appropriated for abstract thinking."[36] Similarly, Gibbs "believe[s] that image schemas are best understood as experiential gestalts which momentarily emerge from ongoing brain, body, and world interactions. Image-schematic reasoning, such as that seen in linguistic understanding, involves the embodied simulation of events, and is not simply a matter of activating preexisting representational entities. Image-schematic reasoning does not simply mean doing something with one's mind, but constructing a simulation of experience using one's body."[37] Image-schema–based metaphors thus are akin to such artifacts as charts, graphs, and meters—in using which we employ our visual and spatial reasoning in order to think about an enormous variety of nonvisual and nonspatial data. Common linguistic expressions of image-schematic projection also include statements that normally may not be considered metaphorical, such as "I found love" (LOVE IS AN OBJECT), "I'm in love" (LOVE IS A LOCATION), and "I keep falling in and out of love with you" (LOVE IS A LOCATION and AN INVOLUNTARY CHANGE OF EMOTIONAL STATE IS FALLING).[38] Such statements are not based on perceived structural similarities between love and physical objects or places. Rather, such metaphors project physical structures onto love and allow it to be thought and talked about as if it were an object or a place. Likewise, MORALITY IS A BOUNDED SPACE, a metaphor analyzed by Slingerland,[39] does not assert a similarity between morality and bounded spaces, but simply is a spatial projection that structures the topic of morality and makes possible certain kinds of reasoning. The temporary and dynamic character of such mappings is shown by the fact that inconsistent projections can be combined even in a single utterance. For example, the inconsistent spatial projections made in the statement "I used to be full of love for him, but I'm not in love anymore" do not seem dissonant.

Image-schematic projection's fundamental cognitive importance emerges in light of the fact that a metaphor's source domain is never more abstract than its target domain. An apparent exception—"a raging storm"—actually conforms to this rule, as the underlying metaphor is not "A STORM IS ANGER" but "A STORM IS AN ANGRY PERSON." Only when two ideas are at equal levels of abstraction can either idea serve as the source domain of a metaphor, hence the metaphors A BUILDING IS A BODY (e.g., "steel beams form the skeleton of a skyscraper") and A BODY IS A BUILDING (e.g., "the eyes are the windows to the soul"). Moreover, metaphors in which source and target are equally abstract demonstrate the interaction of source and target described by Richards.[40] However, when the target is more abstract than the source, the transfer of meaning is much more unidirectional, from source to target. This strong linguistic constraint is explained by Lakoff and Johnson's claim that sensory and motor cortices are recruited in abstract thinking, whereas the brain structures primarily responsible for abstract thought do not directly participate in sensory and motor functioning. Thus, the logic of image-sche-matic projection is determined not by an a priori principle, but by the physi-cal structure of the brain.

A group of image-schematic–projection metaphors that merit special consideration consists of those in which a source domain's ability to elicit a particular affective response is projected onto the target domain.[41] The *Dhammapada*'s metaphors for passion include several examples of this type. One common metaphor for cognitive and affective flaws in the *Dhamma-pada* is impurity.[42] This metaphor functions in part through projection of a physical image schema, as we imagine mental flaws as defilements to be removed through cleansing. Probably more significant, however, is the feel-ing of disgust elicited by the thought of pollution. Boyer points out that the "mind seems to include a specific inference system that" responds to dangers of rot, disease, and dirty or toxic food; and that "triggers strong emotional reactions . . . even to the mere suggestion of such situations."[43] It is there-fore not surprising that purity and pollution are such fertile source domains for ethical metaphors. Another metaphor for passion in the *Dhammapada* is fire.[44] By projecting the image schema of fire onto passion, this meta-phor suggests that, like fire, passion causes pain and destruction and must be extinguished. But the fact that languages throughout the world use heat and hot entities as metaphors for passions, especially lust and anger, suggests an additional motivation for this metaphor. Studies have shown that strong emotions, particularly anger, cause a rise in body temperature.[45] Fire's ability to suggest the embodied experience of passion gives this metaphor its power. Passion is also metaphorically represented in the *Dhammapada* as agitation.[46] The projection of an image schema of physical agitation onto passion sug-gests that passion must be calmed. But what gives this metaphor its power is the fact that mental excitement or distress is actually experienced in the body as physical agitation: butterflies in the stomach, racing heart, and so forth.

Because emotions are essential to human reasoning, and especially to practical decision making, affective-response–projection metaphors should not be regarded simply as colorful or evocative language unimportant to cognition. As Antonio R. Damasio demonstrates, persons who lack the abil-ity to feel their emotional responses to alternative possible courses of action become paralyzed by indecision, even if their mental capacities are otherwise intact.[47] Like sensorimotor image-schematic–projection metaphors, these affective-response–projection metaphors prompt us to understand and re-spond to situations and concepts that might otherwise seem abstract or un-important. Our regular affective responses to particular situations may even usefully be considered an aspect of our image schemas for those situations, as affective responses, like sensory-based image schemas, are regular embodied responses to our environment. Constitutive of these affective responses are our internal sensations of nausea, bodily temperature, heart rate, and so forth. Mark Johnson identifies as a shortcoming of image-schema analysis its exclusive concern with the structure of experience to the neglect of affect and value.[48] However, his assertion that image schemas should be understood primarily not as representations but as regularities in embodied experience leaves open the possibility of a broader definition of image schema that would include emotional response.

I want also to take note of another type of metaphor, in which the categories of mental experience—such as consciousness, thought, intention, and emotion—are projected onto nonhuman beings and inanimate phenomena. Psychologists call the ability to imagine the thoughts of others theory of mind. Theory of mind enables us to interact with other human beings and animals, much as our image schemas enable us to navigate our physical environments. Metaphors in which mental qualities of the source are projected onto the target include most cases of anthropomorphism and personification. This type of metaphor is of particular importance to the academic study of religion. The idea that religion consists in the projection of human qualities onto imagined divine realities is the basis of Ludwig Feuerbach's seminal theory of religion, and it is also central to contemporary theories of religion put forth by Guthrie, Boyer, and Atran.[49] Summarizing this new line of thinking, Paul Bloom argues that religion is a by-product of two basic mental systems: "First, we perceive the world of objects as essentially separate from the world of minds, making it possible for us to envision soulless bodies and bodiless souls. This helps explain why we believe in gods and an afterlife. Second, . . . our system of social understanding overshoots, inferring goals and desires where none exist. This makes us animists and creationists."[50] In other words, religion is created by our inherent tendency to project mental qualities onto the nonhuman world. The tendency to perceive agency is so ingrained that even scientific writing is shot through with expressions of nonhuman purpose, like "plants seek light" or "the tiger's stripes are for camouflage." In the former example, we use a complex phenomenon, human conscious behavior, to understand and make inferences about a simpler phenomenon, the heliotropism of plants. We do so because human mental phenomena are so basic to our experience that they seem simple, even when they are in fact enormously complex, and because such projections enable us to use our human intuitions to make inferences about nonhuman phenomena. In a case like that of the tiger's stripes, creation by a deity seems to many people a more likely explanation for the diversity of life than do the simple mechanisms of mutation and natural selection. Even though the divine designer would have to be inconceivably intelligent and complex, the existence of such a being seems plausible to us because we imagine it as a being much like ourselves, just greater.

Metaphors based on projection of mental qualities also commonly involve image-schematic projection. An example is provided by the *Dhammapada* verses that describe passion as an enemy.[51] These depictions of passion as an intelligent and purposeful opponent demand that the hearer combat this danger with initiative, strategy, and a sense of urgency. By activating multiple sensory- and motor-based inference systems as well as our theory of mind, these metaphors enable us to understand and respond to situations not directly available to sense experience or physical manipulation.

SOME ANALYSES OF BUDDHIST METAPHOR

In my view, conceptual metaphor theory's most important contribution has been to reveal the pervasive role of image-schematic projection in abstract thought. By showing how human reason is shaped by our sensory and motor capacities and experiences, cognitive linguistics offers a way of grounding the comparative study of religious symbol in the universality and cultural variability of embodied human experience. The principal weakness of conceptual metaphor theory—its problematic account of primary metaphors and of their acquisition in early childhood experience—is a nonfatal flaw which the theory's future refinements, no doubt, will correct. In the remainder of this chapter I will demonstrate the theory's usefulness for the study of religion by interpreting some metaphors from the *Dhammapada* and the *Visuddhimagga*.

Although Lakoff and Johnson perhaps understate culture's role in the formation of metaphor, their hypothesis that common embodied experiences give rise to a high degree of commonality in metaphors across cultures is supported by a survey of metaphors in Pāli Buddhist literature. For example, the *Dhammapada's* passion metaphors that I have presented in this chapter—plants, currents, fetters, impurity, fire, agitation, and enemies—also are present in English, or at least can be readily understood by speakers of English. In addition, four of the same basic spatial models of the self that have been identified by Lakoff and Johnson in their analysis of English, and of which Slingerland finds examples in the *Zhuangzi*,[52] are employed in the

Dhammapada's metaphors for passion. First, passion is portrayed in several metaphors as an object or being external to the subject—such as a current, snare, enemy, or chariot[53]—which the subject seeks to control, or whose control the subject seeks to escape. Alternatively, passion is depicted as the subject's clinging, sticking, or connecting to the external objects of desire.[54] A person who lets go of or detaches himself from these objects is liberated from this condition. Second, in some other metaphors, passions are symbolized by qualities of the self, such as agitation and pollution—qualities that, unlike the inherent qualities featured in the ESSENTIAL SELF model, are understood to be accidental traits to be eliminated. Third, the self may be represented metaphorically as a container for mental phenomena. In this conceptual frame, passions are imagined as foreign substances that threaten to enter a person, hence a basic Buddhist term for passion and other mental flaws—*āsava*, or "inflow." The *Dhammapada* teaches that such emotions should be kept out; and that those a person does contain should be discharged, vomited, or thrust out.[55] Fourth, passions and other mental phenomena are rendered as places in which the subject may be located. To attain a mental state is to reach or touch it, to be in a mental state is to dwell in it, and to be free of a mental state is to go beyond it.[56]

Despite differing from the metaphors of other cultures, early Buddhist metaphors can be understood in terms of more basic metaphors shared widely across cultures. For example, English-speakers typically do not think of passions as inflows, but can readily understand this metaphor in terms of the SELF AS CONTAINER metaphor, which they share with speakers of Indic languages. The application of the SELF AS CONTAINER metaphor to emotion is universal or nearly universal, as it is motivated by the universal experience of feeling our emotions within our bodies. However, the inflow metaphor is not a necessary entailment of the container metaphor. The inflow metaphor's culturally contingent character is illustrated by the fact that, in Indic languages, the term *āsava* and its equivalents underwent a reversal of meaning: in Buddhist, Brahmanical, and Jain traditions, the denotation of *āsava* (Sanskrit: *āsrava*) changed from "inflow" to "outflow," even as the term continued to connote passion.[57] Evidence that this shift occurred includes Buddhist passages like *Aṅguttara Nikāya* I 124, a fifth-through-first-century-BCE text which likens a person who displays anger, hatred, and discontent at the slightest provocation to a malignant sore that produces a discharge (*āsava*) when struck; and *Visuddhimagga* 684, which explains that the *āsava*s are so called "because of the exuding (*savana*) [of these defilements] from unguarded sense-doors like water from cracks in a pot."[58] This shift involved an

important change in the sense of the metaphor: whereas the inflow interpretation likens passions to toxins that threaten to enter the body, the outflow
interpretation likens passions to bodily excretions such as tears or vomit—
impure effects of a loss of self-control. Thus images of discharging and exuding, which in the *Dhammapada* symbolize ridding oneself of passion, acquire
in the *Aṅguttara Nikāya* and *Visuddhimagga* the opposite signification—the
loss, during the experience of passion, of self-control. Although these understandings of *āsava* are mutually contradictory, both are based on the Self as
Container metaphor.

Another metaphor that conceptual metaphor theory illuminates is Asceticism Is Heat (*Tapas*), a common metaphor in South Asian religious
literature, including the *Dhammapada*.[59] Because ascetics seek to free themselves from passion, this metaphor appears to conflict with the widespread
metaphor Passion Is Fire. In some Brahmanical traditions, this apparent in-
coherence is avoided by understanding asceticism and passion as two aspects
of a single reality.[60] This understanding informs the mythology of Śiva, who
alternates between asceticism and eroticism, as well as a favorite motif of
Indian myth and folklore, the forest-dwelling ascetic who gives way to anger
or lust and thereby loses his accumulated asceticism (*tapas*). Yet, analogous
stories are not told about advanced Buddhist practitioners, who are thought
of not as building up heat, but as having cooled off. The Sanskrit word
nirvāṇa (Pāli: *nibbāna*) literally means "extinguishing"; and the *Dhammapada* says that a person who has attained this goal is "extinguished" (*nibbuto*),
"has cooled off" (*sītibhūtaṃ*), and is "without *upadhi*" (*nirūpadhiṃ*)—*upadhi*
meaning both "grasping" and "fuel."[61] But how can Buddhist *tapassīs* (pos-
sessors of heat) have cooled off?

Despite this apparent inconsistency, these asceticism and passion metaphors cohere within a Buddhist context, as Lakoff and Johnson would
predict. While historian of religions Walter Kaelber has suggested that the
self-inflicted torment that asceticism involved caused it to be thought of as
heat,[62] a simpler explanation more likely to be accepted by Buddhists is that
asceticism is coded as hot because it consists in exertion. The Asceticism Is
Heat metaphor likely has as its physical basis the heat that physical exertion
causes a person to feel. Indeed, derivatives of the verb *tapati* (to heat) that
mean "energy" or "exertion" appear in *Dhammapada* 143B and 276. Yet, if
ascetic practice heats, its goal—nirvana—cools. This supposition is supported by the analogous way in which the *Dhammapada* uses derivatives of the
verb *yuñjati* (to yoke), including *yoga*. Such "exertion" or "discipline" often
is represented metaphorically as yoking, while *nibbāna* is called *yogakkhema*,

or "rest from yoking."[63] Thus, exertion is represented metaphorically both as heating and as yoking, while the goal of this exertion, both as coolness and as release from yoking. Here, in light of Lakoff and Johnson's prediction that a culture's main metaphors will cohere, a conceptual structure that otherwise could be overlooked is recognized instead.

The *Dhammapada* also provides evidence to support the claim made by George Lakoff and Mark Turner that novel uses of metaphor in poetry usually consist of combinations and extensions of conventional metaphors.[64] One conventional Buddhist metaphor is the field of merit (*puññakkhetta*). In this metaphor, the seed represents a religious donation; and the field, the recipient of the religious donation. Just as the quality of the soil in which seed is planted partly determines its yield, so the worthiness of the religious donation's recipient partly determines the merit of the donation. The *Dhammapada* elaborates this metaphor by combining it with the metaphor PASSIONS ARE PLANTS to assert that the best recipients are ascetics free of the "weeds" of lust, hatred, and delusion.[65] Another metaphor combination occurs in *Dhammapada* 369, which urges, "Bail out this boat, O monk. When bailed out, it will go lightly for you. Having cut off lust and hatred, you will go to nirvana."[66] Here, passions are represented simultaneously as a river that must be crossed and as water flowing into a leaky boat (the self) and weighing it down. That passions are represented as water in both of these metaphors gives this verse's metaphor combination a pleasing consistency. This verse also employs the standard Buddhist metaphor of the religious life as a journey to nirvana, a metaphor that draws on three universal (or nearly universal) image-schematic projections: MENTAL STATES ARE PLACES, CONDITIONS OF EXISTENCE ARE PLACES, and A MEANINGFUL LIFE IS A JOURNEY.

Metaphors are used not only in Buddhist poetic texts, but also throughout Buddhist philosophical and scholastic literature. For example, the *Visuddhimagga* is shot through with image-schematic projections, especially projections of spatial image schemas. Certainly, such schemas appear in Buddhaghosa's definition of meditative concentration, the second of the *Visuddhimagga*'s three primary topics, at *Visuddhimagga* 84–85:

It is concentration (*samādhi*) in the sense of concentrating (*samādhāna*). What is this concentrating? It is the centering (*ādhāna*) of consciousness and consciousness-concomitants evenly (*samaṁ*) and rightly (*sammā*) on a single object [literally, "support"]; placing, is what is meant. So it is the state in virtue of which consciousness and its concomitants remain evenly and rightly on a single object,

undistracted [literally, "not thrown about"] and unscattered, that
should be understood as concentrating.[67]

Here Buddhaghosa uses spatial metaphors not only to describe meditative
concentration, but also to tell his readers how to use their spatial imagination and reasoning in their meditation practice. Just as this passage cannot
be accurately translated or explained without using spatial language, so the
practice that Buddhaghosa describes cannot be performed without using
spatial image schemas to guide one's thoughts. Although the conditions of
embodiment usually are thought to shape more ecstatic forms of religious
experience (such as trance, possession, and devotion), this passage shows that
body-based image-schematic projections deeply inform enstatic experiences
as well.

Some of the many similes that Buddhist authors use indicate that they
recognize physical experience's essential role in constituting meditative practice. For instance, Buddhaghosa, while discussing in *Visuddhimagga* 136–37
the need for a meditator to produce (*pavatteti*—literally, "set in motion") a
meditative sign (*nimitta*—the abstracted or purified object of meditation)
with constant effort (*samena payogena*) in order to attain a state of meditative absorption, illustrates this point extensively with five similes: (1) that a
bee must fly with constant speed (*samena javena*) in order to reach a flower,
(2) that a surgeon's pupil must make a constant effort (*samena payogena*) in
order to cut a lotus leaf in water, (3) that a man must make a constant effort
(*samena payogena*) in order to untangle a spider's web, (4) that a skipper must
raise his sails in light wind and lower them in high wind in order to arrive
safely at his destination, and (5) that a student must make a constant effort
(*samena payogena*) in order to fill an oil tube without spilling the oil. In offering these similes, Buddhaghosa is not explaining the unfamiliar in terms
of the familiar, as—with the exception of pouring oil into a tube—these
similes concern matters not likely to be part of a monk's personal experience.
Rather, Buddhaghosa requires his audience to imagine actively the spatial
relationships and mental states featured in these simile scenarios, which all
involve maintaining a constant speed or effort. Because these scenes generally are unfamiliar to the audience members, they cannot summon from
memory a conventional understanding of these situations but instead must
mentally simulate the actions evoked by the similes, such as applying just the
right amount of pressure to cut a lotus leaf floating on water. The effectiveness of these similes comes not from their exemplifying an abstract notion
of moderation, but from their stimulating the motor cortices to activate an

image schema of balanced effort so that this schema can be used to structure meditative practice. This activation process is similar to that involved in religious ritual: when performing a ritual, a person physically enacts image schemas that have religious meanings within that ritual context. The power of religious rituals, like the power of religious tropes, consists not in making a claim or comparison, but in engaging the embodied mind in thought about religious matters.[68]

Of course, to say that historians of religions should pay attention to the embodied nature of religious experience is to suggest nothing new, as "the body" has become a central concern in religious studies.[69] Cognitive linguists, however, offer a theory that uses cognition's embodied character to explain why there is so much similarity in symbol and metaphor across the world's religions. Although historians of religions may reject parts of this theoretical model—and I acknowledge that the competing definitions of its central category, "image schema," do make problematic the model's adoption—there is much to be gained by engaging in the cross-disciplinary discussion that conceptual metaphor theory has opened up.

NOTES

1. Slingerland 2004b: 336.
2. See especially Jonathan Z. Smith's sympathetic but highly critical review of Eliade's project (2000).
3. I refer especially to the work of Stewart Elliott Guthrie, of Pascal Boyer, and of Scott Atran, which I discuss briefly further on.
4. In addition to Slingerland's studies, noteworthy applications of conceptual metaphor theory to the comparative study of religion include Karl H. Potter's analysis of *karma* in South Asian religions (1988), David L. McMahan's study of the metaphor KNOWING IS SEEING in South Asian Buddhism (2002), and Robert Ford Campany's discussion of early medieval Chinese concepts corresponding to the modern Western idea of religion (2003).
5. The only qualification that I would make of Slingerland's conceptual-metaphor-theory account concerns his statement that, according to the theory, "human cognition is independent of language" (2004b: 324). I think that this formulation overstates the case, as I have not been able to find in Lakoff and Johnson's writings any statements that divorce language from cognition so completely.

6. Lakoff and Johnson 1999: 337; Lakoff and Johnson [1980] 2003: 3, 146, 247.
7. See, among others, Murphy 1996.
8. Lakoff and Johnson [1980] 2003: 248–49.
9. Rohrer 2005.
10. Some important early statements of this criticism were made in Fernandez 1991, including the chapters by anthropologists Naomi Quinn (1991) and Hoyt Alverson (1991).
11. Lakoff and Johnson [1980] 2003: 273–74, 256–57.
12. On these and other representative primary metaphors, see Lakoff and Johnson 1999: 49–57.
13. Lakoff and Johnson [1980] 2003: 57.
14. C. Johnson 1999: 167.
15. Sinha and Jensen de López 2000.
16. Ortony 1988: 101–2; Murphy 1996: 191.
17. Lakoff and Johnson [1980] 2003: 265.
18. Vervaeke and Kennedy 2004: 218.
19. Lakoff and Johnson 1999: 45–59; Lakoff and Johnson [1980] 2003: 254–57.
20. Lakoff and Johnson [1980] 2003: 256, 265.
21. Lakoff and Johnson [1980] 2003: 255.
22. C. Johnson 1999: 166.
23. C. Johnson 1999: 161.
24. An image search of the World Wide Web for "duck rabbit" yields several examples of this type of drawing.
25. C. Johnson 1999: 155, 166.
26. Lakoff and Johnson [1980] 2003: 244–45.
27. In addition to the references cited in this paragraph, see Glucksberg and McGlone 1999; Keysar and Bly 1999; and Blasko 1999.
28. Quinn 1991; Ortony 1988.
29. Murphy 1996.
30. Vervaeke and Kennedy 2004: 217.
31. Gibbs 1996: 313.
32. Lakoff and Johnson 1980 [2003]: 91–96.
33. Plants: *Dhammapada* 250, 262–63, 283–84, 285, 334, 335, 337, 338, 340, 394; currents: *Dhammapada* 218, 251, 339, 341, 347; fetters or snares: *Dhammapada* 31, 221, 342, 345–46, 349–50, 370, 384–85, 397–98.
34. More than seventy years ago, I. A. Richards (1936: 92) remarked on this reliance on metaphor:

In philosophy, above all, we can take no step safely without an un-relaxing awareness of the metaphors we, and our audience, may be employing; and though we may pretend to eschew them, we can attempt to do so only by detecting them. And this is the more true, the more severe and abstract the philosophy is. As it grows more abstract we think increasingly by means of metaphors that we profess *not* to be relying on. The metaphors we are avoiding steer our thought as much as those we accept.

35. M. Johnson 2005: 18–19. This definition follows those offered initially in M. Johnson 1987: xiv, 29, 79. As Hampe and Grady 2005—especially its chapters by Grady (2005) and Gibbs (2005)—makes clear, there are significant differences within the field of cognitive linguistics as to how the term "image schema" should be defined.
36. M. Johnson 2005: 24.
37. Gibbs 2005: 115.
38. For arguments that such statements should not be considered metaphorical, see Glucksberg and McGlone 1999; Murphy 1996; and Jackendoff and Aaron 1991.
39. Slingerland 2004a: 19–22.
40. Richards 1936: 100. Richards's terms for "source" and "target" are "vehicle" and "tenor," respectively. In the metaphor "John is a snake," the human target ("John") constrains the source ("snake") to be understood as embodying human qualities of craftiness and deceit.
41. Richards (1936: 118) was the first scholar to identify metaphors that were based on similarities between the affective responses to sources and to targets.
42. *Dhammapada* 9, 15–16, 87, 125, 158, 236, 241–42.
43. Boyer 2001: 119.
44. *Dhammapada* 202, 251.
45. Ekman, Levenson, and Friesen 1983; Zajonc, Murphy, and Inglehart 1989; Levenson et al. 1992. See also Lakoff's discussion (1987: 407–8).
46. *Dhammapada* 33–34, 231, 249, 255, 349, 397, 413–14.
47. Damasio 1994. Slingerland (2005: 558–64) makes a similar point about the implications of Damasio's work for understanding a primary function of conceptual blends, including metaphors.
48. M. Johnson 2005: 27.
49. Feuerbach 1989: 29–31; Guthrie 1997; Boyer 2001; Atran 2002.
50. Bloom 2005.
51. *Dhammapada* 223, 231, 335–36, 342–43.

52. Lakoff and Johnson 1999: 267–89; Slingerland 2004b.
53. Chariot: *Dhammapada* 222.
54. *Dhammapada* 171, 180, 209, 218, 221, 245, 284, 291, 335, 341, 396, 397, 401, 402, 406, 421.
55. *Dhammapada* 13–14, 39, 89, 124, 150, 292–93, 343, 378, 386, 388, 420.
56. *Dhammapada* 21, 57, 85–86, 141, 221, 397, 413.
57. Enomoto 1978: 158–59.
58. Ñyāṇamoli 1976: 2:800.
59. *Dhammapada* 184, 194, 387.
60. The classic study of this theme is O'Flaherty 1973.
61. *Dhammapada* 414, 418.
62. Kaelber 1989: 49.
63. Yoking: *Dhammapada* 26–27, 91, 185, 209; rest from yoking: *Dhammapada* 23.
64. Lakoff and Turner 1989: 51–52.
65. *Dhammapada* 356–59.
66. Norman 1997: 53 (translation modified).
67. Ñyāṇamoli 1976: 1:85.
68. Lakoff and Johnson ([1980] 2003: 233–35) make some similar suggestions about the relationship between metaphor and ritual.
69. For an introduction to this scholarship, see Law 1995; Coakley 1997; LaFleur 1998; and P. C. Johnson 2002.

REFERENCES

Alverson, Hoyt. 1991. "Metaphor and Experience: Looking over the Notion of Image Schema." In Fernandez 1991: 94–117.

Aṅguttara Nikāya. Igatpuri, India: Vipassana Research Institute, 1999. Chaṭṭha Saṅgāyana CD-ROM Version 3.

Atran, Scott. 2002. *In Gods We Trust: The Evolutionary Landscape of Religion.* Oxford: Oxford University Press.

Blasko, Dawn G. 1999. "Only the Tip of the Iceberg: Who Understands What about Metaphor?" *Journal of Pragmatics* 31, no. 12: 1675–83.

Bloom, Paul. 2005. "Is God an Accident?" *Atlantic Monthly*, December, 105–12.

Boyer, Pascal. 2001. *Religion Explained: The Evolutionary Origins of Religious Thought.* New York: Basic Books.

Campany, Robert Ford. 2003. "On the Very Idea of Religions (in the Modern West and in Early Medieval China)." *History of Religions* 42, no. 4: 287–319.

Coakley, Sarah, ed. 1997. *Religion and the Body.* Cambridge: Cambridge University Press.

Damasio, Antonio R. 1994. *Descartes' Error: Emotion, Reason, and the Human Brain.* New York: G. P. Putnam's Sons.

Dhammapada. 2003. Edited by Oskar von Hinüber and K. R. Norman. Oxford: Pali Text Society, 1994. Reprint, with corrections, Oxford: Pali Text Society.

Ekman, Paul, Robert W. Levenson, and Wallace V. Friesen. 1983. "Autonomic Nervous System Activity Distinguishes among Emotions." *Science*, n.s., 221, no. 4616: 1208–10.

Enomoto, Fumio. 1978. "Āsrava ni tsuite." *Indogaku bukkyōgaku kenkyū* [Journal of Indian and Buddhist Studies] 27, no. 1: 158–59.

Fernandez, James W., ed. 1991. *Beyond Metaphor: The Theory of Tropes in Anthropology.* Stanford: Stanford University Press.

Feuerbach, Ludwig. 1989. *The Essence of Christianity.* Translated by George Eliot. 2nd ed. Amherst, NY: Prometheus Books.

Fillmore, Charles J. 1982. "Frame Semantics." In *Linguistics in the Morning Calm*, edited by The Linguistic Society of Korea, 111–37. Seoul: Hanshin Publishing Company. Cited in C. Johnson 1999: 166.

Gibbs, Raymond W., Jr. 1996. "Why Many Concepts Are Metaphorical." *Cognition* 61, no. 3: 309–19.

———. 2005. "The Psychological Status of Image Schemas." In Hampe and Grady 2005: 113–35.

Glucksberg, Sam, and Matthew S. McGlone. 1999. "When Love Is Not a Journey: What Metaphors Mean." *Journal of Pragmatics* 31, no. 12: 1541–58.

Grady, Joseph E. 2005. "Image Schemas and Perception: Refining a Definition." In Hampe and Grady 2005: 36–55.

Guthrie, Stewart Elliott. 1997. "The Origin of an Illusion." In *Anthropology of Religion: A Handbook*, edited by Stephen D. Glazier, 489–504. Westport, CT: Greenwood Press.

Hampe, Beate, and Joseph E. Grady, eds. 2005. *From Perception to Meaning: Image Schemas in Cognitive Linguistics.* Berlin: Mouton de Gruyter.

Jackendoff, Ray, and David Aaron. 1991. Review of *More Than Cool Reason: A Field Guide to Poetic Metaphor*, by George Lakoff and Mark Turner. *Language* 67: 320–38.

Johnson, Christopher. 1999. "Metaphor vs. Conflation in the Acquisition of Polysemy: The Case of *See*." In *Cultural, Psychological and Typological Issues in Cognitive Linguistics: Selected Papers of the Bi-annual ICLA Meeting in Albuquerque, July 1995*, edited by Masako K. Hiraga, Chris Sinha, and Sherman Wilcox, 155–69. Amsterdam: John Benjamins Publishing Company.

Johnson, Mark. 1987. *The Body in the Mind: The Bodily Basis of Meaning, Imagination, and Reason.* Chicago: University of Chicago Press.

———. 2005. "The Philosophical Significance of Image Schemas." In Hampe and Grady 2005: 15–33.

Johnson, Paul Christopher. 2002. "Models of 'the Body' in the Ethnographic Field: Garífuna and Candomblé Case Studies." *Method & Theory in the Study of Religion* 14, no. 2: 170–95.

Kaelber, Walter O. 1989. *Tapta Mārga: Asceticism and Initiation in Vedic India.* Albany: State University of New York Press.

Keysar, Boaz, and Bridget Martin Bly. 1999. "Swimming against the Current: Do Idioms Reflect Conceptual Structure?" *Journal of Pragmatics* 31, no. 12: 1559–78.

LaFleur, William R. 1998. "Body." In *Critical Terms for Religious Studies*, edited by Mark C. Taylor, 36–54. Chicago: University of Chicago Press.

Lakoff, George. 1987. *Women, Fire, and Dangerous Things: What Categories Reveal about the Mind.* Chicago: University of Chicago Press.

Lakoff, George, and Mark Johnson. 1999. *Philosophy in the Flesh: The Embodied Mind and Its Challenge to Western Thought.* New York: Basic Books.

———. 2003. *Metaphors We Live By.* Chicago: University of Chicago Press, 1980. Reprint, with a new afterword, Chicago: University of Chicago Press.

Lakoff, George, and Mark Turner. 1989. *More Than Cool Reason: A Field Guide to Poetic Metaphor.* Chicago: University of Chicago Press.

Law, Jane Marie, ed. 1995. *Religious Reflections on the Human Body.* Bloomington: Indiana University Press.

Levenson, Robert W., Paul Ekman, Karl Heider, and Wallace V. Friesen. 1992. "Emotion and Autonomic Nervous System Activity in the Minangkabau of West Sumatra." *Journal of Personality and Social Psychology* 62, no. 6: 972–88.

McMahan, David L. 2002. *Empty Vision: Metaphor and Visionary Imagery in Mahāyāna Buddhism.* London: RoutledgeCurzon.

Murphy, Gregory L. 1996. "On Metaphoric Representation." *Cognition* 60, no. 2: 173–204.

Norman, K. R., ed. and trans. 1997. *The Word of the Doctrine (Dhammapada)*. Oxford: Pali Text Society.

Ñyāṇamoli, Bhikkhu, trans. 1976. *The Path of Purification (Visuddhimagga)*. By Bhadantācariya Buddhaghosa. 2nd ed. 2 vols. Berkeley: Shambala Press.

O'Flaherty, Wendy Doniger. 1973. *Asceticism and Eroticism in the Mythology of Śiva*. Delhi: Oxford University Press.

Ortony, Andrew. 1988. "Are Emotion Metaphors Conceptual or Lexical?" *Cognition & Emotion* 2, no. 2: 95–103.

Potter, Karl H. 1988. "Metaphor as Key to Understanding the Thought of Other Speech Communities." In *Interpreting across Boundaries: New Essays in Comparative Philosophy*, edited by Gerald James Larson and Eliot Deutsch, 19–35. Princeton: Princeton University Press.

Quinn, Naomi. 1991. "The Cultural Basis of Metaphor." In Fernandez 1991: 56–93.

Richards, I. A. 1936. *The Philosophy of Rhetoric*. New York: Oxford University Press.

Rohrer, Tim. 2005. "Image Schemata in the Brain." In Hampe and Grady 2005: 165–96.

Sinha, Chris, and Kristine Jensen de López. 2000. "Language, Culture and the Embodiment of Spatial Cognition." *Cognitive Linguistics* 11, nos. 1–2: 17–41.

Slingerland, Edward. 2004a. "Conceptual Metaphor Theory as Methodology for Comparative Religion." *Journal of the American Academy of Religion* 72, no. 1: 1–31.

———. 2004b. "Conceptions of the Self in the *Zhuangzi*: Conceptual Metaphor Analysis and Comparative Thought." *Philosophy East & West* 54, no. 3: 322–42.

Slingerland, Edward G. 2005. "Conceptual Blending, Somatic Marking, and Normativity: A Case Example from Ancient Chinese." *Cognitive Linguistics* 16, no. 3: 557–84.

Slobin, Dan I. 1985. "Crosslinguistic Evidence for the Language-Making Capacity." In *Theoretical Issues*, 1157–1244. Vol. 2 of *The Crosslinguistic Study of Language Acquisition*, edited by Dan Isaac Slobin. Hillsdale, NJ: Lawrence Erlbaum Associates. Cited in C. Johnson 1999: 166.

Smith, Jonathan Z. 2000. "Acknowledgments: Morphology and History in Mircea Eliade's *Patterns in Comparative Religion* (1949–1999). Part 2: The Texture of the Work." *History of Religions* 39, no. 4: 332–51.

Vervaeke, John, and John M. Kennedy. 2004. "Conceptual Metaphor and

Abstract Thought." *Metaphor and Symbol* 19, no. 3: 213–31.

The Visuddhi-Magga of Buddhaghosa. 1920–21. Edited by C. A. F. Rhys Davids. 2 vols. London: Pali Text Society.

Zajonc, R. B., Sheila T. Murphy, and Marita Inglehart. 1989. "Feeling and Facial Efference: Implications of the Vascular Theory of Emotion." *Psychological Review* 96, no. 3: 395–416.

PART II

Figuring Religious Images

5

Bathed in Milk

Metaphors of Suckling and Spiritual Transmission in Thirteenth-Century Kabbalah

Ellen Haskell

T HE FORM OF Jewish mysticism known as Kabbalah is characterized by the use of vivid divine imagery to communicate a complex theology of interdependence between divinity and humanity. Within this vocabulary of images, one of the most unusual is that of God as a nursing mother. This image, appearing in the thirteenth century in some of Kabbalah's most influential texts, is associated more often with elements of Catholic theology than with Jewish thought and also is surprising within the context of traditional Judaism, in which anthropomorphic descriptions of God are dominated by masculine images that in turn reflect male cultural dominance. Nevertheless, the image of a breastfeeding God is an important part of kabbalistic thought, serving as a metaphor for spiritual transmission and expressing a unique theological formulation that both complements and corrects more normative masculine images of divinity.[1]

The image of God as a nursing mother constructs a model for the interactions of divinity and humanity, metaphysically relocating the kabbalist with reference to God and establishing a relationship of profound intimacy, nurture, and reliance by presenting a metaphor for divinity in which concomitant metonymies set up vital contiguous relationships between divinity and humanity that socialize God and the mystic into a coherent and holistic system. This system provides a sensation of cosmological coherence, effecting a "return to the whole," a restoration of humanity's relative place within the ordering of the universe.[2]

In this study, I will examine two influential texts from Kabbalah's classical thirteenth-century period, Ezra of Gerona's *Commentary on the Song of Songs* and *Sefer ha-Zohar* (The Book of Splendor), in order to demonstrate how the metaphor of a breastfeeding God establishes and defines critical relationships between divinity and humanity. I will begin by examining briefly the metaphorical expressions of kabbalistic theology and then will proceed to a presentation of texts that contain suckling imagery.[3] Next, I will analyze how the nursing-mother image uses metaphor and metonymy to achieve a return to the whole. Finally, I will suggest some reasons why such an image developed in the thirteenth century, including the possibility of influence by Christian devotional imagery.

KABBALISTIC THEOLOGY: METAPHORICAL EXPRESSIONS

Originating in southern France and northern Spain during the late twelfth and early thirteenth centuries, theosophical Kabbalah posits a dynamic theology whose metaphorical expressions are creative, beautiful, and at times shocking. In this theology, God (whose concealed and unknowable being is referred to as *Ein Sof*, meaning "Without End") reveals itself to humanity in ten stages of divine life, or divine attributes, known as *sefirot*. These *sefirot* are most commonly referred to as *Keter* (Crown), *Hokhmah*[4] (Wisdom), *Binah* (Understanding), *Hesed* (Love), *Din* (Judgment), *Rahamim* (Compassion), *Netzah* (Eternity), *Hod* (Majesty), *Yesod* (Foundation), and *Shekhinah* (Presence). Each of these individual *sefirot* can be understood as a complex symbol encompassing a broad variety of related metaphorical images. For example, the *sefirah Shekhinah* may be described using the human metaphors of mother, daughter, and bride; the natural metaphors of moon or lily; or the material metaphors of gateway or well.[5]

All of the *sefirot* interact in complex ways, revealing the dynamic processes of the divine inner life. They do not form a linear progression but rather are structured in a form often described as an inverted tree, a system of waterways, or a macrocosmic human body.[6] Each individual *sefirah* is part of the divine whole while also encompassing a variety of individual connotations of gender, emotional content, role within the sefirotic structure, and more. A flow of ongoing divine energy often expressed in terms of blessings, light imagery, and water imagery connects the *sefirot* with one another and continues into the human world, where it provides life and blessings. This flow of blessings is not unidirectional: one of the most important teachings of Kabbalah is a profoundly active acceptance of the doctrine of *imitatio dei*, in which the human being not only reflects the divine being in microcosm but, through this reflection, is able to affect and transform divinity, with the person acting upon God even as God acts upon the person. Thus, the kabbalist also is capable of transmitting blessings from the earthly realm back to divinity, and the whole of reality is connected by an ongoing flow of life. It is the transmission of this divine overflow from divinity to humanity that is expressed so evocatively in the metaphor of God as a nursing mother.

The suckling metaphor is one of a large group of metaphors associated with the kabbalistic idea of divine femininity. Kabbalistic theology posits a God that incorporates both masculinity and femininity—a striking innovation, especially considering the fact that all the early kabbalists were men. Two of the ten *sefirot*, the third and the tenth, consistently are gendered female, and the concept of a feminine aspect of divinity is one of the most complex and characteristic parts of kabbalistic theology. In this regard, Arthur Green, a contemporary scholar of Kabbalah, writes, "The cluster of symbols around the tenth *sefirah*, as she comes to be placed by the latter thirteenth century, is the most highly developed part of Kabbalistic symbolism."[7]

Prior to the emergence of Kabbalah, Judaism did not consider God to have a feminine aspect, and the inclusion of both masculine and feminine characteristics within divinity is one of Kabbalah's most important contributions to Jewish thought.[8] Yet the origins of this symbolism are somewhat vague and confusing, and many theories have been proposed to account for them. The thread that runs consistently through these theories is that the divine feminine is a composite symbolic construction incorporating themes from earlier Jewish literature that came together in a unique way at the end of the twelfth century, when kabbalistic theology made its debut.[9]

Two texts that date from the classical period of this theology's development contain the most significant expressions of the suckling metaphor found in thirteenth-century Kabbalah. Rabbi Ezra ben Solomon of Gerona's *Commentary on the Song of Songs*,[10] written in the 1220s, was one of the first kabbalistic documents made available to a broad public. Before Rabbi Ezra's time, kabbalistic teachings generally were confined to the elite esotericists of southern France and northern Spain. Although his work's ready availability drew criticism from rationalists and kabbalists alike,[11] the *Commentary* became a tremendously influential work: "As the earliest Kabbalistic commentary to the Song of Songs, R. Ezra's work may be seen as one that had a truly pivotal influence on the future development of Jewish mysticism."[12] Indeed, Ezra's *Commentary* is the first kabbalistic text to employ the image of God as a breastfeeding mother as a metaphor for the divine overflow's spiritual transmission.[13]

The other text excerpted in this study, *Sefer ha-Zohar*, is the quintessential work of theosophical Kabbalah and occupies a position of authority and popularity unparalleled in the mystical literature of Judaism. During the centuries following its composition, the Zohar became the only post-Talmudic work of Jewish literature to achieve nearly canonical status within the Jewish community at large, and it is difficult to overestimate its influence on Judaism's mystical thought.[14] The Zohar is a lengthy multivolume work consisting of diverse literary strata and stylistic genres. Although it is a pseudepigraphic text designed to have the appearance of great antiquity, the Zohar can be traced to late-thirteenth-century Castile and the authorship either of the prominent kabbalist Moses de León (1240–1305) or of a group of kabbalists associated with him.[15] The Zoharic text itself represents a major synthesis of earlier rabbinic and kabbalistic literature and contains critical innovations and elaborations of the kabbalistic theological system. Some of the most significant of these elaborations involve the theology and characterization of divine femininity, including the image of God as a mother from whom the *sefirot* and humanity suckle spiritual sustenance.

KABBALISTIC IMAGES OF GOD AS A NURSING MOTHER

The metaphor of God as a breastfeeding mother begins with the inner life of God itself. Drawing on the imagery of Song 8:1 in his *Commentary*, Ezra depicts God as a nurturing, sustaining, feminine figure with divine spirituality flowing from its supernal breasts.

> "If only you were as a brother to me, [suckling from my mother's breasts]"[16] (Song 8:1). The Glory replied: If you desire and yearn that I will unite with you, I also will "direct all of my desire to you" (Psalm 38:10) so that you will be as a brother to me and I will not be separated from you. "Suckling from my mother's breasts." And you will receive suckling from the place of my suckling, [this place] that is the spirit of the living God.[17]

Ezra reads the Song of Songs as an internal dialogue among the *sefirot*, and in this passage the Glory represents the feminine tenth *sefirah* in conversation with the masculine sixth *sefirah*. These two divine aspects are understood as the lovers[18] from the Song, and desire to be united in the flow of divine life that connects the *sefirot*. The metaphor of God as a nursing mother is provided by the language of scripture and used to characterize the source of divine life: "the spirit of the living God."[19] Thus, Ezra describes God's inner self with language of nurturing parent-child relationships while depicting the *sefirot* as desirous of these relationships and the union that they can provide. The metaphor of suckling as spiritual transmission in the *Commentary* on Song 8:1 not only expresses the flow of energy among the divine gradations but also communicates the intimacy of the intradivine relationships.

The most significant aspect of this passage is that it provides a metaphor for understanding divine interiority, with which the human mystic must stand in relation. The metaphor of suckling among the *sefirot* incorporates both structural and affective connotations, with Ezra depicting God as a nurturing figure expressing spirituality, rather than milk, from its supernal breasts. Emphasis on divine unity despite the seeming separation of the *sefirot* is an important aspect of this passage, and Ezra indicates this intimacy through a network of familial relations structured by the image of God as a breastfeeding mother. The suckling desired and enacted by the divine gradations is ideal for demonstrating sefirotic unity, because the suckling metaphor connotes a doubled intimacy: a child partakes of the being of its mother both by its birth from her interior self and through the process of suckling. The suckling act defies separation, linking mother and child in internal substance through the flow of milk from the mother's body into the child's. This physiological model of parent-child connection bears cultural connotations of intimacy, nurture, sustenance, love, and reliance. These senses are heightened by the Glory's reference to "my mother's breasts" in the passage.

Thus, the metaphor of God as a nursing mother in this text stresses the kabbalistic mystery of a God that is both the ultimate expression of oneness and simultaneously divided into ten gradations. By using this metaphor, Ezra also provides insight into the divine emotional state, showing that it is shaped by patterns of closeness, intimacy, and longing for union. The desire of the *sefirot* for parent-child intimacy binds them within the fabric of God's inner life, in which they participate through the medium of the spirit of the living God.

This discussion of the internal divine climate provides the kabbalist with a model for understanding that with which he must connect. Furthermore, because kabbalistic theology teaches that the flow of divine life passes from the divine realm to the human realm, the kabbalist can perceive himself as ultimately connected to this nurturing flow of being. And, because of Kabbalah's focus on *imitatio dei*, the passage implies the affective stance that the mystic should take toward this connection: a stance of longing and desire to achieve spiritual intimacy with God, just as the *sefirot* desire to participate in divine communion.

Another passage from Ezra's *Commentary* applies the metaphor of God as a nursing mother to the human realm, where its use echoes the intradivine dynamics of the previous passage:

> "I am a wall and my breasts are like towers. [Then I was in his eyes as one who finds peace]" (Song 8:10). She is proud that she will be like a fortified wall to strengthen [herself] with her faith and with the two Torahs—the Written Torah and the Oral Torah—that are the [source of] vitality for man, as the breasts are the [source of] life for the infant. "Then," she said, I was in the eyes of the Holy One, blessed be He, "as one who finds peace."

Again, the female speaker from the Song is understood to be the tenth *sefirah*. The very divine aspect that longs for suckling from the spirit of God prepares to transmit the divine overflow to the people of Israel through the medium of sacred scripture. The *sefirah*'s two breasts are used to depict the two forms of Torah, Written and Oral.[20] This anthropomorphic wellspring of Torah is understood to be the true source of human vitality and is likened to a human mother's breasts, which are the life source of an infant. Humanity, like a child, joins in an intimate relationship with divinity in order to receive the life-sustaining spiritual transmission of Torah.

A fuller description of how humanity is meant to relate to God as a nursing mother occurs in the *Commentary* on Song 8:8:

> "We have a little sister [and she has no breasts. What shall we do for our sister on the day that she is spoken for?]" (Song 8:8) This is a parable concerning [the people of] Israel, who are in exile, despised and lowly. "And she has no breasts." They do not have a place of suckling, because they have gone forth from the land of the living and are separated from the place of the Torah. As it is written, "For Torah shall go forth from Zion" (Isaiah 2:3).[21] And concerning the exile it is said, "For many days Israel has not had the God of truth

and the Torah" (2 Chronicles 15:3). "What shall we do for our sister on the day that she is spoken for?" What shall we do for them? With what shall we be able to sustain them and to give them a future and hope in their exile?

Ezra interprets the Song's image of the little sister without breasts as the citizens of a specific nation: the people of Israel. The Israelite people's lack of power in the world is reflected in their personification as a preadolescent girl. This reading also alludes to earlier interpretations of the Song in which Israel, rather than the tenth *sefirah*, is understood to be the bride of God.

Using the image of God as a nursing mother, Ezra creates an interpretation in which the people of Israel are placed in a distressing position. If the people lack a place of suckling, then in Ezra's theology they actually are detached from the source of divine life, the spiritual overflow from within the sefirotic structure. Ezra links Torah transmission to human vitality: the people of Israel cannot suckle, because they have left the "land of the living." This detachment is caused both by their separation from the Holy Land and by their consequent detachment from the Torah, which—as Ezra elegantly interprets Song 8:10—is transmitted from the breasts of the Assembly of Israel, the tenth *sefirah* herself. In fact, Ezra reinforces his link between the Torah and the breasts of the feminine divine gradation by repeating the word "place" in connection with each. The tenth *sefirah*'s breasts are both the "place" of suckling and the "place" of the Torah.

Ezra explains Israel's separation from these loci by linking Song 8:8, in which he interprets the Land of Israel and the Torah as the places of suckling, with 2 Chronicles 15:3. In its original context, this verse serves as a prophetic criticism of the Israelite people during the monarchical period. Here, however, Ezra links the lack of God and Torah to the lack of a suckling place, eloquently reinforcing his interpretation of Israel's dislocation. In addition, this separation from divine suckling has subtle affective resonances. The people of Israel need sustenance while separated from the divine breasts and the spiritual nourishment on which they suckled there. The Israelite people lack hope and may be depressed. Thus, a means must be found to provide a positive emotional context.

Ezra's *Commentary*, which contains the first example of the suckling metaphor in kabbalistic theology, draws the metaphor from the language of the Song itself, infusing the unusual image of God as a breastfeeding mother with the authority of both sacred scripture and traditional exegesis. Without the anthropomorphic language of the Song and its unique character of

sacred sensuality, Ezra would have been unlikely to have settled on this striking metaphor. In fact, in much of his *Commentary*, he employs light and
water imagery to describe the flow of divine life. The language of the Song,
however, affords him interpretive leeway and access to a level of feminine
anthropomorphism unprecedented in kabbalistic literature. Ezra's use of the
Song's breast imagery allows the metaphor of a nursing, motherly God to
take on a concrete, experiential quality. Removed from the realm of abstract
or impersonal imagery, the nursing-mother metaphor produces an extremely
vivid mental picture of a feminized aspect of divinity to whom the kabbalistic reader can relate.

While Ezra's *Commentary* is extremely innovative in its use of the nursing-mother metaphor, his work contains very little affective imagery associated directly with suckling. Although he uses explicit feminine body images
drawn from sacred texts to add structure to the metaphor, he does not structure the affectivity of the suckling act in the same way. Instead, he constructs
suckling as a desirable and positive form of relation while leaving implicit
the emotions involved in the suckling act. Furthermore, his use of the breast-
feeding-mother metaphor is tied directly to the text of the Song itself, with
little additional emphasis on divine femininity. But in *Sefer ha-Zohar* both
affective spirituality and a disruption of the suckling metaphor's reliance on
scriptural citation occur, allowing the metaphor of God as a nursing mother
to take on a fuller theological life. If Ezra's *Commentary* contains the seeds of
the suckling metaphor, then the Zohar contains its fruition.

For example, Zohar 1:203a[22] incorporates this metaphor into its teaching on the "Valley of Vision" of Isaiah 22:1, a text that in its biblical context
begins a prophetic pronouncement against the people of Jerusalem:

> But come and see: "Valley of Vision," this is the *Shekhinah*, who was
> in the Temple, and all the children of the world used to suckle from
> her: they suckled on prophecy. For, although all the prophets surely
> used to prophesy from another place,[23] they used to suckle their
> prophecy from within her. And for this reason she was called "Valley
> of Vision." . . . Because, when the Temple used to stand, Israel used
> to perform services and offer offerings and sacrifices. And the *Shek-
> hinah* rested upon them in the Temple, like a mother covering over
> her children. And all the faces used to shine while blessings were
> found above and below. And there was not a day on which blessings
> and rejoicings were not found. And Israel used to rest in safety in
> the land, and all the world used to be nourished because of them.

Here, the Zoharic authorship radically has shifted the meaning of the biblical verse and interpreted the Valley of Vision as the *Shekhinah* (the tenth
sefirah), considered a source of prophecy. Revelation is relayed from the
Shekhinah to the human prophets, who receive it by suckling directly from
this feminine aspect of God. As in Ezra's *Commentary*, the transmission of
divine spiritual energy flows through the *sefirot* and is passed to the human
world by means of suckling. Yet, in this Zoharic context, the nature of the
transmission is stated explicitly: it is prophecy, the word of God reaching
into the human realm. The transmission of prophecy also is associated with
blessings, and when prophecy is suckled from the *Shekhinah* blessings "[a]re
found above and below." Use of the term "blessings" in the Zohar is another
way of referring to the divine overflow on which the *sefirot* and humanity
suckle. Thus, the divine overflow passes through the sefirotic structure and
is channeled into the *Shekhinah*, who passes it to the Israelite prophets by
means of nursing.

In order for this transmission to happen, the divine and human worlds
must exist in the proper relationship, understood here as the era when the
Shekhinah dwelt within the Temple when it stood in Jerusalem prior to its
final destruction in 70 CE. In this passage, it is not only prophets who suckle
from the *Shekhinah* but "all the children of the world." The passage of divine
spiritual overflow depends on the people of Israel's proper alignment with
the *Shekhinah*, which was achieved in the days of the Temple through the
sacrificial rites. Once Israel has received the overflow, it passes into the rest of
the world, creating a chain of spiritual transmission. The passage emphasizes
this alignment and transmission through literary parallelism. When all is
well, the *Shekhinah* rests upon Israel, and Israel rests within the land.

The idea of being spiritually nourished is linked very closely to the suckling metaphor in the Zohar and often is associated with the transmission of
spiritual energy by means of suckling. This concept of spiritual nourishment
also is found in Ezra's *Commentary*, where it is associated with a spiritual
satiation that transcends human eating or drinking. In fact, "[n]ourishment
imagery is used throughout the kabbalah as a metaphor signifying the flow
of divine blessings from the upper worlds to the lower."[24] Thus, in Zohar
1:203a, Israel and the rest of the world suckle on the spiritual nourishment
of divine blessings and prophetic inspiration. By setting this fortuitous chain
of divine transmission during the Temple period, the Zohar looks back to an
idealized past of the Jewish people.

Though stating explicitly that divine spiritual overflow is transmitted to
the human world by means of suckling, this Zoharic passage is most notable

for its dramatic elaboration of the suckling metaphor's connotations. Here, we see explicit mother imagery linked clearly to suckling imagery, a link establishing a parent-child relationship between divinity and humanity that is reinforced by repeated references to humanity as children. The *Shekhinah* suckles "all the children of the world" with prophecy and rests upon Israel in the Temple "like a mother covering over her children." The term "mother" here, unlike in Ezra's *Commentary* on Song 8:1, is independent of a biblical verse undergoing interpretation. Instead, the Zohar uses the term freely and independently, structuring the connotations of the suckling metaphor explicitly with feminine parental imagery. The *Shekhinah* often is referred to as a mother, and the Zohar feels no need to cite additional scriptural prooftexts to reinforce what has, by the late thirteenth century, become a standard theological formulation.

In addition to exemplifying the explicit use of independent mothering imagery, the suckling image in Zohar 1:203a is associated with affective terminology that structures further the image's connotations. The Zohar tells us that the *Shekhinah* breastfeeds with prophecy and blessings, an act that establishes a direct and ongoing relationship between Israel and God during times of correct interaction between humanity and divinity—a relationship represented in this context by the practice of Temple ritual. But this passage also clearly associates prophecy and blessings passed through suckling with rejoicing, though the identity of the being who rejoices is not stated. I suggest that, because the blessings that are accompanied by these rejoicings occur both above (in the divine realm) and below (in the human realm), it is not only humanity who rejoices at this spiritual transmission but God as well. Moreover, the suckling that occurs when human and divine relationships are enacted properly also is linked with safety, nourishment, and the shining of faces—indications of spiritual fulfillment.[25] This fulfillment is reinforced by the terminology of nourishment found in the text.

The words and ideas brought together in Zohar 1:203a provide additional structure and affective texture for the image of God as a nursing mother, associating it with the positive transmission of joyful blessings to humanity and with the joyfully nurturing relationship between mother and child. Unlike Ezra's *Commentary*, the Zohar is unhesitatingly explicit about the positive emotional connotations of suckling language, highlighting not only the anthropomorphic nuances of the suckling image but the anthropopathic ones as well. It is in passages such as Zohar 1:203a that the full impact of suckling imagery is brought to bear upon the reader, restructuring his concept of the relationships between God and self. In its fullness the suckling image, with its profound depiction of idealized human and divine relationships, serves as a model for the kabbalists' desired and ideal connection with divinity.

The next passage, Zohar 2:122b, is excerpted from a section dealing with the divine countenance. The presence of suckling imagery within such a section of text implies that the concept of suckling as spiritual transmission is connected intimately to kabbalistic ideas of the revelation of divinity. Accordingly, the text provides a description of the interactions of the uppermost *sefirot*:

> The brows of the eyes are called "Place," for they give watching to all the colors, the Lords of Watching. These brows, with regard to [that which is] below,[26] are brows of watching from that river that flows and goes out: a place to draw from that river, to bathe in the whiteness of *Atika*, in the milk that flows from the Mother. So that when Might[27] is stretched forth and the eyes glow with a red color[28] *Atika Kadisha* shines his whiteness and glows in the Mother, and she is filled with milk and she gives suck to these. And all the eyes bathe in that milk of the Mother that flows and goes out continuously. As it is written, "bathed in milk" (Song 5:12). In the milk of the Mother that flows continuously and does not cease. . . . The ears of the King: When pleasure is found and the Mother gives suck and the shining of *Atika Kadisha* is brightened, the light of the two brains is aroused and the shining of the Father and the Mother. All of these are called the brains of the King, and they glow as one. And when they glow as one they are called the ears of the Lord because they receive the prayers of Israel.

Here, *Atika Kadisha* (The Ancient of Days) seems to represent the first two *sefirot*, *Keter* and *Hokhmah*, but also may bear implications of *Ein Sof*, God as infinite and indescribable, existing beyond the sefirotic structure. While *Atika Kadisha* is the Father, *Binah* (the third *sefirah*) is understood as the Mother, with whom this *sefirah*—which often serves as a structural parallel for the feminine tenth *sefirah* in kabbalistic literature—is associated traditionally.

In the color symbolism of Kabbalah, white represents Love, while red represents Judgment.[29] The white milk that flows from the Mother serves as a remedy to the powers of Judgment as it is suckled by the sefirotic structure and its whiteness spreads, eradicating redness. Balancing these two divine characteristics, Love and Judgment, is a central concern of kabbalistic thought. The red color of the eyes under the influence of Judgment in this passage implies an eye inflammation that can be cured by the whitening flow of milk. The white color that Love shares with milk provides another reason for the liquid's inclusion in this passage, where milk helps to structure and define the image of God as a nursing mother.

The passage continues and concludes with a description of the divine countenance, shifting focus from the eyes to the ears. When the *sefirot* are in the correct interrelationships (which are represented by the pleasure of the Father and the Mother), the Mother breastfeeds, spreading the milk of the divine overflow. This configuration allows reception of Israel's prayers, reasserting the kabbalistic theological point that, when the *sefirot* and the people of Israel maintain proper relationships with each other, divine overflow pours into the world, and human prayer and blessings ascend to divinity. As in the work of Ezra, the metaphor of suckling as spiritual transmission is applied to divinity in order to emphasize the intimacy and interdependence of the *sefirot* as they are united in the divine overflow, as well as the nurturing divine environment into which prayer ascends.

Milk not only is depicted as a medium of suckling in this passage but also is identified as a substance in which the total immersion of bathing can be achieved. The *sefirot* (and possibly the angelic potencies as well) receive the milk both internally via suckling and externally by bathing. This startling image of complete inundation with the milk of the divine overflow is achieved by referencing Song 5:12. Thus, the Zohar shows the divine world washed fully and completely in the milk of the divine overflow.

The feminine mothering imagery that structures the suckling metaphor is presented independently again in Zohar 2:122b, without the scriptural citation that Ezra seems to require. *Binah*, generally understood as the Upper Mother when *Shekhinah* is understood as the Lower Mother, allows an uncompromised use of feminine imagery. The mothering imagery here is drawn to cosmic proportions, however, and divinity is represented as flowing continuously with milk in a never-ending stream. Motherhood is drawn beyond the scope of humanity and invested with cosmic and eternal significance, as the text implies by its repeated assertion that *Binah*'s milk flows ceaselessly through the *sefirot*.

In addition, the transmission of this milk is textured by anthropopathic terminology that demonstrates the Zohar's use of affective language to structure this feminine image of God. The Mother's nursing is stimulated by the pleasure that she finds in *Atika Kadisha*. This pleasure, combined with the allusion to Love established by kabbalistic connotations of the color white,

makes a statement about the transmission of divine overflow and about sefirotic immersion in it. The overflow is given in pleasure and love, structured by positive affective terminology and connotations. Moreover, when
the prayers of Israel ascend, they are received in pleasure and love at the
highest levels of God. Thus, the suckling metaphor is a nexus of femininity,
milk, and positive emotional connotations that provides a complete field of
imagery with which to understand the upper levels of divinity. The reader
is able to locate himself in relation to this structure and is encouraged to do
so by the text's description of the joyous atmosphere into which his prayers
ascend.[30]

METAPHOR, METONYMY, AND THE NURSING-MOTHER IMAGE

Anthropologist James Fernandez has defined metaphor as "a strategic predication upon an inchoate pronoun . . . which makes a movement and leads
to performance," and as "a mediating device connecting the unconnected
and bridging the gaps in causality."[31] These characteristics allow metaphors
to become powerful vehicles for cultural transformation, because they fill in
perceived spaces in world organization and, in doing so, construct models
that lead to performative changes in thought and behavior. Fernandez, who
works extensively on metaphor and religious revitalization movements,[32] is
interested particularly in metaphor's potential for resituating humanity in
relation to divinity, a cosmological development that fundamentally alters
the experience of the world for religious participants. He explains that a
theology comprising several metaphors interacting in dynamic ways gives its
adherents a sensation of cosmological coherence and brings about a return
to the whole, a restoration of humanity's relative place within the ordering
of the universe.[33]

The observation that complex religious models grounded in vivid metaphorical images can effect a return to the whole is of interest to scholars of
Jewish mystical literature because this literature draws on experience for its
effect while simultaneously transforming the meanings that are bound to
everyday objects of readers' attention. Jewish mystical texts actively create
meaning in the minds of their readers by using vivid and unusual imagery.
This process is critical to the kabbalists, who are concerned primarily with
relating themselves to the unknown and whose encounter with the mystical
literature alters the accepted meanings of their world and of the words that
describe it. "The language of [kabbalistic] myth thus gives shape to spiritual

consciousness and provides the armature and forms of imagination through which one may conceptualize 'the Whole' and bear it in mind at all times. Myth may therefore comprise and condition a mystical mentality—not by being transcended so much as by being fully subjectivized and lived."[34]

A coherent model for the whole relies upon the ability of metaphor and metonymy to join seemingly disparate areas of experience into a comprehensive system. Anthropologist Deborah Durham and Fernandez explain that metaphor deals initially with two domains, one of which is used to understand the other. In metaphorization, the two domains are juxtaposed and meaning is transferred between them, with one domain "enriching, transforming, or constituting and creating" an understanding of the other.[35] When this process occurs, the boundaries between the juxtaposed domains can become blurred, as the domains act reciprocally upon each other. The mechanism that largely effects the transformation of both domains is the union of metonymy and metaphor.

A metaphor, far more than a trope of word replacement, is a complex statement in which one entity is displaced onto another entity and in turn can be altered by that entity. The metaphorical statement is complex because it does not operate in a void but instead is surrounded by an entire conceptual structure that affects the interaction of the entities within the metaphor. By contrast, metonymy is a trope of contiguity rather than similarity and has been characterized by anthropologist Alice Kehoe as "the contextual linking of concepts within a hierarchy of units (e.g., the 'strong right arm' for 'the powerful man')."[36] Metonymy's use of contiguity may be obvious, as in the part-for-whole relationship of Kehoe's example, or more obscure, as in the relationship between funerals and the color black.[37] Moreover, such metonymical contiguities often take the form of metaphorical entailments, connotative associations that accompany a metaphor and structure it conceptually. In the case of the nursing-mother metaphor, the associations of nurture, parenting, and affection are all associations contiguous to mothering that help to structure the image of it in the reader's mind.

While metaphor and metonymy traditionally have been viewed as separate linguistic phenomena—largely because of the impact of linguist Roman Jakobson's study "Two Aspects of Language and Two Types of Aphasic Disturbances"—some scholars have called for a closer look at the relationship between metaphor and metonymy, particularly in the field of anthropology.[38] Metonymy, far from being separate from metaphor, is a major force behind metaphorical entailments and provides much of the thick perceptual reality of metaphorical assertions. As Fernandez explains, "The complexity of expressive experience lies in the interplay of contiguity and similarity associations in the predications upon the pronouns participating in this experience."[39] More precisely, "[m]etaphor does not simply juxtapose two domains, but ultimately joins them, uniting them metonymically in their parallel structures. [This interdependence of metaphor and metonymy] creates a more concordant model of the world, a single, more encompassing organization."[40] The original similarity relationship posited by a metaphor is upheld by a complex network of contiguity associations, which in turn are linked and able to refer to one another within the framework of the primary metaphorical statement. Thus, a person responding to a metaphorical image will use not only the image itself to develop an understanding of the unknown domain being described but also the relevant contiguous associations that structure the metaphor.

According to anthropologist Terence Turner, metaphors actually can constitute themselves as metonymies "because the emergent common meaning they create constitutes a new 'whole' of which the two otherwise disparate members of the metaphor equally become parts."[41] Thus, as meaning emerges from the metaphor, its two domains are placed into a contiguous metonymical relationship with each other. That is to say, when different entities enter into a metaphorical relationship, they become common members of a metonymical system developed by that relationship. On this view, metaphor structurally develops "a relation of semantic identity . . . between elements of semantic categories not recognized in other contexts as belonging to the same domain." This interaction of different domains involves a "shift in 'recognition'" that can be either "in the structural vantage point or epistemological perspective of the subject."[42]

When a metaphor is expressed, then, all of the metonymical associations on both sides of the metaphorical expression are placed into a relation of mutual equivalence. This process can have many effects on our perception of our place in the world. As Fernandez reminds us, both metaphor and metonymy are capable of constituting statements about "transformation or transcendence of state."[43] Furthermore, Durham and Fernandez see the metonymical restructuring within a metaphor as an important way to challenge the world's structure. In their eyes, one of the most important ways to effect cultural transformation is by restructuring the internal metonymical structure of culturally dominant metaphors.[44] Such action allows the ideas that stand behind social norms to change according to their cultural and historical contexts without creating a radical break within the cosmology that is being transformed.

Similarly, in kabbalistic texts that contain the nursing-mother image, there is a subtle transformation of the metonymical connotations associated with divine anthropomorphism—a transformation that allows a traditional means of envisioning God to receive a very new theological emphasis. By bringing about this transformation, kabbalists developed anthropopathic connotations different from those usually associated with a masculine characterization of divinity. For example, there is a metonymical association of nurturance attributable to a breastfeeding, mothering God that is very difficult to derive from a traditional masculine anthropomorphic image of God, such as a king seated on a throne. Yet both of these images can be derived metonymically from the basic metaphor of humanity because both a mother and a king are types of human figures.

Because metaphor and metonymy seem to telescope in and out of each other with alarming rapidity, they may become difficult to distinguish. But drawing such a distinction with precision often is unnecessary once we understand the metaphorical and metonymical interdevelopments taking place. As Turner has observed, metaphor and metonymy are mutually relativized according to context and can take each other's places at different levels of expression.[45] Progressing from anthropomorphism proper (that is, masculine anthropomorphism) to a feminine anthropomorphism with regard to certain divine aspects allows states that are associated metonymically with the sociocultural female body, such as motherhood and—more specifically—breastfeeding, to be transformed into new divine metaphors.

Embracing the kabbalistic characterization of *Shekhinah* and *Binah* as divine mother figures, kabbalistic literature uses vivid breast imagery, milk imagery, and parent-child imagery to structure divinity, making it accessible to the reader at an experiential level. The nursing-mother metaphor allows a full domain of contiguous associations to be put into place. This domain creates a configuration in which humanity and divinity participate in a reciprocal familial relationship, sharing not only domestic structures but also the emotions that accompany these structures. The use of affective language adds even more emotional texture to the nursing-mother image, explicitly informing the reader that the divine overflow is transmitted in love, nurture, and pleasure and is emotionally as well as physically satisfying. By virtue of being located in "canonical" texts of Kabbalah, the image's innovative cosmological model of divine/human relationship is sanctified. As anthropologist Roy

Rappaport observes of such a sanctified cosmology, "It is no longer merely conceptual. . . . It becomes something like an assertion, statement, description, or report of the way the world in fact *is*."[46]

Metaphor creates meaning by establishing relationships between concrete and inchoate concepts and at its most basic level is a trope of "carrying over." Certainly, the metaphor of suckling as spiritual transmission, as it emerges in thirteenth-century Kabbalah through the image of God as a breastfeeding mother, is concerned precisely and exclusively with carrying over. In other words, the nursing-mother image articulates desirable relationships between concrete humanity and inchoate divinity. The image foregrounds and asserts the quality of relation because the image deals not with an individual term but rather with the connection between beings, forging a decisive cognitive link between self and Other.

By using the nursing-mother image, kabbalists direct their readers' attention to the experience of relation and the means by which it is established between beings. By using this profoundly expressive metaphor of relation, this "metametaphor" (a trope of carrying over about carrying over the milk that flows between mother/God and child/humanity), the Zohar reconstructs its readers' consciousness of self, God, and the relationship between them, establishing humanity and divinity in a relationship of intimacy, nurture, and dependence. In doing so, the Zohar reinforces a key tenet of kabbalistic theology, the interdependence of humanity and divinity. By transforming his idea of God through the use of human terms, the kabbalistic author or reader simultaneously transforms his understanding of himself: creating an anthropomorphic image of God that is focused on the quality of relation, the kabbalist recreates himself as a being who is capable of standing in such a relation.

The image of God as a nursing mother effects a return to the whole by creating a new concept of a whole that incorporates humanity and divinity into a relationship of anthropomorphic similarity and familial, nurturing contiguity. When the human image of the breastfeeding mother is applied to God, divinity and humanity are related to each other. They conceptually become parts of the same thing, belonging to the same organization. Both understood as humanized entities, they are placed into the social relationship of parent and child, a relationship that the kabbalists understand on an experiential basis because Judaism radically denies celibacy and requires participation in family life. Thus, God is humanized to a point at which it can relate to humanity, while humanity is divinized to the extent that it can participate in an interactive relationship with God. The entire structure of relationship between the two is redefined. If God is a nursing mother, humanity is God's child. Because this child is of substance similar to that of its parent, it is capable of receiving its mother's milk—the intimate, sustaining transmission of divine overflow.

The understanding developed by this model is very different from that achieved through more dominant Jewish images of God as a king seated on a throne or as a stern Judge. The image of God as a nursing mother also develops a different model for relationship than does the familial metaphor of God as a father, because the nursing mother continuously pours forth the inner substance of her milk into the person of her beloved child, who not only returns her love but also depends upon her for nourishment. This new understanding of divinity and humanity allows the kabbalists to establish a relationship with God that is experienced as a return to the whole or as a homecoming: a profoundly intimate connection between nurturing mother and loving, devoted child. Thus, the suckling image constructs a metonymical, metaphysical social relationship between God and humanity that is unprecedented in Jewish theological literature. By participating in this new socioreligious relationship, both divinity and humanity are transformed. More precisely, the socioreligious relationship created by the kabbalistic suckling image creates a role for the kabbalist that is both social (child) and religious (child of God). With this image, the kabbalist defines a perceived social role that he chooses to foreground in his description of his relationship with God. By living as a good kabbalist, he enacts this relationship in his daily life. This relationship thus exemplifies the metonymical alignments that Kehoe regards as critical to people's perception of their social roles, the specific qualities of themselves as human beings that they elect to emphasize and enact in their daily lives.[47]

Thus, the image of God as a nursing mother in the Zohar provides a new model for understanding God and self.[48] The nursing-mother image is neither the Zohar's only model for such understanding nor the most dominant model. The nursing-mother image is, however, profoundly evocative, an important complement and corrective to models of thinking about God that remove divinity from direct human social experience, such as the abstract light imagery that plays a large role in kabbalistic discourse, or the kabbalistic water imagery that associates God with the impersonal power of nature. Unlike these more-removed models, the suckling model creates closeness between God and humanity at a cosmological level, redefining the social relationships that each experiences and fulfills.

THIRTEENTH-CENTURY DEVELOPMENTS
OF THE NURSING-MOTHER IMAGE

The question of why an image focused so specifically on divine and human interrelationships develops at this time must remain somewhat open. Yet the image does seem to reflect certain cultural factors of its period. Modern scholars of Jewish mysticism generally see the development of kabbalistic theology in part as a response to the flowering of Jewish philosophy and its model of a divinity that can be encountered solely through intellectual effort.[49] In this sense, Kabbalah can be understood as a religious revitalization movement. Certainly, the image of God as a nursing mother—with its emphasis on relationality, affective spirituality, and divine intimacy—serves as an alternative model for understanding God.

In addition, it is likely that kabbalistic theology developed in part as a consequence of Christian missionizing efforts, which increased dramatically during the thirteenth century. The Cistercians, Dominicans, and Franciscans all rejected the earlier model of the cloistered monk, turning instead toward itinerant preaching and pastoral care.[50] Moreover, many of these monastic orders were eager to impose on Jews the Church's authority over heretics.[51] A central part of the medieval Christian argument against Judaism was the idea that God had turned His back on the Jews because they had denied Jesus as Christ. Hence a theology of relationship like that provided by the image of God as a nursing mother may have served as a Jewish response to and negation of Christian criticism.

Yet kabbalistic theology may have been influenced by contemporary Christian spirituality as well. During the twelfth century, the use of feminine metaphors in Christian theology grew.[52] These feminine images were invoked not only in the theology of the Virgin Mary, which became extremely important in twelfth-century Western Christianity, but also in depictions of Jesus as mother,[53] Ecclesia as mother,[54] and male clerical authority figures as mothers[55]—all of which appeared in conjunction with suckling imagery.[56] This imagery, as in thirteenth-century Jewish theology, provided a model for understanding the relationships between divinity and humanity, often serving as a metaphor for spiritual transmission and instruction.[57]

Both Rachel Fulton and Caroline Bynum connect Christian suckling imagery with an increased interest in affective spirituality and the religious models that such spirituality inspires.[58] But Jewish suckling imagery, while containing an affective component, would be characterized incorrectly as being focused on affectivity. There is a difference between a transmission of affectivity and instruction, as in the Christian model of divine suckling, and the overflow of the divine life itself, as in the kabbalistic model. In kabbalistic texts, affective language simply adds further texture to the suckling image rather than being an end in itself. Yet Christian suckling imagery resembles its Jewish counterpart in its association primarily with male clergy members rather than female mystics or cloistered women.[59]

Despite this similarity between kabbalistic and Christian suckling imageries, other differences remain. Christian suckling imagery is part of a broader twelfth-century theology of Mary as mediator between humanity and divinity. Although her role is similar to that of the *Shekhinah*,[60] Mary mediates in a very different sense. Unlike the *Shekhinah*, who is a part of divinity, Mary in Christian theology occupies a position that is definitively below God, while remaining above humanity. In fact, it is Mary's identity as a "real" human being compassionate to the human condition that makes her such an essential figure in this theology of compassionate mediation.[61]

Furthermore, the suckling image in Christian texts has connotations that are alien to kabbalistic theology. For example, medieval European medicine often conflated various body fluids, associating milk with blood and allowing the suckling metaphor to take on Eucharistic implications.[62] As a consequence of this and similar developments, Christian suckling imagery by the thirteenth and fourteenth centuries was associated with the blood of the Eucharist rather than with milk.[63]

Thus, the use of mothering and suckling imagery for religious figures is common to both Judaism and Christianity though manifesting in very different ways in these religious traditions. Additionally, such imagery has an affective impact in both traditions, although in Kabbalah affective spirituality is not the primary religious focus that it is in Marian devotion. The question of influence that these similarities imply is an issue warranting serious consideration.[64]

Indeed, there are several contexts in which religious dialogue between medieval Jews and Christians occurred and may have influenced the development of the image of God as a breastfeeding mother in Kabbalah. In the twelfth and thirteenth centuries, the Jews of southern France and northern Spain were not a ghettoized people but rather interacted on a daily basis with their Christian neighbors. In Spain particularly, during the times when Jews enjoyed political favor, they often served in positions of authority at royal courts. In these situations, Jews had the opportunity to observe certain aspects of Christian religious observance, including Marian processions, shrines, and exterior church art.[65] Because the Jews observing these cultural phenomena probably experienced a mixture of attraction and aversion,[66] it is possible to understand the kabbalists as dealing with these external cultural challenges and influences by internalizing, transforming, and abstracting appealing aspects of Christian ideas while rejecting alienating ones.

For instance, Ezra's excursus into Song of Songs exegesis—his early-thirteenth-century work being the first kabbalistic commentary on the Song[67]—parallels contemporary Christian exegetical developments. In the twelfth century, Christian writers began to interpret the Song from a Marian perspective, understanding it as a love song between Jesus and his holy mother. Until that point, Christian exegetes had interpreted the Song as a dialogue between Jesus and the soul or between Jesus and the Church,[68] ideas roughly parallel to the earlier Jewish view of the Song as a dialogue between God and the people of Israel. Also, this Christian literature, like Ezra's work, makes notable use of the breast imagery from the Song.[69] Although it is difficult to know exactly what Jews took from their encounters with Christian spirituality, they, like Ezra, likely considered to some extent or at least found topically inspiring the theology presented by the Christian clergy.

Even so, internal drives toward religious revitalization, responses to Christian arguments for Jewish detachment from God, and the sway of Marian spirituality are not sufficient to explain the vivid feminine imagery found in the texts of classical Kabbalah. Indeed, for its elaboration of divine femininity and suckling imagery, the Zohar draws heavily not only on external influences but also on the traditional images of Jewish literature, adapting them to suit its own kabbalistic concerns. But, because the impact of these various cultural factors cannot be proven in the context of the current state of research, the kabbalists' reasons for developing the image of God as a nursing mother must remain somewhat obscure, at least for the time being.

NOTES

1. Readers interested in learning more about the image of God as a nursing mother in Jewish mysticism are welcome to consult my recently published book on the topic (Haskell 2012). Chapters 2, 3, and 4 of my book treat some of this chapter's material from a different perspective that is less focused on metaphor theory.
2. Fernandez 1986: 191, 207–8, 211.
3. The text passages included in this study represent only a small portion of the suckling metaphor's occurrence in the *Commentary on the Song of Songs* and *Sefer ha-Zohar*. I focus here not on intrasefirotic suckling but

on instances of suckling that relate directly to humanity—specifically, those that are associated with mothering imagery—and whose descriptions are accessible to a nonspecialist audience.

4. In this project, I have chosen to adopt a modified system of transliteration using only selected diacritical markings. From this point in the study onward, _h_ represents the Hebrew letter _het_, while _kh_ represents _khaf_ without a _dagesh_ and _k_ represents _kaf_ with a _dagesh_. For the sake of simplicity, vowel length will not be indicated in transliteration.

5. These are only a few of the metaphors used to describe this _sefirah_, which has a broader variety of representative images than do many other _sefirot_.

6. Again, these are only a few of the images used to describe the sefirotic structure.

7. Green 2002: 29.

8. For example, although the feminine tenth _sefirah_, often known as _Shekhinah_, plays an extremely large role in kabbalistic theological literature, it seems that the term _Shekhinah_ itself does not have feminine connotations prior to the medieval period but instead represents a manifestation of the divine presence (Scholem 1991: 140–96; Urbach [1975] 1979: 37–65). Moshe Idel (2005: 46), however, notes that it is possible to question this theory and to suggest an earlier feminization of the term.

9. Green notes that Kabbalah combines two previously distinct themes in its thought on the feminine tenth _sefirah_, that of the _Shekhinah_ as the divine presence and that of the Community of Israel (often bearing female connotations in earlier sources), along with feminized themes of the Torah and the Sabbath. According to Green, these different images are combined into "a single associative cluster." Similarly, Peter Schäfer (2002) demonstrates how divine Wisdom, another feminized image from biblical and rabbinic Judaism, is incorporated into the kabbalistic _Shekhinah_. Both Green (2002: 18–21) and Schäfer (2002: 12–13) believe that the Jewish concept of divine femininity is related directly to the growing trend toward Marian piety in the twelfth-century Church. Idel (2005: 46–47) remains cautious about this connection to Marian theology, noting that "this influence is yet to be demonstrated in a detailed manner."

10. This work is attributed erroneously to the more famous kabbalist Nahmanides as early as 1387 and often is printed under his name. In other cases, the work is attributed to Azriel of Gerona. It is, in fact, the work of Rabbi Ezra. But, in the source for my translations, Charles Chavel's

edition (2002: 473–518), the *Commentary* is included again among the works of Naḥmanides. Gershom Scholem ([1987] 1990: 371) and Georges Vajda (1957: 195), however, have attributed the work to Rabbi Ezra and discussed the history of this confusion.

11. Scholem [1987] 1990: 374, 394.
12. Green 1999: 7. Isaiah Tishby also notes that Ezra's *Commentary* is an important source text for the Zoharic authorship (Tishby and Lachower 1989: 1:80).
13. Ezra's teacher, Isaac the Blind (c. 1165–1235), also uses suckling as a metaphor for spiritual transmission in his *Commentary on Sefer Yetzirah* but does not connect suckling with explicit feminine imagery. In Hebrew, the term "suckling" (*yenikah*) can refer to a child's nursing or a tree's action in drawing nourishing water, so the presence of explicit mothering imagery is necessary to express fully the metaphor of God as a nursing mother.
14. Scholem [1941] 1995: 156.
15. Scholem [1941] 1995: 156–204; Liebes 1993: 85–138. The Zohar is attributed pseudepigraphically to the second-century sage Rabbi Shimon bar Yoḥai and written in a peculiar form of Aramaic—a linguistic choice intended to reinforce the work's supposedly ancient character. Through rigorous analysis of the text's language, vocabulary, writing style, and historical inconsistencies, Scholem assigns the Zohar's authorship to Moses de León. The more contemporary group-authorship theory is the work of Yehuda Liebes.
16. Brackets indicate implied words that are not present within the text. Following traditional Jewish modes of exegesis, Ezra's readers would have filled in the missing part of Song of Songs 8:1 for themselves.
17. The translations of the Chavel edition of the *Commentary* are my own.
18. In Kabbalah, the unity of masculine and feminine divine aspects within the sefirotic system often is described in erotic terms.
19. This phrase may refer to the second *sefirah*, *Hokhmah*.
20. This description of both the Written Torah and the Oral Torah as the two breasts of the feminine tenth *sefirah* is somewhat unusual. Generally, in Kabbalah, the Oral Torah is associated with the feminine Assembly of Israel, while the Written Torah is associated with the masculine sixth *sefirah*, *Raḥamim*. This formulation is found in texts as early as the late-twelfth-century *Sefer ha-Bahir* and the writings of the kabbalist Isaac the Blind (c. 1165–1235) (Scholem [1965] 1996: 47–49; Tishby and

Lachower 1989: 3:1085–86). Though unusual, Ezra's attribution of both the Written Torah and the Oral Torah to the final *sefirah* works well with the imagery of the Song and with the duality of female breasts.

21. In its biblical context, this statement is hopeful. Here, however, Ezra reads the phrase in a curiously inverted manner as an indicator of the going forth of the people of Israel into exile from the land of Israel and the place of the Torah.

22. I have used the Margoliot edition (1999) of *Sefer ha-Zohar* in this study. The translations of that work are my own.

23. "[A]nother place" refers here to the *sefirot Netzah* and *Hod*, usually considered the sources of prophecy in kabbalistic theology.

24. Hecker 2005: 3. Although Joel Hecker (2005: 4) notes the relationship between nourishment and suckling, he prefers to focus on the sexual connotations of divine nourishment rather than on the parent-child connotations.

25. The transmission and reception of the divine overflow often is connected with light imagery in kabbalistic literature. In Zohar 1:203a, we see a context in which the suckling metaphor is enriched with additional light imagery to express the idealized relationship between humanity and divinity during Temple times.

26. The term "below" refers here to entities that are considered metaphysically lower than the specific divine gradation under discussion. In addition, the Zohar often uses "above" and "below" as references to the divine and human worlds.

27. This is the fifth *sefirah*, *Din* (Judgment).

28. In Kabbalah, the color red often is associated with divine Judgment.

29. For an example of this symbolism, see Zohar 3:248b, which describes the redness of *Din* (the fifth *sefirah*) and the whiteness of *Hesed* (the fourth *sefirah*). In this passage, the *Shekhinah* takes on the two colors under various circumstances. Also using the symbolism of white and red is the beautiful passage that cites Song 2:2 at the beginning of the Zohar (Zohar 1:1a). For additional examples, see Zohar 1:9a and Zohar 1:221a.

30. A puzzlement of this passage is the peculiarity of milk (implying the presence of breasts) on the divine countenance. This bizarre juxtaposition is achieved by interpreting Song 5:12 ("His eyes are like doves by streams of water, bathed in milk"), which itself combines eye imagery with milk imagery, although the Zohar changes the relationships between the two, reading the eyes as either sefirotic or angelic potencies. The male of the

biblical verse generally is understood by exegetes to represent God. Thus, Song 5:12 is a fitting source of inspiration for a Zoharic description of the divine countenance and also provides a means to bring milk imagery into the description of *Binah*, the Upper Mother.

31. Fernandez 1986: 8, 46.
32. Fernandez 1986: 191–206. One of the main arguments of Fernandez's book is that metaphors move items through cultural value-space, essentially transforming them in relation to their surrounding societies. These movements then have the power to transform the societies in which they occur.
33. Fernandez 1986: 191–208.
34. Fishbane 2003: 314.
35. Durham and Fernandez 1991: 191–92.
36. Kehoe 1973: 266.
37. Jakobson 1971: 83–84.
38. Turner 1991: 130; Ohnuki-Tierney 1991: 162; Durham and Fernandez 1991: 193.
39. Fernandez 1986: 43–44.
40. Durham and Fernandez 1991: 197–98.
41. Turner 1991: 134.
42. Turner 1991: 128.
43. Fernandez 1986: 57.
44. Durham and Fernandez 1991: 209.
45. Turner 1991: 149.
46. Rappaport 1979: 119.
47. Kehoe 1973: 266.
48. My argument runs counter to that of Elliot Wolfson (1995: 109), who states, "It must be concluded, therefore, that the breast that gives milk is functionally equivalent to the penis that ejaculates. If that is the case, then the righteous described as suckling from the splendor of the breasts of the *Shekhinah* are, in fact, cleaving to and drawing from the corona of the divine phallus." This statement is part of an extensive argument that the *Shekhinah*, the feminine component of kabbalistic divine androgyny, is in fact equated with the corona of the divine phallus. Wolfson (2005: 81–82) has suggested that kabbalistic literature culturally masculinizes motherhood, rather than valorizing it as a feminine quality. But his views on reconstituting divine androgyny as an important kabbalistic goal have been challenged by Idel (Wolfson 1995: 91, 94, 208; Idel 2005: 74–75).

49. Intellect also forms an important link between God and humanity in Kabbalah, which is influenced heavily by medieval Jewish philosophy despite being able to be read as a reaction against philosophical spirituality (Idel 2002: 46–49; Huss 2001: 125). While thirteenth-century Spanish kabbalists' attitudes toward philosophy vary, they tend to be negative. Thus, these early kabbalists see philosophy either as an inferior form of knowledge or as a dangerous lure away from religious observance and prayer (Huss 2001: 130–33). In contrast, the image of God as a nursing mother is a means of defining the interaction between God and humanity without drawing on the language of the intellect, focusing instead on the social and affective aspects of the relationship.

50. Bynum 1982: 12–14; Schäfer 2002: 147–48.

51. Baer 1961: 150.

52. Bynum 1982: 17, 138.

53. Bynum 1992: 58.

54. Bynum 1992: 93; Bynum 1982: 112.

55. Bynum 1982: 112–13.

56. Bynum 1992: 93; Bynum 1982: 115.

57. For example, the founder of the Cistercian Order, Saint Bernard of Clairvaux (1091–1153)—who, according to a popular medieval legend, suckled at the breasts of the Virgin Mary herself—offers a theology in which Jesus nurses the Ecclesia, which in turn breastfeeds Christians with religious influence. In Bernard's theology, suckling represents a flow of instruction or affectivity (Bynum 1982: 115). Thus, Bernard's suckling represents a form of religious transmission similar to the metaphorical suckling in Kabbalah.

58. Fulton 2002: 197; Bynum 1992: 158; Bynum 1982: 115, 160.

59. Fulton 2002: 195. Of course, medieval Judaism has no equivalent to these religious Christian women. Yet, even in Christianity, where women do have the potential for a limited degree of religious authority and innovation, the suckling image remains the province of male clergy members.

60. Schäfer 2000; Schäfer 2002; Green 2002.

61. Fulton 2002: 384; Bynum 1982: 244.

62. Bynum 1982: 133.

63. Bynum 1982: 151.

64. Schäfer 2002: 231–32.

65. Schäfer 2002: 239–40; Green 2002: 27.

66. Schäfer 2002: 215; Green 2002: 28.

67. Green 1999: 7.
68. Fulton 2002: 249.
69. Bynum 1982: 117–19.

REFERENCES

Baer, Yitzhak. 1961. *From the Age of Reconquest to the Fourteenth Century.* Vol. 1 of *A History of the Jews in Christian Spain*. Translated by Louis Schoffman. Philadelphia: Jewish Publication Society of America.

Bynum, Caroline Walker. 1982. *Jesus as Mother: Studies in the Spirituality of the High Middle Ages*. Berkeley: University of California Press.

———. 1992. *Fragmentation and Redemption: Essays on Gender and the Human Body in Medieval Religion*. New York: Zone Books.

Chavel, Charles, ed. 2002. "Peirush le-Shir ha-Shirim." In *Kitve Rabenu Moshe ben Nachman*, vol. 2, 473–518. Jerusalem: Mosad ha-Rav Kook.

Durham, Deborah, and James Fernandez. 1991. "Tropical Dominions: The Figurative Struggle over Domains of Belonging and Apartness in Africa." In Fernandez 1991: 190–210.

Fernandez, James. 1986. *Persuasions and Performances: The Play of Tropes in Culture*. Bloomington: Indiana University Press.

———, ed. 1991. *Beyond Metaphor: The Theory of Tropes in Anthropology*. Stanford: Stanford University Press.

Fishbane, Michael. 2003. *Biblical Myth and Rabbinic Mythmaking*. Oxford: Oxford University Press.

Fulton, Rachel. 2002. *From Judgment to Passion: Devotion to Christ and the Virgin Mary, 800–1200*. New York: Columbia University Press.

Green, Arthur. 1999. "Editor's Note." In *Rabbi Ezra ben Solomon of Gerona: Commentary on the Song of Songs and Other Kabbalistic Commentaries*, edited and translated by Seth Brody and Arthur Green, 7–10. Kalamazoo, MI: Medieval Institute Publications.

———. 2002. "Shekhinah, the Virgin Mary, and the Song of Songs: Reflections on a Kabbalistic Symbol in Its Historical Context." *AJS Review* 26, no. 1: 1–52.

Haskell, Ellen Davina. 2012. *Suckling at My Mother's Breasts: The Image of a Nursing God in Jewish Mysticism*. Albany: State University of New York Press.

Hecker, Joel. 2005. *Mystical Bodies, Mystical Meals: Eating and Embodiment in Medieval Kabbalah*. Detroit: Wayne State University Press.

Huss, Boaz. 2001. "Mysticism versus Philosophy in Kabbalistic Literature." *Micrologus* 9: 125–35.

Idel, Moshe. 2002. *Absorbing Perfections: Kabbalah and Interpretation*. New Haven: Yale University Press.

———. 2005. *Kabbalah and Eros*. New Haven: Yale University Press.

Jakobson, Roman. 1971. "Two Aspects of Language and Two Types of Aphasic Disturbances." In Roman Jakobson and Morris Halle, *Fundamentals of Language*, 2nd ed., 67–96. The Hague: Mouton.

Kehoe, Alice B. 1973. "The Metonymic Pole and Social Roles." *Journal of Anthropological Research* 29, no. 4: 266–74.

Liebes, Yehuda. 1993. *Studies in the Zohar*. Translated by Arnold Schwartz, Stephanie Nakache, and Penina Peli. Albany: State University of New York Press.

Margoliot, Reuven Moshe, ed. 1999. *Sefer ha-Zohar al Hamishah Humshei Torah*. 3 vols. Jerusalem: Mosad ha-Rav Kook.

Ohnuki-Tierney, Emiko. 1991. "Embedding and Transforming Polytrope: The Monkey as Self in Japanese Culture." In Fernandez 1991: 159–89.

Rappaport, Roy A. 1979. *Ecology, Meaning, and Religion*. Berkeley: North Atlantic Books.

Schäfer, Peter. 2000. "Daughter, Sister, Bride, and Mother: Images of the Femininity of God in the Early Kabbala." *Journal of the American Academy of Religion* 68, no. 2: 221–42.

———. 2002. *Mirror of His Beauty: Feminine Images of God from the Bible to the Early Kabbalah*. Princeton: Princeton University Press.

Scholem, Gershom. 1990. *Origins of the Kabbalah*. Edited by R. J. Zwi Werblowsky and translated by Allan Arkush. N.p.: Jewish Publication Society, 1987. Reprint, Princeton: Princeton University Press.

———. 1991. *On the Mystical Shape of the Godhead: Basic Concepts in the Kabbalah*. Edited by Jonathan Chipman and translated by Joachim Neugroschel. New York: Schocken Books.

———. 1995. *Major Trends in Jewish Mysticism*. Jerusalem: Schocken Publishing House, 1941. Reprint, New York: Schocken Books.

———. 1996. *On the Kabbalah and Its Symbolism*. Translated by Ralph Manheim. New York: Schocken Books, 1965. Reprint, New York: Schocken Books.

Tishby, Isaiah, and Fischel Lachower, eds. 1989. *The Wisdom of the Zohar: An Anthology of Texts*. Translated by David Goldstein. 3 vols. Washington: Littman Library of Jewish Civilization.

Turner, Terence. 1991. "'We Are Parrots,' 'Twins Are Birds': Play of Tropes as Operational Structure." In Fernandez 1991: 121–58.

Urbach, Ephraim E. 1979. *The Sages: Their Concepts and Beliefs*. Translated by Israel Abrahams. Jerusalem: Magnes Press, 1975. Reprint, Cambridge: Harvard University Press.

Vajda, Georges. 1957. *L'amour de Dieu dans la théologie Juive du Moyen Âge*. Paris: J. Vrin.

Wolfson, Elliot. 1995. *Circle in the Square: Studies in the Use of Gender in Kabbalistic Symbolism*. Albany: State University of New York Press.

———. 2005. *Language, Eros, Being: Kabbalistic Hermeneutics and the Poetic Imagination*. New York: Fordham University Press.

6

Metaphors and Images of Dress and Nakedness

Wrappings of Embodied Identity

TERHI UTRIAINEN

RELIGION VERY MUCH works by using powerful images and metaphors of embodied social reality. In this essay, I will examine the images and metaphors of dress and nakedness which abound in Christian visual and verbal culture. I will argue that this imagery of dress and nakedness is about different aspects of identity and care of the self. Undressing and dressing figures are not simple metaphors stating once and for all what the Christian identity is about. Instead these figures construct a moving and changing matrix of cultural imaginary concerning identity as an ongoing, fragile, and precarious process. In the Bible and Finnish Lutheran hymns, images and metaphors of dress and nakedness are conceptualized in terms of fundamental social and moral practices of revealing and covering/protecting selves and others. In order to show how these figures refer to and build up identity as a process, I will apply both Gaston Bachelard's notion of image and Paul Ricoeur's notion of metaphor.

RELIGIOUS VISUAL AND VERBAL IMAGES

Religion has strong visual and verbal aspects. According to art historian David Morgan, visual piety plays an important role in the practice of Christianity, as well as of other religions.[1] Yet Catholics, Orthodox Christians, and Protestants have different relationships to images. For Protestants, as opposed to Catholics and Orthodox Christians, images are not an object of veneration or cult but an important mnemonic device: religious imagery helps both in building and in fixing memories of religious teachings, dogmas, and experiences.[2]

In many religious books, images are at least as important an element as text, and a lot of people possess—sometimes nostalgically, sometimes traumatically—among their early (religious) memories particular pictures which have often been very popular in their time. In my country, Finland, probably the best-known such picture (for most of the twentieth century) was a print where a small boy and girl walk over a bridge in a dark forest. They are followed by a beautiful angel with long hair and soft, feathered wings who is dressed in a long, white robe. This image is cherished by many Finns, many of whom connect to it a song from the turn of the twentieth century, "The Guardian Angel" (music by P. J. Hannikainen, lyrics by Immi Hellén). But a negative, even traumatic, image is one that depicts the fate of the damned— for example, the *Hell* panel of Hieronymus Bosch's *Garden of Earthly Delights* triptych (1505–1510), or one of Gustave Doré's illustrations of Dante's *Inferno* (1861) or of the Bible (1865). Along similar lines, the Finnish-Swedish writer Oscar Parland recounts in his 1962 autobiographical novel, *The Year of the Bull*, how much he, as a child, both feared and was fascinated with one particular fallen-angel postcard that he had found in his grandmother's drawer.[3]

In times before common literacy, religious images were even more powerful. In the Middle Ages, for instance, the interiors of churches were practically filled with images that constituted rich and complex visual sign systems depicting often very concrete bodily states and actions. Yet, even in the present time, Protestants as well as Catholics make touristic pilgrimages to churches in Rome and other old European cities, simply to be impressed by famous and powerful Christian images.

One of religious imagery's many tasks is to imagine and represent a community and its conception of truth.[4] Embedded in a religious image and the practices of seeing it are implicit instructions as to how the image should be seen, what the image is about, and what the conception of truth with which it engages is. Very often, a necessary requirement for such an image to be taken as "true" is that it be similar enough to a lot of other images in the same culture. Accordingly, the image's "truth" is built in an often long and persuasive process of repetition. Consequently, the repeated and familiar image—which, with slight variation, is seen almost everywhere—is, in quotidian life, not seldom accepted as unquestionably true. Images can inhabit the same communicative situations and networks as—but need not argue in the same propositional way as—verbal language, since the emotional and neurological mechanisms images use are somewhat different from the mechanisms used by verbal language.[5] Very often, however, images are used in order to emphasize further and sometimes also to simplify the verbal and doctrinal message. For example, Christian missionary work demonstrates the use and power of images in a context where shared verbal language is missing or scant.[6] The emotive power of images can also be seen in the various outbursts of iconoclasm in the history of Western religions.[7]

Image-making and -reading processes cooperate with other social, cultural, political, and religious practices. Pictorial practices can function relatively independently of or can act within larger and more multiform communicative processes. The latter is very much the way images work within verbal language. Such religious practices as praying, reading, singing, giving sermons, and uttering other ritual language—in addition to being connected often with the concrete visuality of different images and symbols—often have a very strong and impressive figurative aspect. Repeated and familiar verbal language—by virtue of its figurative potential—is, perhaps, as strong a means for carving and storing religious memories as are concrete visual images.[8]

The rhetoric and persuasive power of verbal imagery, or figurative language, have been acknowledged and analyzed by scholars in women's studies, philosophy, religious studies, and medical anthropology.[9] In *The Resurrection of the Body in Western Christianity, 200–1336*, historian of medieval religious culture Caroline Walker Bynum analyzes verbal imagery in order to illuminate the theological debates surrounding the question of resurrection.[10] Although she could have focused on the arguments and dogmas presented within the often heated discussions on what precisely guaranteed the identity of the Christian subject, her focus on verbal imagery—namely, such devices as metaphors, analogies, and examples which may sound very exotic to the present reader, as well as all the wild allusions and references that they make—clarifies different and very important aspects of these debates. By shedding light on the figurative rather than argumentative aspects of language, Bynum brings her readers closer to the popular religious thinking of the time that she studies, since visual religious representations were more familiar to the common folk then than were verbal and dogmatic statements. According to her, imagery is much more than mere ornamental paraphernalia added to the dogmatic text. Instead, imagery builds up a living and embodied text, such as the Bible, which itself abounds with imagery. In the Bible, the concepts of mercy and sin are often depicted by figures of flourishing and decay, respectively; the relationship between God and humans is likened to that of man and woman; and the soul is visualized often as a small, naked body. All the visual fields used in these Biblical examples are drawn from fundamental and familiar bodily and social processes and experiential fields. So too are dress and nakedness, which form the object of my analysis.

METAPHORS AND IMAGES OF IDENTITY

I don't make a categorical distinction between metaphor and image. On a rather general level, I understand them both in terms of the figurative and the imaginary. By the "imaginary," I mean both psychic and cultural figurative constructions which often take bodily forms and manifest as modes of action, and thus am identifying a heuristic concept with which to map both the psychological or "lived" side and the cultural and political side of embodiment.[11] By the "imaginary," I also imply a particular perspective on the meanings of the imagery of dress and nakedness, and this perspective I owe to the French philosopher Gaston Bachelard, as he expresses it in *The Poetics of Space*.[12] Bachelard himself, however, does distinguish metaphor from image. In his understanding, a metaphor (much like a concept) condenses information instead of inaugurating a fresh and open-ended process of thought. In this sense, such an expression as "autumn undresses the trees" would be a simple and also rather worn-out metaphor—a cliché, in fact. An image, on the contrary, according to Bachelard, does not follow the same economic. The relationship between an image and the object that it describes does not involve adequate and economic condensation of information but something quite different. An image is dynamic and more free from the object that it describes, and its way of functioning is based purely on imagination. Through dreaming, an image opens up thinking to unforeseen directions and proportions. An image, instead of condensing information about an object, opens up and enriches it.[13]

Since the object I am trying to describe and analyze in this essay is a rich and complex matrix of cultural imagery and imaginary, I think it is important to bear in mind Bachelard's principle concerning the way images work. The verbal images of dress and undress should not be reduced to simple economic condensations of propositions or conditions. Instead, such images deal with processes and significations which are in continuous movement and change. These images are about such things as "being human" and "identity," but do not simply try to fix these conditions. Instead, the images aim at shedding light on the conditions, always from slightly different angles.

I, however, understand metaphor slightly differently than does Bachelard, and here my inspiration is Paul Ricoeur. According to Ricoeur, metaphor does not always describe a thing, or an object; but, rather, a process, or something that happens or takes place. Thus metaphor has to do with verb rather than with noun.[14] Processes or happenings described metaphorically are often fundamental experiences which cannot be depicted in any other way: death, life, suffering, love, ecstasy, melancholy, good, evil, soul, identity . . . all these are rather like processes than like static things. These experiences are starting points of self-understanding, communication, and ethics but by nature are able neither to be depicted or defined analytically or propositionally nor to be observed with the five senses. Yet, these experiences—even though they don't remain the same, but, instead, are changing perpetually (i.e., are becoming and are evading)—can be hinted at, by using language that describes bodily experiences and practices.[15] For example, when trying to describe the soul, starting with the body—and understanding the soul in some relationship to bodily processes or practices—is natural: while the soul feels and experiences, it is like, but not quite the same as, the body. Thus, images and metaphors may often be the most exact depictions possible of experiences and practices which don't have definite locations or forms.

In this essay, I will combine Bachelard's and Ricoeur's conceptualizations as I focus on processes of dress and undress. Instead of simply identifying images/metaphors of dress and undress (nakedness) in my sources, I will focus on what happens in the depicted scenes: Is there an end state of nakedness or of being fully dressed, or is there, instead, a process of dressing up or stripping off? Is this process voluntary, or is it, on the contrary, forcible and violent? And who is the object being dressed or undressed and who is the subject dressing or undressing in the depicted process—do these actors coincide with or differ from each other? And what do Christian images of dress and nakedness tell us about the ways the extremely difficult question of identity can be posed in a culture that has inherited much of the Christian conceptual and imaginary legacy?

When I write "identity," I want to emphasize two closely connected ways of understanding it. In more philosophical and classical thinking, "identity" refers to (relative) continuity and sameness in a temporal process ("Will I still be me after this divorce? After my death?"). In sociological thinking, "identity" refers more to belonging to certain reference groups and, also, to identity work ("Do I identify myself more as a mother or as a scholar? Is this my real identity or should I change it?"). These analytically separate ways of understanding identity are, of course, often inseparable in lived social reality. Nevertheless, distinguishing between them analytically reveals nuances in the ways care of the identity is depicted in the sources. I have borrowed the idea of "care of the self" from philosopher Michel Foucault, as he explicates it in the third volume of his *History of Sexuality*.[16] According to Foucault, care of the self is a historical phenomenon that dates to European Antiquity and its political organization. It is reasonable, however, to think that the Christian culture has inherited this care for either the bodily or the spiritual, psychological, or moral self: members of this culture—in order to secure their identities and to achieve "ontological security"[17] in a world of uncertainties and in order to locate themselves socially—are continuously creating new techniques and practices (such as asceticism, sports, work ethics, meditation, and therapies). Both practices and images of dress take part in this process of self-care in an unpredictable world shared with others.

RELIGIOUS DRESS METAPHORS: SHELTER AND EXTENSION

Dress and nakedness, as well as dressing and undressing, figure in frequently repeated images in Christian visual and verbal culture. The motifs of dress and undress are found in both the first and the last books of the Bible. In Genesis, the human couple is created in order to live naked in the earthly paradise, but, before expelling them from Eden, God prepares clothes of leather for them and dresses them up. In Revelation, the prophetic voice of the text warns people to wash their clothes and to make sure not be found naked at the moment of last judgment, since those who are found then to be naked or dressed in clothes that are filthy will be doomed to damnation.[18] Moreover, the hundreds of intervening pages contain a plethora of variations on the themes of dress and nakedness—as, for instance, in the stories of Noah and Job, in several prophetic allegories, in the Passion of Jesus told in the Gospels, and in the body symbolism of the Epistles of Paul. Outside the Bible—in visual art, prayers, hymns, sermons, novels, and so forth—the imagery of dress and nakedness bears the important tasks of depicting and mediating the unresolved problematic of the human/Christian identity. Some of the most famous dress-and-nakedness images are well-known depictions of the Crucifixion, such as Matthias Grünewald's *Isenheim Altarpiece* (c. 1510–1515), which features a stripped and brutally tortured Jesus. Additionally, in many Christian visual representations of the last judgment, the human figures stand naked, waiting to receive their judgment.[19] The imagery of dress and nakedness can be found also outside explicitly religious ritual contexts, in contemporary language. In my previous studies of contemporary practices surrounding dying people in Finland, I discovered that a lot of Finnish caregivers described death and dying with images of undressing: "'In front of death we must undress ourselves and expose also the unclean parts'"; "'Why were you not allowed to leave this world as a womanly woman made by God? You are being undressed, also physically.'"[20]

Before I analyze some examples of the Christian verbal imagery of dress and nakedness, I will define more carefully what I understand by "dress," this "'visual metaphor for identity.'"[21] Only after one has pondered upon the meanings of dress, can one better understand what it means to be naked—either physically or metaphorically.

Representations connected to physical dressing and/or undressing often function themselves as images or metaphors of adding and lessening or of covering and revealing. And, as soon as one starts to speak about something else than simple physical (un)dressing, one is in the middle of extremely rich verbal imagery to be found almost everywhere. For example, weaving and sewing work in many cultures, and especially in women's language, as metaphors of life.[22] One Finnish caregiver of the dying calls death the "great weaver," i.e., the fabricator of the dress or cloth of life.[23] Expressions about dressing and undressing appear frequently not only in philosophical language and in the language of gender theories (which ask whether gender is but a dress to be put on and off),[24] but also in literature and poetry. Also, everyday talk makes use of dressing imagery in such sayings as "clothing one's thoughts in words."

Often this verbal imagery is easily understood in its context. There are at least two reasons for this trend. The first is simply because dressing and undressing are visible phenomena often used as metaphorical expressions for adding and lessening and for completing and simplifying, as well as for covering and revealing. The second and more profound reason is that dressing and undressing are, as practices and experiences, so very familiar and commonplace to every human being. Besides being a universal human need (like feeding, sex, and dwelling), dressing and undressing are practices that construct our very human "nature"; we very much exist in the processes of dressing and undressing.[25] On a more abstract level, these processes coincide with the multiple ways of covering and revealing ourselves.[26] Thus, dressing and undressing become very easily and quite "naturally" devices for thinking about the question of identity.

Dress shelters people from weather, visibility, and contact. This is a very simple, functional definition of dress. Besides this, dress is also other things. In multidisciplinary research, dress has been characterized both as a means of covering and as a means of revealing its wearer's body. Dress is also a means to express or perform selfhood, as well as a means to extend the borders of self to reach the world. Moreover, dress is not only a physical shelter but also a very powerful and manifold symbolic shelter against, for instance, supernatural forces. Dress is, all in all, a multiform bodily, social, and symbolic practice.[27] It is possible, sometimes, to interpret a whole cosmology, by "reading" somebody's dress. Thus, dress bears both social and ontological meanings related to identity, as religious dress attests.[28]

For example, the dress of a shaman is a shelter and also often a weapon against both natural and supernatural powers. The shaman's dress helps to distance unwanted forces, but can also summon or invite desired forces. Thus, it functions not only as protection but also as an extension of the self and the same toward life-giving otherness. Through the cosmological sign system of her dress, the shaman is connected to the whole universe of her culture and community. For instance, the red color of the hat of the ancient Finnish shaman was believed to please important spirits that liked to reside in the headpiece, and the shoes of the Siberian shaman could be decorated with the pattern of bear bones because the journey to the other world required a bear's strength.[29] Furthermore, the religious specialist's dress can act as a "boundary mechanism" between the sacred and the profane, or between the otherworldly and this world.[30] The material of the dress; its model, patterns, and traditional ways of being made; and its ultimate ownership and status in trade or gift-giving systems are sometimes mythologically sanctioned by ancestors or gods of the community.[31]

A lot of religious groups use dress as an identity and boundary mechanism that helps to make them into visually and morally coherent groups and to distinguish them from others.[32] For example, Protestants have often valued simple dress which does not draw too much attention to the individual body, because this is not an aspect of the self that they desire to be seen or emphasized; and some Protestant groups have strongly objected to very conspicuous dress. For these groups, dress is an important part of tradition that should not be changed. The Amish, for instance, still dress very much in the same simple manner as when they arrived in North America from Europe; and their traditional religious identity (as well as their gender identities) can be easily seen by anyone who simply looks at their dress. The Mormons, on the contrary, dress outwardly pretty much as any relatively conservative American does, but they wear a boundary maker against their naked bodies: their sacred dress is special underwear sanctified in the temple. They wear this clothing all their life, day and night, against the skin, as a sacred touch and reminder of the precarious holiness of their bodies.[33]

Folk dress also often bears religious and magical significance. Folk dress is not seldom decorated with magical signs resembling writing, and in the Carpathian regions in Eastern Europe women have in fact modeled embroidery on writing worn by members of the community.[34] In Norway, the traditional shirts have metal brooches which protect their wearers from evil forces who see their own reflections in the shining metal and shun away.[35] In Greece and Macedonia, an important element of women's traditional dress is the embroideries and fringes that decorate and guard the critical openings of the dress. When malevolent spirits try to enter the dress and reach the vulnerable human body inside, they are trapped by these teasing and aesthetic edges and borders of the dress, and this way the body is saved from the alien invasion.[36]

Another magico-religious function of dress, the function of communicating messages from this world to the other world, is fulfilled by the dress of the ancient Egyptian aristocrat: once the body of the deceased has been cleansed and embalmed, it is wrapped in layers of linen shrouds before being closed in a coffin; and all these layers of wrapping can be decorated by magical charms that help the deceased in her journeying to the other world.[37] Together the layers of cloth and the coffin construct a sheltering wrapping around the deceased, a wrapping that connects the meanings of dressing and dwelling at home as two practices that are the most important in the process of securing the very vulnerability and fragility of identity. In fact, dressing the deceased is ritually sanctioned in most cultures.[38] Perhaps only in situations when communities are in severe crisis do they leave their dead without decent dress. This was the case during the Holocaust[39] and other genocides. Moreover, my previous study of Finnish suicides shows that many people who think about taking their own lives express, in their suicide notes, their wish to be buried in particular dress.[40]

As important as funeral dress is the first dress, that is, the dress of the newborn. In fact, birth is the sole moment of life when it is absolutely necessary to be naked, for it is possible to be at least partly dressed when bathing, making love, or engaging in any other postnatal activity. The newborn is the only naked human being who has never been undressed. But, very soon after the child is born, she is wrapped in a cloth or swaddle, or dressed up in some other, often meaningful way. In this regard, I will give two examples. First, in premodern Eastern Finland, the newborn was wrapped in her father's shirt in order to strengthen the bond between her and him.[41] Second, in the traditional Czech and Slovak culture, one and the same shawl was used at three critical moments of life: the garment was worn by the bride at her wedding, was wrapped around her newborn, and was spread over the mother's deceased body.[42]

In some cultures, the myths narrating human beings' origin tell about the importance of dress, albeit in different ways. In the Old Testament, God creates man and woman naked and without shame. It is only after the Fall that people start to be ashamed of their nakedness and try to cover it. After its very first occurrence, nakedness in Biblical texts is never without the slight flavor of shame or ultimate vulnerability. The myth of human origin told by Latin American Incas, however, is different. According to them, the first humans came out of a cave while fully dressed in their native costume—there is no original nakedness in this story. And, following the same cultural logic, the Incas always value dress on people—living and dead—as well as on their sacred objects, which are most carefully wrapped in traditionally decorated cloths.[43]

DRESS AND NAKEDNESS: SOME DEFINITIONS

The central vocabulary of dress research is diverse and complex.[44] In this essay, I will use only the most central concepts: dress (dressing), garment, and cloth (clothes, clothing). Dress is a wider category and practice than garment and cloth, although the three terms can be synonymous. Sometimes one simple garment or item of clothing (for example, a hat) can function as a metonymy of the whole process of dress. For example, in Greece, as well as in Finland, a married woman was traditionally never to be seen without her headpiece; devoid of it, she was in a state equivalent to nakedness.[45] The lack of veil can be a sign of similar "nakedness" in some other cultures.

Sociologist Mary Ellen Roach-Higgins and anthropologist Joanne B. Eicher define dress broadly enough for the concept to cover many kinds of things added or done to the body, such as clothes, accessories, tattoos, jewelry, piercings, plastic surgery, cosmetics, implants, and even athletic bodily changes.[46] All of these things work as important boundary mechanisms[47] in ongoing social, moral, and imaginary identity work.[48] Dress is a most important visual and often also tactile metaphor or image of identity when identity is understood as a process of caring of the self, which is always precarious and full of desires. Dress is our second skin, which often becomes as natural and as intimate as our first skin. Our second skin is often but not always placed upon our first skin. Sometimes dress—such as tattoos, piercings, and chirurgical implants—extends under skin, and so the first and second skins become interlocked.[49]

If dress is as important a practice as there is in the process of being human, nakedness is something that can best be understood in relation to dress. Indeed, we are very seldom completely naked: "Where other animals go about unclad, or clad only in the garments bestowed on them by their human owners or protectors, only in privacy or in very exceptional social circumstances are human beings found without at least some garments, if only the fig leaf equivalent."[50] Complete nakedness is often very strictly regulated and is conceptualized and imagined as lack of dress, even when nakedness is valued positively, as in the case of some emancipatory practices. For example, in nudism, nakedness is seen as breaking free from clothes enforced by society; and, in the figurative speech of New Age adherents, old clothes should be "dropped" so that the authentic "naked" self will be emancipated.[51] Moreover, philosopher Charles Taylor has described the attitude of the Enlightenment as that of standing nakedly in front of the Truth.[52]

In this essay, I conceptualize nakedness and the naked human body, respectively, as an experience and as one important figure of the incompleteness, fragility, and vulnerability of the human subject. The newborn is one example of this incompleteness and vulnerability, the dying and dead person is another. Life between birth and death bears this vulnerability in its heart. Of Huynh Cong Ut's famous 1972 photograph of a young Vietnamese girl who runs naked on the street and tries to save herself from destruction by napalm, historian of photography John Pultz writes, "The girl's nude body appears as something vital, essential to continued human life on earth";[53]

and I would continue that the naked human body is a necessary but not yet sufficient condition for human life. Philosopher Kate Soper reminds us how undressing a victim is a very common part of torture all over the world, and how forced nakedness threatens the victim's very humanity.[54] Since it is possible to understand humanness as something which can be stripped naked, dress symbolizes all those fragile shelters that we build in front of death and decay.[55] Thus nakedness is (both concretely and figuratively) lack of dress and, potentially, of life. Nakedness brings us in touch with bare life without its necessary (albeit sometimes restricting and thus, in themselves, violent) sheltering and empowering wrappings.

BIBLICAL (UN)DRESSINGS

As already mentioned, the imagery of dress and nakedness is abundant in Biblical narratives. In this chapter, I will take up three of them—Genesis, Job, and the Epistles of Paul—in more detail and will make short references to others. In a larger study,[56] I have also analyzed the story of Noah, as well as several Old Testament prophets who tell basically the same allegory about Israel repeatedly turning to the service of foreign gods. The allegory depicts Israel as an unfaithful wife who undresses herself in front of her many lovers and who finally will be punished, by being totally and violently undressed by her husband—Jahve. I have also analyzed the narratives in the Gospels and focused on the episodes of dressing and undressing Jesus (which are especially important in the scene of the Passion), as well as the imagery of dress in Revelation. Besides these "grand narratives," there are multiple sections of the Biblical texts where the imagery has an important bearing.

TWO WAYS OF BEING NAKED, AND THE GARMENTS OF SKIN

In Genesis, the nakedness of the human couple is on the front stage three times. First we confront the innocent and unconscious nakedness before the Fall. After this, the man and the woman, after having eaten from the forbidden tree, suddenly become aware of their own nakedness and hasten to find fig leaves in order to hide their nakedness. They also hide themselves from God's view. The third time when nakedness occurs is right before He dresses the couple in garments of skin.

From the very beginning, Genesis 2:24–25 binds man and woman together through the sexual act—man and woman become "one flesh": "Therefore shall a man leave his father and his mother, and shall cleave unto his wife: and they shall be one flesh. And they were both naked, the man and his wife, and were not ashamed." The first bodily encounters between man and woman bear a seemingly innocent nature: "and [they] were not ashamed." Very soon, however, nakedness and shame become tightly bound to each other. As a result, man and woman's initial and innocent connection is polluted: in the beginning there was no shame, but afterward nakedness is and will always be shameful. Innocent nakedness is a lost state into which humans can never return (at least by themselves) after the Fall.

> And the eyes of them both were opened, and they knew that they were naked; and they sewed fig leaves together, and made themselves aprons. And they heard the voice of the LORD God walking in the garden in the cool of the day: and Adam and his wife hid themselves from the presence of the LORD God amongst the trees of the garden. And the LORD God called unto Adam, and said unto him, Where art thou? And he said, I heard thy voice in the garden, and I was afraid, because I was naked; and I hid myself.

Here, in Genesis 3:7–10, nakedness is directly linked to the opening of the eyes and to seeing—or at least to seeing differently than ever before. Thus, one single act has changed the human being's relationships to herself and to the other—to the fellow human as well as to God. Being together has become something which is at least potentially shameful. Awareness of this potential emphasizes vision, as if the text recounts a moment of second birth or creation: this is the birth of a seeing, reflecting, and shaming subjectivity. Nakedness which was innocent was nakedness that was not reported as an object of vision, whereas this new nakedness is precisely something to be seen, and at the very same moment something that needs to be hidden from the eyes of the humans as well as from the Godly eye. It is a forbidden sight and a forbidden knowledge.

The dress (the aprons made of fig leaves) the human couple tries to prepare themselves is not sufficient. Their new nakedness requires another, better, more opaque and solid dress. This dress is prepared for them by God Himself, in Genesis 3:21: "Unto Adam also and to his wife did the LORD God make coats of skins, and clothed them." The pieces of clothing that the humans were able to make for themselves, which were not capable of covering their nakedness, now become shameful. Proper covering (as the text would have it) can be accomplished only by the dress God makes them. Because He not only makes the dress but also dresses the couple in it, He is presented both as the provider (or even owner) of the dress and as the dresser of the humans. The human beings are mere objects (or puppets or, perhaps, infants) to be dressed. This emphasis can be seen also in other Biblical texts, such as Job and the prophetic texts mentioned earlier. In the Paulian texts of the New Testament, however, the human becomes more like the subject or agent of her own act of dressing, as we shall soon see.

In sum, nakedness in the Genesis narrative is of two sorts. First there is the initial and innocent nakedness without shame, and after that there is the shameful and vulnerable nakedness caused by human initiative and action. This new nakedness leaves the human beings in a state of helplessness and incapacity. The dress they make themselves out of vegetation will not do. Rather, they need the very Other to dress them up in a different kind of dress. And the dress they receive is made out of dead animals' skins. How can this be understood?

Clothing of skin is discussed much by early Christian theologians (i.e., Origen and Gregorius of Nyssa) and continues to be a prominent theme in Greek Orthodox theology.[57] Garments of skin have been understood as a complex gift from God. The garments were made of dead animals' skins, and thus bear the meanings of death and decay: like other animals, humans will be objects of death—although the Godmade dress will shelter them in the hard life outside paradise, they, in the end, will die. Thus, these garments possess the positive and negative aspects of clothing: the garments are solid and protect the humans, but, in doing so, continuously call to mind the death awaiting them.[58] This clothing has also been interpreted as the traveler's garment needed during the earthly journey toward death and resurrection.[59] This theme of the traveler's garment becomes the key metaphor in such a classic of Puritan literature as John Bunyan's *Pilgrim's Progress* (1678), where a man called Christian travels through a route of perils to the city of Heaven. In nearly all the important phases of his journey, his dress changes and becomes a central theme.

In addition, the contemporary Greek Orthodox theologian Panayiotis Nellas compares the earthly leather garment with the initial, virginal garment of paradisiacal nudity.[60] The latter is, in the Greek Orthodox theological tradition, a "psychosomatic" dress that was made of both psyche and soma and thus combined the spiritual and the material and that perfectly

connected the human subject to her environment. This dress was no boundary mechanism (since no boundary was needed), but was pure connection
made out of Godly breath. Thus, in some interpretations, even the initial
nakedness can be understood as a very peculiar and perfectly fitting dress!

MOTH-EATEN CLOTH

In another oft-cited Biblical passage, Job 1:20–22, the title character describes his misery after having become the object of betting in a cruel competition between God and Satan: "Then Job arose, and rent his mantle, and
shaved his head, and fell down upon the ground, and worshipped, And said,
Naked came I out of my mother's womb, and naked shall I return thither:
the LORD gave, and the LORD hath taken away; blessed be the name of
the LORD." In this story, Satan has undressed Job in many ways and on
many levels, in order to test his loyalty to God. Job expresses his misery and
mourning in the same way as is done in many Old Testament texts (e.g.,
Gen. 37:29, 2 Sam. 13:31, Ezra 9:3): he tears his clothes and shaves his head.
He tells us that he doesn't possess anything in this life, and that the fate of
humans is to leave this world as naked as the newborn. The same image is
found in Ecclesiastes 5:14–16.

According to Job 10:8–11, the Old Testament God has made the human
being very concretely by molding and fashioning her out of different materials: "Thine hands have made me and fashioned me together round about; yet
thou dost destroy me. Remember, I beseech thee, that thou hast made me
as the clay; and wilt thou bring me into dust again? Hast thou not poured
me out as milk, and curdled me like cheese? Thou hast clothed me with skin
and flesh, and hast fenced me with bones and sinews." The human being is
materialized, molded, sewn up, put together, and dressed up, skin and flesh
being the garment. Neither the materials needed in this process of fabrica-
tion nor the fabricated whole belongs to her. She is, rather, like a marionette
in the hands of God, as Job 13:27 attests: "Thou puttest my feet also in the
stocks, and lookest narrowly unto all my paths; thou settest a print upon the
heels of my feet."

In Job, the human being is nothing but an always ultimately (at least
potentially) undressed body. Or, on the contrary, she is nothing substantial
at all—not even a body but merely a border of cloth (of skin and flesh), a
piece of sheer materiality, as seen in Job 13:28: "And he, as a rotten thing,
consumeth, as a garment that is moth eaten." Inherent in this image is a

model of thought—or its possibility—that humans are but garments, not something wrapped in them. Hence, the human being is but exteriority and dead materiality. In Job (as elsewhere in Christian thinking), the condition of being human is called "flesh." In both suffering and death, this flesh is torn and tortured and, in the end, is completely torn off—as if flesh were a many-layered material reality, as clothing or a garment can be. Humans are molded, dressed up, mobilized, and—in the end, when the Biblical God so wishes—undressed, torn off, and destroyed, layer after layer. On her own, then, a human being has no guarantee of her identity. This guarantee, in its totality, is a gift from the Other.

In the prophetic allegory of Ezekiel 16 is another powerful, violent, and this time even pornographic[61] story of Godgiven and Godtaken dress.[62] In Ezekiel 16:36–39, Jahve says explicitly that Israel, as a feminized human being, is naked and completely helpless without the dress given to her by Him. In this narrative, the metaphor of Godgiven dress assumes a human being whose subjectivity is complete submissiveness: all human agency is judged negatively and its value is denied. This image is juxtaposed with the scene of dressing in Ezekiel 16:6–14. Here the Lord, who is promenading in the streets, finds a naked newborn girl (who is to become His wife) covered with blood. The Lord takes up the abandoned child then grown maiden; covers her with His skirt; and gives her clothing and thus life, shelter, and a place in a community. In this scene, His action can be interpreted as a tender and caring gesture, offering at once ontological and social identity and security— a gesture of a good (foster) parent and husband. Yet it conveys the same message concerning the subjectivity of the human being as does the rest of the story: without the Godly action, there would have been no dress, shelter, continuity, or belonging.

DRESSED IN IMMORTALITY

Like many other religious and philosophical texts of Antiquity, the Epistles of Paul contain many metaphorical notions of dress and nakedness.[63] These notions can be found in all Paulian epistles, as well as in those which probably were not written by Paul himself. In my analysis, I will not separate these two categories of texts, as both have been active in constructing the later Christian and even modern consciousness and its care for the self.

Bodily metaphors are important in the Paulian texts. Together, Christians form the body of Christ, which, according to 1 Corinthians 12:12, is thus both the "model *of*" and the "model *for*" the Christian congregation:[64]

"For as the body is one, and hath many members, and all the members of that one body, being many, are one body: so also is Christ." In 1 Corinthians 12:23–24, Paul emphasizes how important it is to take care not only of the more valuable body parts but also of those with less value, and how the latter need all the more careful covering. The less valuable body parts should be understood against the background of the historical context and its hierarchical social structure comprising common folk (and women) as distinguished from the elite (and men). In the cultural scale of honor, the meaning of the nakedness of people differs, depending on their social positions. The lower one's social position, the more shameful one's nakedness potentially is.[65]

One influential image drawn by 1 Corinthians 15:54 is that of an individual who, in order to save her identity throughout the process of death, has to undress herself and, after undressing, dresses herself again. What she needs to take off is her very mortality, which is thus understood to be something like clothing. And, just as mortality can be likened to a dress, so too can immortality, which is a new and radically different dress: "So when this corruptible shall have put on incorruption, and this mortal shall have put on immortality, then shall be brought to pass the saying that is written, Death is swallowed up in victory."

There is also an elaborated image that depicts the individual not at all willing to strip herself naked. Nakedness is thus implied to be a mostly unwanted state (like death itself), but, according to 2 Corinthians 5:4, is a necessary or, rather, inevitable liminal state before the new dress: "For we that are in this tabernacle do groan, being burdened: not for that we would be unclothed, but clothed upon, that mortality might be swallowed up of life." In Galatians 3:27–28, garments are a very explicit metaphor of Christ. The converted or baptized individual wears the very Christ, and this Christ-garment is a uniform that dresses all people—men and women, slaves and the free alike. It connects all Christians while wrapping them in the same identity: "For as many of you as have been baptized into Christ have put on Christ. There is neither Jew nor Greek, there is neither bond nor free, there is neither male nor female: for ye are all one in Christ Jesus."

For Paul, identity is not anything original in the sense that it can be revealed simply by peeling off outer layers of "clothing," which is, in fact, the model of salvation in some forms of Platonic and Gnostic thinking.[66] On the contrary, in the Paulian texts, there is no necessary core or essence of human being under the clothes. Undressing is important, but only as a transitory stage before a new dress. Except for this transitory nakedness, there always are dresses in human life, but, importantly, the dresses differ from each other. The responsibility of the individual subject (as well as the community) is to take care of her own dress, to take off the wrong one and change it into the right one.[67] For Paul, if this care of the self and its dress is well mastered, then even death need be not a state of nakedness but a possibility to receive the ultimate garment. The Paulian texts construct an image of continuous identity work where identity is resolved and put together in an ongoing process.

This Paulian model of identity as a process of dress and undress can be found in many other Christian texts, such as the Finnish Lutheran hymns that I will soon discuss. This model can be found also in less explicitly religious texts. It is in use, for example, in the twenty-first-century life stories of two young Finnish women, who discuss their identity crises associated with experiencing anorexia nervosa and childhood incest, respectively:

> With food one can do all possible evil to oneself. . . . It is always possible to strip off the old life and to start a new one. . . . I suppose my dream was to be purified, and that in the process of purification all evil would just drop off. . . . I wanted to be dressed in the robe of an angel, and is it a wonder if all that I lost was my hunger for life?[68]

> Like rain and wind
> this morning
> stripped the leaves from the trees
> thus revealing the branches and trunks
> I would like to be undressed
> of things
> that have covered me
> for decades.
> Safely,
> trusting
> that I would receive a new dress without a gown of shame.[69]

These passages show that the metaphorics of dress and nakedness is based on a constitutive human process of covering and revealing; and that religious language and its metaphors sometimes provide a very longliving and powerful symbolic resource for expressing the care of the self, even in a secular context.

IMAGES OF DRESS AND NAKEDNESS IN FINNISH LUTHERAN HYMNS

Hymns, which are religious ritual language with many functions, are sung collectively not only during sermons but also in other rituals taking place in the church as well as elsewhere. Furthermore, hymns can be sung, read, and meditated in the privacy of homes (I remember my grandmother singing or humming hymns while working in the farm) and are also not seldom cited in death notices. Indeed, in eighteenth-century Finland, the Lutheran hymnal was the most widely distributed and read book of all.[70] Thus, the language and imagery of its hymns have made their imprint on the Finnish consciousness. Part of the hymns' central imagery about the nature of human being is the imagery of dress and nakedness. This imagery is an important means to describe and to imagine both God and the mutual relationship between God and humanity.

In the two most recent Finnish Lutheran hymnals—those from 1938 and 1986—the human being's nakedness is a metaphor of helplessness, defenselessness, and poverty, as well as shame. The human subject, having been a spendthrift, now begs not only to be taken to the mercy of the Lord, but also for healing and purification and for a garment of righteousness to cover her fallen and impure state. She is blind, poor, and crippled; and sin has stripped her naked. In front of death, she has been undressed totally—she has been torn both from her clothes and from her earthly dwelling. In this world she is an alien, and at the moment of death she wants something to cover and shelter her alien nakedness: the heavenly/Godly dress.

> I shall undress this earthly house
> I may throw away this sinful dress
> Jesus has brought with Him the bliss
> He covers my nakedness.[71]

When the human subject tries to cover herself by her own means, the result is but a sinful and shameful dress that needs to be stripped off at once. This humanmade dress, which is described as being false and as having transitory beauty,[72] can disappear or drop off without warning, at any moment. As a dress that reveals more than it covers, it emphasizes nakedness even further. The dress or pieces of clothing that the humble human subject begs from her God are to be given to her when she dies in strong faith with Christ. In this way, as in the Epistles of Paul, death with Christ itself becomes a garment:

> I am dead and
> buried with Christ
> I am dressed in the
> delightful garment
> of righteousness.[73]

There are also many other names given to this begged garment. In some hymns, it is the wedding dress, the dress of the bridegroom, the garment of bliss, the garment of mercy, or a sacred garment. In other hymns, the begged habiliment is an armature, a sword, a crown, a special belt, or a traveler's garment that protects and empowers her or him.[74]

God, too, has a garment, for the singer of the hymns imagines the rims of the Godly gown that He uses to shelter her. Jesus (God in human form) has also a special body inside which the human being can desire to be taken. In one hymn, she desires to be let inside His very wounds. Thus, the Godly body is porous or layered—a little like a many-layered cloth—so as to include, hide, and shelter the human at least until she receives the ultimate heavenly shelter:

> Dear Jesus, I beg You to
> hide me in Your wounds
> completely,
> hide me till You will come and
> take me to the bliss of heaven.[75]

God himself is without clothes when in the form of Jesus, who, in the poems of other hymns, is shown naked both at birth and when dying. His humble birth is described through the image of His nakedness—He is so poor that He is without a proper swaddle—and this Godly nakedness is contrasted to His heavenly majesty that is evinced by the statement that even all possible clothes made out of pure gold cannot be a sufficiently valuable dress for Him.[76] The mystery of incarnation thus is expressed by describing the very human nakedness of the newborn God.[77] But this nakedness is not only a sign of the Christian God's humanity, since this very divine nakedness has also a magical potency to dress up the naked souls of humans.[78]

There seems to be a kind of reciprocity between the nakedness of the human subject and the nakedness of God-Jesus. Both are metaphors of human poverty and fragility, but somehow the Godly nakedness at least partly sanctifies and purifies the human (shameful and polluted) nakedness in an act of imitation by incarnation as God decides to become human. But imitation works both ways: the nakedness of the suffering and crucified (incarnated) Jesus becomes a model for the suffering human being (*imitatio Christi*). Stripping naked into the fragile human state is a means for God to receive the human form, while nakedness, for the human, is a means to become close and at least a little bit similar to God.

The human being depicted through the imagery and metaphors of dress and nakedness in Finnish Lutheran hymns is helpless, in shame, and in need of shelter. She has no dress of her own, and she begs both for a dress and for a sheltering dwelling from her God. Only God can give the human this sheltering dwelling as He covers her nakedness with the rim of His own gown. The singer of the hymns also wishes her God to take her inside His suffering body; and, in the end, even death is depicted as a Godly dress. The hymns' Jesus can be described as being undressed by humans and as begging them to give Him clothing. At the same time, however, He is able to cover the nakedness of the humans with His own nakedness. The hymns, by presenting not only human nakedness but also Godly nakedness, construct an image of an arresting and disturbing reciprocity: the human and God can dress or undress each other and can take care of each other's dress and—as the metaphor of dress is unraveled—identity.

(UN)DRESSING RELIGION

Identity is a precarious and vulnerable ontological and social process which cannot easily be captured in definitions. In descriptions of processes like identity, images and metaphors become important devices; and verbal imagery is part of a visual religiosity that works side by side with religion's other aspects, such as linguistic and conceptual ones (as, for example, Morgan and Bynum show). In this essay, I have made an excursion into Christian literature to show important images and metaphors of caring for identity, namely, those of dress and nakedness. And, since identity is not only a thing but also a process, its metaphors and images should be read not only as nouns but also as verbs, as Ricoeur suggests. Processual imagery of dress and nakedness—or of dressing and undressing—is one way of expressing the process of identity in a bodily as well as religious sense, because (un)dressing is a basic, constitutive, and inevitable bodily, social, moral, and imaginary practice and experience in human life. Dress is a boundary mechanism with which we identify and distinguish ourselves. It is our second skin with which we communicate with worlds and others.

Biblical as well as other Christian texts abound with the imagery of dress and nakedness. In this essay, I have been able to treat only a few examples. The Bible, of course, serves as a subtext and cultural reservoir of imagery that affect the rest of Christian literature and language. The Bible, however, does not determine the use of the imagery in other Christian texts, but merely gives the tools and the coordinates to be used imaginatively in subsequent culturally and historically specific texts—even across the Old and New Testaments, episodes and depictions of dressing and undressing differ.[79] Consequently, Bachelard's notion of image has been important for my work: images of identity imagine new and unforeseen variations and possibilities.

In the present essay, I have shown how basically Biblical imagery varies in twentieth-century Finnish Lutheran hymns. In a larger study,[80] I have analyzed also such texts as Bunyan's *Pilgrim's Progress*, Greek Orthodox liturgical texts, and nineteenth-century Finnish Lutheran sermons, in order to detect not only how their imagery of identity very much uses Biblical texts as a reference and resource but also how culturally specific texts twist, repeat differently,[81] and add to Biblical imagery so as to make possible and to emphasize different aspects and interpretations of the process of identity. Sometimes dress is forced upon a human being, and sometimes it is violently torn off, but it can also be given as a gift in an act of care and compassion. Sometimes the right dress is a nostalgic dream (of a golden past) or a deep desire (of future bliss). Nakedness is either a shameful and feared state in which the human being is not in possession of means of living, or a fragile but inevitable transitory state between dresses and identities. In other Christian texts, and in more secular or less Christian texts, nakedness can also bear meanings more directly related to freedom and authenticity, but these meanings have not been my focus in the present essay.

My analysis of the Finnish Lutheran hymns also shows that it is not only the human being whose identity can be expressed metaphorically as a precarious process of dress and undress, but also God. Jesus is sometimes shown naked, and God is depicted through the metonymy of the rim of His gown. On a subsequent level of analysis, it would be possible to focus also on the very notion of God, as well as that of religion, as these ideas are metaphorically implied in the hymnic texts. Their imagery and metaphorics of dress hint at a notion of religion as one means of both protecting and extending (and sometimes also exposing) identity. Very much as dress does.

NOTES

1. Morgan 1998; Morgan 2005.
2. Morgan 2005: 11–13, 46, 71, 124–25.
3. Parland 1991: 18–24.
4. Morgan 2005: 55. See also Anderson 1991.

5. Whitehouse 2000.
6. Morgan 2005: 147–87.
7. Besançon 2000.
8. Morgan 2005: 30–31, 51–52; Whitehouse 2000.
9. See, for example, Cornell 1995; Gatens 1996; Jantzen 1999; and Pouchelle 2004.
10. Bynum 1995.
11. Utriainen 2006b: 206, 218 n. 2. See, for example, Grosz 1994: 40; and Gatens 1996.
12. Bachelard 1994.
13. Bachelard 1994: xv–xxxix, 74–75.
14. Ricoeur 1986: 15–16.
15. See, for instance, Lakoff and Johnson [1980] 2003.
16. Foucault 1988.
17. Giddens 1991.
18. Gen. 1:27–28; 2:21–25; 3:21, 23; Rev. 3:4, 18; 7:14; 16:15 (Authorized [King James] Version).
19. Liepe 2003: 177–90.
20. Utriainen 1999: 157, 164; Utriainen 2004: 134, 133.
21. Davis 1992: 25.
22. Schneider and Weiner 1989: 2–3; Vilkko 1997.
23. The source of this quotation is one of over five hundred texts written by Finnish caregivers of the dying in the first half of the 1990s. This material—produced in the context of a nationwide project, the "Good Death," which was supervised by the Finnish Ministry of Health—was the focus of my doctoral dissertation (Utriainen 1999).
24. Soper 2001; Butler 2006.
25. Soper 2001.
26. Lévinas 2000.
27. See, for example, Horn and Gurel 1981: 17–35; Kaiser 1998: 14–27; Goffman 1966; and Stone 1995.
28. Arthur 1999; Arthur 2000.
29. Siikala 1992: 239–41; Hoppál 2003: 112.
30. Poll 1995: 220; Arthur 1999; Arthur 2000.
31. See, for instance, Hoskins 1989; Crippen and Mulready 2000; and Meisch 2000.
32. Arthur 1999.
33. Hostetler 1995; Hamilton and Hawley 1999; Davies 2001.
34. Barthes 1990; Welters 1999c; Kelly 1999.

35. Gilbertson 1999.
36. Welters 1999b; Mladenovic 1999.
37. Taylor 2001: 58–63.
38. See, for example, Feeley-Harnik 1989 and Darish 1989.
39. Bauman 1989: 145.
40. Utriainen and Honkasalo 1996.
41. Keinänen 2003: 217–18.
42. Williams 1999.
43. Meisch 2000. On the importance of wrapping in Japanese culture, see Hendry 1993.
44. Kaiser 1998: 4.
45. Welters 1999c; Talve 1990: 227.
46. Roach-Higgins and Eicher 1995: 7. See also Arthur 1999: 3.
47. Poll 1995: 220.
48. Entwistle 2001: 48; Welters 1999c.
49. Entwistle 2001: 45; Warwick and Cavallaro 1998; Soper 2001: 24.
50. Soper 2001: 17. See also Entwistle 2001: 33–34 and Hollander 1993: 83–87.
51. See, further, Heelas 1996: 18–20.
52. Taylor 1989: 404.
53. Pultz 1995: 116.
54. Soper 2001. See also Goffman 1961.
55. Soper 2001: 21–24.
56. Utriainen 2006a.
57. See, for example, Smith 1966 and Nellas 1987.
58. Nellas 1987: 86; Soper 2001.
59. Brown 1988: 244–45.
60. Nellas 1987: 51–52, 88.
61. Griffin 1981; Brenner 1997.
62. See also Day 2000.
63. Cannuyer 2000; Uro 2003: 65.
64. Geertz 2000: 93–94.
65. Brown 1988: 315–16.
66. Uro 2003: 74–77; Williams 1989.
67. Unlike Paul, Revelation, the sole apocalyptic text in the New Testament, gloats over the nakedness of the damned—but then, of course, "apocalypse" means ultimate revelation and exposure.
68. Hakala 2000: 115 (translation mine).

69. Laitinen 2002: 84 (translation mine).
70. Väinölä 1995: 17.
71. *Suomen evankelisluterilaisen kirkon virsikirja* 1986, 605:2 (translation mine).
72. *Suomen evankelisluterilaisen kirkon virsikirja* 1938, 241:5.
73. *Suomen evankelisluterilaisen kirkon virsikirja* 1938, 326:5 (translation mine).
74. See, for example, *Suomen evankelisluterilaisen kirkon virsikirja* 1938, 151:5, 582:2, 169:2; and *Suomen evankelisluterilaisen kirkon virsikirja* 1986, 319:3, 318:4.
75. *Suomen evankelisluterilaisen kirkon virsikirja* 1938, 365:4 (translation mine).
76. See, for example, *Suomen evankelisluterilaisen kirkon virsikirja* 1938, 21:6; and *Suomen evankelisluterilaisen kirkon virsikirja* 1986, 51:4.
77. Art historian Leo Steinberg (1996) studies a similar theme in the context of Renaissance painting.
78. *Suomen evankelisluterilaisen kirkon virsikirja* 1938, 22:13; *Suomen evankelisluterilaisen kirkon virsikirja* 1986, 26:5.
79. The Bible is also strongly influenced by literature and language preceding and surrounding it.
80. Utriainen 2006a.
81. See Butler 2006.

REFERENCES

Anderson, Benedict. 1991. *Imagined Communities: Reflections on the Origin and Spread of Nationalism*. Rev. ed. London: Verso.
Arthur, Linda B., ed. 1999. *Religion, Dress and the Body*. Oxford: Berg Publishers.
———, ed. 2000. *Undressing Religion: Commitment and Conversion from a Cross-Cultural Perspective*. Oxford: Berg Publishers.
Bachelard, Gaston. 1994. *The Poetics of Space*. Translated by Maria Jolas. Boston: Beacon Press.
Barthes, Roland. 1990. *The Fashion System*. Translated by Matthew Ward and Richard Howard. Berkeley: University of California Press.
Bauman, Zygmunt. 1989. *Modernity and the Holocaust*. Ithaca: Cornell University Press.

Besançon, Alain. 2000. *The Forbidden Image: An Intellectual History of Icono-clasm*. Translated by Jane Marie Todd. Chicago: University of Chicago Press.

Bible, King James Version. Electronic Text Center, University of Virginia Library. http://etext.lib.virginia.edu/kjv.browse.html.

Brenner, Athalya. 1997. *The Intercourse of Knowledge: On Gendering Desire and 'Sexuality' in the Hebrew Bible*. Leiden: E. J. Brill.

Brown, Peter. 1988. *The Body and Society: Men, Women, and Sexual Renunciation in Early Christianity*. New York: Columbia University Press.

Butler, Judith. 2006. *Gender Trouble: Feminism and the Subversion of Identity*. London: Routledge.

Bynum, Caroline Walker. 1995. *The Resurrection of the Body in Western Christianity, 200–1336*. New York: Columbia University Press.

Cannuyer, Christian. 2000. "Autour du Logion 4 de l'Évangile selon Thomas: L'ancien à l'école du nouveau-né." *Acta Orientalia Belgica* 13: 107–26.

Cornell, Drucilla. 1995. *The Imaginary Domain: Abortion, Pornography & Sexual Harassment*. New York: Routledge.

Crippen, L. Kaye, and Patricia M. Mulready. 2000. "Continuation and Change in Tenganan Pegeringsingan, Bali." In Arthur 2000: 183–200.

Darish, Patricia. 1989. "Dressing for the Next Life: Raffia Textile Production and Use among the Kuba of Zaire." In Weiner and Schneider 1989: 117–40.

Davies, Douglas J. 2001. "*Gestus* Manifests *Habitus*: Dress and the Mormon." In *Dressed to Impress: Looking the Part*, edited by William J. F. Keenan, 123–39. Oxford: Berg Publishers.

Davis, Fred. 1992. *Fashion, Culture, and Identity*. Chicago: University of Chicago Press. Quoted in Entwistle 2001: 47.

Day, Peggy L. 2000. "Adulterous Jerusalem's Imagined Demise: Death of a Metaphor in Ezekiel XVI." *Vetus Testamentum* 50, no. 3: 285–309.

Entwistle, Joanne. 2001. "The Dressed Body." In Entwistle and Wilson 2001: 33–58.

Entwistle, Joanne, and Elizabeth Wilson, eds. 2001. *Body Dressing*. Oxford: Berg Publishers.

Feeley-Harnik, Gillian. 1989. "Cloth and the Creation of Ancestors in Madagascar." In Weiner and Schneider 1989: 73–116.

Foucault, Michel. 1988. *The History of Sexuality, Volume 3: The Care of the Self*. Translated by Robert Hurley. New York: Vintage Books.

Gatens, Moira. 1996. *Imaginary Bodies: Ethics, Power and Corporeality*. New York: Routledge.

Geertz, Clifford. 2000. *The Interpretation of Cultures.* 2nd ed. New York: Basic Books.

Giddens, Anthony. 1991. *Modernity and Self-Identity: Self and Society in the Late Modern Age.* Cambridge: Polity Press.

Gilbertson, Laurann. 1999. "To Ward Off Evil: Metal on Norwegian Folk Dress." In Welters 1999c: 199–210.

Goffman, Erving. 1961. *Asylums: Essays on the Social Situation of Mental Patients and Other Inmates.* Chicago: Aldine Publishing.

———. 1966. *Behavior in Public Places: Notes on the Social Organization of Gatherings.* New York: Free Press.

Griffin, Susan. 1981. *Pornography and Silence: Culture's Revenge Against Nature.* London: Women's Press.

Grosz, Elizabeth. 1994. *Volatile Bodies: Toward a Corporeal Feminism.* Bloomington: Indiana University Press.

Hakala, Laura, ed. 2000. *Siskonmakkarat: Miltä syömishäiriö tuntuu.* Helsinki: Tammi.

Hamilton, Jean A., and Jana Hawley. 1999. "Sacred Dress, Public Worlds: Amish and Mormon Experience and Commitment." In Arthur 1999: 31–51.

Heelas, Paul. 1996. *The New Age Movement: The Celebration of the Self and the Sacralization of Modernity.* Oxford: Blackwell Publishers.

Hendry, Joy. 1993. *Wrapping Culture: Politeness, Presentation, and Power in Japan and Other Societies.* Oxford: Clarendon Press.

Hollander, Anne. 1993. *Seeing through Clothes.* Rev. ed. New York: Avon Books.

Hoppál, Mihály. 2003. *Samaanien maailma.* Jyväskylä, Finland: Atena Kustannus Oy.

Horn, Marilyn J., and Lois M. Gurel. 1981. *The Second Skin: An Interdisciplinary Study of Clothing.* 3rd ed. Boston: Houghton Mifflin Company.

Hoskins, Janet. 1989. "Why Do Ladies Sing the Blues? Indigo Dyeing, Cloth Production, and Gender Symbolism in Kodi." In Weiner and Schneider 1989: 141–73.

Hostetler, John A. 1995. "Dress as a Language of Protest." In Roach-Higgins, Eicher, and Johnson 1995: 221–23.

Jantzen, Grace M. 1999. *Becoming Divine: Towards a Feminist Philosophy of Religion.* Bloomington: Indiana University Press.

Kaiser, Susan B. 1998. *The Social Psychology of Clothing: Symbolic Appearances in Context.* 2nd ed. New York: Fairchild Publications.

Keinänen, Marja-Liisa. 2003. "Creating Bodies: Childbirth Practices in Premodern Karelia." PhD diss., Stockholm University.

Kelly, Mary B. 1999. "Living Textile Traditions of the Carpathians." In Welters 1999c: 155–78.

Laitinen, Merja. 2002. "Insestitilanteen ulottuvuuksia. Pahaa, pahempaa vai pahinta?" In *Pahan kosketus: Ihmisyyden ja auttamistyön varjojen jäljillä*, edited by Merja Laitinen and Johanna Hurtig, 63–85. Jyväskylä, Finland: PS-kustannus.

Lakoff, George, and Mark Johnson. 2003. *Metaphors We Live By*. Chicago: University of Chicago Press, 1980. Reprint, with a new afterword, Chicago: University of Chicago Press.

Lévinas, Emmanuel. 2000. *God, Death, and Time*. Edited by Jacques Rolland and translated by Bettina Bergo. Stanford: Stanford University Press.

Liepe, Lena. 2003. *Den medeltida kroppen: Kroppens och könets ikonografi i nordisk medeltid*. Lund: Nordic Academic Press.

Meisch, Lynn A. 2000. "Christianity, Cloth, and Dress in the Andes." In Arthur 2000: 65–82.

Mladenovic, Vesna. 1999. "Threads of Life: Red Fringes in Macedonian Dress." In Welters 1999c: 97–110.

Morgan, David. 1998. *Visual Piety: A History and Theory of Popular Religious Images*. Berkeley: University of California Press.

———. 2005. *The Sacred Gaze: Religious Visual Culture in Theory and Practice*. Berkeley: University of California Press.

Nellas, Panayiotis. 1987. *Deification in Christ: Orthodox Perspectives on the Nature of the Human Person*. Crestwood, NY: St Vladimir's Seminary Press.

Parland, Oscar. 1991. *The Year of the Bull*. Translated by Joan Tate. London: Peter Owen.

Poll, Solomon. 1995. "The Hasidic Community." In Roach-Higgins, Eicher, and Johnson 1995: 224–35.

Pouchelle, Marie-Christine. 2004. "Postures guerrières de la médecine." Paper presented at the colloque de l'Association Guerre et médecine, Paris.

Pultz, John. 1995. *Photography and the Body*. London: Calmann and King.

Ricoeur, Paul. 1986. *The Rule of Metaphor: Multi-disciplinary Studies of the Creation of Meaning in Language*. Translated by Robert Czerny, Kathleen McLaughlin, and John Costello. London: Routledge & Kegan Paul.

Roach-Higgins, Mary Ellen, and Joanne B. Eicher. 1995. "Dress and Identity." In Roach-Higgins, Eicher, and Johnson 1995: 7–18.

Roach-Higgins, Mary Ellen, Joanne B. Eicher, and Kim K. P. Johnson, eds. 1995. *Dress and Identity*. New York: Fairchild Publications.

Schneider, Jane, and Annette B. Weiner. 1989. Introduction to Weiner and Schneider 1989: 1–29.

Siikala, Anna-Leena. 1992. *Suomalainen šamanismi: Mielikuvien historiaa*. Helsinki: Suomalaisen Kirjallisuuden Seura.

Smith, Jonathan Z. 1966. "The Garments of Shame." *History of Religions* 5, no. 2: 217–38.

Soper, Kate. 2001. "Dress Needs: Reflections on the Clothed Body, Selfhood and Consumption." In Entwistle and Wilson 2001: 13–32.

Steinberg, Leo. 1996. *The Sexuality of Christ in Renaissance Art and in Modern Oblivion*. 2nd ed. Chicago: University of Chicago Press.

Stone, Gregory P. 1995. "Appearance and the Self." In Roach-Higgins, Eicher, and Johnson 1995: 19–39.

Suomen evankelisluterilaisen kirkon virsikirja. 1938. Porvoo, Finland: Werner Söderström Osakeyhtiö.

Suomen evankelisluterilaisen kirkon virsikirja. 1986. Helsinki: SLEY-Kirjat.

Talve, Ilmar. 1990. *Suomen kansankulttuuri*. 3rd ed. Helsinki: Suomalaisen Kirjallisuuden Seura.

Taylor, Charles. 1989. *Sources of the Self: The Making of the Modern Identity*. Cambridge: Cambridge University Press.

Taylor, John H. 2001. *Death and the Afterlife in Ancient Egypt*. Chicago: University of Chicago Press.

Uro, Risto. 2003. *Thomas: Seeking the Historical Context of the Gospel of Thomas*. London: T&T Clark.

Utriainen, Terhi. 1999. *Läsnä, riisuttu, puhdas: Uskontoantropologinen tutkimus naisista kuolevan vierellä*. Helsinki: Suomalaisen Kirjallisuuden Seura.

———. 2004. "Naked and Dressed: Metaphorical Perspective to the Imaginary and Ethical Background of the Deathbed Scene." *Mortality* 9, no. 2: 132–49.

———. 2006a. *Alaston ja Puettu: Ruumiin ja uskonnon ääret*. Tampere, Finland: Osuuskunta Vastapaino.

———. 2006b. "The Modern *Pietà*: Gendered Embodiment and the Religious Imaginary by the Side of the Dying." In *Materializing Religion: Expression, Performance and Ritual*, edited by Elisabeth Arweck and William Keenan, 202–20. Aldershot, UK: Ashgate Publishing.

Utriainen, Terhi, and Marja-Liisa Honkasalo. 1996. "Women Writing Their Death and Dying. Semiotic Perspectives on Women's Suicide Notes." *Semiotica* 109, nos. 3–4: 195–220.

Väinölä, Tauno. 1995. *Vanha virsikirja: Vuoden 1701 suomalainen virsikirja.* Helsinki: Kirjaneliö.

Vilkko, Anni. 1997. *Omaelämäkerta kohtaamispaikkana: Naisen elämän kerronta ja luenta.* Helsinki: Suomalaisen Kirjallisuuden Seura.

Warwick, Alexandra, and Dani Cavallaro. 1998. *Fashioning the Frame: Boundaries, Dress and the Body.* Oxford: Berg Publishers.

Weiner, Annette B., and Jane Schneider, eds. 1989. *Cloth and Human Experience.* Washington: Smithsonian Institution Press.

Welters, Linda. 1999a. "Gilding the Lily: Dress and Women's Reproductive Role in the Greek Village, 1850–1950." In Welters 1999c: 71–96.

———. 1999b. "Introduction: Folk Dress, Supernatural Beliefs, and the Body." In Welters 1999c: 1–12.

———, ed. 1999c. *Folk Dress in Europe and Anatolia: Beliefs about Protection and Fertility.* Oxford: Berg Publishers.

Whitehouse, Harvey. 2000. *Arguments and Icons: Divergent Modes of Religiosity.* Oxford: Oxford University Press.

Williams, Michael A. 1989. "Divine Image—Prison of Flesh: Perceptions of the Body in Ancient Gnosticism." In *Fragments for a History of the Human Body, Part One*, edited by Michel Feher, Ramona Naddaff, and Nadia Tazi, 128–47. New York: Zone Books.

Williams, Patricia. 1999. "Protection from Harm: The Shawl and Cap in Czech and Slovak Wedding, Birthing and Funerary Rites." In Welters 1999c: 135–54.

PART III

Figuring Religious Activities

7

Poetry, Ritual, and Associational Thought in Early India and Elsewhere

LAURIE L. PATTON

> In reality, . . . the contiguity and resemblance of stimuli do not precede the
> constitution of the whole. 'Good form' is not brought about because it would be
> good in itself in some metaphysical heaven; it is good form because it comes into
> being in our experience.
> —Maurice Merleau-Ponty, *Phenomenology of Perception*[1]

THE FRAMEWORK OF METONYMY AND ASSOCIATIONAL THOUGHT

W HAT IS METONYMY, aside from associative thought based on contiguity?
And what is its significance for the study of religion, distinct from the burgeoning studies of metaphor in the same vein? Raymond W. Gibbs Jr. gives
Honoré de Balzac's use of image as a wonderful literary example of a concrete
object or person that stands in for or represents larger objects or domains of
experience. Consider the opening of his novel *Père Goriot*:

> Madame Vauquer is at home in its stuffy air, she can breathe with-
> out being sickened by it. Her face, fresh with the chill freshness of
> the first frosty autumn day, her wrinkled eyes, her expression, vary-
> ing from the conventional set smile of the ballet-dancer to the sour

179

frown of the discounter of bills, her whole person, in short, provides a clue to the boarding-house, just as the boarding-house implies the existence of such a person as she is.

Balzac shows us something about the boarding-house from her face, and the boarding-house in turn implies something about the person she is.[2] Each element is associated and shares features with something else nearby. The person and the boarding-house are in the same conceptual domain and share the same features of stuffiness and convention.

The differences between metonymy and metaphor are crucial to this discussion. Scholars have disagreed with one another, and still do, on the relationship between the two—on whether metonymy is a subset of metaphor, whether they are diametrically opposed, and so on. Many agree, however, that the two can be distinguished in terms of how they make connections between things. In metaphor, two elements from different conceptual domains are related. In metonymy, two elements from the *same* conceptual domain are related.

To take an everyday example, in the sentence "The creampuff was knocked out in the boxing match," the term "creampuff" metaphorically refers to the boxer because he is soft and easy to beat, but the human boxer and the creampuff come from two different domains. In contrast, metonymy connects concepts from the same domain: "We need a new glove to play third base." A "new glove" is the third baseman in a baseball game. Unlike the boxer, who is like the creampuff, the third baseman is not like the glove. The glove that he wears becomes the signifier of his role.[3] Thus, the metonymical relationship of the two different elements here is one of contiguity within the same conceptual domain, whereas the metaphorical relationship of the two elements in the creampuff example is one of similarity between different domains.[4]

Roman Jakobson proposed a theory that similarly distinguishes metaphor and metonymy. After testing aphasic patients, he argued that any linguistic sign can be combined with or substituted for by other linguistic signs. In one kind of aphasia, there is a loss of semantic knowledge, and speakers find something contiguous to it in order to regain meaning—that is, they create metonymies. Other aphasics retain the ability to give synonyms for the words that they cannot find, and thus look instead for terms similar to the words that they have forgotten—that is, they create metaphors.[5]

SOME PROPERTIES OF METONYMY

Framing

While the debate about Jakobson's definitions has since become much more complex,[6] the larger issue for early Indian, or Vedic, thinking is that metonymy is a form of conceptual contiguity, and that such contiguity occurs within a larger framework from which the composer, reader, and reciter of early Indian texts draw. This larger "frame" is usually a cultural one, the content and shape of the frame depending upon our everyday experience and world-knowledge. Beings, things, processes, and actions that generally or ideally occur together are represented in the human mind as a frame.[7] Because frames of reference—those types of "extralinguistic knowledge" that give linguistic knowledge specificity—are so different, many metonyms are hard to translate across cultures. For example, the frame of the metonym "breakfast" for a Southern Baptist might include "toast, butter, ham, eggs, milk, and coffee" but would be different for an observant Brooklyn Heights Jew who did not eat ham, and for a South Indian brahmin who ate spicy vegetables and *masala dosa*.

Merleau-Ponty articulates the inherent existence of framing in human experience in his *Phenomenology of Perception*.[8] In the chapter "'Association' and the 'Projection of Memories,'" he argues with both associationists and psychologists, and asserts that the law of association in its own right cannot be an operative fact of perception without a larger perception of a whole that precedes the perception of similarity. As he writes,

> There are not arbitrary data which set about combining into a thing because *de facto* proximities or likenesses cause them to associate; it is, on the contrary, because we perceive a grouping as a thing that the analytical attitude can then discern likenesses or proximities. This does not mean simply that without any perception of the whole we would not think of *noticing* the resemblance or the contiguity of its elements, but literally that they would not be part of the same world and would not exist at all.

The world that is perceived therefore precedes all associative thought, or in Merleau-Ponty's words, "In reality, . . . the contiguity and resemblance of stimuli do not precede the constitution of the whole. 'Good form' is not brought about because it would be good in itself in some metaphysical heaven; it is good form because it comes into being in our experience."[9] That is to say, the form or shape of resemblance is something that emerges from bodily experience.

In short, the rules of association are governed by a frame—our perception and experience of what constitutes a world. Part of that world is the fact of identification (similarity) with other elements in that world through a set of patterns and conceptions. Thus, a study of mental associations in early India must always carry with it an understanding of indigenous ideas and social principles and of the dynamic relationship between them. The mental associations and the world of action they posit are so integrally connected that, when one of them shifts, the pattern of interaction between them shifts accordingly. To add to the aforementioned everyday Indian example: a child visiting South India for the first time stayed in a seaside hotel and ate *masala dosa* and *sambhar* for breakfast. He commented, "We ate lunch for breakfast everyday in Madras! But only by the beach." His way of coping with the new breakfast was to switch the frame so that the world of breakfast included the world of lunch. But this new world was also defined by his association of it with his hotel by the sea and with no other place: the world of lunch-for-breakfast was in strict contiguity to the place in which he consumed it.

PRAGMATISM

As such, the frames that are activated in any given metonymy have a "pragmatic" function—that is, they are defined by usage and not by concept. The presence of this pragmatism explains why literal language is not the prevailing language for communication. For instance, in the aforementioned baseball example, one might say "the third baseman" instead of the "glove," but the point of the communication is that someone good with a glove, at catching and throwing, is optimally needed. Thus philosophical anthropologists Dan Sperber and Deirdre Wilson's "principle of relevance": "Every act of ostensive communication communicates a presumption of its own optimal relevance."[10] One might say a communication is optimally relevant if it produces maximal contextual effects with a minimum of processing effort. Klaus-Uwe Panther and Günter Radden give an example of this through a conversation between two nurses: "It's time for my gall bladder's medication" versus "It's time for Randolph's medication."[11] In the particular pragmatic context of the hospital, the gall bladder designation is the most effective means of identifying a patient—not his name, his education, his looks, and so forth. (The nurses would not have been communicating efficiently if they had said, "It's time for the PhD in economics who lives on Spruce Lane's medication.") Outside the hospital context, of course, this form of pragmatic communication is neither efficient nor appropriate—but it is intensely efficient and appropriate within that context.

Referentiality

Contributing to metonyms' "maximal efficiency" in pragmatic contexts are the referential capacities operating within metonymies, capacities on which many linguists prefer to focus. As linguist Beatrice Warren puts it, the two elements of a metonymy tend to refer to each other because they are based on relations that presuppose actual coincidence and thus—as mentioned earlier—contiguity within the same conceptual domain.[12]

While there are many kinds of referential metonymies, they each generally involve two nominal expressions—one of which being the modifier and the other, the head and referring item—that are implicitly linked. Let us take one simple example: "The silver is in the drawer" is a common metonymy, "silver" here meaning "that cutlery which consists of silver." The implicit head and referring item is "that cutlery which," its modifier is "silver," and the implicit link between them is "consists of." A similarly implicit relationship occurs within the sentence "It is time for the gall bladder's medication," where "gall bladder" means "the man who has an ailment in his gall bladder," because of the implicit link ("has an ailment in") between the head ("the man who") and its modifier ("his gall bladder"). Thus referential metonymy is a kind of abbreviation having potentials as a naming and/or rhetorical device that focuses on one particular quality of a thing.[13] As I will describe further on, metonymies are prevalent in the nominal compounds that we find in Sanskrit in general, and particularly in Vedic ritual texts—in epithets for deities, as well as in many other instances.

Prototypicality

The question of selectivity in referential metonymies is related to our understanding of metonymy "as a particular type of mental mapping . . . whereby we conceive of an entire person, object, or event by understanding a salient part of a person, object or event."[14] This question of the salient part (i.e., the salient part of Randolph is his gall bladder) is relevant to our purposes, for it raises the issue of the "prototype effect." Such an effect has been observed by cognitive psychologists in studies "demonstrat[ing] that participants judge certain members of categories to be more representative of those categories than other members."[15] For example, the subcategory "robin" is more representative of the category "bird" than is "chicken," "ostrich," or "penguin." Likewise, the subcategory "desk chair" is more representative of the category "chair" than is "beanbag chair," "barber chair," or "electric chair."[16] And "housewife mother" is more representative of "mother" than is any other kind of mother.[17] Thus the salient subcategory actually reveals a basic structure of social thought: "working mother" and "adoptive mother," among others, cannot stand in for the whole category of "mother," whereas "housewife mother" can. "Working mother" and "adoptive mother" deviate from the prototypical "housewife mother" stereotype.[18]

Prototypical metonymical thinking has a number of social consequences. As is obvious in the aforementioned case of "mother," there are clearly principles behind the selectivity of associational thought such that one subcategory becomes more prototypical than another (indeed, Vedic ritual ideas also are thus selectively constructed). It is, in fact, this selectivity that has led literary theorist Wai Chee Dimock to call metonymy that form of literary composition which is most open to social manipulation. In her example of early-twentieth-century London and the propaganda of Britain at the time, the strength, robustness, and good cheer of the working-class woman is used to represent the entirety of British society.[19] To choose those qualities of the working-class woman, however, is to tell only a small part of her story; her use and abuse in the vicissitudes of everyday working life are not represented, nor is the social system in which she must operate. The power, as well as the problem, of prototypical metonymical thinking is that it is fundamentally a partial truth that, through its intensity and repeated use, can become representative of the whole truth.

IDENTIFICATION

The selectivity in metonymy can also create an identification between the agent and the act or between the agent and the instrument of the act.[20] In thinking about this phenomenon, one linguist, Brigitte Nerlich, began observing her son construct what she called "creative metonymies." She writes,

> Matthew started school in January. At first we thought he might eat the school dinners. But he didn't like them and insisted on bringing his own lunch box like most of his friends do. So in the end we relented and, walking to school in the morning, he brandished his lunch box saying to everybody he met: "I love being a **lunch box**." Then he thought a bit and said: "I love being a sandwich, I really like being a **sandwich**"—one could really see the metonymical chain extend from his arm through the lunch box to the sandwich and back. What he meant by this metonymical utterance was that he liked to be part of the children who were allowed to bring a lunch box (i.e., a sandwich) to school and were not forced to have this horrible stuff like potatoes and veg served at the school dinner![21]

There is a kind of identification between the actor and the instrument—in this case, the boy and his sandwich—that creates that particular metonymical reality.

Even early on, Jakobson observed that this kind of identification between actor and object also works in realist fiction. As in the aforementioned example of Balzac's *Père Goriot*, the realist author "[f]ollow[s] the path of contiguous relationships, . . . metonymically digress[ing] from the plot to the atmosphere and from the characters to the setting in space and time."[22] The metonymies thus belong to both description and narration, being based on the contiguity of things and people and the contiguity of events. In fiction, objects can serve as elements of description and motivators of narrative action. The device that Toni Morrison uses as such in *Song of Solomon* is an earring. Indeed, jewelry—associated as it is with social and personal identity and with power and status—is seen in many cultures as a metonymical means to identify a person, as "a means of identifying the whole by an outward part."[23]

But there is even more to the role of metonymy in realist narrative. Michael Rifaterre has argued that it is repetition and embeddedness that make a metonym effective.[24] There must be a prolonged sequence, dispersed throughout the narrative and weaving in and out of it, forming part of the referential frame of the text. The earring in *Song of Solomon*, for example, is a metonym that is constantly recontextualized; repetition thus allows it to move from its immediate context to the whole textual structure. Acting as the kind of frame discussed earlier, the fictional world must have its own consistency or truth and is understood by the assumed reader in terms of a real experienced world and a rich personal encyclopedia of knowledge and beliefs.[25]

METONYMY AND RITUAL: PERFORMANCE STUDIES

All of metonymy's properties explored so far in narrative are keenly present in ritual as well. Here, performance studies can contribute a great deal to our understanding of this phenomenon, building as it does on the essential interaction between text and context, between the creativity of individual performers and the interpretations offered by their observers.

First, ritual involves a highly specific contextualized world or "frame," which is as or even more specific than the gall bladder ward in the hospital. This framing is what Dennis Tedlock and many other performance theorists are trying to get at when they speak of an oral poetics[26]—the fullness of context in which every ritual is carried out. For Tedlock, ritual "is not the imperfect realization of a playwright's lofty intentions by lowly actors, nor is it an incomplete obedience to the rules set forth in an imaginary mental handbook of the poetic art. Instead, performance is constitutive of verbal art" in which the actors use every part of their context to create effective performances.[27] Ritual is its own frame or world, with a wealth of possible and actual metonymies present at any given moment. As Charles L. Briggs puts it, "[T]he emergence of contextual and performance-based approaches is crucial, since they point to the status of contextual elements as central elements of the performance, not just external conditions."[28]

Performance studies has suggested that metonymical expression, because of its highly contextualized nature, is more the norm in ritual situations than is nonmetonymical expression. Ritual is a created world governed by roles and instruments; hence the higher likelihood of actors to use pragmatic forms of communication and metonymically to refer to and identify with those roles and instruments. While others have examined the religious aspects of performance in contexts similar to the highly structured world of early Indian ritual,[29] Briggs's work on the Easter liturgy in a Mexican/Texan town comes closest to the kind of analysis that I am attempting here. Briggs makes a study of the set texts of hymns and prayers in the Easter liturgy and of their relationship to the actors' liturgical gestures and movements during Holy Week. As an interpretation of a "formal" performative context, the liturgy is analogous to mantras and the ritual directions about their usage in the Śrauta and Gṛhya texts—early Indian works dealing respectively with public and domestic sacrificial rules of the usage of poetic verses in ritual. While space does not permit an intensely detailed analysis, it is worth pausing to show how Briggs's treatment of this Easter liturgy indicates all of the metonymical properties outlined earlier.

First, he outlines the kind of pragmatic selectivity present in the Holy Week performance, whereby participants "select elements of the ongoing linguistic, social, cultural, political, historical, and natural environment and . . . accord them a meaning and role within the performance."[30] Thus, the rigidly set texts of Holy Week are modified creatively by all these selected elements in metonymical association.

Second, Briggs argues that the "referential content" of the texts and holy images focuses the worshipers' attention on the events of Holy Week and their transformative properties. He notes that there is a kind of mutual referentiality between the images of the Holy Week liturgy and the words of the liturgy. Because the words of the liturgy are said to have been handed down from Christ, there is a kind of eternal quality to them. Thus, when the words refer to the images (those painted by the liturgical actors on the church walls, those created by the actors in costumed procession), they also are confirming the images' eternal status. The images then refer back to and confirm the words.[31]

So too Briggs argues that the words of Holy Week liturgies effect an identification between the actors and their referents—the characters in the Passion of Christ. As such, the words are transformative in nature, and their meaning matters. Briggs writes, "[T]he mere locution of a particular set of illocutionary formulae is seen as utterly useless. To be successful in achieving symbolic unification with Christ and the Virgin, a worshiper must be fully engaged, physically, cognitively and emotionally, in the rituals."[32]

Relatedly, there is a prototype effect in which certain characters are better examples of the category "human" than are others. The crucial element is that the worshiper experience his own words, actions, and emotions as "matching" those of Christ and of the Virgin to such an extent that unification is achieved. Thus, the Virgin and Christ are the prototypes of humanness, and the worshiper's task is to place him- or herself in metonymical juxtaposition with them, to "match" them.

While Briggs gives us an exhaustive account of the relationship between a fixed-text ritual and its context, we can also work with more mundane examples. Let us take two familiar statements from Jewish and Christian rituals: in a Jewish synagogue, from the rabbi to the congregation: "Would the Bar Mitzvah please come to the podium?"; and in an Anglo-Catholic church, from one worshiper to another: "The crucifix is slow today!" These two statements contain all of the metonymical properties that were discussed in Briggs's treatment. First, both are highly pragmatic forms of conversation. One doesn't need other information about the person having the Bar Mitzvah (he's nervous, he lives nearby) or the crucifix (he's late, he overslept) to communicate the basic idea. So too both statements involve mutual referentiality: the crucifer and the moving crucifix imply each other; the Bar Mitzvah is the person who has the Bar Mitzvah. Moreover, these two metonymies also involve identification of the actor with the instrument of causation: the Bar Mitzvah must identify with the Bar Mitzvah process or else he wouldn't get through the ceremony; likewise, the crucifer must identify with his role or else he wouldn't get through the procession. Finally, the prototype effect is also in force: the crucifer is the best example of a Christian worshiper that day; the Bar Mitzvah is the best example of a mensch that day. (Bar Mitzvah, of course, originally referred to the person and then to the ceremony, so there is a double metonymy at work here in both directions.)

Thus, we can see from these everyday examples that it is not so far, linguistically speaking, from "Mommy, I love being a sandwich" to the Eucharist's "I am the bread of life" or "Take, eat, this is my body, which is given for you." And, to take this somewhat humorous and blasphemous comparison one step further, repetition is key to ritual as well as metonymical effectiveness in fiction. The metonymical construction of person and bread was and is repeated several times throughout the Christian liturgy (perhaps more intentionally than Matthew repeated his self/sandwich metonymy). The effectiveness in ritual of the person/bread metonymy is therefore somewhat similar to that of the earring in *Song of Solomon*: it becomes its own subtext, its own set of referential meanings.

EARLY INDIAN RITUAL METONYMY

Given the sense of metonymy in ritual explained previously, how are Vedic ideas constructed by metonymy by virtue of being ritually associated with canon—linked with sacred words through their actions? Comparison through contiguity is perhaps one of the basic modes of thought in Vedic ritual, particularly in the Sūtra (comprising aphorisms) and Vidhāna (concerning the use of mantras) material that I will discuss here.

Vedic ritual is similar to other rituals in that it is the manipulation of sacrificial objects, texts, and persons. These manipulations in their own right can be read as a myriad of metonymies—ways in which "the concrete depiction of some object or person stands for or represents larger objects or domains of experience."[33] The presence of such metonymies does not mean that every ritual movement is "symbolic of" something. Rather, concrete objects or actors connect in ritual with a domain of associations or worlds that are known to the ritual actors.

Let us take a concrete example from a documentary film about a Vedic ritual: Frits Staal's *Altar of Fire*, used in classrooms all over America, Europe, and India.[34] At one point in the proceedings, the filmmaker asks one of the priests why a particular mantra about being reborn is being recited. The priest says that in sacrificing the sacrificer is undergoing a rebirth and is using the language of Indra in the mantra to "stand in" for Indra as he is being reborn. In Warren's view, "Mary is Cinderella in the play" is a metonymy that implies that Mary is playing the role of Cinderella in the play. So too the sacrificer is "standing in" for Indra and for the entire set of associations with Indra at the moment of the mantra's recitation. (I will refrain from doing more than simply remarking on the irony that this lovely interpretive statement by a brahmin actor in the ritual comes in the middle of a film made by a scholar who has argued that brahmin ritual actors do not semantically interpret their rituals.) In the priest's own interpretation, there is a mutual reference between the sacrificer's words and ritual act: just as the mantra to Indra itself describes the act of being reborn, so too does the ritual act of the sacrificer uttering the mantra.

We find metonymical thought—association through contiguity and context—to be the basis for the composition of Sūtras themselves, both Śrauta (or public ritual texts) and Gṛhya (or domestic ritual texts). As Indologist Jan Gonda rather wryly remarks, "The *śrautasūtras* deal with the intricate and elaborate ritual sacrifices in a concise language which, while vigorous in brevity and exactness, leaves much to be tacitly understood."[35] In one Vedic ritual school, for instance, there is a complex technique of recitation called the *hautra mantra*, which involves many multileveled rules that are in fact only implied by ritual context.

Moreover, the specific qualities of metonymical thinking (framing, pragmatism, referentiality, prototypicality, and identification) are prevalent in colorful ways in Vedic ritual. First, the frame of Vedic ritual is all-important, as it is in metonymical thinking. Staal has written eloquently of ritual procedures that become the "frames" of or "embed" other rituals.[36] This mode allows for an elaborate set of possibilities for ritual substitution. Such is also the case with mantra usage. In Staal's view, one can trace this embeddedness from prototype to ectype with almost mathematical precision. Thus, the Soma sacrifice—when it is the frame of one particular offering, or *iṣṭi*—creates a whole different set of metonymical associations for that offering than does the *aśvamedha*, or horse sacrifice, when it is the frame of that offering.

We can deduce the role of the frame in Vedic ritual from the fact that in many different Śrauta manuals, the actor—literally, the subject of the sentence—is entirely omitted. For example, *Baudhāyana Śrauta Sūtra* 1.2.7 simply reads, "He undertakes the vow; he sets out [to gather] a twig." "He" in the first sentence means the sacrificer, but "he" in the second sentence means the *adhvaryu*—a completely different person in the ritual. One would know this fact only from an assumed ritual frame. The power of context can also be seen in the frequent omission of the names of deities. To take another example from our Āśvalāyana *śākhā*, a particular Vedic school, its manual (*Āśvalāyana Śrauta Sūtra* 2.1.22) states, "Everywhere on the arrival of a deity there is absence [of the names] of the regular [gods, mentioned in the model sacrifices]." That is to say, the model sacrifices provide the prototype and therefore supply the context in which the names of deities are to be remembered.

Second, ritual pragmatism is prevalent in elegant Vedic economies of expression in the Sūtras. In fact, "[n]umerous [ritual] expressions . . . attest not only to a thorough familiarity with various techniques but also to a considerable proficiency in expressing complicated processes with great precision by means of technical terms—e.g. [one verb in the] BŚS. [the *Baudhāyana Śrauta Sūtra*] 3, 5: 73, 10 *abhidyotayati* [conveys the phrase] 'he illuminates the offering by means of an ignited blade of straw.'"[37] This shortened language indicates an assumed set of ritual actions. Here again, compare the contemporary metonymical response to the question "How did you get here?": "I hailed a taxi." The simple verb "hail" means "to stop," but in its metonymical use means: "to stop, to get in, to give the cab driver directions, and to drive to the destination."[38] We are often unaware of how many complex actions are implied and assumed by the use of a single verb, which in its simplest meaning has a single referent.

Third, referential qualities of metonymies are also basic to the structure of Vedic rituals. Remember that in referential metonymy a referent that is explicitly mentioned is implicitly linked to a referent that is implied.[39] This type of metonymy is well known as a basic linguistic concept in the construction of compounds even in early Sanskrit: the *bahuvrīhi*. *Bahuvrīhi* (literally, "much rice") most commonly means "a man who possesses much rice." And, when the reader is parsing compounds, she proceeds exactly the way in which Warren would analyze "redhead" as "a person who possesses a head of red hair." Here, "a person," the implicit referring item, is connected through the implicit relationship of possession to its explicit modifier "redhead." Of course, the analysis of a *bahuvrīhi*, or Sanskrit referential metonym, may become more complicated than Warren anticipated,[40] involving not just one grammatical relationship between the modifier in such a compound and its referring item but several.

There is an unwavering commitment to *bahuvrīhi* compounds in Vedic ritual. Let us take, for example, the epithets for deities that are used in almost any mantra. These *bahuvrīhi* compounds usually connote the essential activity and attributes of any given deity. For instance, the term *jātavedas* is not just "knowledge of creatures" but also "that being who has knowledge of creatures," and is usually applied to Agni (the deity of fire). Similarly, the term *mahāyoni* means not just "great womb" but "one who has been produced by copulation" (i.e., "one for whom there was a great womb"). So too *mahāvrata*, the term for the winter-solstice festival, is rich with metonymical meanings. Most simply *mahāvrata* signifies a "great vow" but also means a particular verse recited at the end of the yearlong *gavāmayana* ceremony that follows the rays of the sun. *Mahāvrata*, in a metonymical spree, also can mean the final *gavāmayana* day itself of the *mahāvrata* ritual, or any of this day's ceremonies or ritual rules. We can also see this referential metonymy in the names of ritual objects. In a more political vein, *gataśrī* has as its literal meaning "gone glory" but also can mean "one who has obtained glory or wealth"—one who is a victorious king, a learned brahmin, or a *vaiśya* (commoner) who is the leading figure of his village.[41]

There are myriad examples of such referential metonyms. Indeed, the *Nirukta*, an etymological dictionary dating from the fifth century BCE, can be said to be made up entirely of such metonyms. And, as states a famous later text, *The Laws of Manu* (which was composed roughly between 100 BCE and 100 CE), "no sacrificial rite can be performed without an etymologist."[42] Thus we can infer the centrality of referential metonyms in early Indian thought and practice.

Fourth, prototypicality is one of the main properties of Vedic ritual metonymy, a crucial organizing principle of the Vedic ritual texts, as Staal and many others have observed. The contents of most of the Śrauta Sūtras are arranged systematically, with "prototypes" (*prakṛtayaḥ*) of the sacrificial ceremonies being described first. They are followed by topics or ectypes (*vikṛtayaḥ*) that require separate treatment but still can occur in a condensed form because they follow the basic pattern of the prototypes.[43] Hence Rosch's notion of prototype—that some members of a category are more representative than others—definitely applies here. The basic *agniṣṭoma* rituals, for instance, are the prototypes and members of the category of Soma sacrifice that are most representative of that category. This prototypical mode of thought was an explicit organizing principle for the entire corpus of ritual Sūtras.

In another example, again in the Āśvalāyana school, there are formulaic expressions to inform the student that the preceding rite is a prototype. *Āśvalāyana Śrauta Sūtra* 2.1.1 states the rule: *paurṇamāseneṣṭipaśusomā upadiṣṭāḥ*—"by the sacrifice of the full moon the *iṣṭis* (rituals involving vegetable offerings) and animal and Soma sacrifices are taught." According to this text, the full-moon sacrifice is the prototype, and the other sacrifices are the variants.

We also see prototypes of the deities themselves in the recitation of mantras referring to the deities themselves. A sacrificer says, "I lift this grass with the arms of Indra," or in the aforementioned example of the Staal film *Altar of Fire* the sacrificer is "standing in" for Indra in reciting the mantra about rebirth. This act is a metonymical reference to a prototype: the category of Indra is the most representative of all those who are reborn, of all those who lift purifying *darbha* grass. One is reminded of the movie *Castaway*, where the central character stands by his newly built fire on the deserted island and shouts, beating his breast, "Fire! I have built FIRE!" There, by his actions and his tone of voice, he is metonymically extending himself to the prototypical "first man" who discovered fire.

Finally, the ritual literature is also filled with the kind of efficacious repetition that makes a successful use of metonym in literature. While the contemporary reader may not find in the Sūtra literature an image with the same compelling force as Pilate's earring in *Song of Solomon*, the very embeddedness of ritual procedures and ritual mantras requires a high degree of repetition. As a means of instruction to the sacrificer, this constant repetition is one way of helping him to become familiar with the ritual material. In my observations of contemporary Vedic sacrifices, I often heard laughter at the moments when the Śrauta Sūtras were consulted, only to be told that a particular procedure had "already been explained [*vyākhyātam*]." The Śrauta Sūtras are filled with abbreviations that indicate cross-referencing, precisely in order to finesse repetition. For example, the *Āśvalāyana Śrauta Sūtra* cautions the ritualists that a repetition is coming with the term *uktam*, as in *uktam agnipranayanam*—"the bringing forth of the fire has already been mentioned," or the phrase *siddham iṣṭiḥ saṃtiṣṭhate*—"the sacrifice is completed in the established way." In fact, we might argue that, unlike Pilate's earring, these explicit references to repetition make the metonymies quite obvious. But the Vedic ritual repetitions do, in fact, carry with them a whole set of assumptions and worldviews every time they are used. My favorite: *śeṣam pūrvavat*—"the rest is as before." I understood the powerful metonymical properties of this phrase in the howls of frustrated laughter in contemporary Vedic revivals when someone encountered "*śeṣam pūrvavat*" and realized that this meant that an entire complex ritual procedure had to be repeated.

CONCLUSIONS

Ritual actors would say they were up to something other than "magic" in their utterance of mantras. Certainly the exclusive use of the term "magic" can lead us conceptually astray in many ways in our thinking about early Indian ritual. Instead, we might argue that, in many of its various properties (framing, pragmatism, referentiality, prototypicality, and identification), the Vedic ritual world is informed by metonymical thinking. In effect, through the lens of metonymy, a model of magic in early India may be reenvisioned as a model of performance, wherein ritual actors make imaginative linkages between poetic image and gesture. Vedic texts show different uses of resemblance for different exegetical purposes. Viewed thus as a set of hermeneutical acts, the intellectual operations involved in the ritual use of mantras become interesting in their own right, not simply as instances of magical thought.

What is more, such a view of ritual manuals also implies that brahmins participating in the rituals are self-conscious, reflective actors. As the brahmins of the Śrauta, Gṛhya, and Vidhāna texts seem to know quite well, making resemblances between mantras and their environment, between canon and context, entails making claims about the nature, function, and privilege of canonical texts (both oral and written), their authors, and their physical worlds. In performing this study of ritual uses of metonymy mainly in early India, I hope that my micrological concerns can be of some use to scholars of religion in addition to serving as the basis upon which to theorize the dynamics of other ritual and poetic traditions that may have analogous forms of imagistic connections between word and world.

NOTES

I am grateful to Jonathan Z. Smith, Paul Griffiths, Brannon Wheeler, Joseph Wawrykow, Benjamin Ray, Bruce Chilton, and Charles Hallisey for their comments on earlier drafts of this essay, which was presented originally at the panel "Commentarial Acts" at the annual meeting of the American Academy of Religion in November 1994, was published subsequently in my book *Bringing the Gods to Mind* (Patton 2005: 38, 45–58), and is reprinted here in an emended form with the permission of the University of California Press.

1. Merleau-Ponty 1962: 16.
2. Balzac 1951: 33; Gibbs 1999: 61.
3. Gibbs 1999: 62–63.
4. Brown [1927] 1966: 149–50.
5. Jakobson 1971: 83–84, 86, 90.
6. Since Jakobson began writing about metaphor and metonymy, his twofold schema has been much elaborated or criticized: it is said that it is too simplistic and that it is difficult to make hard and fast distinctions between the two categories in many instances (see Happ 1985 and 1993 and Blank 1999). Effective metaphors can be based in part on syntagmatic contiguity, and effective metonyms can be based in part on paradigmatic similarity. Sylvia Plath's line "How long can my hands be a bandage to this hurt?" is a perfect example of how metaphor and metonymy can be linked: in fact, hurt hands can be syntagmatically contiguous to the bandage (metonymy) and at the same time can be paradigmatically compared to the bandage, which occupies a conceptual realm other than that of body parts (metaphor).
7. Blank 1999: 173.
8. Merleau-Ponty 1962. See also Bergson 2002.
9. Merleau-Ponty 1962: 16.
10. Sperber and Wilson 1995: 158.
11. Panther and Radden 1999: 12.
12. Warren 1999: 130–31.
13. Warren 1999: 123, 124.
14. Gibbs 1999: 66.
15. Gibbs 1999: 66.
16. Heider 1971; Rosch et al. 1976: 432, 434. For further discussion of Rosch's research on prototypicality, see Lakoff 1973: 458–61 and Lakoff 1987: 39–45.
17. Lakoff 1987: 79–82.

18. Gibbs 1999: 66.
19. Dimock 1994: 87–91.
20. Nerlich, Clarke, and Todd 1999: 363.
21. Nerlich, Clarke, and Todd 1999: 370.
22. Jakobson 1971: 92; Pankhurst 1999: 386.
23. Pankhurst 1999: 387. See also Norrick 1981: 96–97.
24. Rifaterre 1990: 21.
25. Langacker 1987: 388.
26. Tedlock 1983. See also Tedlock and Mannheim 1995.
27. Tedlock 1983: 17.
28. Briggs 1988: 372.
29. Tedlock 1983; Gill 1987; Grimes 1990, 1995, and 2000; Laderman 1991; Driver 1993; Nájera-Ramírez 1997; Mudimbe 1997; Spiziri 1997.
30. Briggs 1988: 359.
31. Briggs 1988: 327.
32. Briggs 1988: 337.
33. Gibbs 1999: 61.
34. Gardner and Staal 1977.
35. Gonda 1977: 629.
36. Staal 1989.
37. Gonda 1977: 635.
38. Gibbs 1999: 66.
39. Warren 1999: 123.
40. Warren 1999: 131.
41. *Katyāyana Śrauta Sūtra* 4.13.5; *Śatapatha Brāhmaṇa* 1.3.5.12.
42. *Manu-Smṛti* 2.5.
43. Gonda 1977: 630.

REFERENCES

The Āśvalāyana Śrauta Sūtra, with the Commentary Anāvilā of Haradattāchārya. 1923. Edited by T. Ganapati Sastri. Trivandrum: Government Press.

Balzac, Honoré de. 1951. *Père Goriot.* Translated by Marion Ayton Crawford. Harmondsworth, UK: Penguin Books. Quoted in Gibbs 1999: 61.

The Baudhāyana Śrauta Sūtra Belonging to the Taittirīya Saṃhitā. 1982. Edited by W. Caland. 2nd ed. 3 vols. New Delhi: Munshiram Manoharlal.

Bergson, Henri. 2002. "Images and Bodies." In *Henri Bergson: Key Writings*, edited by Keith Ansell Pearson and John Mullarkey, 86–124. New York: Continuum.

Blank, Andreas. 1999. "Co-presence and Succession." In Panther and Radden 1999: 169–92.

Briggs, Charles L. 1988. *Competence in Performance: The Creativity of Tradition in Mexicano Verbal Art*. Philadelphia: University of Pennsylvania Press.

Brown, Stephen J. 1966. *The World of Imagery: Metaphor and Kindred Imagery*. London: Routledge & Kegan Paul, 1927. Reprint, New York: Russell & Russell.

Dimock, Wai Chee. 1994. "Class, Gender, and the History of Metonymy." In *Rethinking Class: Literary Studies and Social Formations*, edited by Wai Chee Dimock and Michael T. Gilmore. New York: Columbia University Press.

Driver, Tom Faw. 1993. *Life in Performance: Reflections on Ritual, Religion, and Social Value*. Washington: Society for Values in Higher Education.

Gardner, Robert, and Frits Staal. 1977. *Altar of Fire*. VHS. Berkeley: University of California Extension Media Center.

Gibbs, Raymond W., Jr. 1999. "Speaking and Thinking with Metonymy." In Panther and Radden 1999: 61–77.

Gill, Sam D. 1987. *Native American Religious Action: A Performance Approach to Religion*. Columbia: University of South Carolina Press.

Gonda, Jan. 1977. *The Ritual Sūtras*. Vol. 1, fasc. 2 of *A History of Indian Literature*, edited by Jan Gonda. Wiesbaden, Germany: Otto Harrassowitz.

Grimes, Ronald L. 1990. *Ritual Criticism: Case Studies in Its Practice, Essays on Its Theory*. Columbia: University of South Carolina Press.

———. 1995. *Beginnings in Ritual Studies*. Rev. ed. Columbia: University of South Carolina Press.

———. 2000. *Deeply into the Bone: Re-inventing Rites of Passage*. Berkeley: University of California Press.

Happ, Heinz. 1985. *'Paradigmatisch'—'syntagmatisch': Zur Bestimmung und Klärung zweier Grundbegriffe der Sprachwissenschaft*. Heidelberg: C. Winter.

———. 1993. "Polysemie und semantische Relationen im Lexikon." In *Wortschatz und Fremdsprachenerwerb*, edited by Klaus Vogel and Wolfgang Börner, 22–56. Bochum: AKS-Verlag.

Heider, Eleanor Rosch. 1971. "On the Internal Structure of Perceptual and Semantic Categories." Unpublished paper, Department of Psychology, University of California, Berkeley.

Jakobson, Roman. 1971. "Two Aspects of Language and Two Types of Aphasic Disturbances." In Roman Jakobson and Morris Halle, *Fundamentals of Language*, 67–96. 2nd ed. The Hague: Mouton.

Katyāyana Śrauta Sūtra. 1972. Edited by Albrecht Weber. Reprint, Varanasi: Chowkhamba Sanskrit Series Office.

Laderman, Carol. 1991. *Taming the Wind of Desire: Psychology, Medicine, and Aesthetics in Malay Shamanistic Practice*. Berkeley: University of California Press.

Lakoff, George. 1973. "Hedges: A Study in Meaning Criteria and the Logic of Fuzzy Concepts." *Journal of Philosophical Logic* 2, no. 4: 458–508.

———. 1987. *Women, Fire, and Dangerous Things: What Categories Reveal about the Mind*. Chicago: University of Chicago Press.

Langacker, Ronald W. 1987. *Theoretical Prerequisites*. Vol. 1 of *Foundations of Cognitive Grammar*. Stanford: Stanford University Press.

Manu-Smṛti, with Nine Commentaries by Medhātithi, Sarvajñanārāyaṇa, Kullūka, Rāghavānanda, Nandana, Rāmacandra, Maṇirāma, Govindarāja and Bhāruci. 1972–1982. Edited by Jayantakrishna Harikrishna Dave. 5 vols. Bombay: Bharatiya Vidya Bhavan.

Merleau-Ponty, M. 1962. *Phenomenology of Perception*. Translated by Colin Smith. New York: Humanities Press.

Mudimbe, V. Y. 1997. *Tales of Faith: Religion as Political Performance in Central Africa*. Atlantic Highlands, NJ: Athlone Press.

Nájera-Ramírez, Olga. 1997. *La Fiesta de los Tastoanes: Critical Encounters in Mexican Festival Performance*. Albuquerque: University of New Mexico Press.

Nerlich, Brigitte, David D. Clarke, and Zazie Todd. "Mommy, I Like Being a Sandwich." In Panther and Radden 1999: 361–85.

Norrick, Neal R. 1981. *Semiotic Principles in Semantic Theory*. Amsterdam: John Benjamins Publishing Company.

Pankhurst, Anne. 1999. "Recontextualization of Metonymy in Narrative and the Case of Morrison's *Song of Solomon*." In Panther and Radden 1999: 385–400.

Panther, Klaus-Uwe, and Günter Radden, eds. 1999. *Metonymy in Language and Thought*. Amsterdam: John Benjamins Publishing Company.

Patton, Laurie L. 2005. *Bringing the Gods to Mind: Mantra and Ritual in Early Indian Sacrifice*. Berkeley: University of California Press.

Rifaterre, Michael. 1990. *Fictional Truth*. Baltimore: Johns Hopkins University Press.

Rosch, Eleanor, Carolyn B. Mervis, Wayne D. Gray, David M. Johnson, and Penny Boyes-Braem. 1976. "Basic Objects in Natural Categories." *Cognitive Psychology* 8, no. 3: 382–439.

Śatapatha Brāhmaṇa. 1940. 5 vols. Bombay: Laxmi Venkateshwar Steam Press.

Sperber, Dan, and Deirdre Wilson. 1995. *Relevance: Communication and Cognition*. 2nd ed. Oxford: Basil Blackwell.

Spiziri, Frank S. 1997. *A Cobbler's Universe: Religion, Poetry, and Performance in the Life of a South Italian Immigrant*. Edited and translated by Catherine L. Albanese. New York: Continuum.

Staal, Frits. 1989. *Rules without Meaning: Ritual, Mantras and the Human Sciences*. New York: Peter Lang Publishing.

Tedlock, Dennis. 1983. *The Spoken Word and the Work of Interpretation*. Philadelphia: University of Pennsylvania Press.

Tedlock, Dennis, and Bruce Mannheim, eds. 1995. *The Dialogic Emergence of Culture*. Urbana: University of Illinois Press.

Warren, Beatrice. 1999. "Aspects of Referential Metonymy." In Panther and Radden 1999: 121–39.

8

Spatial Metaphors and
Women's Religious Activities
in Ancient Greece and China

Yiqun Zhou

M EN AND WOMEN were commonly associated with different spheres in premodern societies. Whereas women belonged to the house and their major responsibilities involved housekeeping and childrearing, men moved in extradomestic spaces and pursued success in political, economic, military, and intellectual occupations. The gendered spatial differentiation—female and domestic versus male and extradomestic—was both physical and conceptual, and both descriptive and normative. The categories "inside" and "outside" (in relation to the domestic space), which simultaneously denote actual spaces identified with male and female activities and convey an argument about the proper understanding of gender ethics, provide the fundamental literal and metaphorical representation of the sexual segregation that has governed the working of many traditional societies.[1]

Just as women's experience varies from culture to culture, there is no single version of the commonplace inside-outside metaphor. The boundaries of "inside" and "outside" can be configured differently, and distinct values can be attached to each of the two spheres in different societies. In this essay, I will illustrate the cultural variations of the same gendered spatial metaphor by examining the cases of ancient Greece and China (c. tenth–fourth centuries BCE), two classical civilizations that are often viewed as paradigmatic because of their lasting legacies.[2] I will investigate the workings of the inside-outside metaphor in ancient Greek and Chinese religious contexts. As I will show, religion played a key role in maintaining or disrupting the boundaries between "inside" and "outside" and also in determining the values associated with the two spheres in the two societies. My comparative analysis has two aims: to shed light on how different forms of religion play different roles in women's lives, and to contribute to the understanding of how different experiential bases underlie different systems of metaphorical concepts.[3]

In the first section of this essay, which presents a general discussion of how the inside-outside metaphor epitomized the basic principle of sexual separation in ancient Greece and China, I will show that "inside" and "outside" connoted different values and participated in different systems of metaphorical concepts in the two societies while exhibiting cultural coherence within the same system. In the next section, I will examine how women's participation in religious activities affected the normal configurations of the inside-outside boundary in each of the two ancient societies. I will focus on those activities that played the most important roles in defining women's social statuses and identities in ancient Greece and China. My comparison will emphasize the continuity and alignment between women's religious activities and daily gender norms in the Chinese case, and the disruption and tension between such activities and norms in the Greek case. To substantiate this broad contrast, I will analyze some examples from literary, ritual, and historical texts in the subsequent two sections of this essay, which I will end by drawing some comparative conclusions about the religious practices of Greek women and Chinese women.

"INSIDE" AND "OUTSIDE"

The earliest theoretical formulation of the principle of gendered social spaces in the Western tradition may be found in the *Oeconomicus* (Household Management), in which the author, the Athenian philosopher Xenophon (c. 430–c. 354 BCE), discusses household management under the persona of his mentor, Socrates. In book 7 of the *Oeconomicus*, Socrates meets Ischomachus, a model Athenian citizen and farmer, in the agora (marketplace) and asks him about his lifestyle, since Ischomachus's appearance suggests that he does not pass his time indoors. To this question, he answers, with a smile,

"I certainly do not pass my time inside the house. For, you know, my wife manages the house quite capably by herself."[4] Later, he goes to great lengths to demonstrate that such separation of spaces has its basis in nature. In brief, women are more adapted for indoors, and men, for outdoors, on account of women's and men's possession of opposite attributes in mental toughness, endurance of adverse natural conditions, and affection for infants.[5] Such natural reason is to receive moral sanction: "Thus for the woman it is more decent to stay indoors than to spend time in the open air, but for the man it is more shameful to stay indoors than to take care of the work outside."[6]

A gender-based, inside-outside spatial distinction also existed in ancient China. According to chapter 37 of the *Book of Changes*, one of the Five Confucian Classics, "[a] woman's proper place is in the inside, and a man's proper place is in the outside. It is a fundamental principle of heaven and earth for men and women to be properly placed."[7]

Despite the division of gender structure into the "inside" and the "outside" in both ancient Greece and ancient China,[8] the two spaces were associated with different values in the two societies, and such difference may also be understood in terms of spatial metaphors. In ancient Greece, the "outside"—from law court, assembly, and agora to gymnasium and battlefield—was where the "center" of social life was located and where the "highest" forms of individual and collective accomplishments were pursued. Juxtaposed with the "outside" and viewed comparatively, the "inside"—the space bounded by the house—represented the "periphery" of social life and occupied the "lower" ends of human values.[9] The Greek structure of social organization and values may be spatially represented as follows:

FIG. 8.1

Outside———Center———Higher

Inside———Periphery———Lower

The inside-outside dyad did not enter into the same system of spatial metaphors in the ancient Chinese tradition. Whereas in Greece success in public life was endowed with greater value than was success in family life, and the civic community claimed a higher level of allegiance from the citizens (who were, by definition, male), in ancient China the patrilineal kinship organizations furnished the basic model for the structure and functioning of society and polity, and filial piety enjoyed the privilege of being the supreme ethical and political virtue.[10] Life in the "inside" was therefore not relegated to a peripheral and lower status vis-à-vis the "outside" sphere of public life. Rather, achievements in the outside world were considered in terms of an extension of the most fundamental training one had acquired in the "inside" for the ultimate purpose of the perpetuation and prosperity of the family. The following chart brings out the different spatial relationship between the "inside" and "outside" spheres in the Chinese tradition, which form concentric circles rather than a hierarchy:

FIG. 8.2

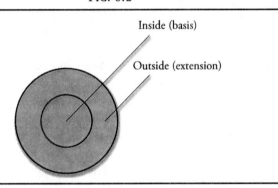

Whereas male dominance in ancient Greece was reflected in the hierarchical relationship between "inside" and "outside," in ancient China—an unquestionably male-dominant society—the physical and conceptual identification of women with "inside" did not make it a marginal and subordinate sphere vis-à-vis "outside." Here, "inside" provided the site for lifelong training and practice in the most exalted Chinese virtue, and women played a crucial role in such training and practice, by contributing indispensably to reproduction, childrearing, and household management. As I will show in the next section, the different relationships between the gendered social spheres in ancient Greece and China were reflected in these societies' spatial structures of religion.

WOMEN AND THE SPATIAL CONFIGURATION OF RELIGION

Consisting of sacrifices, processions, and competitions in music and athletics, public festivals dedicated to various deities formed the centerpiece of ancient Greek religious life. Participation in the festivals indicated one's membership in the civic communities, victories in the musical and athletic competitions conferred great honor on the winners and their families and cities, and artistic and literary works celebrating both the splendor of the festivals and the competitive excellence of their participants preserved some of the most cherished memories of the Greeks.[11]

The sanctuaries and the procession routes linking major landmarks (such as the agora and the city gates) and the sacred precincts occupied the spotlight in the celebration of Greek public festivals.[12] Their preeminence eclipsed the importance of the house as the site of many religious rituals conducted to mark lifecycle transitions in the family (such as birth, death, and marriage) and to honor deities on other occasions of special significance to family members. The household cults were of a clearly secondary status in the Greek religious system, and were not the subject of enthusiastic commemorations.[13] The scant evidence that has survived about Greek domestic cults forms a striking contrast with the voluminous sources pertaining to various aspects (from logistical and physical to symbolic and ideological) of the public festivals. This state of the evidence is also true of the extant knowledge about Greek women's religious life.

Women were an active presence in Greek public festivals. While some festivals were open to both males and females of all ages, other festivals were limited to individuals of a certain sex or a specific age group (e.g., men, women, married women, boys, girls).[14] If the festivals provided one among other major public arenas for Greek men to assert their memberships in the civic community and to demonstrate their competitive excellence in the presence of their peers, for Greek women the festivals constituted the only regular and most important institutionalized contexts in which to participate in public life.[15] It was a great honor for a young woman to be chosen to bear baskets in the festival processions and to grind grain for ritual cakes and weave robes for dedication to deities in the sacrifices. Moreover, it was an indication of good birth to perform in a festival chorus (typically organized by gender and age), and victories in the choral contests gave women rare public opportunities to claim their fair share in the renowned agonistic culture of the Greeks.[16] Although Greek women undoubtedly played regular, essential roles in the household cults, both as managers and as attendants, evidence of all genres and of both male and female authorship shows that, as was the case for men, participation in the festivals formed the center of Greek women's religious experience.[17] Allowing women to put aside their quotidian domestic duties and to pursue friendships with other women and win public recognition for their own beauty and talents under the aegis of the gods, the festivals lifted women out of their generally invisible and segregated existence in the "inside" and launched them into the "outside," the sphere of competition, power, and fellowship. As a result, women avidly embraced the festivals (especially the all-female ones) and their associated activities (for training and preparation), whereas men viewed their womenfolk's participation in the festivals with a mixture of fascination and anxiety.[18]

A paradox emerges from this discussion of the privileged role of the public festivals in Greek women's religious life. On the one hand, in that they allowed women to transcend the normal physical and conceptual constraints on their conduct, the festivals illustrated the often-observed emancipatory and empowering function of religion for subordinate groups.[19] On the other hand, the centrality of the festivals in Greek religion in general and in Greek female religiosity in particular confirmed the hierarchical relationship between the "outside" and "inside" domains in Greek society. Women's designated sphere was the "inside," but household cults were peripheral and lower forms of religious practice in Greece, and the recognition of women's excellence and value ironically found its highest religious expression in women's participation in the festivals that took them away from home and saw them engaging in activities that were at odds with the normal social expectations for mothers and wives. The fact that women only momentarily flourished in the public festivals and then returned to the domestic world—with its unsung routine duties and mundane ties, as well as sacred rites—points up the lack of sufficient recognition for domesticity, and the strong valorization of the spirit of public competitiveness and civic fellowship in Greek religion.

The spatial configuration of religion was different in ancient China. Here ancestor worship, regularly performed rites that honored patrilineal ancestors (male and female), was the most important form of religious practice; and the ancestral temple, where lineage descendants gathered to conduct ancestral sacrifices, was the ritual center.[20] The welfare of the patriline was the basic goal of the ancestral sacrifices, and the ritual activities in which descendants made offerings and paid obeisance to ancestors formed a continuum with the daily life in which children performed services for and demonstrated love and obedience to their parents and other senior patrilineal kin. Ancestral piety as a religious virtue and filial piety as an ethical and political virtue thus mirrored each other, and ancestor worship consecrated the domestic realm as the site for the realization of the most deeply cherished Chinese values.[21]

The Chinese also celebrated numerous public festivals in honor of various deities, and there is no mistaking the importance of these occasions in providing rhythms for people's lives and opportunities for the forging and renewal of communal ties (that is, besides satisfying individuals' religious feelings).[22] Unlike the Greek festivals, however, the Chinese festivals did not play a key role in defining people's social identities and relationships, nor did the activities at these festivals embody the values and ideals that the Chinese held most dear. If the Greek festivals showcased the solidarity and competitiveness of the civic community, and as such represented the highest Greek ideal of sociability, the Chinese festivals were basically occasions of pleasure and relaxation. Instead, it was the ancestral sacrifices that best illustrated the Chinese conception of the ideal human community: a lineage consisting of an unbroken line of ancestors and descendants, all of whom strove to contribute to the well-being of their common patriline.[23] Like its ancient Greek counterpart, the spatial structure of Chinese religion replicated the relationship between "inside" and "outside" in its society at large. Whereas Greek religion affirmed the preeminence of the "outside" sphere, in China the "inside" was in full spotlight, due to the ritual centrality of ancestor worship.

Women were an integral part of Chinese ancestor worship. As wives and mothers, women performed managerial functions in the ancestral rites—in particular taking charge of the preparation of food, drink, and textiles for use in the sacrifices—and also attended the sacrifices alongside their kinsmen, as members of the patrilineal descendant group. When women passed into the status of ancestors in the afterlife, then they received sacrificial offerings from their patrilineal descendants, sometimes in separate rites and sometimes jointly with male ancestors.[24] All the roles that women played in ancestor worship (managers, sacrificers, and eventually ancestors) recognized their contributions to the well-being of the family, from its basic biological survival to its daily functioning. In defining the family as the anchor of every male or female individual's social identities and life goals, ancestor worship affirmed women's value to the continuation and prosperity of the patrilineal family institution. The numerous ancestral sacrifices sanctified women's domestic roles and served as constant, solemn reminders of their indispensability to the fulfillment of the highest Chinese ideal about human flourishing.

Yet, in the lives of ancient Greek women, as I have discussed, festivals—the centerpiece of Greek religion—played a paradoxical role. The honor and emotional gratification that Greek women gained by momentarily abandoning their domestic roles to participate in the festivals only threw into higher relief the disjunction between women's daily experience at home and the special opportunities the festivals afforded them. Only by transgressing the physical boundary of the house and the normal social expectations for female conduct, did Greek women temporarily have a share in the prestige of public life. But the centrality of ancestor worship to Chinese religion obviated such disjunction and transgression and instead created a strong alignment between Chinese women's quotidian existence and their (socially defined) most important religious experience. Religion's different roles in the lives of Greek women and Chinese women can be represented on the charts shown in the previous section. In the case of ancient Greece, upward arrows are added to indicate spatial movement: participation in the festivals involved women in a movement from inside to outside, from periphery to center, and from lower to higher (see figure 8.3). No movement is involved in the case of ancient China (see figure 8.4). Dark shading is added to emphasize that the "inside" spatially overlapped with the ritual center defined by ancestor worship. Thus, whereas transgression/disjunction is a major motif in ancient Greek representations of women's public religious activities (especially the all-female festivals), alignment/continuum characterizes ancient Chinese depictions of female ancestor worshipers—a contrast illustrated by the following examples from Greek and Chinese texts.

FIG. 8.3

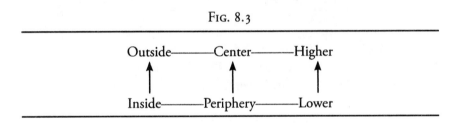

FIG. 8.4

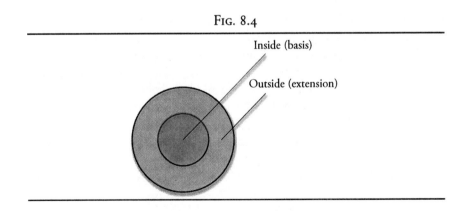

THESMOPHORIANS AND OTHER FEMALE FESTIVAL GOERS

Celebrated in largely similar manner all over the Greek world, the Thesmophoria was a major festival honoring Demeter, the Greek goddess of grain and fertility, and her daughter, Persephone. The participants—wives and mothers from citizens' families—gathered in the center of the city for three consecutive days every year, conducting rites in honor of the two goddesses (called the Twain by the Greeks) and aimed at securing a good harvest.[25]

The most notable fact about the Thesmophoria, as it appears in ancient sources, is the mystery shrouding its activities. The rule that the festival's participants be female (violations by men were punishable by death) and keep secret what happened during the rites seems to have been strictly enforced. The female celebrants of the Thesmophoria (Thesmophorians) were entrusted with a task critical to the survival of the civic community, and to fulfill that task they left home and moved to the center of the city. In Athens, the Thesmophoria appears to have been celebrated on the Pnyx, the regular site for the gathering of the Athenian Assembly, the city's supreme political organ.[26] The high-profile celebration of the Thesmophoria shows that, although women were excluded from politics and other pursuits in the "outside," women's importance to the welfare of Greek society was recognized in the religious area and in a way in keeping with the Greek hierarchy of social domains. The most valued activities and accomplishments had to take place "outside" of the home and at the "center" of public life. Providing the most fitting testimony to the limited albeit regular recognition of Greek women's crucial contributions to society, the Thesmophorians' three-day occupation of the city center also bore out the paradox of Greek women's festival participation discussed earlier.

While being wives and mothers of citizens, the Thesmophorians did not come together in their domestic roles but rather, completely unattached to any man during the festival, lived and associated with one another and ran their own affairs. The festival did not present a celebratory view of marriage and family life, either. According to tradition, the Thesmophoria was founded to celebrate the reunion of Demeter and Persephone, who had been kidnapped by Hades (king of the Underworld) as his wife and was allowed to return to her mother for two-thirds of the year, after the wrathful Demeter deprived the earth of its fertility and unleashed widespread famine.[27] In the light of this founding myth, the Thesmophoria can be seen as a tribute to the strong bonds between mothers and daughters that defied the distraction and sometimes violent disruption caused by marital duties. The festival, from the sentiment of the myth on which it was founded to the women's activities that it featured, represented a severe disjunction between normal social expectations for mothers and wives and their public religious experience.

Such disjunction was clearly in the awareness of Greek men, and what has survived of their recorded imaginations about the Thesmophoria is pervaded by a feeling of suspicion and anxiety about the women who had moved into the sphere normally reserved for men and had engaged together in unknown activities.[28] Aristophanes' comedy *The Thesmophorians* (staged in 411 BCE) offers some entertaining and yet serious insights into the male perception of the women at the Thesmophoria.

In Aristophanes' play, the Thesmophorians are to pass a decree to put Euripides to death, on charges that the tragedian has defamed women by revealing all of their secret crimes and unspeakable vices. In a desperate attempt to save himself, Euripides cajoles a clueless kinsman into infiltrating the women's gathering, under a female guise, in order to challenge the verdict. The bulk of the play consists of the comic exchanges between the disguised kinsman and the Thesmophorians. Although he valiantly exposes them as greedy, slothful, and conniving creatures, thereby justifying Euripides' portrayals, the kinsman cannot but lose out in the face of his united female opponents. His disguise is uncovered, the death sentence on Euripides is passed, and the kinsman only barely manages to escape in one piece.

Underlying the whole play are motifs of gender conflict, female solidarity, and male discomfort about the mysterious character of the activities of women left to their own devices. These related motifs are brought together in the marvelous turn of phrase that the Thesmophorians use to refer to themselves, a "commonwealth of women."[29] Momentarily formed of women who usually are dispersed in individual households as mothers and wives but are now gathered on a site where normally men exercise their political power as members of a civic community, this female commonwealth is a comical construct that wonderfully encapsulates the spatial and conceptual transgression entailed in the activities of the Thesmophorians (and, for that matter, of all the participants in women-only festivals).[30] Leaving home and house behind, the festival celebrants enter into a commonwealth of their own and show themselves to be men's equals in deliberating and adopting collective decisions on matters of common concern to them (in the Thesmophoria celebrated in Aristophanes' play, such decisions include a decree against male misogyny allegedly represented by a famous playwright). The fantastic commonwealth of the Thesmophorians excellently dramatizes the drastic displacement of the inside-outside boundary during the all-female festivals, as well as the suspicion and unease that these religious occasions elicited in Greek men.

The potential political implications of women's collective presence in the festivals were exploited in another Aristophanic comedy staged in 411 BCE, *Lysistrata*. In this play, an Athenian woman named Lysistrata successfully organizes a sex strike by the wives all over Greece to boycott the long war between the Athenians and the Spartans (and their allies). Under the pretext of making a sacrifice to Athena, the patron goddess of Athens, the sex strikers seize the Acropolis, site of Athena's temple and the Athenian treasury, and barricade themselves against the men who attempt to take back the citadel. Before an armed clash breaks out between the sex strikers and their male opponents, the two sides engage in a fierce debate in which the men accuse the women of gross transgression of their designated boundaries but the women counter that they have both the responsibility and the capability to intervene in state affairs:

> Here we begin, all you citizens, to deliver
> advice that will benefit the city;
> and rightly so, for she nurtured me in sumptuous splendor.
> As soon as I was seven years old, I was an Arrephoros;
> then I was a Grinder; when I was ten, at the Brauronia,
> I shed my saffron gown as one of the Foundress's Bears;
> and I was also once a basket-bearer, a beautiful girl, wearing
> a string of dried figs.[31]

For Greek men participation in the festivals was an important marker of civic membership, which simultaneously carried political rights and obligations, but for Greek women the festivals only constituted isolated opportunities to find public religious representation, which did not convert into political representation. This gender asymmetry was recognized and made fun of in *Lysistrata*. In the passage just quoted, the women proudly name a list of the functions that they have served at various festivals, and thus make a logical argumentative move that seeks to establish for women (as has been the case for men) the connection between public religious representation and political representation. The women—in opposition to the men who charge them of being transgressive and unfeminine and who try to drive them out and restore the order of things—argue that they have marched into the center of the city and taken politics into their hands to live up to the religious representation and honors that the city conferred on them. In the words of the leader of the female squad that occupies the Acropolis, "I owe it to the city to give her some good advice."[32] Participation in public religious activities becomes the basis for women to make political claims, and women's collective experience in the festivals gives them the solidarity that enables them to pull off a pan-Hellenic sex strike and stage a successful seizure and defense of the Acropolis, one of the most important symbols of the city of Athens.

As fantastic as *The Thesmophorians*, *Lysistrata* brings out through its comic plot the disjunction between Greek women's daily life and their public religious experience, and highlights the inconsistency of giving women public religious representation but completely severing its link to political representation. *Lysistrata*, in showing women actually to be capable of organizing themselves to intervene effectively in politics, also expresses in a lighthearted manner Greek men's fears about women's collective power, which found on public religious occasions the most likely site for its exercise. Like the Thesmophorians who have to go home after their three-day celebration, the sex strikers on the Acropolis leave with their husbands after their purpose to stop the war has been achieved. The brief moments in which women shine together in public form a contrast with what they must deal with at home on most days, and this demonstration of collective female power becomes material for celebration rather than for suspicion and speculation.

The most poignant literary expression of the tension between Greek women's domestic existence and public religious experience can be found in Euripides' tragedy *The Bacchae*. In this play, the maenads, entranced devotees of the god Dionysus, roam the mountains and refuse to obey the Theban king's order to disband and return home.[33] They annihilate the troops he sends, and eventually prevail even over him and tear him into pieces. The greatest pathos of the play lies in the fact that the king, Pentheus, is torn apart by the hands of his own mother, Agave, the co-leader (with her two sisters) of the maenadic army.[34] Thinking that she is holding the head of a dismembered young lion, Agave proudly pronounces the martial superiority of the maenads under her leadership, calling on the Thebans to come to view the prized prey:

> Come, see the beast we, Cadmus' daughters, caught and killed;
> Caught not with nets or thronged Thessalian javelins,
> But with our own bare arms and fingers. After this
> Should huntsmen glory in their exploits, who must buy

Their needless tools from armourers? We with our hands
Hunted and took this beast, then tore it limb from limb.[35]

Shortly, Agave invites her father, Cadmus, to share in her pride:

Father! Now you may boast as loudly as you will
That you have sired daughters best by far of mortals!
I speak of all three, but myself especially.
I have left weaving at the loom for greater things,
For hunting wild beasts with my bare hands. . . .[36]

Here, Agave explicitly rejects women's prescribed work at the loom and has
her eye on "greater things" (*meízon*), namely, glory-bringing public pursuits
that men have attempted to appropriate for the citizen-soldiers only.[37] In a
single battle, Agave, worthy of her aspirations, proves her fellow maenads
and herself better warriors by far and stands in a position to vaunt the force
of their bare arms, to the humiliation of the all-too-conventional heroes.

Agave's heroics, however, come at the expense of femininity, domesticity, and motherhood. At the end of the play, Agave is finally brought to
her senses and grieves over both her son's death and her own exile. The
mourning mother—erstwhile warlike leader of the maenads, and ferocious
filicide—represents a stirring self-reflection of the Athenians, who glorified
public competitiveness to an extreme but understood the implications of
such glorification for women's lives. Despite the significant differences between the maenads' orgiastic Dionysiac festival and civic festivals like the
Thesmophoria, all the rites took women away from home, organized them,
provided them with public recognition, and thereby confirmed the "outside"
as the privileged sphere vis-à-vis the "inside" in the Greek value system.[38]
Despite its radical grimness, *The Bacchae* soberly illustrates the paradoxical role of public religious activities in Greek women's lives, as well as the
Greeks' conscious struggles with some contradictions inherent in their social
design.[39]

ANCESTOR WORSHIPERS

In keeping with the intention to present a prosperous and orderly descent
group in the presence of the ancestors, Chinese women were typically

represented as forming a harmonious unit with their kinsmen during the ancestral sacrifices. The chapter on an ancestral rite called "offering a single beast to the ancestor" in the *Book of Etiquette and Ceremonial* (written c. 450–350 BCE) illustrates this point.

At each ancestral sacrifice, the chief sacrificer and his wife lead the men and women of their descent group to perform tasks that are well orchestrated to demonstrate both distinction and interdependence between the two sexes.[40] In the central part of the ritual, after the Personator (the person who impersonates the honored ancestor and receives offerings on behalf of him or her) has consumed the offered food and drink, the ceremony proceeds as follows:

> The Chief Sacrificer Gives a Digestif to the Personator.
> The Personator Toasts the Chief Sacrificer and Blesses Him.
> The Chief Sacrificer Offers Wine to the Liturgist and the Waiter.
> The Chief Sacrificer's Wife Offers Wine to the Personator, and He Toasts Her.
> The Chief Sacrificer's Wife Offers Wine to the Liturgist and the Waiter.
> The Senior Guest Offers Wine to the Personator.
> The Chief Sacrificer's Wife Hands a Cup of Wine to Him, in Order That He Himself May Drink a Toast.
> The Chief Sacrificer Hands a Cup of Wine to His Wife, in Order That She Herself May Drink a Toast.
> The Personator Offers a Toast to the Guest. The Guest Offers Wine to the Liturgist and the Waiter, and Hands a Cup of Wine to the Chief Sacrificer and His Wife, in Order That They Themselves May Drink a Toast.
> The Chief Sacrificer Offers Wine to the Senior among His Brethren,[41] and Himself Drinks a Toast.
> The Chief Sacrificer Offers Wine to All His Brethren.
> The Chief Sacrificer Offers Wine to the Womenfolk among the Descendants, and Himself Drinks a Toast.[42]

As this list shows, the activity of the chief sacrificer's wife largely matches that of her husband, but an important difference sets them apart. Although both the chief sacrificer and his wife exchange toasts with the Personator, offer wine to the officiators, and toast each other, only the chief sacrificer—in his capacity as the representative of his entire descent group—is blessed by the

Personator (second on the list of activities). In keeping with the patrilineal nature of ancestor worship, the wife's ritual identity is subsumed under her husband's. Nonetheless, as indicated by the parallel activities prescribed for the chief sacrificer and his wife, she is fully recognized as an integral part in the ritual unit that represents all the men and women in the patrilineal descent group to secure the blessings of their ancestors (male and female). Although the extent to which the meticulous ritual prescriptions governing each activity just enumerated reflected the practice of actual sacrifices is unclear, the parallel activities prescribed for men and women in the ritual text make perfect sense in light of the basic rationale of ancestor worship. Side by side in the ancestral temple, men and women were expected to demonstrate their resolve to cooperate and to contribute to the well-being of the family.[43]

The alignment between women's normal sphere of activity and the space for the highest expression of female religiosity in ancient China contrasts with the discontinuity and tension that characterized the spatial configuration of Greek religion. Whereas the supreme form of Greek religion momentarily involved women in the public pursuit of friendships and competitive excellence, Chinese women garnered approbation and authority for being pious attendants in the ancestral temples and for observing the ethical tenets of ancestor worship. For a Chinese woman, becoming the mother of good sons was the most essential achievement before her eventual ascendancy to the status of ancestor; and the prestige of motherhood and the honor of being an ancestor held out the greatest promise to young wives who struggled to negotiate the daily pressures of being good wives and daughters-in-law. The numerous names of women, as dedicatees (ancestresses) or dedicators (usually ancestresses' daughters-in-law), that appear in inscriptions on ritual bronzes dedicated to ancestors testify to the continuum between the stages in the female life cycle—from wife to daughter-in-law to mother to ancestress.[44] This continuum corresponded to the intimate intertwining between ancestor worship and its ethical corollary of filial piety and to the spatial overlap between the site of a woman's daily life and the locality of the religious experience that defined her most essential social identity.

To illustrate the alignment and continuum between female domesticity and religiosity as represented in ancient Chinese sources, I will look at the image of Jing Jiang, one of the most famous female paragons in early Chinese history. The mother of Gongfu Wenbo, who came from an illustrious aristocratic lineage in the state of Lu and served as a minister in the Lu court in the sixth century BCE, Jing Jiang was known for a number of related things. She was a strict disciplinarian of her son and a serious moral advisor to her grandnephew (when both men were already high officials); she demonstrated unfailing reverence to the memories of her deceased parents-in-law; and she rigorously followed ritual principles, both those that pertained to the ancestral sacrifices and those that governed daily conduct and interpersonal relationships (particularly in the area of sexual decorum).[45]

Underlying these qualities of Jing Jiang's were her impeccable ancestral piety and filial piety. Her ancestral piety was manifested as her fastidious insistence on observing rules in the performance of ancestral rites, but was not just about correct conduct in ancestral sacrifices. As she invoked not only descendants' obligations to ancestors but also the teachings of her deceased parents-in-law when advising her son and grandnephew or when imposing harsh punishment on her son for his misbehavior, Jing Jiang demonstrated her belief in the homology of ancestral piety and filial piety. Moreover, the authority that Jing Jiang continued to wield over her son and grandnephew in their full adulthood, as well as her own continued honoring of the teachings of her deceased parents-in-law when she herself was a powerful matriarch, points to the fact that Chinese women derived their power and influence from their commitment to defending the interests of the patrilineal family institution. While the defense of family interests was a supreme obligation shared by all family members—past, present, and future—whether they moved in the "outside" or in the "inside," mothers assumed special responsibilities because of their role in the upbringing of children. In the name of the perpetuation and prosperity of the family line, Chinese matriarchs like Jing Jiang claimed power from the "inside" and wielded authority and influence over their kinsmen who were expected to contribute to family welfare from the "outside."

COMPARING THE RELIGIOUS PRACTICES
OF GREEK WOMEN AND CHINESE WOMEN

In the sources I have examined about Chinese ancestor worshipers and Greek festival goers, different uses of the trope of female work (weaving, spinning, and woolwork) evince different configurations of "inside" and "outside" in ancient China and Greece. In *Bacchae* 1236–37, an enraptured Agave boasts that she has abandoned weaving for "greater things," namely, leading an army to victory and thereby demonstrating her valiance. Here, weaving and fighting represent the quintessential female work and the core activity of the Greek citizen-soldier, respectively. Agave, in her spatial movement and in her conduct on the "battlefield" that she and her maenadic troops make of the villages and mountains, demonstrates graphically the superiority of pursuits in the "outside." The sex strikers in *Lysistrata* 567–70 and 574–86 also make important use of the trope of female work, though they appear to follow a different logic. They argue that they have the capability to handle politics, because solving the state's problems requires the same skills as does treating a skein of wool: women who know how to rid a fleece of dirt and burrs will know how to remove bad people from the city, and selecting and employing good people is just like carding the good wool for spinning and weaving.

The difference between the uses of the trope of female work in *The Bacchae* and *Lysistrata* is only apparent. Agave declares her aspirations for excellence in the public sphere by straightforwardly asserting the inferiority of women's domestic role. The Aristophanic rebels, in order to justify their interference in state affairs, argue that shouldering domestic responsibilities qualifies them to manage political matters; but this argument assumes that women deserve for their homemaking skills participatory roles in politics. When female work is presented thus as women's credentials for politics, it is not appreciated for its own sake but rather invites the inference that the most valued recognition of talents has to take place in the public domain, the site for a higher order of business.

Weaving also appears as an important subject in two records on Jing Jiang that are found in *Discourses of the States* (compiled by 300 BCE) and *Biographies of Women* (compiled in the first century BCE). In one story, Wenbo urges her to give up weaving, lest he be criticized for not being able to provide his mother with the leisurely lifestyle deserved by someone of her status. Jing Jiang responds with a long lecture on the virtue of industry. To ensure the prosperity of both the family and the state, she asserts, men and women should work hard at their duties assigned according to the sexual division of labor. Weaving, the most essential female work, has both economic and ritual significance—in this regard, Jing Jiang mentions women's responsibility to weave the garments worn during sacrifices.[46] She goes on to explain that by her diligence at the loom she has merely striven to do her part in maintaining the well-being of the family and to fulfill her obligations to the ancestors, and that Wenbo's failure of comprehension makes her fear for the survival of her husband's line.[47] In the other Jing Jiang story that features weaving, she draws for Wenbo an analogy between the art of government and the skill of weaving. She likens the functions of eight offices to eight parts of the loom. For example, the General can be considered as the selvedge that keeps the fabric in formation; the Director of Messengers sends envoys back and forth like the shuttle; and the Minister, in his upright and responsible guidance of the country, stands firm like the axle.[48]

The second Jing Jiang story immediately recalls the *Lysistrata* simile in which the Athenian women illustrate their "philosophy of government" by comparing governing to working wool. There is, nevertheless, an important difference. The Athenian women attempt to prove that, despite their previous exclusion from the management of their city's affairs, mastery of the analogous domestic skills both entitles and enables the women to move over smoothly to ruling positions. By contrast, the points that Jing Jiang wishes to make to her son are that weaving is important to women, just as government is to men; and that the well-being of the state depends on the sexes' properly acquitting their respective duties (the same message conveyed in the other story about Jing Jiang and weaving). In other words, although she interacts with a man in an authoritative and forceful way like that of the Aristophanic women, she uses the governing/weaving analogy for an almost opposite purpose, seeking to drive home the separate yet interdependent social functions of the sexes. Instead of presenting accomplishment in female work as justification for taking up male work, a woman who is exemplary in fulfilling her responsibilities in the "inside" gains the authority to advise men on the fundamental importance for men and women to carry out their respective duties in family and society so as to prove themselves to be worthy descendants of their ancestors.

The impact that women's participation in the highest forms of religion had on gender ethics varied between ancient China and Greece. In ancient China, the dominance of ancestor worship, which took place in the domestic space and exalted familial values, upheld the normative inside-outside gender structure and endowed women—who played roles in the "inside"—with power and influence. In ancient Greece, however, the preeminence of the festivals, which promoted both competitiveness and extradomestic ties, resulted in a disjunction between women's daily mode of existence and their public religious experience and ironically affirmed the "outside" as the sphere of higher pursuits.

Moreover, different social relationships are foregrounded by Chinese and Greek sources about women's participation in the dominant forms of religious activities. In the Chinese sources, the female ancestor worshipers form ritual units either with their kinsmen (most importantly, husband-wife and mother-son) or with their kinswomen (most importantly, mother-in-law–daughter-in-law). In the Greek sources, by contrast, the mother-daughter relationship (epitomized by the celebration of the Demeter-Persephone bond in the Thesmophoria) and female friendships are at the fore. Whereas the Chinese cluster of relationships locates women firmly within the domestic space and the patrilineal and patriarchal kinship network, Greek women are shown flourishing in the public sphere and embracing bonds that—from the perspective of the patrilineal and patriarchal family—constitute a centrifugal force.

The different configurations of the inside-outside gender structure in ancient Greek and Chinese religious contexts may recall the distinction that has been made between religion's emancipatory and sacralizing functions with respect to women. According to this distinction, religion in its emancipatory function enables women to transcend the normal constraints on female conduct, whereas religion in its sacralizing function interprets women's traditional roles as sacred.[49] Seemingly, then, the Greek festivals, while ironically confirming the "outside" as the "center" and as the site for "higher" pursuits, fulfilled an emancipatory function for women; but Chinese ancestor worship, in exalting the contributions that women made to family and society while being firmly located in the "inside," performed a sacralizing function.

Yet, there is an important difference between my findings and those of the studies informed by the emancipation-sacralization distinction. Those studies, which tend to emphasize women's empowerment in religion, usually weigh heavily the autonomy of action that women demonstrate in emancipatory and sacralizing religious activities.[50] While reflecting and validating women's common concerns and experiences as wives and mothers (such as marriage, childbirth, and the health and safety of family members), the sacralizing rituals are considered empowering, in that they often are organized and celebrated by women who are related or unrelated (with little or no male participation) and take place outside of the structure of mainstream, male-dominant religion.[51]

Thus understood, the sacralizing function of religion does not amount to the role of ancestor worship in Chinese women's lives. As the dominant form of ancient Chinese religion, ancestor worship defined the family as the ritual center for every person and painstakingly presented men and women as interdependent units in a hopefully endlessly extending line of ancestors and descendants. Ancestor worship empowered women not by giving them autonomy, but instead by recognizing them as fully co-opted members of the patrilineal and patriarchal family institution.

To different degrees, emancipatory and sacralizing religious activities as commonly understood highlight women's articulation of their religiosity through distinctive or independent ritual actions.[52] Moreover, emancipatory and sacralizing activities take place in settings that, in different ways, testify to the subordinate status of the domestic ritual space. Unlike emancipatory activities, sacralizing activities may not involve open violations of conventional gender boundaries but tend to stand in the shadows of a society's dominant religion. Yet, in Chinese ancestor worship, the highest religious and ethical virtues were homologous both for men and for women, and women's ritual identities and activities were inseparable from those of the women's husbands and sons. If Chinese ancestor worship, in affirming the normative gender ethics, can be said to perform a sacralizing function, then this ritual represents a unique form in doing so.

There is no evidence of what the remarkable alignment between religious and ethical values and between ritual and domestic spaces in ancestor worship implied for ancient Chinese women's subjective religious experience. Clearly, however, the dominant form of religion in ancient China did not fulfill the emancipatory and transcendental function commonly associated with religion; and Chinese women's experience in ancestor worship provided no basis for the kind of suspicion, anxiety, and fantastic imagination sparked by Greek women's presence in public festivals.

Ancestor worship, which placed Chinese women in the "inside" and recognized and rewarded them for their contributions there, certainly did not have potential political implications as did Greek women's representation in public religious events. The women at the Greek festivals, who together demonstrated competitiveness and solidarity, were without too great a stretch perceived as forming a commonwealth of their own and as having the ambition to crack into the male-dominant public sphere. The tantalizing feminist potential of Greek women's festival presence remained only a fantasy in Greek drama, but the fact that such potential was first manifest in a society marked by a clear hierarchy between the "outside" and "inside" spheres is historically significant.[53] Yet, the modern feminist concepts that echo ancient Greek portrayals of female festival goers do not find parallels in the ancient Chinese tradition, where the "inside" and "outside" spheres formed concentric circles, and men and women presented themselves as harmonious and orderly units before their ancestors.

NOTES

1. The spatial metaphors discussed in this essay are also called orientational metaphors and spatialization metaphors (Lakoff and Johnson [1980] 2003: 14–21). For studies on the relationship between spatial

arrangements and women's status, see Spain 1992; Ardener 1993; and Shands 1999.

2. Since 1985, twenty books (including one conference volume) have appeared in the field of China-Greece comparative studies. Articles and book chapters comparing various aspects of the two ancient societies (philosophy and science being the most dominant subjects) are even more numerous. For the latest bibliography, see Zhou 2010: 1.

3. The roles of religion in the lives of women in world cultures: Falk and Gross 1980; Sharma 1987. The experiential grounding and cultural coherence of metaphors: Lakoff and Johnson [1980] 2003.

4. *Oeconomicus* 7.3 (translation mine).

5. *Oeconomicus* 7.22–26.

6. *Oeconomicus* 7.30 (translation mine).

7. *Book of Changes*, 50 (translation mine).

8. Ancient Greece: Walker 1983; Vernant 1983. Ancient China: Raphals 1998: 195–234; Hinsch 2003.

9. On the subordinate status of the family in ancient Greek civic ideology, see Vernant 1982: 49–68; Humphreys 1983; Schmitt-Pantel 1990; and Redfield 1995.

10. On the cornerstone status of the lineage organizations (corporate patrilineal kinship groups tracing descent to a common ancestor and bound by common property and ritual) in ancient Chinese society and politics, see Qian 1991; Zhu 2004; Sena 2005; and Falkenhausen 2006. On filial piety as the highest Chinese virtue, see Holzman 1998 and Zhang 2008.

11. Parke 1977; Burkert 1985: 99–109; Cartledge 1985; Phillips and Pritchard 2003.

12. Burkert 1985: 84–92.

13. Rose 1957; Sourvinou-Inwood 2000a and 2000b; Zhou 2010: 41–98.

14. Sourvinou-Inwood 1988; Calame 2001; Dillon 2002.

15. The exceptional role of religion in allowing Greek women to participate in public life is commonly noted (e.g., Redfield 1995: 167; Parker 1996: 80).

16. Calame 2001; Dillon 2002: 37–106; Kowalzig 2004; Zhou 2010: 161–216. For comparative perspectives on competitiveness as a hallmark of ancient Greek culture, see Lloyd 1996; Lloyd and Sivin 2002; and Zhou 2010.

17. Dillon 2002; Zhou 2010: 161–216.

18. Lefkowitz 1996; Dillon 2002; Zhou 2010: 161–216. I will discuss further the male attitude shortly.

19. Falk and Gross 1980.

20. Rawson 1999; Li 2008: 165, 244; Kern 2009.
21. Zhou 2010: 99–157.
22. Granet 1932.
23. See Zhou 2010: 99–157 for more discussion of the different types of solidarity and authority relationships represented and celebrated in the dominant religious practices of ancient Greece and China.
24. Chen 2003; Cao 2004; Zhou 2010: 161–216.
25. Brumfield 1981; Simon 1983; Nixon 1995.
26. MacDowell 1995: 259–60.
27. The myth of Demeter and Persephone is preserved in the Homeric *Hymn to Demeter*.
28. Zeitlin 1982; Winkler 1990: 188–209.
29. *Thesmophoriazusae* 307–8 (". . . tòn dêmon . . . / . . . tôn gunaikôn"), 334–35 (". . . tôi dêmôi . . . / tôi tôn gunaikôn . . .") (translation Sommerstein's).
30. Classicist James Redfield (1995: 167) observes "that the [Greek] city-state as it excluded women evoked from the start a fantasy of the alternative city of women, a fantasy given ritual form in the Thesmophoria, when the women for a time withdrew and formed a kind of ritual city of their own."
31. *Lysistrata* 638–47 (translation Sommerstein's). The Arrephoroi (plural for Arrephoros) began the weaving of the robe dedicated to Athena at the festival of the Panathenaia, and also marched in the procession there. The Grinders ground grain for ritual cakes, probably for the rites in honor of Demeter at Eleusis. The Brauronia was a quadrennial festival celebrating girls' passage to adulthood. See Henderson 1996: 216 nn. 139, 140, 142 for succinct explanations of these terms.
32. *Lysistrata* 648 (translation Sommerstein's).
33. On the Dionysiac festivals of the maenads, see Dodds 1951: 270–82 and Kraemer 1992: 36–49.
34. The battle motif appears early in the play, when Dionysus enters and declares that, if Thebes tries to bring the maenads home by force, he "will join that army / [o]f women possessed and lead them to battle. . . ." (*Bacchae* 50–52 [translation Vellacott's]). On their way to the mountains, the maenads fall on two villages lying in their way and ransack both. A fierce battle ensues when the enraged villagers arm themselves to resist, and it results in an "amazing sight":

. . . The spears those men were throwing drew
No blood, but the women, hurling a thyrsus like a spear,

> Dealt wounds; in short, those women turned the men to flight.
> (*Bacchae* 760, 761–64 [translation Vellacott's])

35. *Bacchae* 1203–10 (translation Vellacott's).
36. *Bacchae* 1233–37 (translation Vellacott's).
37. Near the beginning of the play, the chorus describes the maenads as being taken away from their looms and shuttles, by Dionysiac frenzy (*Bacchae* 117–19). Pentheus, in his initial reaction to the roaming maenads, plans to round them up and force them to work at the loom (*Bacchae* 514). Weaving, the classic female work, represents femininity and domesticity. On fighting as an essential part of the Greek definition of citizenship, see Garlan 1995 and Canfora 1995.
38. Classicist Charles Segal (1997: 349–94) analyzes the disruptions of physical and conceptual boundaries as the maenads move between house, city, and mountain in *The Bacchae*.
39. Classicist E. R. Dodds (1960: xlv) interprets *The Bacchae* in terms of the Greeks' ambiguous attitude toward human rationality and what can be called primitive and irrational forces in their society. My reading identifies a different kind of tension in the play. All the unresolved ambivalence and tension make the play powerfully tragic.
40. The chief sacrificer was supposed to be the eldest son born to the wife (versus consorts of a secondary status) of the most senior male in each generation of the patriline.
41. The term "brethren" refers to the chief sacrificer's brothers and paternal cousins.
42. *Book of Etiquette and Ceremonial*, 2:137–46 (translation Steele's).
43. The chapter on the ancestral rite called "offering the smaller set of beasts to the ancestors" in the *Book of Etiquette and Ceremonial* (2:158–78 [translation Steele's]) contains a very similar protocol for the ritual proceeding.
44. For studies on the female dedicators and dedicatees in Chinese bronze inscriptions, see Chen 2003 and 2008; Cao 2004; and Zhou 2010: 161–216.
45. Raphals 1998: 30–33, 92–98; Raphals 2001 and 2002; and Zhou 2003 and 2010: 161–263 are detailed studies on the Jing Jiang stories. Zhou 2010: 161–216 focuses on Jing Jiang's image as a filial daughter-in-law and a meticulous follower of rules in ancestral sacrifices. There is no reason to doubt the historical existence of Jing Jiang the sixth-century-BCE aristocratic matron, though it is difficult to tell idealization from reality in interpreting the narratives about her. Without attempting to

determine to what extent Jing Jiang's image was a result of hagiographic construction, I use the sources on her to fathom the attitudes and perceptions about female religiosity among the ancient Chinese male elite, much in the same way I treat the Greek literary evidence on the female festival goers.

46. *Discourses of the States*, 2:205.
47. *Discourses of the States*, 2:208.
48. *Biographies of Women*, 1.7ab.
49. Falk and Gross 1980.
50. Falk and Gross 1980; Procter-Smith 1993; Pintchman 2004.
51. See, for example, the five anthologized essays in part 3 of Falk and Gross 1980, which examine rituals for wives and mothers in India, Central America, and Iran.
52. Scholars tend to understand the positive role of religion in women's lives in terms of the opportunities it allows for women to exercise agency or to receive equal representation in a community of the faithful. For example, anthropologist Erika Friedl (1980: 163) shows how the tribal women in an Iranian village feel that the Islamic religion was "made for men and not for women," because they "have no religious rituals that are exclusively or specifically for them and no religious gatherings in which they receive instructions or can actively engage in a communal religious activity."
53. Patterson 1991: 106–32 and Redfield 2003: 12 are among the studies tracing modern feminist ideas and movements to the ancient Greeks. The modern feminists and the female rebels on the ancient Greek stage both make two contentions, namely, that women as a sex group have been subjected to unequal and unfair treatment by men, and that women must develop a sense of sisterhood and unite to change their subordinate position and gain access to equal rights. For these two essential elements of feminism, see Cott 1987: 4–5 and Lerner 1993: 274.

REFERENCES

Ardener, Shirley, ed. 1993. *Women and Space: Ground Rules and Social Maps.* Rev. ed. Oxford: Berg Publishers.

Aristophanes. 1990. *Lysistrata.* Edited and translated by Alan H. Sommerstein. Warminster, UK: Aris & Phillips.

———. 1994. *Thesmophoriazusae.* Edited and translated by Alan H.

Sommerstein. Warminster, UK: Aris & Phillips.

Book of Changes (Zhouyi). 1959. In *Shisanjing zhushu*, edited by Ruan Yuan. 1815. Reprint, Beijing: Zhonghua shuju.

The I-Li, or Book of Etiquette and Ceremonial. 1917. Translated by John Steele. 2 vols. London: Probsthain.

Brumfield, Allaire Chandor. 1981. *The Attic Festivals of Demeter and Their Relation to the Agricultural Year*. New York: Arno Press.

Burkert, Walter. 1985. *Greek Religion: Archaic and Classical*. Translated by John Raffan. Cambridge: Harvard University Press.

Calame, Claude. 2001. *Choruses of Young Women in Ancient Greece: Their Morphology, Religious Role, and Social Functions*. Translated by Derek Collins and Janice Orion. Lanham, MD: Rowman & Littlefield Publishers.

Canfora, Luciano. 1995. "The Citizen." In Vernant 1995: 120–52.

Cao Zhaolan. 2004. *Jinwen yu Yin Zhou nüxing wenhua* (Bronze Inscriptions and Women's Culture in Yin-Zhou China). Beijing: Peking University Press.

Cartledge, Paul. 1985. "The Greek Religious Festivals." In *Greek Religion and Society*, edited by P. E. Easterling and J. V. Muir, 98–127. Cambridge: Cambridge University Press.

Chen Chao-jung. 2003. "Zhoudai funü zai jisi zhong de diwei" (Women's Roles in Zhou Dynasty Ancestor Worship). *Tsinghua Journal of Chinese Studies* 31, no. 4: 395–440.

———. 2008. "Liang Zhou qingtongqi de nüxing jieshouzhe yu nüxing zhizuozhe" (Female Dedicators and Dedicatees in Zhou Bronze Vessels). Paper presented at the March 8 Early China Seminar, Columbia University, New York, NY.

Cott, Nancy F. 1987. *The Grounding of Modern Feminism*. New Haven: Yale University Press.

Dillon, Matthew. 2002. *Girls and Women in Classical Greek Religion*. London: Routledge.

Discourses of the States (Guoyu). 1988. Edited by Du Yu. 2 vols. Shanghai: Guji.

Dodds, E. R. 1951. *The Greeks and the Irrational*. Berkeley: University of California Press.

Euripides. 1960. *The Bacchae*. 2nd ed. Edited by E. R. Dodds. Oxford: Oxford University Press.

———. 1974. *Euripides: The Bacchae and Other Plays*. Translated by Philip Vellacott. Harmondsworth, UK: Penguin Books.

Falk, Nancy Auer, and Rita M. Gross, eds. 1980. *Unspoken Worlds: Women's Religious Lives in Non-Western Cultures*. San Francisco: Harper & Row.

Falkenhausen, Lothar von. 2006. *Chinese Society in the Age of Confucius (1000–250 BC): The Archaeological Evidence*. Los Angeles: Cotsen Institute of Archaeology.

Friedl, Erika. 1980. "Islam and Tribal Women in a Village in Iran." In Falk and Gross 1980: 159–73.

Garlan, Yvon. 1995. "War and Peace." In Vernant 1995: 53–85.

Granet, Marcel. 1932. *Festivals and Songs of Ancient China*. Translated by E. D. Edwards. London: George Routledge & Sons.

Henderson, Jeffrey, ed. and trans. 1996. *Three Plays by Aristophanes: Staging Women*. New York: Routledge.

Hinsch, Brett. 2003. "The Origins of Separation of the Sexes in China." *Journal of the American Oriental Society* 123, no. 3: 595–616.

Holzman, Donald. 1998. "The Place of Filial Piety in Ancient China." *Journal of the American Oriental Society* 118, no. 2: 1–15.

Humphreys, S. C. 1983. *The Family, Women and Death: Comparative Studies*. London: Routledge & Kegan Paul.

Kern, Martin. 2009. "Bronze Inscriptions, the *Shijing*, and the *Shangshu*: The Evolution of the Ancestral Sacrifice during the Western Zhou." In *Early Chinese Religion, Part One: Shang through Han (1250 BC–220 AD)*, edited by John Lagerwey and Marc Kalinowski, 143–200. Leiden: E. J. Brill.

Kowalzig, Barbara. 2004. "Changing Choral Worlds: Song-Dance and Society in Athens and Beyond." In *Music and the Muses: The Culture of 'Mousikē' in the Classical Athenian City*, edited by Penelope Murray and Peter Wilson, 39–65. Oxford: Oxford University Press.

Kraemer, Ross Shepard. 1992. *Her Share of the Blessings: Women's Religions among Pagans, Jews, and Christians in the Greco-Roman World*. New York: Oxford University Press.

Lakoff, George, and Mark Johnson. 2003. *Metaphors We Live By*. Chicago: University of Chicago Press, 1980. Reprint, with a new afterword, Chicago: University of Chicago Press.

Lefkowitz, Mary R. 1996. "Women in the Panathenaic and Other Festivals." In *Worshipping Athena: Panathenaia and Parthenon*, edited by Jenifer Neils, 78–91. Madison: University of Wisconsin Press.

Lerner, Gerda. 1993. *The Creation of Feminist Consciousness: From the Middle Ages to Eighteen-seventy*. Oxford: Oxford University Press.

Li, Feng. 2008. *Bureaucracy and the State in Early China: Governing the Western Zhou.* Cambridge: Cambridge University Press.

Liu Xiang. 1983. *Biographies of Women (Lienü zhuan).* Edited by Liang Duan. In *Sibu beiyao.* 1924–1931. Reprint, Taipei: Zhonghua shuju.

Lloyd, G. E. R. 1996. *Adversaries and Authorities: Investigations into Ancient Greek and Chinese Science.* New York: Cambridge University Press.

Lloyd, Geoffrey, and Nathan Sivin. 2002. *The Way and the Word: Science and Medicine in Early China and Greece.* New Haven: Yale University Press.

MacDowell, Douglas M. 1995. *Aristophanes and Athens: An Introduction to the Plays.* Oxford: Oxford University Press.

Nixon, Lucia. 1995. "The Cults of Demeter and Kore." In *Women in Antiquity: New Assessments,* edited by Richard Hawley and Barbara Levick, 75–96. London: Routledge.

Parke, H. W. 1977. *Festivals of the Athenians.* Ithaca: Cornell University Press.

Parker, Robert. 1996. *Athenian Religion: A History.* Oxford: Oxford University Press.

Patterson, Orlando. 1991. *Freedom: Volume 1; Freedom in the Making of Western Culture.* New York: Basic Books.

Phillips, David J., and David Pritchard, eds. 2003. *Sport and Festival in the Ancient Greek World.* London: Classical Press of Wales.

Pintchman, Tracy. 2004. "Courting Krishna on the Banks of the Ganges: Gender and Power in a Hindu Women's Ritual Tradition." *Comparative Studies of South Asia, Africa and the Middle East* 24, no. 1: 23–32.

Procter-Smith, Marjorie. 1993. "'In the Line of the Female': Shakerism and Feminism." In *Women's Leadership in Marginal Religions: Explorations outside the Mainstream,* edited by Catherine Wessinger, 23–40. Urbana: University of Illinois Press.

Qian Hang. 1991. *Zhoudai zongfa zhidushi yanjiu* (A Study of the History of the Zhou Lineage Law System). Shanghai: Xuelin chubanshe.

Raphals, Lisa. 1998. *Sharing the Light: Representations of Women and Virtue in Early China.* Albany: State University of New York Press.

———. 2001. "Arguments by Women in Early Chinese Texts." *Nan Nü* 3, no. 2: 157–95.

———. 2002. "A Woman Who Understood the Rites." In *Confucius and the Analects: New Essays,* edited by Bryan W. Van Norden, 275–302. New York: Oxford University Press.

Rawson, Jessica. 1999. "Ancient Chinese Ritual as Seen in the Material Record." In *State and Court Ritual in China,* edited by Joseph P. McDermott, 20–49. Cambridge: Cambridge University Press.

Redfield, James. 1995. "Homo Domesticus." In Vernant 1995: 153–83.

———. 2003. *The Locrian Maidens: Love and Death in Greek Italy*. Princeton: Princeton University Press.

Rose, H. J. 1957. "The Religion of a Greek Household." *Euphrosyne* 1: 95–116.

Schmitt-Pantel, Pauline. 1990. "Collective Activities and the Political in the Greek City." In *The Greek City: From Homer to Alexander*, edited by Oswyn Murray and Simon Price, 199–213. Oxford: Clarendon Press.

Segal, Charles. 1997. *Dionysiac Poetics and Euripides' Bacchae*. Expanded ed. Princeton: Princeton University Press.

Sena, David. 2005. "Reproducing Society: Lineage and Kinship in Western Zhou China." PhD diss., University of Chicago.

Shands, Kerstin W. 1999. *Embracing Space: Spatial Metaphors in Feminist Discourse*. Westport, CT: Greenwood Press.

Sharma, Arvind, ed. 1987. *Women in World Religions*. Albany: State University of New York Press.

Simon, Erika. 1983. *Festivals of Attica: An Archaeological Commentary*. Madison: University of Wisconsin Press.

Sourvinou-Inwood, Christiane. 1988. *Studies in Girls' Transitions: Aspects of the Arkteia and Age Representation in Attic Iconography*. Athens: Kardamitsa.

———. 2000a. "What Is *Polis* Religion?" In *Oxford Readings in Greek Religion*, edited by Richard Buxton, 13–37. Oxford: Oxford University Press.

———. 2000b. "Further Aspects of *Polis* Religion." In *Oxford Readings in Greek Religion*, edited by Richard Buxton, 38–55. Oxford: Oxford University Press.

Spain, Daphne. 1992. *Gendered Spaces*. Chapel Hill: University of North Carolina Press.

Vernant, Jean-Pierre. 1982. *The Origins of Greek Thought*. Ithaca: Cornell University Press.

———. 1983. "Hestia-Hermes: The Religious Expression of Space and Movement in Ancient Greece." In *Myth and Thought among the Greeks*, translated by Janet Lloyd and Jeff Fort, 127–75. London: Routledge & Kegan Paul.

———, ed. 1995. *The Greeks*. Translated by Charles Lambert and Teresa Lavender Fagan. Chicago: University of Chicago Press.

Walker, Susan. 1983. "Women and Housing in Classical Greece: The Archaeological Evidence." In *Images of Women in Antiquity*, edited by Averil Cameron and Amélie Kuhrt, 81–91. London: Croom Helm.

Winkler, John J. 1990. *The Constraints of Desire: The Anthropology of Sex and Gender in Ancient Greece*. London: Routledge.

Xenophon. 1992. "Oeconomicus." Edited and translated by E. C. Marchant. In *Memorabilia. Oeconomicus. Symposium. Apology*, 361–526. Cambridge: Harvard University Press.

Zeitlin, Froma I. 1982. "Cultic Models of the Female: Rites of Dionysus and Demeter." *Arethusa* 15, nos. 1–2: 129–57.

Zhang Jijun. 2008. "Xian Qin (The Pre-Qin)." In *Zhongguo lunli daode bianqian shigao* (A Preliminary History of the Transformation of Chinese Ethics), edited by Zhang Xiqin and Chai Wenhua, 1:9–166. Beijing: Renmin.

Zhou, Yiqun. 2003. "Virtue and Talent: Women and *Fushi* in Early China." *Nan Nü* 5, no. 1: 1–42.

———. 2010. *Festivals, Feasts, and Gender Relations in Ancient China and Greece*. New York: Cambridge University Press.

Zhu Fenghan. 2004. *Shang Zhou jiazu xingtai yanjiu* (Studies on Family Forms in Shang-Zhou China). Rev. ed. Tianjin, China: Tianjin Guji.

9

In Search of Equivalence

Conceiving Muslim-Hindu Encounter through Translation Theory

TONY K. STEWART

From the sixteenth century to the early colonial period, the region of Bengal was notable for its vibrant religious activity, activity that was often closely allied to political and military fortune, economic expansion, and the opening of new lands for cultivation. As population grew, the delta region became the site of numerous encounters of religious communities, not so much in the sense of active proselytizing or efforts to lay claim to a land in the name of religion, but in the considerably more casual process of individuals and groups from different backgrounds meeting as they moved into previously unsettled territories and tried to keep something of their religion about them. This is especially important to remember in the study of Islam in Bengal because of an often naive assumption that Bengal was innately "Hindu" and then gradually converted to Islam, when, in fact, only portions of western Bengal and the periphery around the delta were initially Hindu in orientation, while much of the remaining territory was unsettled or sparsely so. This frontier territory—much of what constitutes Bangladesh and southern parts of western Bengal today—was domesticated by practitioners of one or the other tradition on a more ad hoc basis. Those areas east of the Gaṅgā tended to yield more readily to Muslim development because of certain explicit restrictions on *brāhmaṇa* settlement and the more general fact that much of that land was insufficiently domesticated for Hindu habitation of a kind favored elsewhere. Many of the small communities that carved their niches in the un- or partially settled land were often remote and isolated, only eventually linking to larger metropolitan trading and political networks that we assume today to be the norm in the region that is now so heavily populated. In these outposts it comes as no surprise that religious power—the ability for individuals to negotiate and impose a meaningful moral order on an often wild and unruly physical and cultural landscape—was not automatically an issue of theology or doctrinal purity and even less so an issue of religious practice. The evidence suggests that what was deemed right was what was powerful (and vice versa), and what was religiously powerful in these regions was often simply what worked to help people endure. Regardless of their background, nearly everyone in this precolonial period acknowledged certain forms of local and regional power, and because of this, apposite religious structures (e.g., the ascetic Hindu *saṃnyāsin* and the Sufi *pīr*) operated with a kind of exchange equivalence.[1] Doctrine seems often to have had little bearing in these situations, but that in no way should imply that doctrine was not present; it was simply used and understood differently than is the academic norm today.

If we approach the development of religious belief and practice in Bengal as a function of the local and assume that in this environment improvisation was central to survival—as it would have to be in an area without the strong institutions that accompany more organized religion—then we must reconceive the nature of the religious encounter that characterizes the region in this pre- and early colonial period. The reason is straightforward enough: old academic models for articulating this encounter label it "conflict," in which case there is little left to say apart from that one succeeded and the other did not, or label it "syncretism," which produces something new and different from either original part. Seldom do we see any analysis that articulates how two or more traditions in this region might encounter one another without this ontological shift in the makeup of the tradition; and the change most often assumed is the latter. Syncretism is predicated on the assumption that preexisting and discrete doctrinal or ritual systems are mysteriously combined to form some unnatural admixture. But the myriad forms of the concept of syncretism (when used as an interpretive, rather than strictly descriptive, category) become highly problematic in nearly all of their applications because they nearly uniformly read into the history the very institutional (ritual, theological, social) structures that are not yet present in any enduring way. But this is to say that the constituent parts that are brought together to create this syncretistic entity are historical back formations of a kind that could be made only once the tradition was successfully rooted. And precisely because the end product is conceived as the unholy alliance of religious entities that should be kept apart in an ideal world—again because the constituent parts are idealized, essentialized, and completely stripped of their historical grounding—the focus is on the result, rather than the process, and that product is routinely described in negative terms. Until very recently, this has been the case with nearly all of the studies of Islam in the Bengali environment.[2] Ultimately, this kind of theorizing constructs models that have little or no relation to what actually happens in the course of practice except as an arbitrary measure of deviation from some presupposed norm, a measure that is rhetorically effective for religiously committed reformers but that should be highly problematic for historians.

The experience attested in the extensive literatures of precolonial Bengal, however, suggests a very different kind of religious experience, an experience that did not produce unviable end products as syncretists would argue, but established enduring frameworks of religious organization and interpretation that eventually grounded the traditions as we understand them today in their regional forms. These encounters emphasized the local, the creative efforts of individuals trying to make sense of an environment that did not always cooperate. The textual evidence of early Bengali Islam, which by virtue of this dearth must be considered potentially idiosyncratic, individualistic, and highly localized, points to very pragmatic applications of doctrine to practice, from the ragged and incomplete to very sophisticated creations. These texts portray the struggle of individuals and their groups—various persuasions of Sufis, but also Sunnis and Shi'ahs—to understand their Hindu counterparts—Vaiṣṇavas, Śaivas, Śāktas, and others, and never in terms of the gross categories of Hindu and Muslim, which are the stock and trade of syncretistic formulations. These early Bengali Islamic texts document the way authors attempted to make their understanding "fit" with those they encountered, and that process of understanding became an extended act of "translation." Translation in this context defines a way that religious practitioners seek "equivalence" among their counterparts. As will become apparent, it is this act of translation that offers an alternative interpretive strategy for conceptualizing the way these various Sufi communities formulated their understandings of the contours of power in Bengal. Because of the local nature of this religious expression, power that could be translated could be effective for everyone, regardless of persuasion; by extension, we might argue that only those constructions that were translated were truly effective, and in that dynamic process of translation comes the creative application of doctrine to real life. The results of the encounter of traditions can best be appraised in the process of this interaction, not in the static instantiated end product that is often falsely understood to result. But before examining how the processes of translation can provide a model for reconceptualizing the issue, it is necessary to understand first why the concept of syncretism fails in most cases as a viable interpretive category to explain the encounter of Islam with the various Hindu traditions of Bengal. It is important to note that both arguments hinge on common but complex issues of language and category formation that are shared by nearly all religious writers of the time and region.

LANGUAGE AND CATEGORY FORMATION
IN THE BENGALI MIDDLE PERIOD

In the premodern, precolonial literature of Bengal, it is not at all uncommon to find overtly religious texts using common technical vocabularies that today we routinely identify as significant markers of sectarian affiliation. From our late twentieth-century perspective, this language allows us to categorize the orientation of these texts as Muslim or Hindu, and those categories themselves are deemed transparent and generally unambiguous to the contemporary reader. Yet many texts from the older period do not lend themselves to such easy marking, not only in the common Bengali folk genres such as *pāñcālī* and *pālā gān*, but in romance and semi-epic, and even certain overtly religious speculations and instructional manuals. Among the latter, it is the Sufi literature that is perhaps most difficult to interpret because of the mixture of technical and nontechnical terms from sometimes unexpected sources, but other less overtly religious genres have adopted similar lexical strategies, so the analysis of the Sufi approaches should yield insights into the full range of forms.

Because many among today's scholastically oriented, as well as many among the general educated populace, judge these texts by holding them to a standard of value that equates a purity of language to a purity of religious intention, these Sufi and related texts are all too frequently deemed so sufficiently problematic that they are not seriously examined as documents of a Bengali Islam. For many modern interpreters of South Asian Islam, a text is often assumed to be unworthy of study when the technical vocabulary for key theological concepts suggests anything other than a consistent use of a strict and unambiguous Islamic vocabulary that is derived from Urdu or Persian (and ultimately from Arabic). A text that mixes Islamic vocabularies with others, especially those apparently Hindu, can be acknowledged in only a limited way, if at all, but is more often simply avoided as a perhaps well-intentioned, but somehow confused, or at least confusing—and therefore potentially dangerous—work. The effect of this approach is to divert the gaze from an important formative dimension of the history of Bengal. This negative result is further exacerbated when the depiction of Islamic life found in some of these texts appears to overlap with other religious traditions—again especially various modalities of Hindu religion—or when its praise extends to specific religious figures, mythical or historical, who are promoted or shared across these boundaries (e.g., Satya Pīr), or, more problematic yet, when opposing sectarian ethical or religious systems of value are espoused that appear at least on the surface to be transparently the same in their working effect (e.g., *adab* and *dharma*). In today's often highly charged political climate where language and religion and politics are often aligned to define mutually exclusive identities, the reason for this response is actually rather unambiguous: for most contemporary interpreters, whether in Bangladesh, India, Pakistan, or the West, the concept of religious encounter—which this shared vocabulary and shared experience imply—is almost automatically understood in terms of ideological "contest," if not conflict, an assumption that pits two opposing groups in eternal enmity. These rigid monolithic constructs play a very important role in nearly all theories of their interaction, as will become apparent. Historically this has not always been the case.

Because of the nature of this commonly held presupposition about the exclusive nature of religions and religious experience, the contemporary interpreter is generally blind to the fact that this attitude is itself the result of historical processes that have conflated religious orientations with political identities in the colonial and postcolonial periods. Since the reform movements of the late eighteenth and nineteenth centuries, starting with the Wahhabis, but eventually including others of different religious persuasions, a general and very unreflective assumption in the intellectual (and certainly the political) community of Bengal has gradually taken hold: people routinely assume that when an author uses a specialized vocabulary to talk of religious matters, that author is making a political statement about his religious intentions.[3] Since the mid-nineteenth century, it has become increasingly difficult when declaring a religious preference not to declare a political proclivity, if not a clearly demarcated identity, because of the various state-imposed institutions that have historically conflated the two; this was especially precipitated in the effects of the first census taken in 1872 and then translated into other state apparatuses, such as domestic law and parliamentary representation, which guaranteed separation of religions as a standard for public polity.[4] An overt religious declaration or the equally obvious choice of technical language to speak of significant issues is now generally assumed to signify a political orientation that reveals the author's "real" or underlying intention in writing a religious work.

But today the possibility of ever determining "authorial intent" precisely is now moot, with most modern analysts arguing that no matter what an author claims to be doing, the reader can never really know; or, in the extreme, the author cannot know fully what he is about, thereby making any estimate of intention little more than informed speculation that often reflects more the concerns of the interpreter and his world. In its worst case, this hermeneutical skepticism can produce an outright epistemological impasse for analysis.[5] While this debate about intentionality generally focuses on fiction, it has important ramifications for other forms of writing, especially where religious values are articulated. So whenever a religious text uses a mixed language that seems to confuse "proper" religious ideals—ideals that are determined in advance by these nineteenth- and twentieth-century standards of purity and exclusion—the precolonial author is judged to be either confused or just ignorant, or alternatively his work can comfortably be ignored in a way that allows the text to be manipulated toward the ends of the interpreter. Either way, the text seems to disappear from public view as an independent document with any historical or intrinsic value.

In his pioneering Bengali literary histories, Muhammad Enamul Haq (Bengali: Muhammad Enāmul Hak) cataloged Muslim writers from this early period, classifying their works into genres, such as *śarā-śarāyit* (legal and moral code), *kāhinī* (historical tales), *sṛṣṭitattva* (cosmogony), *darśana* (theology and philosophy), *sūphītattva* (Sufi metaphysics), *premopākhyāna* (romance literature), *marsīyā* (lamentations), *itihāsika-kāvya* (historical poetry), *rūpaka* (rhetoric), *padāvalī* (lyric poetry), and a miscellaneous category for leftovers.[6] He also did much the same for Sufi literature in his *Bange Sūphi Prabhāva*.[7] It is significant that in those early works an entire class of religious literature was simply eliminated, texts that were to his eyes a hodgepodge of Sufi, Vaiṣṇava, Nātha, general *tāntrika*, and other religious ideas both mainstream and not. It is easy to speculate that these texts were omitted precisely because in their language they failed to fit the exclusive categories he had constructed. Their apparent hybridity was, not surprisingly, problematic for those construing religious or ideological purity as a litmus test for inclusion in a "proper" literature and was just as problematic for those compiling a "national" literature, both impulses applying to the Pakistan in which he wrote.[8]

Among those texts omitted, and therefore worthy of additional scrutiny, were two books called *Āgama* and *Jñānasāgara* by one Āli Rajā, and one of these will retain our attention as an example for analysis.[9] These books, often paired as two parts to a single book, present a sophisticated systematic theology, grounded in an extensive cosmology that serves to justify the yogic mode of Sufi practice. Sharif considers Āli Rajā, whose precise dates are uncertain, to be one of the most significant thinkers of the eighteenth century, with a metaphysical acumen equal to the great Vaiṣṇava scholar Kṛṣṇadāsa Kavirāja or the Muslim scholar Hājī Muhammad.[10] Āli Rajā (alt. Rājā, Rejā, Riḍā), who also wrote under the alias of Oyāhed Kānu Phakir, was a Sufi from the village of Ośa Khāin, Ānoyārā District, in Caṭṭagrāma (Chittagong), whose family still claims a tract of land there. He had for his *murshid* (spiritual guide) and *dikṣāguru* (initiating teacher) the famous Śāh Keyāmuddin, and in that association he wrote extensively, in addition to the two aforementioned works, a book of meditations put to music titled *Dhyānamālā* and the speculative *Sirājkulupa*. He was also a poet of some stature, with no fewer than forty-seven of his *pada*s surviving, all of which are on the theme of Rādhā and Kṛṣṇa's love.[11] His sons were also authors of some note.[12] All of this suggests that Āli Rajā was a fairly prominent member of the Islamic literati around the prosperous region of Chittagong, who left a significant literary and religious legacy—yet Haq's original classification scheme could find no comfortable place for Āli Rajā's metaphysical works. It was only much later that Haq reluctantly recognized Āli Rajā and others like him in his English *A History of Sufi-ism in Bengal*, where, as an obvious afterthought, he tacked on two short chapters at the end of his book to create a new category called "Muslim Yoga Literature." This reflects a more discrete and somewhat more neutral acknowledgment of its "hybrid" or "admixed" character previously noted by Karim, who had published Āli Rajā's *Jñānasāgara* nearly a half century earlier.[13] By creating a separate category of syncretistic labels for this literature, Haq and his followers have operated on the assumption that these authors were engaged in an intellectual and religious activity that was somehow fundamentally different from what other "mainstream" authors did, that writers like Āli Rajā were trying to create a new religious identity or praxis that was perhaps ingenious but ultimately confused. With this assumption hinging on Āli Rajā's use of an explicitly non-Muslim vocabulary, the literary gaze is turned to works of perceived greater value. But if we begin with a different proposition about his use of this non-Islamic vocabulary, assuming that it was a search for equivalence, assuming that he and others were attempting to articulate sophisticated ideas of their own using the locally available lexicon with its limiting conceptual structure, these texts suddenly come alive as examples of Islamic expansion in an entirely new mode, a linguistic and cultural appropriation, not an Islamic dissipation.

Before attempting to classify by genre the texts of Āli Rajā and others like him, and automatically implying in that classification a value judgment, we might fruitfully start one step earlier in the hermeneutic process by asking ourselves about the availability and limits of language in the historical time and place of these texts. It becomes clear that no unambiguously Islamic idiom existed in Bengali during the time, or at least it was only beginning to emerge by the end of the period. Such specific Islamic technical vocabulary would not prevail until sometime later, largely with the development of institutional infrastructures, and even that language—in spite of attempts by certain factions to identify a "Musalmani" Bengali—has never been, nor could it be, completely "pure" in ideational terms. The reason it cannot be pure in exclusively Islamic terms is because the Bengali language itself has its roots in Sanskrit, which has been the bearer of a traditional culture that operates according to assumptions that are common to the religious traditions of the Hindus, and of course Jains, Sikhs, early Buddhists, and others. It has been well documented that religions and languages share many features as formal, albeit now widely understood to be open-ended, semiotic systems, regardless of how that structural similitude is construed. For our purposes, one of the most relevant points of convergence is in the ability of both language and religion to capture, preserve, and reify basic cultural values, to structure experience according to shared conceptual elements. Language of course is not religion, but the two rely heavily on each other in this process of articulating what is of value, because language itself structures the conceptual world of any culture to the point where certain thoughts cannot be entertained in a given language, and those structures that prevail in a language will reflect what is significant to its host culture.[14] It is important to note that religion is often the most pronounced articulator and repository of those key structures of meaning and value, and in its use of texts—whether oral or written—language becomes the medium of the experience; hence the close relation. Any analysis should, then, account for the ways that Bengali Muslims chose to use this Bengali language that has from its inception been imbued with a religious or ideational sensibility that is other than Islamic.

The problem was not simply that these authors were attempting to use the Bengali language to express ideas that were not in the Bengali language's original conceptual structure, for many of the key concepts that control an Islamic cosmology and theology were in fact present (and this, as will become apparent, is vitally important to our strategy of interpretation). Precisely because these concepts were present—even though the terms frequently carried or at least implied additional conceptual entailments that were alien to Islam as an extension of the terms' semantic fields—Bengali offered a potentially malleable medium for the message of Islam, which is to say that the ideas were not so alien that they could not be expressed in the extant vocabulary of the sixteenth, seventeenth, and eighteenth centuries. That Bengali should be so used is paramount to the Islamic conception of its own message, for Islam claims for itself a transnational and universal status; that is, Muslim practitioners argue that the sublime object of their religious world is transportable across all national and cultural boundaries, and its tenets can be conveyed in any language (in spite of the caveat that the Holy Qur'ān can only be in Arabic). Had this not been so, Islam would have remained exclusively limited to Semitic-language speakers in a tightly confined geographic area; yet Islam has been a vibrant force in South Asia for well over a thousand years, and in Bengal for a good portion of that. Given the developing nature of the language during the premodern period, coupled with the proposition that the language itself structures the very ideas being conveyed, we might not unreasonably ask how it is that a Muslim author can use Bengali successfully to convey his religious sensibility, without compromising his commitments or inadvertently changing Islam itself. To answer this question may be the first step in determining what constitutes a distinctively Bengali Islam, as opposed to the more usual strategy of measuring Islam in Bengal against some essentialized ideal. And the few extant Sufi texts are among the most extensive Islamic Bengali documents of the formative period, capturing the struggle of these early practitioners as they tried to articulate a Muslim vision in the local vernacular, a language that bore the weight of centuries of Hindu adaptation.

THE PROBLEM OF SYNCRETISM

The language of the texts composed by the likes of Āli Rajā, especially the technical vocabulary, appears to our contemporary sensibility to be largely Hindu, perhaps most obviously in the yogic terminology, but that appearance only disguises to our modern eyes what were thoroughly Islamic conceptions.

Most interpreters characterize this language as somehow "hybrid." Hybridity is only one version of the larger interpretive strategy that hinges on the concept of "syncretism." But the model of syncretism is never simply applied to the language itself but—and this is one of its biggest flaws—operates on the assumption that the language transparently and faithfully reflects the traditions behind the language (not just their conceptual structures), and so the analysis almost imperceptibly shifts from language to tradition, naively extrapolating the form of religion from its limited expression in texts. As it has been used in the history of religions, this model of syncretism assumes that two distinct entities—in these examples, "Islam" and "Hinduism," as if those were somehow truly monolithic entities—were brought together to form some new construction that shared parts of both but could be classified as neither.[15] But the concept of this syncretism is ultimately faulty as an interpretive model for two closely related reasons, which have been hinted at earlier. First, syncretism assumes at the outset its own conclusions, in a curious form of the logical fallacy of *petitio principii*, by articulating the inappropriate alliance of two things that in their essential form are mutually exclusive and distinct from each other—yogic meditation in ecstatic practice in the case of early Bengali Sufis, for example—and which do not "naturally" belong together because they have been defined as such. Second, the unstated object of the model of syncretism is its end product, pointing to the creation of some kind of static "entity" that is by virtue of its violation of exclusive categories inherently unstable. This model, which conveniently sidesteps any attempt to understand the process by which these seemingly disparate or disjunctive religious beliefs and practices interact, is forever damned to project unseemly (i.e., "impure") entities that cannot reproduce themselves (i.e., they are not viable), if in fact they are anything more than the product of the scholastic imagination in the first place. It is the way this end product is articulated that reveals the problem most vividly, because any resort to interpretive models of syncretism appears on the surface to produce neutral descriptions, but the descriptions are never direct nor are they precise: they are always metaphoric and value laden. And the metaphoric constructs not only free the interpreter from examining syncretism itself but generally reveal their almost universally negative implications. The metaphors, which only hint at processes (but never explicitly articulate the combining action directly, leaving it to the reader to imagine), imply that the resulting form is unnatural, and therefore unstable, if not doomed to eventual destruction. There are four basic categories of metaphor that control these images, each of which demonstrates how the underlying notion of invalidity is disguised but omnipresent: (1) borrowing and influence, (2) the "cultural veneer" or overlay, (3) alchemy, and (4) organic or biological reproduction.[16]

Borrowing and Influence

Often not even understood as a form of syncretism, the economically derived metaphor of "borrowing" suggests that members of one group (here Sufis, especially in Bengal the Chishtīyya and Naqshbandīyya) are not sufficiently creative or independent to think for themselves and must take prefabricated ideas or rituals from somewhere else (here Hindu, largely Vaiṣṇava theology, or from yoga in modalities of meditative practice) to articulate its truths— and of course with that limited understanding the borrower inevitably uses the "borrowed" ideas and rituals improperly, that is, not as they were "meant to be" used. Similarly, the astrologically based metaphor of "influence," originally explained as emanations from the stars and planets, is understood to exert mysterious unseen force, often articulated through sophisticated hydraulic metaphors, causing someone or some group to be persuaded without fully understanding why. The explanation then suggests that volition was absent in the decision-making process, which thinly disguises the borrowing metaphor, making one group dependent, passively receptive, and therefore of less value than the source. For example, the Sufi poets of this early age could only imagine their religious path in already well-developed yogic terms.

The "Cultural Veneer" or Overlay

Another common metaphor of syncretism is that of "cultural veneer," an overlay of one alien culture on another, which in our examples is inevitably an imported Islam overlaid onto a Bengal that is assumed to be Hindu. While giving the appearance of accounting for historical change, since Hindus were assumed to be there first, the resulting amalgam describes no process but rather a static condition, an end result. The entailment of the metaphor, however, is decidedly pointed with respect to an obviously anticipated result, for veneers are generally thin layers of fragile ornamental wood or other material bonded to a foundation that is coarse and sturdy. Subject to delamination, the veneer is easily damaged or destroyed; that is, it is impermanent, while the permanent base continues to function as it always had, perpetrating by the choice of metaphor a not-so-subtle political commentary. Occasionally this approach is articulated as the "false mask," with many of the same entailments.

Alchemy

Alchemy is arguably the most popular metaphor of syncretism, one that secondarily shares in the hydraulic metaphor of influence, while maintaining a chemical basis of interaction and reaction. The combinations that can be forged in the alchemical crucible produce either permanent change or reversible temporary conditions. Understood as bad or quack science, the irreversible combination of fluids or the dissolution of a compound results in the creation of a solution that is often construed as a dangerous process by combining elements that should not be. Such daring processes create new entities that often have little or no use, and can in fact be fatal to those who come into contact with them, as religious reformers are quick to point out. The more common alchemical model of syncretism, however, is the "mixture," a colloidal suspension of two ultimately irreconcilable liquids that will inevitably separate, or the admixture of solids that with little effort will disintegrate. In both versions of this more commonly conceived mixture of religious beliefs and practices, the parts retain their unique identities, implying that their essences are unchanged and their concoction is little more than a momentary juxtaposition.

Biological Reproduction

The biological is arguably the most persuasive model of syncretism: two or more contributing "parents" produce through miscegenation an offspring that cannot be classed with either parent (even Manu invokes this image to explain the multitude of *varṇa* designations); equally often the offspring is a "bastard" of unacknowledged provenance, for example, the mother was raped by some unknown assailant. The potential inflammatory nature of this kind of metaphor lends itself to an obvious polemic. When the offspring's characteristics are identifiable to a parent, the "mixture" metaphor is subsequently invoked and those features are understood to be dominant, that is, its "real" characteristics come through. If the product is blended in such a way that dominant features from both parents are incorporated, it is a hybrid (plant) or half-breed (animal), again classifiable with neither source. But the negative entailment of the hybrid metaphor is that these offspring do not reproduce because they are sterile, or if they manage to reproduce, they do not "breed true"; that is, most will disaggregate in one or two generations.

None of these models of syncretism adequately characterizes the process by which the religious practitioner actually encounters the other and addresses it, leaving those processes to the imagination invoked by the metaphor itself, a move that shifts the focus onto the ostensible end product, itself a metaphoric creation. And, of equal import, each of the models of religious syncretism carries in its metaphor the implicit expectation of failure, falsity, or impermanence, a decidedly negative valuation in nearly every case, the only possible exception being the occasional good alchemical solution or the rare hybrid that does manage to reproduce. On the whole, the models presuppose essentialized, dehistoricized, monolithic entities that interact in ways that cannot be described directly, only metaphorically, with the conclusion that they are unnatural and inappropriate not only built into their original category formation, but reinforced in the entailments of the metaphors themselves. Further, the evidence that is marshaled to make the arguments for syncretism is largely linguistic, punctuated by the occasional physical monument or record of ritual but predicated on the all-too-easy assumption that the language of these texts transparently and directly reflects experience and practice, an assumption that uncritically, although not necessarily intentionally, extends the original Whorfian hypothesis (i.e., that language reflects categories of meaning) to the instantiation and reification of religious traditions that are at best idealized constructions read back into the material. The reader can see in the passage further on how seductive and easy these models would be to apply, which should in itself give pause. So to offer an alternative that does not naively assume that the language of the text is a literal replica of religious belief or practice, we must return to the initial language through which we understand these early Bengali Sufis and other Islamic practitioners and theologians. I would like to propose a different interpretive strategy that would refocus the question onto the active dimension of these texts and their authors and consumers, that is, to account for the "process of production," rather than a description of the static end product of this complex and challenging cultural and religious interaction.

In contrast to the model of syncretism that proposes to describe the new amalgam created by these Sufi texts, I would propose that we can reconstruct a process by which the premodern Sufi or other Muslim writer, working within the constraints of a Bengali language whose extant technical vocabulary was conditioned largely by Hindu ideational constructs, attempted to imagine an Islamic ideal in a new literary environment. These texts become, then, historical witnesses to the earliest attempts to think Islamic thoughts in the local language, which is to say, to think new thoughts for Bengali, ideas that had never previously been explicitly expressed, otherwise there probably would have been an explicit vocabulary to support them, as there now is. In order to express their ways of imagining the world, we must assume that these Muslim authors did not "borrow" terms but, in a more intellectually astute process, sought the closest "terms of equivalence" in order to approximate the ideas they wanted to express. Put another way—and here the direction of this method should become clear—these early Bengali Islamic authors "translated" their concepts into the closest locally available terminology as a step toward articulating a different kind of religious orientation, but as we shall see, terminology is not just words, but entire conceptual worlds, metaphoric worlds. If we assume that the authors were fully cognizant of what they were doing, that is, they were not confusing Islam and various traditions of Hinduism, then we can see that while appearing to write in their own language (Bengali), they were in effect translating into that language ideas and concepts that were at least somewhat alien to it. Eventually a technical terminology derived from Persian and Arabic would take its place in the Bengali of the Muslim author, and this vocabulary would prove to be formidable in size and effect;[17] but in the earliest stages of this process, which date to the sixteenth through eighteenth centuries, that particular technical terminology was not a common or widely agreed-upon part of the Bengali language, so the texts from this period illustrate the initial experiments of these innovative and adventurous authors. In order to understand how translation itself can become the model for interpreting these texts, I propose that different styles of translation imply, if not explicitly dictate, systematic decisions regarding the act of translating; that in turn suggests that formal theories of translation can help to illustrate the complexity of the process by providing a logical structure against which to measure the extent of these early authors' struggle to use Bengali to a new end. What follows is an all-too-brief outline of the proposed approach, based on an extended close reading of a single passage of an eighteenth-century Bengali Sufi text.

"TRANSLATION THEORY" AS HERMENEUTIC MODEL

All of translation is a search for equivalence, but obviously the kind of equivalence that is sought is dictated by the nature of the concept being translated from the source language (SL) and the desired result in the target or receiving language (TL). In our examples, however, the language appears at first glance to be just Bengali, but in this premodern period, it is the special relationship of Bengali to its "parent" languages, especially Sanskrit, that makes this "translation" possible. In this precolonial period, when a Bengali author wished to speak technically about matters of religion, or economics, medicine, or any specialized branch of knowledge, he tapped Sanskrit for its rich and precise vocabulary, often appropriating words and phrases in toto without modification. This special diglossia, which was marked by the learned who were frequently multilingual and could shift easily from Bengali to Sanskrit—or, more often, who used a highly Sanskritized Bengali in complex acts of "code-switching"—gradually enriched the Bengali language to the point where it could express ideas that previously had only been possible in Sanskrit itself.[18] The process was quickened by the many translations of Sanskrit epics and other works that had been commissioned by various royal patrons during the fifteenth through eighteenth centuries, translations such as the *Mahābhārata* and *Rāmāyaṇa*, the stories of the *Bhāgavata* and other *Purāṇa*s, and so on. When the first authors of distinctly Islamic texts began to write in the vernacular—something that apparently was considered unnecessary at first, since the language of the courts was generally Persian, which was considered a more appropriate vehicle for the lofty ideas of Islamic scholarship—most of the Bengali technical terminology and its concomitant conceptual structures were of Sanskrit origin. Problematic was the fact that the conceptual structure these Sufi authors were seeking to translate derived ostensibly from Arabic, although it was actually primarily through Persian; it was decidedly not Bengali. It is interesting to note that Bengali speakers in general, but especially notably, Bengali Muslims, resisted the domination of the higher languages of the Muslim elite, unlike vernacular speakers in other regions that underwent the Islamization process.[19] This is borne out today by the role language played in the independence of Bangladesh in 1971 and how that functioned as a unifier of diverse peoples. Consequently, after several centuries of active use of Bengali by Muslim authors, the situation is different for the users of the language, for Bengali enjoys what Bakhtin would call a polyphonic relation to the languages of its high culture (Sanskrit, Arabic, Persian, and even Urdu).[20] Before that level of adaptation could occur, however, the initial move was to seek appropriate, albeit apparently not altogether comfortable, terms of equivalence.

Relying on contemporary translation studies, we can isolate a number of often radically different formal approaches to this search for equivalence that can account for many, if not all, of the incredible linguistic manipulations found in these early religious texts, such as Āli Rajā's. Religious encounter seen as translation, however, is not just an act of utterance followed by the emotional, political, and ideological conflict of conversion, but ultimately reveals a movement of accommodation by the receiving or target language and the culture it represents, which when sufficiently pursued eventually becomes an act of appropriation. The target language incorporates fully the new terms and concepts that result from this encounter, a process that is patently different from syncretism. The act of incorporating what is alien ultimately changes its host—and here is where we can trace some of the processes of religious change, the making of a Bengali Islam. For example, the Muslim *pīr* and his teaching are not just accepted as legitimate expressions of Bengali religiosity; when appropriated into the language and culture, the image of the *pīr* has actually had an effect on analogous, that is, "equivalent," theological and institutional structures of Hindus by modifying their images of the holy man. This process is especially obvious in the Vaiṣṇava case where the power of the *pīr* was more readily recognized because of strong theological affinities, among other factors. The initial act of this Muslim encounter with a Hindu religious figure leads the authors to search for some kind of parallel or analogue in an effort to find an equivalent term or concept, for example, *saṃnyāsī*, *vairāgī*, and so forth, that signifies the original term's common features as found in *pīr*, a strong match in the semantic fields of the term and its gloss. But as the terms of equivalence are actively used, the target language concept—in this example, the Hindu holy man—slowly yields to a dialectic of differentiation with the alien concept—in this example, the *pīr*—that gradually incorporates the alien term and its concept as similar to but uniquely distinct from its analogue, so that today *pīr* and *saṃnyāsī* are both recognized as Bengali words with related but distinct meanings. When the "translation" is successful, the new term becomes a part of the target culture's extended religious vocabulary, and carries with it, or at least points to, another conceptual world. Yet this process of seeking equivalence invariably leaves out some of the original idea, while introducing new ideas into the equation. José Ortega y Gasset captured something of the paradox inherent in the effort to express the thoughts of one language and its culture in those of another: "Two apparently contradictory laws are involved in all uttering. One says, 'Every utterance is deficient'—it says less than it wishes to say. The other law, the opposite, declares, 'Every utterance is exuberant'—it conveys more than it plans and includes not a few things we should wish left silent."[21] As do languages, when religious traditions encounter one another, they translate, and when they do, they inevitably observe this paradoxical rule of discursive transformation. This is a creative and improvisational act that enriches and strengthens both participants, but this dialectic is uneven, and it does not automatically or predictably lead to the creation of some strange new creation but augments the existing entities, enriching all. To impose some logical order on our analysis of these varying processes, we will briefly sample four different strategies of increasing complexity that are in evidence in Āli Rajā's text and others like it, although it would be easy to multiply the numbers: (1) formal literal equivalence, (2) refracted equivalence, (3) dynamic equivalence, and (4) metaphoric equivalence.[22]

Let us turn, then, to Āli Rajā, to look at a snippet of the *Āgama* text that deals with cosmogony:

The Foundation of Creation: The Metaphysics of Light (Nur-Tattva)

In the beginningless space the prime mover and creator (*karatā*) alone existed. The Stainless One (*nirañjana*) was a creamy essence in the thick of the enveloping universe of bleak inertia (*tama guṇa*). When the one called Stainless (*nirañjana*) rent the interior of that orb, he transformed into the Lord Īśvara. Forms (*ākāra*) began to differentiate within that universe and the unitary formless (*nirākāra*) metamorphosed into seventy-one forms. When the formless (*nirākāra*) assumed form, the Stainless (*nirañjana*) took the name of Viṣṇu. The blazing effulgence (*ujjvala*) of the formless (*nirākāra*) quickened the formed (*ākāra*); and the darkness enveloped the blazing light with its dazzling colors: white (*sattva*), black (*tamaḥ*), and reddish-orange (*rajaḥ*) were latent and undifferentiated. No one could distinguish among the three qualities (*guṇa*) what was pleasing.

When the unsegmented universe was segmented into parts, consciousness (*cetana*) drifted in the primal waters. Emotional Being (*bhāva*) inferred its own existence within those primal waters. As it labored to unite (*yoga*) with the Lord, it experienced the essence of love (*prema rasa*). No part (*kalā*) can be under the control of passionate love in a form that is unsegmented. In the absence of syzygies (*yugala*) the intellect (*manas*) cannot discern name [and form]. Unable to distinguish pairs, neither action nor naming can occur. Without the conjunction [of opposites], neither speech nor love is possible. When the Stainless (*nirañjana*) conceived a love for an opposing lover, consciousness (*cetana*) permeated the realm of the unmanifest (*nirākāra*). The Prime Mover (*karatā*) was concealed within the realm of creation, and through his independent immaculate power parted the waters and cleansed the darkness. From that which was without form (*nirākāra*), the formed (*ākāra*) was born as the initial sonic-form "a" (*akāra*). The formless (*nirākāra*) generated the sonic-form "u" (*ukāra*) through the sonic-form "a." From the union of the sonic-forms "a" and "u," the sonic-form "m" (*makāra*) was born. Its power (*śakti*) was realized as [the qualities] *sattva*, *rajaḥ*, and *tamaḥ*. The sonic-form "m" (*makāra*) pulled himself from the waters. Looking at himself [reflected] in the waters, he was smitten (*mohita*) with the love of a devotee (*bhakta*). As he gazed at the reflection of his own initial image (*nija ākāra*), he gained consciousness of himself, yet he remained absorbed, undifferentiated from the sonic-form "a" (*akāra*) and the sonic-form "u" (*ukāra*). For aeons they remained coiled together as a single form, the universe of the sonic-form "m" (*makāra*) within the sonic-form "u" (*ukāra*) within the sonic-form "a" (*akāra*). The sonic-form "m" (*makāra*) grew fiercely hot within the sonic-forms "a" (*akāra*) and "u" (*ukāra*). From the unified one came the two a coupled pair [like] the archer with his bow properly strung. The unifying single name of the triple world remained hidden, the sonic-form "m" (*makāra*) and the sonic-form "u" (*ukāra*) together preserving the unifying essence. The Imperishable Syllable (*akṣara*) remained in solitude within the triple forms. It was from this single Imperishable Syllable (*akṣara*) that the triple world arose.[23]

While others more knowledgeable of the niceties of the explicit and implied cosmological systems in this not altogether transparent text may not agree with every line of my translation, there are some unmistakably distinct acts of Āli Rajā's translation that we can identify, and which will in the final analysis show him to be using this vocabulary for his own very distinct Islamic objectives.

FORMAL LITERAL EQUIVALENCE

While serving as a logical starting point, "formal literal equivalence" in practice was seldom sought in the early Bengali Muslim writings, because formal equivalence operates on the naive assumption that each idea or concept can be literally translated from the source language into the target language without addition or subtraction of meaning. In the West, this formalism has grounded nearly all classical theories and confounded more than a few interpreters over the last two millennia. But perfect one-to-one correspondences simply seldom existed in the materials that the early Bengali Muslim writers sought to describe, and this is tacitly acknowledged by its absence; on this simplistic level, perfect equivalence makes translation invisible, which is only possible for very simple, nontechnical concepts. In practice this literalism in matters of religious import functions more as an ideal generally held by the unreflective, by those who do not translate at all, or by those who wish to make a point that deliberately runs roughshod over subtlety and nuance, as, for example, in the Vaiṣṇava figure Kṛṣṇa Caitanya's argument with a *pīr* wherein he equates the *Bhāgavata Purāṇa* and the Qur'ān, the point of course being conversion.[24] Beyond that basic semantic level, literal equivalence loses much of its practical value because it works only for the simplest terms or for the broadest generalizations. Take, for instance, such limited concepts as recitation of the name, *dhikr* and *japa*; but even here supposed equivalence requires immediate clarification, which is to admit its failure. While noting that this strategy is useful for setting a baseline in our analysis, there is little evidence within these works that the semantic fields of religiously significant terms were ever conceived to be identical, transparent, or literally equal to their adopted equivalents—our examples would be limited here to very general mythic constructs such as the primal waters, the chaos before order, or the darkness that pervades prior to creation, all of which are sufficiently vague that they require little or no reflection until they are later manipulated. Most of the equivalences, however, are more realistically seen as "approximations of equivalence," which leads to the more common conception of translation that today is called, among other things, "refraction."

Refraction and Mirroring

Refraction theory suggests that one be not so much concerned with literalness as with locating approximations—and this strategy was historically useful for establishing equivalent grounds of meaning between Muslims and Hindus. To describe refraction, André Lefevere coined the expression "mirroring," for a translation reflects the original idea but refracts it in the process; that is, it does not capture the identical semantic field but approximates it, often with distortions, the latter being key.[25] With this approach, central religious or other concepts can be established as analogues. For instance, a Hindu notion of god, Viṣṇu-Nārāyaṇa, is held to be the equivalent of Allah, especially through the shared concept of "stainlessness" or *nirañjana*, as Āli Rajā uses the term throughout the first paragraph of the sample text. This concept, explicitly denoting one of Viṣṇu's features, resonates strongly with the equivalent characteristics of God that are enumerated in *dhikr*. This kind of refraction works best in those areas where obvious and overt similarities of character or action can be aligned. In this way an author can compare in general terms an institution such as the Hindu *tola* with the Islamic *madrasa*, or a *guruparamparā* with a Sufi *silsilah*, with a certain confidence that he will not be misunderstood as equating the two; they are roughly similar in function or form, but they are not the same. Refraction theory reaches its limit of usefulness, or is prone to confusing the reader, when it reaches the point where the communities place different values on these apparently equivalent practices or expressions, especially in their specific and technical functions. To handle this differentiation, the authors turn to a more complex strategy of establishing "functional analogues" that bear strong resemblance to the translation theories of Eugene A. Nida that emphasize the context of a term or phrase.

DYNAMIC EQUIVALENCE

Nida, who rejects the "literal" and "refraction" approaches as logically formal theories that describe impractical ideals, offers an alternative in his theory of "dynamic equivalence."[26] Dynamic equivalence not only accounts for overlapping semantic domains but also gives priority to cultural context, which can begin to account for the different values ascribed to equivalent terms. The emphasis shifts away from the precise content and contours of the idea being translated, toward that idea as it is used in its social context, its role and function within the target language and culture, which then allows for a kind of creative latitude in seeking equivalence. Āli Rajā in this short passage uses a *sāṃkhya*-derived terminology to describe the basic dualism that is inherent in all Islamic cosmogonic portrayals according to which the world depends on the opposition of paired elements, the syzygies (*yugala*), necessary for discrimination and cognition to arise. Yet, by invoking the classical *sāṃkhya darśana* or philosophical system, he instantly finds himself embroiled in its implications, especially notable here in the generation of the three *guṇa*s, the elements of *sattva*, *rajas*, and *tamas*. While I can find nothing in the Islamic cosmogonies that corresponds directly to this process of generation, it is the mechanism by which the "unfolding" of creation takes place and represents a prominent Pāñcarātra cosmogonic concept that bears strong resemblance to the mitosis that characterizes Islamic cosmogonies, especially some of the more elaborate among Ismailis and others. The point is that according to Nida's suggestion, the distinctive Bengali vocabulary for creation, which is nearly universally grounded in the terminology of *sāṃkhya*, is the best vehicle to translate the idea of duality, even if exact matches cannot be made and the concomitant concepts blur other distinctions. Put another way, we can say that the translation is dynamic to context. There are numerous such examples from the literatures of this period that by comparison can clarify the range of the dynamic translation even further.

Vaiṣṇavas, for instance, talk of the descents of god or *avatāra*,[27] figures who descend to guide the wayward back to the path of proper conduct (*dharma*), and as such these figures can easily be conceived as the "dynamic equivalent" of the Islamic concept of "prophet" or *nabī*. For the obvious reason that only Allah can be divine, a Muslim author would clearly deny as heresy that dimension of the semantic domain that designates "divinity" for the Vaiṣṇava term of *avatāra*; but because prophethood functions in an Islamic environment in a way analogous to that of the *avatāra*, that is, to guide people to the proper religious path, the terms could be established as parallel or equivalent. So, in response to the popular and underlying notion of "inspired guidance," which can be found in both *nabī* and *avatāra*, authors such as Saiyad Sultān could adopt the term *avatāra* to describe the Prophet Muhammad, as he did with some regularity in his monumental work *Nabī Vaṃśa*.[28]

To suggest that Saiyad Sultān understood *nabī* and *avatāra* to be identical, or that this represented a shift in basic Islamic theology (a shift that would inevitably be considered a degradation and heresy), or to propose that he was constructing some kind of new hybrid or syncretistic religious modality, is utterly to misread his text, for it is clear he did none of these. Rather, he articulated this function of inspired guidance in terms common to a Bengali-speaking world; that is, he "dynamically translated" the idea in context. But the effect of this dynamic translation was not unidirectional, because while Saiyad Sultān may have been simply seeking a Hindu functional analogue for *nabī*, in choosing *avatāra* he actually expanded the semantic domain of the concept of *avatāra* itself. In the *Nabī Vaṃśa*, Śiva and Hari and other figures become *nabī*s or prophets, as much as Muhammad becomes an *avatāra* (although their functions were differentiated). And with this exchange, the two terms become paired in the premodern period as twinned concepts, not identical, but sharing in that common core of meaning in specific local contexts. At the same time, Saiyad Sultān provided sectarian Vaiṣṇavas, Śaivas, and Śāktas with a different reading of their own traditions in a way that makes them more palatable to a broader audience and in so doing permanently altered the conception of *avatāra* itself to include this somewhat expanded meaning.[29] Elsewhere, the semantic trajectories of the two terms diverge in opposing ways. Yet when Saiyad Sultān equated *nabī* and *avatāra*, or Āli Rajā translated his basic dualism into *sāṃkhya*-derived terms, there were implications, which were not always spelled out, but which pointed to a much more complex process of translating entire conceptual worlds. It is not clear just how far Saiyad Sultān was prepared to go in this direction because most of his efforts to seek equivalence in the Bengali of his day were limited to refracted and dynamic choices, but others such as Āli Rajā did take the process further.

SHARED METAPHORIC WORLDS AND THE DOMAIN OF THE INTERSEMIOTIC

Linguistic activity that embraces more than equivalent concepts to include larger structures for negotiating the exigencies of the world moves us into more complex acts of appropriation and assimilation that are required to transcend the purely interlingual. Roman Jakobson refers to this as the highest level of complexity, the category of the intersemiotic.[30] On the intersemiotic level of translation we find an interchange and interpolation of ideas among mythologies, between rituals that are (to a certain extent) mutually observed, and even in the fixing of translation equivalents among the parts of extended theological systems. At this stage, which is the most vexing type of translation—a cultural translation—an entire conceptual world is understood in terms of another, not just in its single terms or phrases. Because these worlds are not identical, yet admit to being understood in terms of direct or implied comparison, they are extended, complex metaphorical constructs, which can be conceived as "shared" or "emergent" metaphorical worlds (and we might even argue that to call it translation is itself a metaphoric leap). Linguistically, the impulse behind this analysis is what Gideon Toury has called "polysystem theory," which attempts to extend the processes of translation to the cultural, intersemiotic level, wherein different features of culture participate in increasingly complicated, often disjunctive, systems of discourse.[31] Polysystem theory assumes that no single mode of discourse or cultural construct can account for the varieties of lived experiences or types of exchanges within which people routinely operate and that people comfortably shift from system to system, often without reflection, depending on the situation. The system in operation is context-dependent; the domains of meaning are not limited to exclusively verbal significations; and the application of them is necessarily imprecise, if not inconsistent. Translation, then, will shift from purely linguistic to symbolic and other forms of cultural expression in ways that are not naively arithmetic; different modes of translation will embody greater and lesser degrees of conformity in the same complex act, so that depending on what is being emphasized, the various dimensions of cultural expression will be more or less translated into their equivalents. If in our examples each expression of religiosity attempted by these precolonial authors is understood to participate in a range of semiotic systems, then its translation will likewise reflect these multiple referents as well. A theological term could conceivably imply, then, certain ritual actions, cosmological expectations, political allegiances, and so forth, in an ever spiraling complication as one attempts to account for the encounter of one religious culture with another through a shared language and its metaphoric and symbolic systems.

It must be remembered, however, that what is sought is not the precise equation of the parts of one symbolic or semiotic system with another in clear one-to-one matches. Rather, this overt use of an apparently alien terminology and conceptual system is an attempt to establish the basis for a common conceptual underpinning so that the matching systems and their parts are demonstrated to be coherently conceived, or at least rectifiable—hence the possibility of equivalence—while almost certain to remain inconsistent in their particulars.[32] Equivalence in this mode suggests that two conceptual worlds are seen to address similar problems in similar ways, without ever proposing that they are identical; to express one in terms of the other—the quintessential metaphoric step—remains an act of translation, not an assertion of identity or some mysterious change of allegiance on the part of the author. This might help explain how Āli Rajā's attempt to articulate the cosmogony in the opening passage of the *"nur tattva"* of his *Āgama* text can appear to appropriate wholesale a generic Hindu cosmogonic act of differentiation through the sacred syllable *"aum."* When we see how he seeks to locate some measure of symbolic equivalence through comparing parallel cosmological constructs—a move that would allow him to express a Muslim truth in a language and conceptual structure that is at

least nominally Hindu—the text suddenly illuminates a very different cultural and religious process. In its application, this process of translating on
a higher conceptual plane can be understood as an extension of the previously noted processes, which have upped the ante of complexity. And there
is in this passage an important hermeneutic move that makes clear that Āli
Rajā is looking for equivalence, not voicing preference for a Hindu creation
scheme.

In general but precise terms, Āli Rajā asserts from the first phrase of
this passage the unity of the creator before creation, while noting the ineffable connection between this unity and the dualism necessary for all existent
things to interact with the divine, the dualism necessary for a relationship
of love to exist. This position of *tawhid* (*tauḥīd*)—which becomes clear in
the passage in the second paragraph beginning with the phrase "The Prime
Mover (*karatā*) was concealed within the realm of creation"—is wholly consistent with any mainstream Islamic theology, yet this same ineffable connection resonates strongly with the mainstream theology of the Vaiṣṇavas of
Bengal and their emphasis on *acintya bhedābheda*—a simultaneous distinction and nondistinction between the ultimate and the created world that is
cognitively unresolvable, that is a mystery.[33] It is no accident, then, that he
chose the already noted use of the term *nirañjana*, here connecting Viṣṇu
with Allah. It is the treatment of the processes of creation through the aural
power of *auṃ* that suggests Āli Rajā's attempt to establish an analogy with
common Islamic cosmogonies. In the next few lines of the text, which re-
describe the process of differentiation through which the formless becomes
formed, as he noted initially in the opening paragraph, the world unfolds
through sonic mitosis: it is the "a" (*akāra*) that produces "u" (*ukāra*), and together they generate the "m" (*makāra*). It is important to note that the latter
two are somehow mysteriously contained within the original *akāra* and are
not just discrete linear unfoldings from it. At this juncture, Āli Rajā portrays
the process in a way that mimics a generic Islamic cosmogony so that direct
parallels can be drawn between a number of different Sufi, and even Shi'ah
and Sunni, cosmogonies. The sonic transformation of creation begins with
God, Allah, as represented by the character from which all characters flow,
alif, the number one, the uncreated who creates; from *alif* is then generated
mīm, Muhammad, and through him eventually all of creation. *Alif* and the
akāra, *mīm* and the *makāra*—these are the two points of action in the creation of the world, the vowel and the consonant as the progenitors of speech
and the world. The ambiguous *ukāra*, which at first glance appears to have
no direct analogue positioned between *alif* and *mīm*, is not superfluous, nor

is it simply glossed over. In Āli Rajā's conceptual world (as noted later in this same text), creation does not move directly from Allah to Muhammad but is mediated by a formless form, the *nur muhammadī*, the *nur tattva*, which separates and connects the world from God, the worldly Prophet Muhammad from his Creator; it is the Muhammad of guiding light. Yet the relationship of *nur* to Muhammad and that of those two to Allah is vague and mysterious, yet hierarchically progressive as the individual parts of *auṃ*. It is Āli Rajā's treatment of the *ukāra* that reveals his hand and makes clear his choice of symbolic homologies.

Neither the fact that Āli Rajā does not spell out that connection, nor the fact that his handling of the problematic *ukāra* is imprecise, should be taken as a sign of some abortive attempt at fusing theologies. Rather, it is this apparent imprecision, especially in the vagueness with which the *ukāra* and *makāra* are generated from the *akāra*, that alerts us to his attempt to find an analogous structure within which to translate the mystery of Sufi cosmogony. Had the *auṃ* been presented as a progression of discrete steps followed by the all-important silence with which it symbolically closes in the traditional Hindu cosmogonies of the *Upaniṣad*s, Āli Rajā might be understood to have attempted some synthesis or even to have adopted a Hindu perspective, but his manipulation of the parts of *auṃ* so that they mimic and parallel the relationship of the creation through *alif* and *mīm* suggests a search for equivalence, a translation of a fundamental but complex concept into the target culture's conceptual lexicon. And precisely because it is a search for equivalence—not an assertion of positive identity—the parts must remain vague, analogous, or at best homologous. The use of one conceptual structure to express another suggests the coming together of metaphoric worlds that operates according to a logic of both metonymic and synecdochal displacements, where parts can be exchanged and substituted in ways that allow one cultural system (the equivalent of a source language) to interact with and be understood by another (the equivalent of a target language). We might conceptualize this search for equivalence taking place on the level of a cultural metalanguage, a kind of conceptual hyperglossia that allows these critically important figures to speak in a conceptual idiom that brings different cultures together, while acknowledging and even justifying their own independent conceptual—and in this case religious—worlds. In our last example, it is an Islamic theology that uses and appropriates a Hindu cosmology to its own purposes, explaining the "real" meaning of the sacred syllable *auṃ* to an audience that might not otherwise have seen the connection, an act that is substantially apart from syncretism; at the same time it demonstrates that the truth of God's creation has been observed by Hindus, even if they did not fully comprehend it. The result is a thoroughly Islamic view of the world in a text that uses an ostensibly Hindu terminology to express it.

CONCLUSION

In conclusion we argue that the search for equivalence in the encounter of religions—when understood through the translation models we have characterized as literal, refractive, dynamic, and metaphoric—is an attempt to be understood, to make oneself understood in a language not always one's own; it does not necessarily reflect religious capitulation or theological ignorance or serve as the sign of a weak religious identity. A hermeneutic strategy that acknowledges the unusual linguistic and cultural confluence found in the Bengali-speaking world clearly will help to explain how so many cultural productions could appear on the surface to violate or be inconsistent with contemporary notions of the pristine ideal standard of religious exclusion, when in fact they project a coherence of conception. The texts that reveal these actors attempting to locate commensurate analogues within the language tradition capture a unique historical "moment" in the process of cultural and religious encounter, as each tradition explores the other and tries to make itself understood. Once the translation process can be shown to have moved from the simplistic modes of seeking equivalence to the complex realms of conceptual sharing that we have designated as metaphoric in nature, the analysis must, of necessity, shift. Because this current analysis seeks to describe the nature of the discourse within which new (and old) ideas are expressed through translation, the focus is deliberately shifted away from the ontological nature of the conceptual entity that is produced, the falsely ascribed new religious idea or end product that results from all models of syncretism, to an analysis of the conditions, both creative and constraining, within which that production, that experimentation, is possible, that is, to the way such encounter can take place. It is a shift from preoccupation with the final form to a greater understanding of the process of its creation, a shift that dramatically alters our estimation of what results from this process. From this point, any number of plausible and useful strategies may be adopted to further explain and refine this discursive activity. The method of looking at these texts through the model of translation should, if applied rigorously, demonstrate a different kind of social and religious interaction among the diverse populations of Bengal, not just among different groups of Hindus and Muslims. And it may well point to previously unaccounted factors that have contributed to that perspective on the world that appears to be so uniquely Bengali, an element of identity that is perhaps Bengali first and sectarian second.

NOTES

This essay originally appeared in *History of Religions* (vol. 40, no. 3 [2001]: 261–87) and is reprinted here in a slightly modified form with the permission of the University of Chicago Press. A number of people have contributed to the argument of this article since it was first proposed during the National Endowment for the Humanities (NEH) Summer Seminar for College Teachers, titled "Hindu and Muslim: Rethinking Religious Boundaries in South Asia" (University of North Carolina at Chapel Hill, summer 1995), which I co-directed with Carl W. Ernst. The paper was subsequently delivered in nascent form in a seminar on religious encounter at the College of Charleston (September 1996), as part of the Lyman-Coleman Lectures at Lafayette College (October 1996), to the Department of South Asia Regional Studies at the University of Pennsylvania (March 1997), at the Bengal Studies Conference at the University of Chicago (April 1997), at an annual conference of the Association for Asian Studies in Honolulu (March 1998), in a seminar on premodern Bengali Islam at Emory University (October 1998), in a religious studies seminar at the University of North Carolina at Greensboro (April 1999), and finally at a Triangle South Asia Consortium Colloquium (September 1999). I would like especially to thank David Gilmartin of North Carolina State University, Carl W. Ernst of the University of North Carolina at Chapel Hill, Bruce B. Lawrence of Duke University, Robin C. Rinehart of Lafayette College, Richard Eaton of the University of Arizona, Charles D. Orzech of the University of North Carolina at Greensboro, Natalie Dohrmann of the University of Pennsylvania, and Charles Kurzman of the University of North Carolina at Chapel Hill, all of whom contributed substantially.

1. For more on this phenomenon, see Stewart 2000.
2. The most sophisticated use of the problematic concept of syncretism for Bengali religion can be found in the important book Roy 1983. It was Eaton 1993 that marked the shift away from models of syncretism to more historically nuanced and historically contextualized studies.
3. The impulse to ignore centuries of historical change within Islam itself,

and to eliminate the inevitable subtle shifts that take place when a universal religion moves into another cultural arena—in this case, a Perso-Arabic Islam taking root in Bengal—motivates a classical fundamentalist decision to "purify" Islam of perceived foreign accretions and to try to recreate the experience of an archaic, pristine Islam as conceived by its original founding members. The implications should be obvious.

4. See Jones 1981 and Cohn 1990.

5. The most commonly cited individuals responsible for this shift in perspective include Roland Barthes, Jacques Derrida, and Mikhail Bakhtin. But more immediately germane are reception aesthetics, starting with that initiated by Hans Robert Jauss at the University of Konstanz, and its follow-on in reader-response criticism. The latter diverges specifically from the initial inquiries of the phenomenology of reading (e.g., Georges Poulet) and, while refining certain propositions of deconstruction, has greatly enhanced our understanding of the role the reader plays in creating the text. The text of course becomes a variable entity based on what the reader brings to it and how he or she understands it. There is an obvious debt here to basic hermeneutic theory, but of more specific reader-response interest is the approach adopted by Iser 1974 and 1978 and Rabinowitz 1987; see also the very useful anthology Tompkins 1980.

6. Haq [1965] 1991b; for summary, see Haq [1965] 1991b: 375–79.

7. Haq [1935] 1991a.

8. After Bangladesh independence Haq (1975) expanded his doctoral dissertation in English under the title *A History of Sufi-ism in Bengal* and significantly appended two new chapters that included this unique literature. It is not unreasonable to imagine that he was signaling the nature of the new Bangladeshi democracy that was more inclusive than its Pakistani counterpart.

9. These texts can be found in the anthology of premodern Sufi texts compiled and edited by the contemporary literary historian Ahmad Sharif (1969). Abdul Karim ([c. 1917] 1969) first publicized the works of Āli Rajā, and it is from the introduction to his published edition of the *Jñānasāgara* that all biographical information has been gleaned by subsequent scholars.

10. Sharif 1969: 311–13.

11. Bhaṭṭācārya 1984: 43–57. Āli Rajā's surviving collected output of Rādhā-Kṛṣṇa lyrics by Muslim authors is greater than all others, save two.

12. Karim ([c. 1917] 1969: 401) provides a genealogical chart on the second page of his introduction, giving his grandfather as Mohammad Ākbar,

father as Mohammad Śāhi, son by his first wife as Erśād Ullā Miyā, son by his second wife as Ephāj Ullā Miyā, and another son called Sarphat Ullā Miyā. The lineage today is traced through the first son.

13. It was, in Karim's words, "*hindu musalmānī bhāvera saṃmiśreṇa*," lit., "an admixture of Hindu and Muslim religious sentiment," with an implication of "confusion"; see Karim [c. 1917] 1969: 400.

14. The first to argue this now widely accepted position were perhaps Edward Sapir (1949a and 1949b) and Benjamin Lee Whorf (1956). There are of course cognitive science specialists who challenge this view, starting with the initial formulations of Noam Chomsky and then pushing the implications of his propositions about the predetermined nature of grammatical deep structures; see Chomsky 1965.

15. Since the first modern use of the term (1615 CE), "syncretism" has described "misguided" attempts at reunion of the Protestant and Catholic churches, and its earliest use was to compare the "mixed" religions of the Hellenistic and Roman eras to "pure" Christianity. See the *Oxford English Dictionary*, 1971 compact edition, for early use of the term.

16. For a more detailed study of this problem, which is here only summarized, see *South Asian Folklore: An Encyclopedia*, s.v. "syncretism." The analysis itself is much indebted to the understanding of the metaphors of everyday speech developed by George Lakoff and Mark Johnson ([1980] 2003).

17. One need only consult any of the several dictionaries of "foreign words" in Bengali to see the extent of this vocabulary, e.g., *Dictionary of Foreign Words in Bengali*.

18. Sheldon Pollock (1996 and 1998) has recently argued that the use of Sanskrit in the various regions often functioned as a hyperglossia (rather than diglossia), because Sanskrit cut across regional boundaries in ways that made it and its claims universal but also because, in this transcending mode, Sanskrit was the ideal vehicle for expressing what was "really real," the most important ideas (in contrast to the vernaculars that were used for the mundane).

19. See Eaton 1993.

20. Bakhtin (1981) characterizes monoglossia as the use of a single uniform language, diglossia as the complex interaction of a language and its parent, and heteroglossia as the interaction of two or more contributing parents when these are in conflict with each other. He resorts to polyphony to describe the conflict-free use of multiple parent contributors. While analytically useful, the practical distinction of heteroglossia and polyphony seems somewhat strained, if not artificial, in this context. For Bakhtin's position relative to members of his school, see Morris 1994.

21. Ortega y Gasset 1959: 2.

22. It should be noted that to use different styles of translation (explained by the underlying translation theories) as a way of conceiving the encounter of religious traditions, or to better understand the apparent encounter, is to use "translation" as a metaphor in its most general sense as the expression of one thing in terms of another. This is fundamentally different from the metaphoric basis of the concept of syncretism itself and therefore not subject to the same critique. The reason the metaphoric use of translation escapes this critique is simple: translation is an identifiable, analyzable act, a concrete process that seeks to express one set of concepts in another language with a potentially different conceptual structure. Syncretism is itself a metaphor, no matter how it is construed, and generally one with no identifiable process to be uncovered; in contrast, the classic metaphors of syncretism serve to cover over what is not understood about the process they ostensibly seek to describe, all too often making syncretism a pseudo-explanation. To deploy translation as a model of religious encounter (i.e., to use it metaphorically) is really to use it on the metadiscursive level, not on the primary level as metaphor is used by the constructions of syncretism.

23. Sharif 1969: 323–25. Where the sample passage speaks directly of the letters that compose the *bīja mantra* (seed sound) "*auṃ*," I have translated *akṣara/-kāra* as "syllable" or "sonic-form"—rather than as the more common gloss of "letter"—in order to convey the aural quality of the cosmogonic act. And I have translated *ākāra* simply as "form" or "the formed."

24. *Caitanya Caritāmṛta* 2.18.175–203.

25. Lefevere 1975 and 1982b; see also Lefevere 1981 and 1982a. In a related vein, see also Catford 1965.

26. Nida 1964; see also Nida and Taber 1969.

27. *Avatāra* is usually misleadingly translated into English as "incarnation," but in the Hindu conception there is no "flesh" (Latin: *carn-*) involved, making the translation an example of "refraction."

28. Sultān 1978.

29. According to Nida, this reading would in fact have to be a more complete reading on the assumption that dynamic translation is possible in the religious context because the material being translated has at its deepest level an "invariant core" that will always manage to transfer across the language barriers in spite of the surface dissimilarities. The idea of the invariant core stems from his assertion that religious

texts (which in his endeavors were limited to Christianity, especially the Bible) were inspired or revelatory and therefore were immune to the conceptual vagaries of different languages (defying the assertions of Sapir and Whorf). This was further justified for Nida, however, by a deliberate misreading of Chomsky's ideas of linguistic "deep structures," which were avowedly not universal, even though Nida chose to read them that way. For an incisive critique of Nida's approach and misuse of Chomsky, see Gentzler 1993: 43–73.

30. Jakobson (1959) argues that translation is "intralingual" within different parts or dialects of the same language, "interlingual" between different languages, and finally, "intersemiotic" between different cultural signification systems.

31. Toury 1980; for the implications of such an approach, see the interesting essays in Talgeri and Verma 1988. See also Edwin Gentzler's critique of polysystem theory (1993: 105–43). A slightly different approach that seeks to quantify discretely the complex levels of translation that account for the rich cultural context can be found in the "variational" model as described by Lance Hewson and Jacky Martin (1991). In this model, the highest level of intersemiotic translation involves the isolation of multifaceted "homologons" that lead to more tightly controlled paraphrastic constructions. This seems to be a promising model for translators to conceptualize what they do, but less useful descriptively in conceptualizing the problem I have described in the encounter of religious traditions.

32. I am here following the lead of Lakoff and Johnson ([1980] 2003), who argue in their work on metaphor in everyday speech that the mechanics of this process can be envisioned as seeking the "coherence" of conceptions without worrying about the consistency of the details of the expression, image, or symbol being manipulated.

33. For a summary of the *acintya bhedābheda* theory as it was adapted by the Gauḍīya Vaiṣṇavas, see *Gauḍīya Vaiṣṇava Darśana*, 1:137–43 (for a brief introduction); 1, 2, 3 (passim). For an English summary, see Dimock 1966.

REFERENCES

Bakhtin, Mikhail Mikhaĭlovich. 1981. *The Dialogic Imagination*. Edited by Michael Holquist and translated by Caryl Emerson and Michael Holquist. Austin: University of Texas Press.

Becker, A. L. 1995. *Beyond Translation: Essays toward a Modern Philology.* Ann Arbor: University of Michigan Press.

Bhaṭṭācārya, Yatīndramohan. 1984. *Bāṃlāra Vaiṣṇava-Bhāvāpanna Musalamāna Kavira Padamañjuṣā.* Calcutta: Calcutta University Press.

Catford, J. C. 1965. *A Linguistic Theory of Translation: An Essay in Applied Linguistics.* London: Oxford University Press.

Chomsky, Noam. 1965. *Aspects of the Theory of Syntax.* Cambridge: MIT Press.

Cohn, Bernard S. 1990. "The Census, Social Structure and Objectification in South Asia." In *An Anthropologist among the Historians and Other Essays,* 224–54. Delhi: Oxford University Press.

Dimock, Edward C., Jr. 1966. "Doctrine and Practice among the Vaiṣṇavas of Bengal." In *Krishna: Myths, Rites, and Attitudes,* edited by Milton Singer, 41–63. Honolulu: East-West Center Press.

Eaton, Richard M. 1993. *The Rise of Islam and the Bengal Frontier, 1204–1760.* Berkeley: University of California Press.

Gentzler, Edwin. 1993. *Contemporary Translation Theories.* London: Routledge.

Haq, Muhammad Enamul. 1975. *A History of Sufi-ism in Bengal.* Dacca: Asiatic Society of Bengal.

———. 1991a. *Bange Sūphi Prabhāva.* In *Muhammad Enāmul Hak Racanāvalī,* edited by Mansur Musa, 1:39–195. Kalikata: Mohsin, 1935. Reprint, Dhaka: Bangla Academy.

———. 1991b. *Muslim Bāṃlā Sāhitya.* In *Muhammad Enāmul Hak Racanāvalī,* edited by Mansur Musa, 1:197–437. 2nd ed. Dhaka: Pakistan Publications, 1965. Reprint, Dhaka: Bangla Academy.

Hewson, Lance, and Jacky Martin. 1991. *Redefining Translation: The Variational Approach.* London: Routledge.

Iser, Wolfgang. 1974. *The Implied Reader: Patterns of Communication in Prose Fiction from Bunyan to Beckett.* Baltimore: Johns Hopkins University Press.

———. 1978. *The Act of Reading: A Theory of Aesthetic Response.* Baltimore: Johns Hopkins University Press.

Jakobson, Roman. 1959. "On Linguistic Aspects of Translation." In *On Translation,* edited by R. A. Brower, 232–39. Cambridge: Harvard University Press.

Jones, Kenneth W. 1981. "Religious Identity and the Indian Census." In *The Census in British India: New Perspectives,* edited by N. Gerald Barrier, 73–101. Delhi: Manohar.

Karim, Abdul, ed. 1969. *Jñānasāgara of Āli Rajā*. Calcutta: Bangīya Sāhitya Pariṣat Mandir, c. 1917. Reprint, in Sharif 1969: 400–532.

Kavirāja, Kṛṣṇadāsa. C. 1961. *Caitanya Caritāmṛta*. Edited with the commentary *Gaurakṛpatāranginī* by Rādhāgovinda Nāth. 4th ed. 6 vols. Calcutta: Sādhanā Prakāśanī.

Lakoff, George, and Mark Johnson. 2003. *Metaphors We Live By*. Chicago: University of Chicago Press, 1980. Reprint, with a new afterword, Chicago: University of Chicago Press.

Lefevere, André. 1975. *Translating Poetry: Seven Strategies and a Blueprint*. Assen, The Netherlands: Van Gorcum.

———. 1981. "Theory and Practice—Process and Product." *Modern Poetry in Translation* 41–42: 19–27.

———. 1982a. "Literary Theory and Translated Literature." *Dispositio* 7, nos. 19–21: 3–22.

———. 1982b. "Mother Courage's Cucumbers: Text, System and Refraction in a Theory of Literature." *Modern Language Studies* 12, no. 4: 3–20.

Morris, Pam, ed. 1994. *The Bakhtin Reader: Selected Writings of Bakhtin, Medvedev, Voloshinov*. London: Edward Arnold.

Nāth, Rādhāgovinda. 1957–1960. *Gauḍīya Vaiṣṇava Darśana*. 5 vols. Calcutta: Prācyavāṇī Mandir.

Nida, Eugene A. 1964. *Towards a Science of Translating, with Special Reference to Principles and Procedures Involved in Bible Translating*. Leiden: E. J. Brill.

Nida, Eugene A., and Charles R. Taber. 1969. *The Theory and Practice of Translation*. Leiden: E. J. Brill.

Ortega y Gasset, José. 1959. "The Difficulty of Reading." Translated by Clarence E. Parmenter. *Diogenes* 7, no. 28: 2. Quoted in Becker 1995: 5.

Pollock, Sheldon. 1996. "The Sanskrit Cosmopolis, 300–1300 CE: Transculturation, Vernacularization, and the Question of Ideology." In *Ideology and Status of Sanskrit: Contributions to the History of the Sanskrit Language*, edited by Jan E. M. Houben, 197–247. Leiden: E. J. Brill.

———. 1998. "India in the Vernacular Millennium: Literary Culture and Polity, 1000–1500." In "Early Modernities," edited by Shmuel Eisenstadt, Wolfgang Schluchter, and Björn Wittrock. Special issue, *Daedalus* 127, no. 3: 41–74.

Rabinowitz, Peter J. 1987. *Before Reading: Narrative Conventions and the Politics of Interpretation*. Ithaca: Cornell University Press.

Roy, Asim. 1983. *Islamic Syncretistic Tradition in Bengal*. Princeton: Princeton University Press.

Sapir, Edward. 1949a. *Language: An Introduction to the Study of Speech.* New York: Harcourt Brace Jovanovich.

———. 1949b. *Culture, Language, and Personality.* Berkeley: University of California Press.

Sharif, Ahmad, ed. and comp. 1969. *Bānlāra Sūphī Sāhitya: Ālocanā o Nayakhāni Grantha Sambalita.* Dhaka: Bangla Academy.

Stewart, Tony K. 2000. "Alternate Structures of Authority: Satya Pīr on the Frontiers of Bengal." In *Beyond Turk and Hindu: Rethinking Religious Identities in Islamicate South Asia,* edited by David Gilmartin and Bruce B. Lawrence, 21–54. Gainesville: University Press of Florida.

Sultān, Saiyad. 1978. *Nabī Vaṃśa.* Vol. 1 of *Rasul Carita,* edited by Ahmad Sharif. Dhaka: Bangla Academy.

Talgeri, Pramod, and S. B. Verma, eds. 1988. *Literature in Translation: From Cultural Transference to Metonymic Displacement.* London: Sangam Books.

Tompkins, Jane P., ed. 1980. *Reader-Response Criticism: From Formalism to Post-Structuralism.* Baltimore: Johns Hopkins University Press.

Toury, Gideon. 1980. *In Search of a Theory of Translation.* Tel Aviv: Porter Institute for Poetics and Semiotics.

Whorf, Benjamin Lee. 1956. *Language, Thought, and Reality: Selected Writings of Benjamin Lee Whorf.* Edited by John B. Carroll. Cambridge: MIT Press.

Afterword

Glen Alexander Hayes

As Wendy Doniger observes in her foreword to this volume, comparative religion has been through at least three major hermeneutical phases. The first (exemplified by Mircea Eliade) tended to essentialize and universalize religious phenomena, while the second (championed by Jonathan Z. Smith) sought to emphasize differences, in order to bring out nuances and context and to avoid the reductionism "of the first wave." The volume you have before you represents a distinct "third wave," for, as Doniger observes, it "seizes a moment when the pendulum has swung back again from the extreme emphasis on difference, to recapture some of the good parts of the old agenda of comparatism—without falling into the worst of the deep pits that it dug for itself." And how have the scholars involved in this volume largely avoided falling back into the reductionist pit? As the title of this volume suggests, they have done so by examining the diverse ways of "figuring religions"— that is, by exploring not only how different religious traditions and their followers employed religious metaphors and tropes, but also how we ourselves, as modern scholars, can develop entirely new methodologies for comparison by utilizing the power and function of metaphor, metonymy, and other tropes to understand religious phenomena better. Each of the authors uses a somewhat different approach, just as they examine different traditions. But, by confronting existing methodologies and classificatory systems and by suggesting new hermeneutical pathways, these scholars have brought us to an important and emerging intersection of comparative religion, philosophy,

263

linguistics, anthropology, and cognitive science. We are just in the early stages of this third wave, but the results are exciting to behold.

In her introduction, Shubha Pathak provides a useful overview of the recent history of comparison in religious studies and sets up the three areas that the volume examines: religious ideas, religious images, and religious actions. She observes that, while some recent scholarship has indeed tried to correct the essentializing and ethnocentrism of the first wave of comparative religion, arguing anew for "why scholars should compare aspects of religions and how they can better do so," the current volume "shows how current comparativists can apply the general lessons that they have learned about examining differences and contexts, while adopting a particular set of approaches appropriate for studying a variety of religious expressions." By applying trope theories developed recently in the three disciplines of philosophy, linguistics, and anthropology, the volume's authors elucidate religious ideas, images, and rituals.

In the volume's first essay, "Marking Religion's Boundaries: Constitutive Terms, Orienting Tropes, and Exegetical Fussiness," Thomas A. Tweed clarifies the second wave's concern for attention to differences and to precision when using categories, definitions, and tropes in the study of religious phenomena. Using a philosophical perspective, he argues that we need to revisit and be more selective in our own uses of the tropes that are used in the study of religion. We also need to be aware of the effects that such metaphors may have on the scholars who employ them. Because any given trope used heuristically can reveal only some aspects of a wider religious world, we must use greater care and precision as we develop methodologies for our explorations of wider religious phenomena, or else we risk overlooking or neglecting important aspects of them. This obligation of scholars to be precise, argues Tweed, "means being clear about the type of definition offered and attending carefully to the choice of orienting trope, since definitions imply theories and employ tropes." Thus, there are tropes—quite often metaphors, but also metonymies and synecdoches—not only beneath the religious phenomena we study, but also within our very own theories and definitions. Since tropes have this sort of dual implication in the study of religion, Tweed reminds us that we "have a professional duty to be self-conscious in [our] use of [this] central categor[y]." His useful overview of different attempts to define religion, covering efforts from throughout the twentieth century, leads him to plead for us to demonstrate "exegetical fussiness," for, in so many ways, "[d]efinitions matter."

He skillfully counters the argument that we may as well refrain from any attempt to define religion, swatting away the usual objections (lexical, historical, moral, applicability, alternatives) like so many methodological nuisances. Despite legitimate concerns about this or that definition, at the end of the process "we have only returned to the sort of fundamental definitional problems that drove many to befuddlement—or silence—when attempting to characterize religion." Citing Melford E. Spiro, and very much in the spirit of Smith, Tweed argues that "interpretive terms need not be 'universal' to be useful." As Smith would often argue in his classes at the University of Chicago Divinity School, the most honest comparativist method must be subjected to what he called "cost accounting": simply put, at the end of the day, has the comparative term helped us to learn more about the subject, or not? All definitions can be problematic, but the best-crafted of these can also be useful tools.

They can serve as useful tools because, as Tweed shows, definitions have an intrinsic connection to theories: "Definitions, in my view, imply theories and employ tropes." This triad of definition-theory-trope is one of mutual influence, and a cycle of consequence and implication. For example, Sigmund Freud's employ of the trope of religion as a childhood neurosis had rather large consequences on his subsequent theories. Tweed notes—and all of the other contributors to this volume may agree—that metaphor is a widely used trope and, since "most language is figurative in some sense, . . . metaphor is an important figure." Reflecting recent insights regarding the deeper functions of metaphor from the fields of cognitive science and linguistics, Tweed also shows how metaphor can serve as both a lens and a vehicle, as "it prompts new sightings and crossings." In other words, metaphors can influence how one perceives and senses the world, and can also influence how one makes sense of, and construes, that world. Metaphors redirect our attention from one domain to another, illuminating some features of the terrain while obscuring others. Metaphors and other tropes—in their richness, depth, and variety—are of value both to religious followers and to religion scholars.

In the conclusion to his essay, Tweed surveys the functions of different types of "orienting metaphors" as tropes in scholarly definitions of religion. As he observes,

At least a dozen orienting metaphors have had some influence in the history of scholarly definitions of religion. Most definitions employ

more than one of these, so there is no pure type, only hybrid forms
that approximate the categories in this taxonomy. And some orienting metaphors have had much more influence than others. Religion
has been analogized as capacity, organism, system, worldview, illness, narcotic, picture, form of life, society, institution, projection,
and space.

This is a most useful list, for it neatly summarizes the gist of many scholarly
approaches, ranging from Edward B. Tylor to Clifford Geertz. And, again,
Tweed's point is that we must be aware of the tropes we are using, for indeed
that choice will greatly influence how our hermeneutical journey will unfold.
As the different contributors to this volume have amply shown, there are different definitional and tropic choices to make, leading to different insights
regarding epic literature (Pathak), concepts of self (Edward Slingerland),
mental experience (James Egge), spiritual transmission (Ellen Haskell), identity (Terhi Utriainen), ritual (Laurie L. Patton), sociospatial relationship
(Yiqun Zhou), and cross-cultural encounter (Tony K. Stewart). Tweed has
skillfully raised most of the major issues of this volume, with his appropriate
request for exegetical fussiness. Let us now consider how the other contributors show such concern as they engage the comparative process with regard
to a wide range of traditions.

In "'Epic' as an Amnesiac Metaphor: Finding the Word to Compare
Ancient Greek and Sanskrit Poems," Pathak leads us through a careful philosophical consideration of the uses and complexities of the term "epic." Following Tweed's exhortation to be aware of one's categories, definitions, tropes,
and theories, Pathak demonstrates that, since the early twentieth century,
scholars have often uncritically applied this term for ancient Greek poems
to also-ancient Sanskrit poems. It is one thing to state that the *Iliad* and the
Odyssey are "epics," for this is what the ancient Greeks themselves regarded
them to be. This statement is an identity, for these two lengthy ancient Greek
poems are indeed "epics" in the original sense of "words" and narrative verse.
But it is really quite another thing for scholars to apply this properly Greek
genre category to the two ancient Sanskrit poems called the *Rāmāyaṇa* and
the *Mahābhārata*. In their original contexts, these two classical and lengthy
Hindu poems are known as *kāvya* (a poem that expresses emotion) and *itihāsa*
(an account of the way things had been), respectively. As Pathak argues, the
use of the Greek term "epic" for the Hindu Sanskrit *kāvya* and *itihāsa* constitutes in fact a type of metaphor, one in fact which we have "forgotten" is
even a metaphor. Hence her use of the term "amnesiac." Following Tweed's

agenda, Pathak discusses the many features of the four poems, and considers their differences as well. Of special note is her warning of the three implications of the choice of "epic" in studying the Hindu texts. The first implication is that the original or "primitive" meaning of the Greek term is lost when it is taken out of context and applied to poems from another cultural and religious context. The second, equally problematic, is that this usage tends to accentuate only certain aspects of the Sanskrit poems, while obscuring or neglecting others. This type of selective emphasis is exactly what Tweed has warned us about! Finally, the third implication is that the original term "epic" has been expanded to include aspects of the Sanskrit poems that were not part of the ancient Greek poems themselves. Thus, when the term "epic" is used as an "amnesiac metaphor" in modern scholarship, we end up losing particularities specific to each of the two sets of original texts. Pathak advises us that her analysis and critique of these (mis)uses of "epic" are just an analytical point of departure, not a terminus, but she has convincingly demonstrated that there are deceptive pitfalls in the comparative pathway. Just because Western scholars are comfortable with a particular term, such as "epic," does not mean that it can be used to show all of the attributes of certain texts from another culture. Again, we should be aware of Tweed's caution regarding the problematic triad of definition-theory-trope, as Pathak's discussion of "epic" has shown. We should not forget this, so to speak.

The next two essays in the volume, "Conceptions of the Self in the *Zhuangzi*: Conceptual Metaphor Analysis and Comparative Thought" by Edward Slingerland and "Theorizing Embodiment: Conceptual Metaphor Theory and the Comparative Study of Religion" by James Egge, both deal with relatively recent developments in the study of metaphor first proposed by George Lakoff and Mark Johnson.[1] Lakoff and Johnson's groundbreaking 1980 book, *Metaphors We Live By*, further developed the argument that metaphors are not just woven into everyday speech ("I find your thesis hard to digest") but also operate more deeply in our minds, influencing how we perceive, construe, and behave in the world. A number of other books developed out of this one, including Lakoff's 1987 *Women, Fire, and Dangerous Things*, in which he deepens the explorations of metaphor across a range of concerns; and his collaboration with Mark Turner in 1989's *More Than Cool Reason*, in which they provide powerful analyses of poetry simple and complex. Also of note is Johnson's 1987 *The Body in the Mind*, which takes us on an amazing journey through metaphor, the senses, embodiment, and cognition. These books are just some of the better-known works, but should suffice here to illustrate the emerging trend.[2]

The essays by Slingerland and Egge have made good use of Lakoff and Johnson's approach. Slingerland, for his part, does a masterful job of applying Lakoff and Johnson's ideas to the *Zhuangzi* and thereby enables us to explore what Johnson has called the "'geography of human experience.'" Slingerland also confronts one of the main critiques of Lakoff and Johnson, namely, that which concerns the issue of universality. Simply put, are there some metaphors of embodiment (e.g., THE SELF IS A CONTAINER, BETTER/ MORE IS UP, CONSCIOUSNESS IS A DESTINATION) which are in fact universal among humans? While Slingerland, in his essay, does not clearly answer this question, he addresses it directly in his 2008 book, *What Science Offers the Humanities.*[3] Ongoing research in neuroscience, which Slingerland and others have been using, is indeed showing us that some very basic metaphors may be based upon what are called "image-schemata," which are innate ways in which the brain organizes space and "maps out" the human body. Some of these very basic schemata may indeed be practically universal, although instantiated locally according to culture.

Additionally, Slingerland details in his essay an important consequence of Lakoff and Johnson's theory, which is that all metaphors have "entailments," or nuances (think back to Tweed again here). For example, some of the "good" entailments of THE SELF IS A CONTAINER metaphor are realizing that the Real Self is inside the container; avoiding the False Self outside of it; and maintaining the "barrier" or boundaries of the contained self/body, where an impervious barrier is good, and a permeable one (letting in bad influences/substances) is bad. As Slingerland shows, conceptual metaphor theory allows the scholar access to the working metaphorical worlds and structures of the religions under study, revealing the "'deep grammar'" of human experience and imagination. Thus, for the author of the *Zhuangzi*, the world is one where SELF-CONTROL IS OBJECT CONTROL, quite the reverse of the modern English phrase of "losing yourself." This discovery of deeper metaphorical worlds and their expression in texts and actions provides a solid theoretical grounding for comparison, and thus an invaluable tool for the comparative effort.

Egge's concerns overlap with many of Slingerland's, as Egge is both critical of the first phase of comparative religion (as embodied by Eliade) and intrigued by the possible uses of conceptual metaphor theory. He raises salient issues regarding the place of "culture" in the theory, and opines that perhaps there are indeed some universals among embodied metaphors. His review of the debates surrounding conceptual metaphor theory is useful, and echoes in its own way Tweed's warning that we maintain exegetical fussiness. Egge's analysis of the intricacies of the source/target model helps us to appreciate the theory more fully, and his argument that we project our source domains of embodiment onto the mind and emotions is quite insightful. For example, his statement that "religion is created by our inherent tendency to project mental qualities onto the nonhuman world," resulting in anthropomorphism and personification, suggests a valuable pathway for applying Lakoff and Johnson's theory.

Finally, Egge brings many of these theoretical concerns together when he observes,

> Although Lakoff and Johnson perhaps understate culture's role in the formation of metaphor, their hypothesis that common embodied experiences give rise to a high degree of commonality in metaphors across cultures is supported by a survey of metaphors in Pāli Buddhist literature. For example, the *Dhammapada*'s passion metaphors that I have presented in this chapter—plants, currents, fetters, impurity, fire, agitation, and enemies—also are present in English, or at least can be readily understood by speakers of English. In addition, four of the same basic spatial models of the self that have been identified by Lakoff and Johnson in their analysis of English, and of which Slingerland finds examples in the *Zhuangzi*, are employed in the *Dhammapada*'s metaphors for passion.

Together, then, Slingerland and Egge make a strong argument for conceptual metaphor theory as an important avenue for figuring religions.

A very different set of theoretical and historical concerns is addressed by Ellen Haskell in "Bathed in Milk: Metaphors of Suckling and Spiritual Transmission in Thirteenth-Century Kabbalah." Haskell analyzes the vivid imagery of God as a suckling mother that is found in two major kabbalistic texts composed in Spain in the thirteenth century: Ezra of Gerona's *Commentary on the Song of Songs* and the *Sefer ha-Zohar* of Moses de León or his associates. In these texts, the divine flow of milk not only is regarded as a metaphor for divine nourishment and spiritual transmission, but also serves as a metonymy which reconnects the mystics to the divine realm. Although the context details of this mystical imagery remain obscure (they may have been influenced by contemporary Christian Marian traditions), it does seem that these kabbalists were trying to refashion their theology and cosmology.

Indeed, Haskell, following Deborah Durham and James Fernandez, "see[s] the metonymical restructuring within a metaphor as an important way to challenge the world's structure. In [these anthropologists'] eyes, one of the most important ways to effect cultural transformation is by restructuring the internal metonymical structure of culturally dominant metaphors." The kabbalistic imagery, even while challenging the patriarchal paradigm in classical Judaism, is legitimated by virtue of being Biblically based. Furthermore, as Haskell observes, "[w]hen the human image of the breastfeeding mother is applied to God, divinity and humanity are related to each other. They conceptually become parts of the same thing, belonging to the same organization." The end result of this process is that "God is humanized to a point at which it can relate to humanity, while humanity is divinized to the extent that it can participate in an interactive relationship with God. The entire structure of relationship between the two is redefined. If God is a nursing mother, humanity is God's child." Thus, we see here a very active use of trope, not just to figure religion, but in fact to refigure it.

We make another theoretical and historical shift with Terhi Utriainen's "Metaphors and Images of Dress and Nakedness: Wrappings of Embodied Identity." Deriving her theoretical insights from the works of philosopher Gaston Bachelard and theologian Paul Ricoeur, she explores diverse imageries of dress and undress in the Biblical and Finnish Lutheran traditions. In Genesis, for example, there are different kinds of nakedness, including the innocent form before and the more shameful versions after the Fall. But the process also includes the "dressing" of Adam and Eve, first in a covering of fig leaves, and then in the more ambivalent garments of animal skins. Of note is Utriainen's argument that any single item of clothing is a metonym for the entire dress—and for the ontological and soteriological states associated with it. In some cases, dressing indicates an "adding" or "covering" of identity, while undressing implies a "lessening" or "revealing" of it. The meaning all depends on the context.

In the Pauline epistles, bodily metaphors are essential and have an astonishing semantic field. Beyond the well-known metaphor of the Christian community as the "'body'" of Christ, Utriainen also discusses "'immortality'" as a dress, Christ as a garment to be "'put on,'" and the trope of the heavenly garments that must be worn by the faithful. She notes, "For Paul, if this care of the self and its dress is well mastered, then even death need be not a state of nakedness but a possibility to receive the ultimate garment. The Paulian texts construct an image of continuous identity work where identity is resolved and put together in an ongoing process." After a similarly informative analysis of images of dress and undress in Finnish Lutheran hymns, she observes, "Processual imagery of dress and nakedness—or of dressing and undressing—is one way of expressing the process of identity in a bodily as well as religious sense, because (un)dressing is a basic, constitutive, and inevitable bodily, social, moral, and imaginary practice . . . in human life. Dress is a boundary mechanism with which we identify and distinguish ourselves. It is our second skin with which we communicate with worlds and others." As an important aspect of figuring religions, the many traditions of human dressing, undressing, and nakedness serve as obvious and rich metaphors for deeper notions of identity and human-divine relationships.

The final three essays in the volume explore the figuring of religions in terms of their activities. In "Poetry, Ritual, and Associational Thought in Early India and Elsewhere," Laurie L. Patton examines the rich traditions of Hindu rituals and mantras from the Vedic period. Whereas most of the other essay authors focus on metaphor, she analyzes metonymy. Readers will find great value in her discussion of the five properties of metonymy (framing, pragmatism, referentiality, prototypicality, and identification), as they are vital to many expressions of religious experience. Beyond the basic function of metonymy in the sense of "part-as-whole," she argues that metonyms provide a powerful form of framing, establishing dynamic forms of conceptual contiguity that emerges from bodily experience. She notes, "In short, the rules of association are governed by a frame—our perception and experience of what constitutes a world. Part of that world is the fact of identification (similarity) with other elements in that world through a set of patterns and conceptions." In many ways, this concern for "frame," conceptual structure, and associational worlds lies beneath our concerns for the roles of tropes throughout this volume and echoes the recent theories of Lakoff and Johnson and of Fauconnier and Turner (more on these in my concluding remarks).

Patton shows how the frames that are activated in metonymies are also governed by a clear pragmatism: they must have usage relevance if they are to work in the real world. Thus, a hospital worker may refer to a patient on a ward as "the gall bladder" rather than, say, "Mr. Jones the lawyer," as doing so makes more pragmatic sense than not. Vital metonymy also involves referentiality, referring to aspects of the frame and associated elements, as when the term "silver" refers to the many types of cutlery in a drawer. Thus, a useful metonym serves as a kind of abbreviation, focusing on one quality of a thing. A powerful metonym must also function as an ideal prototype, though may express only some aspects of the semantic field being referred to, as in the metonym "housewife mother." Of course, as Tweed reminds us, when a culture chooses such a metonym, this choice may have social consequences, maintaining power relationships and stereotypes. Finally, metonymy is quite "selectiv[e,] . . . creat[ing] an identification between the agent and the act or between the agent and the instrument of the act." For example, a child in a school where many children eat from the cafeteria may identify himself with his lunch box and state that he, in contrast to the others, is a lunch box. Such a trope is common in many types of literature—we can find, for instance, many cases of jewelry as an identifying metonym.

Applying these insights as well as ideas from the field of performance studies, Patton shows how all five aspects of metonymy are present in the Vedic case. For example, the sacrificer often "stand[s] in" for the god Indra, but, only by knowing the details of the ritual context and frame, can one discern the many things "omitted" from the literal text itself. Moreover, Vedic metonyms are thoroughly pragmatic, involving actual actions; and are decidedly referential, as are the numerous Sanskrit compounds used as epithets for the gods. Ontologically and grammatically, then, the epithets are also prototypical metonyms, serving as the basis for all subsequent variations of the sacrifice. Used repetitively, the epithets renew and reinforce the cosmology of the Vedic sacrifice and provide the models of its performance. "Viewed thus as a set of hermeneutical acts, the intellectual operations involved in the ritual use of mantras become interesting in their own right, not simply as instances of magical thought," as earlier generations of scholars assumed.

Another scholar who, like Patton, takes care to define her categories and to situate them in their cultural contexts—and thereby follows Tweed's advice—is Yiqun Zhou, who examines the underlying social dimensions of gendered spatial differentiation in "Spatial Metaphors and Women's Religious Activities in Ancient Greece and China." Applying an anthropologically oriented feminist approach akin to those of sociologist Daphne Spain, anthropologist Shirley Ardener, and literary critic Kerstin W. Shands, Zhou explores the cultural and social variations of gendered spatial metaphors in ancient Greece and China, showing how the basic pairing of "'inside'" (female, domestic) and "'outside'" (male, public) was developed and valued differently in these two classical and patriarchal traditions. In ancient Greek society, the configuration valorized the "'outside'" public domain, a type of "center" where men engaged in political and martial pursuits. Women, however, were typically relegated to the "periphery" of the "'inside'" domestic sphere, to raise children and largely avoid politics. In ancient China, by contrast, the existence of the system of filial piety and ancestor worship significantly affected the basic spatial metaphor, so that the "'inside'" domestic sphere was a place where vital religious rituals were conducted by women as well as men, and the "'outside'" sphere of the world was but a projection of the inner domain. Thus, "the inside-outside metaphor" conveyed a strict hierarchy in Greece, while revealing a continuity of overlapping circles in China. In Greece, women generally were expected to stay "'inside,'" away from the centers of power and influence; but, in China, even women, who were "firmly located in the 'inside,'" would eventually become revered ancestors, thus shifting the valence of femaleness in a more neutral, if not positive, direction.

Zhou also analyzes how the different cultures regarded transgressions of their basic spatial metaphors. In Greece, women left their homes for the occasional public festivals and ceremonies, thus temporarily violating their place while being accorded great honor as they sang and marched. The men, however, were ambivalent about this temporary transgression; and Zhou cites passages from the plays of Aristophanes and Euripides to show how even these "public" moments ended up reinforcing the gender hierarchy. The plays present women who venture "'outside'" as casting off their typical chores of weaving, spinning, and woolwork. In China, however, a famous matriarch—Jing Jiang of Lu—defends "[w]eaving . . . [as] the most essential female work," because of its "economic and ritual significance." Chinese women, bearing the "responsibility to weave the garments worn during sacrifices," were respected as wives and mothers even while participating in these public rituals. Thus, both the Greek and the Chinese societies used the basic inside-outside spatial metaphor but did so in ways that reflected their social and gendered worldviews and cosmologies.

The final essay of this volume addresses how different forms of figuring religions may occur when two different cultures and religions encounter one another. "In Search of Equivalence: Conceiving Muslim-Hindu Encounter through Translation Theory," by Tony K. Stewart, provides us with a nuanced overview of different academic models for studying religious encounter, focusing on Muslim-Hindu interactions in precolonial Bengal. Stewart argues that the old models of "conflict" and "syncretism" are not usefully applied to the Bengali context, as their application assumes a first-wave–academic choice of essentialism where "Islam" and "Hinduism" are discrete, idealized, and opposing forms of religion. Following these old models, the resultant Sufi Islam was an "impure," less Islamic, Hinduized hybrid. Yet precolonial Bengali religion was highly local, often growing in the marshy frontiers; and boundaries between what was "Muslim" and what was "Hindu" were not so clear. The dominant form of Sufi Islam that was emerging at this time (as exemplified in the works of Āli Rajā) made extensive usage of Sanskritized Bengali terms, in an attempt "to translate" Islam for a burgeoning Bengali audience. Hence Stewart argues for the use of a "translation theory" model both to express best the actual encounter and to serve the scholar most adequately (back to Tweed again here: clarify your definitions and tropes, and consider the consequences).

Some of the problems with studying this precolonial form of Bengali Sufism can be traced to its authors' usage of numerous words from Bengali and Sanskrit, rather than from Persian or Arabic. These authors' word choices were part of what Stewart calls "a search for equivalence"—an attempt not to mix or dilute Islam with Hinduism, but rather to translate Islamic concepts and cosmologies into the vernacular Bengali of the region. Stewart shows how using models of syncretism prejudges the ensuing analysis by suggesting that the result is somehow less pure or natural than the original traditions. Models based on syncretism are thus "the product of the scholastic imagination in the first place. It is the way this end product is articulated that reveals the problem most vividly, because any resort to interpretive models of syncretism appears on the surface to produce neutral descriptions, but the descriptions are never direct nor are they precise: they are always metaphoric and value laden." This is exactly the type of thing to which Tweed has alerted us: the unintended obfuscatory consequences of our theoretical and hermeneutical choices!

To demonstrate an alternative approach, Stewart reads closely a complex passage from one of Āli Rajā's cosmogonic texts (wherein he uses Hindu terms to explain Islamic creation) and finds therein several levels of translation, the most important of which are "dynamic equivalence" and "metaphoric equivalence." For example, Āli Rajā uses the Sanskrit terms *yugala* and *auṃ* to refer to the original Islamic concepts of cosmogonic dualism and creation through *alif* and *mīm*, respectively. Stewart argues that Sufi use of Sanskrit terms eventually led to their expansion in Bengal to include Islamic valences (much as Pathak asserts that the term "epic" is given a broader semantic field when applied to Sanskrit poems). Moreover, Sufi "translation" and "appropriation" of once-Hindu words and concepts led to shared metaphoric worlds (which are reminiscent of those characterized by Lakoff and Johnson).

Amid Āli Rajā's "creative [translation] efforts," we can still detect two different conceptual worlds at play, both the Muslim and the Hindu. His comparisons remain dynamic and metaphorical, and no original essences are harmed in these processes. We are best advised to utilize methodologies that can illuminate these profound feats of imagination, not to obscure them with our own assumptions and biases.

Crafting an afterword to this fine collection of essays has been quite challenging and, I hope, useful. Each of the essays has cast light on an essential aspect of the world of religions, on the comparative process, and on figuring religions. The diversity of traditions covered—as well as the range of employed approaches from philosophy, linguistics, and anthropology—should situate this volume in Doniger's third wave of the comparative study of religion. I would like to close with some comments on conceptual metaphor theory, the cognitive science of religion, and a promising new cognitive-linguistic methodology: conceptual blending theory. Although Lakoff and Johnson helped to popularize and establish the modern study of metaphors,[4] it is really the more recent efforts of Fauconnier and Turner that have extended conceptual metaphor theory.[5]

At the risk of oversimplifying their methodology, we can say that conceptual blending is a process whereby we take information and meanings from two or more "mental spaces" (neuronal assemblies called "inputs") and, using an overarching "frame" (or organizing pattern) provided by a "generic space," we create an entirely new "blended space" that combines aspects of the inputs and frame. The result is a range of "conceptual integration networks," from the most basic "simplex" network to the "mirror" network to the "single-scope" network of traditional source/target metaphors studied by Lakoff and Johnson; and culminating in the amazing "double-scope" and "multi-scope" networks that are at the heart of language, art, religion, and most daily life.[6] These networks refer to the many ways that the brain accesses and combines mental spaces, creating meaning and thought.[7] All networks involve the "compression" of different aspects of the inputs—using the "organizing frames"—to create the new blended spaces. In brief, this is how our imagination and perception work, in a most dynamic (but largely unnoticed) way.

What Fauconnier and Turner refer to as single-scope networks are better known as the conventional source/target metaphors of the type studied by Lakoff and Johnson and analyzed throughout this volume. In other words, there are two input spaces with two different organizing frames (as opposed to the single frame of a mirror network), but only one organizing frame is projected into the blend. For example, in the metaphor of two CEOs who are in competition, we might say that they are fighting as two boxers: "Ted Turner is fighting it out with Rupert Murdoch." The generic organizing frame is that of competition. The source domain is "boxing" (which provides the organizing frame and framing input), while the target domain is "business" (the focus of understanding). Although the two men may have never struck one another, their roles as "boxers" make sense in the blend and we are able to gain wider insight from the network. Like any such metaphor, the network provokes insight into one thing (boxing) which is then projected onto another thing (business). The same is true of basic religious metaphors like GOD IS LOVE. We use inferences available from the framing inputs (e.g., boxing, love), which themselves already have many compressions of meaning. And even these inputs are blends themselves—thus, complicated systems of blended spaces can become inputs for further blending.

Double-scope and multi-scope networks are perhaps the most intriguing concepts to be used in the study of religion, as they produce the most imaginative and creative blends. In these types of networks, there are not only at least two different inputs and at least two different organizing frames, but those frames also typically clash with one another, so that only parts of each frame are projected into the blend—leading to an entirely new blended space which has its own "emergent structure" and frame. This process is a key to understanding the function of conceptual blending in religion and the imagination. One example that Fauconnier and Turner use to illustrate this useful hermeneutic is that of the Computer Desktop. The first input—that of "office work"—includes things like desks, files, folders, trash cans, and paper clips. The second input is that of "computer commands" (e.g., find, replace, copy, paste, save, print, point-and-click). In the blended space of the Computer Desktop, of course, we never actually touch or lift any folders nor toss paperwork into a basket. Concomitantly, pointing and clicking was not part of traditional precomputer office work.[8] Only certain parts of the inputs are projected into the blended space and really make sense together only in the new emergent structure of that space. The frames of offices and computers clash in some ways (and the topology of a 3-D office is relaxed for the 2-D screen in the blend), yet result in an incredibly creative and imaginative blended network: "This emergent structure is not in the inputs—it is part of the cognitive construction in the blend. . . . The blend is an integrated platform for organizing and developing those other spaces."[9]

A final critical aspect of blending is what Fauconnier and Turner call "counterfactual reasoning," which allows us "to operate mentally on the unreal"—to run scenarios, check outcomes, and then make choices. For example, "If I were you" and "I see nothing" are powerful counterfactual statements. But we make such statements all the time, creating seemingly "absurd" possible worlds that—while actually powerful conceptual blends—seem to be just a routine feat of the imagination.[10] Indeed, we have seen this creation process described throughout *Figuring Religions*. In addition to using the conditional sense of "if" and consequent clauses, counterfactuals also make use of the clash between analogy and disanalogy, between what seems to be possible and what seems to be impossible. Fauconnier and Turner observe "that the capacity to juggle counterfactual spaces is a consequence of the evolution of cognitively modern human beings and their remarkable capacity for double-scope blending. Counterfactuals are a good exemplar of double-scope blending because the oppositions between the spaces are so manifest. One cannot overstate the importance of counterfactuals in human life."[11] Counterfactuals not only are at the root of scientific and mathematical reasoning, but also underlie just about every religious worldview and cosmology. To draw inferences about an unseen deity or heavenly realm, to communicate with spirits, and to fly in a spiritual body to an invisible realm all involve complex counterfactuals and double-scope blending. Thus, many religious traditions have made great use of what we might call "blended worlds," as an expression of their cosmologies and cosmographies; and of "emergent beings," in regard to their ontologies, theologies, and soteriologies. To be sure, the religious person who is involved in "running the blend" will not regard it as such, but instead will attribute profound ontological, soteriological, cosmological, and epistemological status to the blend. It, like most blends, is very much experienced as "real" by this person.[12]

As we face the future of scholarship and of the comparative effort, I feel that the study of religion can benefit not only from the methodologies used in this volume, but also from the use of blending theory and other discoveries from the emerging field of the cognitive science of religion.[13] There have been many ways of figuring religions, and many more remain to be seen.

NOTES

1. Lakoff and Johnson 1980; Johnson 1987; Lakoff 1987; Lakoff and Turner 1989; Lakoff and Johnson 1999; Lakoff and Núñez 2000; Turner 2006.
2. On recent uses of conceptual metaphor theory in the study of Hinduism, see Hayes 2003 and 2005.
3. In this important work, Slingerland also introduces the "next step" in cognitive linguistics and conceptual metaphor theory, called "conceptual blending theory." This is based on the groundbreaking work by Gilles Fauconnier and Mark Turner (2002). I will make some brief comments

on this promising theory in the conclusion to this afterword. For wonderful and detailed examples of metaphor and blending, see Slingerland 2008: 151–218.

4. A useful collection of earlier approaches may be found in Sacks 1979 and Ortony 1993.

5. For a range of updated information on blending theory, see Turner's excellent website (http://markturner.org/blending.html).

6. Fauconnier and Turner 2002: 113–37.

7. For an excellent overview of recent connections between cognitive neuroscience and religious studies, see Bulkeley 2004 and 2005. Also see Barrett 2007 for an overview of the new field of cognitive science of religion. For a useful survey of the history of the field of cognitive science, including some of its applications to the study of Hinduism, see Goldberg 2007.

8. For more examples of clashes in the Computer Desktop blend, see Fauconnier and Turner 2002: 340.

9. Fauconnier and Turner 2002: 133.

10. Fauconnier and Turner 2002: 217–48.

11. Fauconnier and Turner 2002: 231.

12. Kelly Bulkeley (2006) has persuasively argued that the modern cognitive scientist should avoid recent scientific biases against religion as being essentially "pathological." This reductionism by many cognitive scientists illustrates the ongoing gap between religious studies and cognitive science, which this essay is attempting to bridge.

13. At the 2009 meeting of the American Academy of Religion, a new program unit in the cognitive science of religion met, including a cosponsored session with the Tantric Studies Group. At that session, this author presented a paper entitled "Conceptual Blending Theory, 'Reverse Amnesia,' and the Study of Tantra," an initial attempt to use blending theory in the study of South Asian Hindu Tantra.

REFERENCES

Barrett, Justin L. 2007. "Cognitive Science of Religion: What Is It and Why Is It?" *Religion Compass* 1, no. 6: 768–86.

Bulkeley, Kelly. 2004. *The Wondering Brain: Thinking about Religion with and beyond Cognitive Neuroscience.* New York: Routledge.

————, ed. 2005. *Soul, Psyche, Brain: New Directions in the Study of Religion and Brain-Mind Science.* New York: Palgrave Macmillan.

————. 2006. "Less Than Meets the Eye: What Cognitive Science Adds to Tantric Studies." Paper presented at the annual meeting of the American Academy of Religion, Washington.

Fauconnier, Gilles, and Mark Turner. 2002. *The Way We Think: Conceptual Blending and the Mind's Hidden Complexities.* New York: Basic Books.

Goldberg, Ellen. 2007. "Cognitive Science and Hinduism." In *Studying Hinduism: Key Concepts and Methods,* edited by Sushil Mittal and Gene Thursby, 59–73. New York: Routledge.

Hayes, Glen Alexander. 2003. "Metaphoric Worlds and Yoga in the Vaiṣṇava Sahajiyā Tantric Traditions of Medieval Bengal." In *Yoga: The Indian Tradition,* edited by Ian Whicher and David Carpenter, 162–84. London: RoutledgeCurzon.

————. 2005. "Contemporary Metaphor Theory and Alternative Views of Krishna and Rādhā in Vaishnava Sahajiyā Tantric Traditions." In *Alternative Krishnas: Regional and Vernacular Variations on a Hindu Deity,* edited by Guy L. Beck, 19–32. Albany: State University of New York Press.

————. 2009. "Conceptual Blending Theory, 'Reverse Amnesia,' and the Study of Tantra." Paper presented at the annual meeting of the American Academy of Religion, Montreal.

Johnson, Mark. 1987. *The Body in the Mind: The Bodily Basis of Meaning, Imagination, and Reason.* Chicago: University of Chicago Press.

Lakoff, George. 1987. *Women, Fire, and Dangerous Things: What Categories Reveal about the Mind.* Chicago: University of Chicago Press.

Lakoff, George, and Mark Johnson. 1980. *Metaphors We Live By.* Chicago: University of Chicago Press.

————. 1999. *Philosophy in the Flesh: The Embodied Mind and Its Challenge to Western Thought.* New York: Basic Books.

Lakoff, George, and Rafael E. Núñez. 2000. *Where Mathematics Comes From: How the Embodied Mind Brings Mathematics into Being.* New York: Basic Books.

Lakoff, George, and Mark Turner. 1989. *More Than Cool Reason: A Field Guide to Poetic Metaphor.* Chicago: University of Chicago Press.

Ortony, Andrew, ed. 1993. *Metaphor and Thought.* 2nd ed. Cambridge: Cambridge University Press.

Sacks, Sheldon, ed. 1979. *On Metaphor.* Chicago: University of Chicago Press.

Slingerland, Edward. 2008. *What Science Offers the Humanities: Integrating Body and Culture.* New York: Cambridge University Press.

Turner, Mark, ed. 2006. *The Artful Mind: Cognitive Science and the Riddle of Human Creativity.* New York: Oxford University Press.

Contributors

WENDY DONIGER is the Mircea Eliade Distinguished Service Professor of the History of Religions at the University of Chicago Divinity School.

JAMES EGGE is Professor in the Department of History and Philosophy at Eastern Michigan University.

ELLEN HASKELL is Assistant Professor in the Department of Religious Studies at the University of North Carolina at Greensboro.

GLEN ALEXANDER HAYES is Professor in the Department of Religion at Bloomfield College.

SHUBHA PATHAK is Assistant Professor in the Department of Philosophy and Religion at American University.

LAURIE L. PATTON is Professor of Religion and Dean of Arts and Sciences at Duke University.

EDWARD SLINGERLAND is Professor in the Department of Asian Studies and Canada Research Chair in Chinese Thought and Embodied Cognition at the University of British Columbia.

TONY K. STEWART is the Gertrude Conaway Vanderbilt Chair in Humanities and Chair of the Department of Religious Studies at Vanderbilt University.

THOMAS A. TWEED is the Gwyn Shive, Anita Nordan Lindsay, and Joe and Cherry Gray Professor of the History of Christianity in the Department of Religious Studies at the University of Texas at Austin.

TERHI UTRIAINEN is Senior Lecturer in the Study of Religions in the Department of World Cultures at the University of Helsinki.

YIQUN ZHOU is Assistant Professor in the Department of East Asian Languages and Cultures at Stanford University.

Index